SOUTHERN BIOGRAPHY SERIES

GENERAL LEONIDAS POLK, C.S.A.

University of the South

Bishop-General Leonidas Polk, 1861 "Sword over the Gown"

Joseph H. Parks

GENERAL
LEONIDAS POLK
C.S.A.

The Fighting Bishop

Louisiana State University Press
Baton Rouge and London

To
Alliene and Joe

Acknowledgments

ALL WHO WRITE on Southern subjects must of necessity visit the Southern Collection at the University of North Carolina. Director J. W. Patton and his efficient staff make work in their manuscript collections as pleasant as it is profitable. If one's subject is related to the Episcopal Church a visit to the University of the South, Sewanee, Tennessee, will also be rewarding. This author is particularly indebted to the late Mrs. O. N. Torian, archivist of the University of the South, and Arthur and Betty Chitty. Mrs. Torian was custodian of the Leonidas Polk Papers and Arthur Chitty, Director of Public Relations, is the author of a history of the University. Special thanks for valuable assistance are also due Dr. C. C. Crittenden and the staff of the North Carolina State Archives and History, Raleigh; Dr. Dan M. Robison and Miss Isabel Howell of the Tennessee State Library and Archives, Nashville; and Dr. Joe Gray Taylor, Nicholls State College, Thibodaux, Louisiana.

The University of Georgia made liberal financial contributions in the form of research grants.

J. H. P.

Contents

Illustrations and Maps

ILLUSTRATIONS

MAPS

GENERAL LEONIDAS POLK, C.S.A.

(1)

Carolina Background

AMONG THE mid-seventeenth-century immigrants to America was the family of Robert Bruce Pollock, direct forbears of General Leonidas Polk. Pollock was from North Ireland where his Scottish ancestors had settled during the reign of James I. In the struggle between Parliament and Charles I, Robert Pollock had served in a Parliamentary regiment commanded by one Colonel Tasker. He later married the Colonel's daughter, Magdalen Tasker Porter, the widow of Pollock's companion in arms, Colonel Porter. The Tasker family was of French descent.

Dates given by members of the family and by genealogists for the year in which Robert and Magdalen Pollock, their six sons, and two daughters landed on the East Shore of Maryland vary from 1659 to 1686. The name was gradually changed to Polk, and the family soon acquired extensive land holdings. John Polk, eldest son of Robert and Magdalen, married Joanna Knox, and to this union were born William and Nancy. William married Priscilla Roberts and moved to Pennsylvania, settling near Carlisle. After Priscilla's death he married Margaret Taylor. William fathered at least eight children, but it is not certain which wife was the mother of some of the eight.[1]

As far as is known, all of the earlier Polks were farmers and married into farm families. The William Polk family followed the Scotch-Irish pattern of migration. Led by the fourth son, Thomas, with most if not all members of the family following soon afterward, they "skirted the eastern slope of the Blue Ridge, crossed the Dan and Yadkin rivers," and by the early 1750's arrived in the

[1] His grandson William claimed Margaret Taylor as his grandmother, but William's grandson William Mecklenburg claimed to be descended from Priscilla Roberts.

section of the North Carolina back country that later became Mecklenburg County.[2] There in 1755 Thomas Polk married Susan Spratt, a member of another Scotch-Irish family from Pennsylvania.[3]

Thomas Polk immediately assumed a position of leadership among back-country farmers. Although he had little formal education, he was much interested in schools. He had a prominent part in the opening of Liberty and Salisbury academies and the chartering of Queen's College at Charlotte. The Queen's charter was disallowed by the Crown (apparently because there were too many Presbyterians on the board of trustees). With both Thomas Polk and his brother Ezekiel serving as trustees, this frontier institution began operation without a charter and continued until "reestablished" by North Carolina law in 1777. By this date Mecklenburg County had little desire to honor the Queen, so the name of the college was changed to Liberty Hall. It continued to operate until the building was destroyed during the British invasion of the Carolina back country.[4]

Thomas Polk promoted the creation of Mecklenburg County in 1762 and was named among the first justices of the peace, representing the Sugar Creek settlement. He represented the new county

[2] This sketch of early history and other genealogical data relating to the Polk family is based upon Mary Winder Garrett, "Pedigree of the Pollock or Polk Family," *American Historical Magazine* (Nashville, 1896–1904), II, 376–95, and III (1898), 42–73; William H. Polk, *Polk Family and Kinsmen* (Louisville, 1912); Mrs. Frank M. Angelotti, "The Polks of North Carolina and Tennessee," *New England Historical and Genealogical Register,* LXXVI and LXXVIII (Boston, 1847–   ); William M. Polk, *Leonidas Polk, Bishop and General* (New York, 1915), I, 1–4; "Autobiography of Colonel William Polk," in William H. Hoyt (ed.), *The Papers of Archibald D. Murphey* (Raleigh, 1914), II, 400; [James K. Polk and Leonidas Polk], *A Genealogical Tree of the Polk Family* (n.p., 1845), said to have been prepared by the Bishop and his cousin.

[3] Children of this union were Thomas, Jr. (killed in battle of Eutaw Springs); William (married Grizel Gilchrist); Ezekiel (died at sea); Charles (married an Alexander); Martha (married Dr. Ephraim Brevard); Margaret (married Governor Nathaniel Alexander); Mary (married Daniel Brown of South Carolina); James (married a Moore). Garrett, "Pedigree of the Pollock or Polk Family," *loc. cit.* III, 45 ff.

[4] William L. Saunders (ed.), *The Colonial Records of North Carolina* (Raleigh, 1890), VIII, 486–89; Albert R. Newsome, "Thomas Polk," in *Dictionary of American Biography* (30 vols., New York, 1928–36), XV, 42–43. Marshal D. Haywood, *Governor William Tryon and His Administration* (Raleigh, 1903), 26–27.

in the State House of Commons almost continuously from 1766 to 1774.[5]

As a community leader he was especially active in the "War of Sugar Creek," a farmers' riot of 1765 staged by tenants on the grant of George Augustus Selwyn in protest against the price demanded for the lands on which they had already settled. When Henry Eustace McColloh, acting as agent for Selwyn, arrived in Mecklenburg County bringing with him surveyors to mark off lands for those who were willing to pay the price, he was met by Thomas Polk and "large of 100 of his Gang many of whom were Armed with Guns" and acting "in a most ignominious and taunting manner."

McColloh, refusing to be intimidated, ordered his surveyor to begin running lines for those who were ready to purchase. The surveyor "proceeded to fix his Compass and the Chain Carriers having the chain in their hands,—Mr. Polk's People—gathered tumultuously round them. . . . And Tom Polk . . . with his own hand took the Compass off the Staff."

McColloh, reporting the incident to Governor William Tryon, insisted: "There are some particular Circumstances in the Conduct of the said Mr. Polk . . . worthy of being observed upon; being the only Man who has any pretense to sense or weight among these deluded People." He considered Polk "the sole apparent Cause of the Opposition Mr. Selwyn meets with in his just Rights." McColloh further accused Polk of asking to see his certificate of power of attorney granted by Selwyn and then refusing to return the document.[6]

Before McColloh could get any action from the governor a still more serious event occurred. He was not present, having been "Providentially detained by particular business" elsewhere, but he reported that on May 7 a mob in Mecklenburg severely whipped several of his surveyors. He was convinced that had he been present "I most assuredly & without any ceremony [would have] been murdered . . . their Guns were brought for that particular pur-

---

[5] Daniel A. Tompkins, *History of Mecklenburg County and the City of Charlotte from 1740–1903* (Charlotte, 1903), II, 29; Saunders (ed.), *Colonial Records*, VI, 799; Newsome, "Thomas Polk," *loc. cit.*

[6] Memorial to Governor William Tryon, April 25, 1765, in Saunders (ed.), *Colonial Records*, VII, 12–31.

pose.—They declare solemnly—publicly, they will put me to
Death:—they may be damned for a pack of ungrateful brutal Sons
of Bitches:—I dont care." [7]

On May 18 Governor Tryon issued a proclamation calling attention to the action of rioters in Mecklenburg County on May 7,
declaring them in "Great Breach and Disturbance of His Mag-
esty's Peace and Government" for having "violently outrageously
and riotously" assaulted and beaten John Frohoch and others in
the employ of Henry E. McColloh. Any two participants in this
mob action who would come forward and furnish the names of
others would be "exonerated and freed" from punishment.[8] There
is no record of any testimony.

Thomas Polk was not a consistent champion of the interests of
the so-called common man. When the uprising known as the Reg-
ulator Movement reached a climax in 1771 he allied himself with
the side of government and power and captained a company in
Governor Tryon's army. He and Moses Alexander also served as
the governor's commissaries for the counties of Mecklenburg,
Rowan, and Tryon.[9]

When the controversy between Britain and the Colonies became serious, Thomas Polk assumed leadership among back-
country radicals. In response to considerable public enthusiasm, he
called together on May 31, 1775, two representatives from each of
the Mecklenburg County militia companies for discussion of what
assistance should or could be given to the suffering people of
Boston. On this same day news of the Battle of Lexington arrived
in Charlotte. The assembled delegates adopted a group of resolutions declaring all crown commissions null and void and proclaim-
ing that henceforth each Colony should control the exercise of
executive and legislative powers within its borders. It was further
resolved that Mecklenburg County should choose its own military
officials and organize its own local government. All so-called crown
officials who insisted on exercising power were to be considered
enemies of their country. The closing resolution authorized

[7] Henry E. McColloh to Edmund Fanning, May 9, 1765, *ibid.*, 32–34.
[8] Proclamation of Governor William Tryon, May 18, 1765, *ibid.*, 38.
[9] John Spencer Bassett, "The Regulators of North Carolina, 1765–1771,"
American Historical Association *Annual Report* for 1894 (Washington, 1895),
141 ff; Haywood, *Governor Tryon*, 116, 119, 168; Saunders (ed.), *Colonial
Records*, VIII, 674, 698.

Thomas Polk and Joseph Kennedy to purchase 300 pounds of powder, 600 pounds of lead, and 1000 flints for use by the local militia.

Standing on the courthouse steps at Charlotte, Thomas Polk read these resolutions to the largest crowd that had ever assembled in Mecklenburg County.[10] Although these resolutions were printed in both of North Carolina's newspapers and an official copy sent by messenger to the President of the Continental Congress at Philadelphia, they received little attention and were almost completely forgotten during the exciting months ahead.[11]

Thomas Polk was given an opportunity to assist in implementing the principles expressed in the Mecklenburg Resolutions when he was chosen representative to the North Carolina Provincial Congress, which sat during August and September, 1775, and made provisions for a provisional state government. On September 9 he was appointed colonel of militia and in response to an appeal from South Carolina for the assistance of his six companies, he participated in the "snow campaign" against a group of South Carolina Loyalists during the following winter.[12] In the spring of 1776 he was made colonel of the Fourth North Carolina Regiment and authorized to recruit 750 men to join General George Washington in New Jersey the following year. He saw service at Brandywine but was not at Germantown, having been assigned guard duty in the removal of military supplies and public property from Philadelphia. With these supplies also went the bells of the city. As the British approached Philadelphia a citizens' committee had been appointed to take down all church bells and the State House bell (later known as the Liberty Bell) for transportation to safety. On September 24, 1777, Polk, commanding a guard of 200 men

[10] For a copy of these Mecklenburg Resolutions see William Henry Hoyt, *The Mecklenburg Declaration of Independence* (New York, 1907), 22–26; or John H. Wheeler, *Historical Sketches of North Carolina to 1851* (Philadelphia, 1851), 255–56; or Saunders (ed.), *Colonial Records*, IX, 1282–85. There is a tradition in the Polk family that Thomas Polk's son-in-law, Ephraim Brevard, drafted these resolutions the previous evening at Polk's home. Polk, *Leonidas Polk*, I, 11 n.

[11] Captain James Jack, who claimed to have been the messenger to Congress, reported many years later that he delivered the resolutions to Richard Caswell and William Hooper, North Carolina's delegates in Congress. For Jack's statement see Hoyt, *Mecklenburg Declaration*, 251–52.

[12] Saunders (ed.), *Colonial Records*, X, 206, 335.

and a train of 700 wagons, arrived in Bethlehem, where stores were to be deposited.[13]

In late fall Colonel Polk rejoined Washington and shared the suffering at Valley Forge during the following winter. In February, 1778, he was ordered back to North Carolina to assist in recruiting men and collecting supplies. During his absence from the army his Fourth North Carolina was combined with the Second, and he was left a colonel without a command. Although specifically authorized to do so, he was unable to raise a new regiment. His disappointment was further increased by his failure to secure a promotion he thought due him. Francis Nash, a brigadier general from North Carolina, had died of wounds received at Germantown. Polk considered himself the logical choice for Nash's successor, but a junior officer received the appointment.

In a state of disappointment mixed with anger Colonel Polk resolved to retire from active service and made known his intentions in a letter to General Washington: "Such a flagrant demonstration of partiality and injurious preference, without alleging a single article of disqualification against me, has determined me no longer to serve my ungratefull country in so painful and so hazardous a capacity." [14]

Though officially in retirement, Thomas Polk was too aggressive to "sulk in his tent." Instead, he was ever active in denouncing Tories and encouraging Rebels. By now the British had begun active operations in the South, and the fall of Charleston and Savannah left the region open to invasion. In July, 1780, Continental Congress ordered General Horatio Gates, the hero of Saratoga, to take command of Continental forces in the South. On July 25 he arrived at camp on Deep River near Hillsborough, North Carolina. Two days later he started his poorly organized and even more poorly supplied army on a march along the most difficult route toward Camden, South Carolina.

---

[13] Extracts from Moravian diaries copied and translated from the original by Charles C. Jones and included in a letter to Ida Polk, June 21, 1886, Leonidas Polk Papers (University of the South Archives, Sewanee, Tenn.).

[14] Polk to Washington, June 26, 1778, in Walter Clark (ed.), *State Records of North Carolina* (Winston and Goldsboro, 1895–1905), XIII, 451. This work is a continuation of the *Colonial Records* and begins with Volume XI.

Gates learned of Colonel Thomas Polk's enthusiasm for the Rebel cause and through Major Thomas Pinckney sent Polk an appointment as commissary general of provisions for North Carolina and commissary of purchase for Continental forces. This appointment was approved by the North Carolina Board of War.[15] But before Polk could be of real service, Gates had been disastrously defeated at Camden and was in flight to Hillsborough two hundred miles away. The fleeing General spent only one night in Charlotte and made no attempt to defend the town.[16]

Patriot spirit in Western North Carolina had been dampened but not destroyed. As Lord Cornwallis moved near to Charlotte, Thomas Polk rushed a plea to Gates: ". . . we shall be reduced to the Necessity of fighting in two or three days," he concluded, "or passively suffer the Enemy to ravage the Country." [17] No assistance was forthcoming. Small groups of Rebels did clash with the British, but Lord Cornwallis entered Charlotte late in September and established headquarters in Thomas Polk's home, "The White House," said to have been the only painted house in town. The Thomas Polk family had joined others in flight as the British approached.[18]

These Mecklenburg refugees hailed the defeat of Patrick Ferguson's British and Tory force at King's Mountain as "a glorious affair." Thomas Polk gleefully reported it to the North Carolina War Board, concluding with the wishful prediction: "In a few Days doubt not but we will be in Charlotte & I Will take Posses-

[15] See Leonidas Polk Papers under date September 15, 1780; Polk to Pinckney, August 6, 1780, in Clark (ed.), *State Records*, XIV, 535–36. Polk stated: "My Zeal to Serve My Country, and Seeing that the Army is not likely to be well Supplied Otherwise, induce me to Accept of Genl Gates's offer."

[16] Christopher Ward, *The War of the Revolution*, edited by John R. Alden (2 vols., New York, 1952), II, 717 ff.

[17] Polk to Gates, September 10, 11, 1780, in Clark (ed.), *State Records*, XIV, 606, 608–609.

[18] Ezekiel, Thomas' younger brother, took what he considered a more practical view of the situation. He had seen some service in the Patriot cause but had been absent more often than present when battles were fought. When Cornwallis' men passed Ezekiel's Sugar Creek farm he followed them into town and "took protection," agreeing to give no further assistance to the Rebel cause. Leonidas Polk to Benson J. Lossing, May 20, 1854, and Lossing to Leonidas Polk, July 12, 1854, both in Leonidas Polk Papers; Charles G. Sellers, *James K. Polk, Jacksonian, 1795–1843* (Princeton, 1957), 16.

sion of my house & his Lordship take the Woods." [19] He might have added that he would also reclaim what was left of his mill near Charlotte and his store in the town.[20]

The Mecklenburg patriots did not drive Cornwallis out of Charlotte, but upon learning of Ferguson's fate he quickly withdrew his forces toward Winnsboro. The scattered, poorly organized, and inadequately supplied Rebel forces, state and Continental, continued to harass the retreating British. It was Thomas Polk's task to furnish supplies, a task too great for any man, especially when forced to rely on a region already drained of supplies. The scanty records available do not prove inefficiency nor negligence on the part of Polk, yet the great shortage of supplies made complaints inevitable. At one time General Gates and three other high ranking officers called attention to "a number of suspicious Circumstances respecting the Conduct & behavior of Colonel Thomas Polk" and urged that he "be directly Ordered to Salisbury to answer for his Conduct." General William Smallwood also complained to the Board of War, but in a second letter he admitted that at least a part of his charges were not justified.[21]

Before receiving the second letter from Smallwood, Gates had a conference with Polk and informed him of the numerous charges and that "his conduct was deemed doubtful and suspicious." Polk replied that since "his Countrymen suspected his Fidelity" he would continue as commissary no longer than was required to deliver "Five Hundred Beeves, and One Thousand Bushels of Corn" he had collected.[22] Obviously a man who could collect this quantity of meat and bread in the ravaged areas of North Carolina was not a complete failure as commissary. The Board of War did not accept Polk's offer to resign.

Having forfeited the confidence of both civil and military authorities, General Gates was soon replaced by General Nathanael Greene. Greene arrived in Charlotte on December 2, 1780, and was reported to have gone immediately to the home of Thomas Polk. On the following day Polk was said to have observed that

[19] Clark (ed.), *State Records*, XV, 414.
[20] *Ibid.*, 179.
[21] *Ibid.*, XIV, 720, 736, 737, 740–43.
[22] Horatio Gates to North Carolina Board of War, November 17, 1780, *ibid.*, XV, 416.

General Greene already knew more about the situation than General Gates had learned during several months experience.[23]

Colonel Polk, smarting under criticism, feeling the strain of too great a task, and wishing to give some time to private affairs, refused to do more than remain commissary for the district. Major William Davie was assigned the task of supplying forces in the field.[24]

In mid-February, 1781, General Greene informed Colonel Polk that the Salisbury District had been without a brigadier since the death of General William Davidson and that he was recommending to the Governor of North Carolina that Polk be promoted to brigadier general and assigned to this command.[25] About three weeks later General Greene received a petition from the field officers of the Salisbury militia expressing "special confidence in Colo. Thomas Polk" and urging that he be appointed to command them.[26] Greene immediately ordered Polk to take command, pending favorable action by North Carolina authorities.[27] Henceforth he addressed Thomas Polk as "General."

As Greene approached Camden in April, 1781, he found the garrison there too strong to be stormed by the force at his command. To Polk he rushed an inquiry as to how many men the Salisbury district could furnish. But Polk was no longer in command; North Carolina authorities had appointed Colonel Francis Locke instead. General Greene, however, refused to give up. "I am sorry that those in power cannot distinguish popularity acquired by improper indulgences from that of real merit and important services," he wrote Polk. "The appointment of Mr. Lock is not less mortifying to me than unjust to you, and I have not failed to tell Governor Nash that I had rather have half the number of militia with you than double their number with Mr. Lock, who I doubt not is a good citizen but I am persuaded will never make a soldier.

---

[23] Elkanah Watson, *Men and Times of the Revolution* (New York, 1856), 259.

[24] For several letters between Greene and Polk relative to supplies for troops, see Nathanael Greene Papers (Clements Library, University of Michigan, Ann Arbor, Mich.) and Leonidas Polk Papers.

[25] Greene to Polk, February 16, 1781, Leonidas Polk Papers.

[26] See *ibid.*, March 5, 1781.

[27] Greene to Polk, March 6, 7, 1781, Greene Papers and Leonidas Polk Papers, respectively.

I shall never rest satisfied until I get you at the head of Salisbury District." [28]

After Governor Nash was succeeded by Thomas Burke, Greene continued to express lack of confidence in Locke and urge the promotion of Polk. Locke, he insisted, had failed to bring the Salisbury militia to the aid of the army when assistance from his command was badly needed. Could not the incompetent Locke be replaced by the more aggressive Polk? Burke, though apparently in sympathy with the request, saw a great danger in such an action. "The superseding an officer of Col. Locke's rank without inquiry or trial might prove an act from which might result very troublesome consequences," he wrote Brigadier General John Butler. At the same time, realizing the seriousness of the situation, he concluded that to take no action at all would be "entirely inadmissable." Consequently he ordered Butler to take command of "the whole force" and rush to the assistance of General Greene.[29]

What might have been the results had Greene's recommendation been followed and Polk promoted to command can only be surmised, but Butler's appointment did not solve the problem. A month later a band of Tories led by Colonel David Fanning captured Hillsborough, the governor, and the council. Butler not only failed to prevent the capture but also failed in his effort to recapture the prisoners, who were taken to jail at Wilmington.[30]

Fanning's action, however, was of minor importance; the war was almost over. After the surrender of Cornwallis at Yorktown in October, 1781, organized fighting gradually came to an end. The few troops "General" Polk had hoped to command melted away.

[28] Greene to Polk, April 21, June 11, 1781, Greene Papers.
[29] Burke to Butler, August 15, 1781; *id.* to Colonel Locke, August 15, 1781, in Governors Letter Book (North Carolina Department of Archives, Raleigh, N. C.).
[30] Robert O. DeMond, *The Loyalists of North Carolina During the Revolution* (Durham, 1940), 146–47.

(2)

Foundation for Fortune

THREE OF THOMAS POLK's brothers and at least two of his sons also participated in the American Revolution. The most extensive as well as the most distinguished service was performed by his son William. William was born near Charlotte, July 9, 1758. At the beginning of British hostilities he was a student at Queen's College in Charlotte.[1] Like many other youths he was eager for action, so he left college and secured a second lieutenant's commission in the Third South Carolina Regiment, composed of men from both Carolinas. While engaged in small-scale operations against Tories he was shot from his horse, receiving a serious shoulder wound. In after-war-years he liked to claim that his was "the first American blood spilt south of Lexington." [2]

While convalescing William Polk resigned his South Carolina commission and, in November, 1776, was appointed major in the Ninth North Carolina Regiment. He joined this regiment at Halifax in March, 1777, and soon moved to the assistance of General Washington in New Jersey. Young Polk was now nineteen years of age.

He saw service at Brandywine and was again wounded at Germantown. Along with his father, who commanded the Fourth North Carolina, he suffered the winter at Valley Forge. Also as in the case of his father, he was left without a command when the North Carolina regiments were consolidated in the spring of 1778.[3]

For the next two years Major William Polk engaged in recruit-

[1] "Autobiography of Colonel William Polk," Hoyt (ed.), *Papers of Archibald D. Murphey*, II, 400–410.
[2] *Ibid.*, 404.
[3] *Ibid.*; Polk, *Leonidas Polk*, I, 38–41.

ing work in his home section. He returned to active duty when General Gates assumed command in the South and served under General Richard Caswell at Camden. Subsequently, he was shifted to the staff of General William Davidson and was present when the General was killed at Cowan's Ford.

Following the disintegration of the militia that had been commanded by General Davidson, Polk returned to the service of South Carolina, accepting a commission as lieutenant colonel, and saw action under both Sumter and Marion. As the British fell back toward Charleston, Polk's command was among those who continued small-scale harassing attacks until the close of the war.[4]

The Revolutionary careers of Thomas Polk and his son William were sufficiently distinguished to mark them as men of prominence in the new state of North Carolina. Thomas Polk, now advanced in years, had no further desire for public service. He died in Charlotte, January 26, 1794.[5]

William Polk inherited his father's ability. Equipped with a better education and enjoying a distinguished record as a soldier, he was destined for prominence in public affairs and even greater success in private business. These two accomplishments were often closely related, for opportunity knocked loudest at the doors of those in position to act immediately. This was especially true of land speculation. William Polk founded the family fortune in the western lands of North Carolina and Tennessee.

In 1783 the North Carolina legislature established at Hillsborough a new land office for the sale of lands in its Tennessee country. The Confederation Congress was urging the cession of these lands to the United States, but North Carolina preferred to use them to retire war debts and compensate veterans.

Provision had been made in 1782 for marking off a military district in the central part of the Tennessee country in which veterans' land warrants were to be located. To provide local government for this region a new county, Davidson, was created.

[4] "Autobiography of Colonel William Polk," in Hoyt (ed.), *Papers of Archibald D. Murphey*, II, 408; Polk, *Leonidas Polk*, I, 41–45; J. G. deR. Hamilton, "William Polk," in *Dictionary of American Biography*, XV, 43–44; Clark (ed.), *State Records*, XII, 152–54.
[5] Hamilton, "William Polk," in *Dictionary of American Biography*, loc. cit.

The state act of 1783 placed lands outside the military reservation on sale at ten pounds per hundred acres. Continental and state bills were receivable at 800 to 1. Since speculators could buy such bills on the market at a much more favorable ratio, the actual purchase price of such lands amounted to only about five cents per acre. Persons wishing to acquire such lands first had to go to the domain and stake out the tract desired. A crude sketch was then "entered" at the office of John Armstrong, the appointed entry-taker. Armstrong would issue a warrant authorizing an official survey. The plat drawn by the surveyor was submitted to the Secretary of State who would issue an official grant, subject to signature by the governor.[6]

Armstrong's office remained open only about seven months (October 20, 1783 to May 25, 1784); however, this was long enough for persons in favored positions to make entries totaling about three million acres. By the closing date only a small fraction of these entries had been surveyed. The legislature then divided the Tennessee country into eastern, middle, and western districts and named an official surveyor-general for each. William Polk was named for the middle district.[7] No more favorable position could have been desired by one interested in buying up entries and veterans' warrants at bargain prices and locating them on fertile lands.

William Polk immediately opened an office at French Lick (later named Nashville), the center of a few struggling settlements. This central Tennessee country was a part of the hunting grounds for Cherokee, Creek, and Shawnee Indians. However, since these Indians had given aid to the British during the Revolution, North Carolina no longer respected their land claims.

Polk kept an eye on both the fertile lands of Tennessee and public affairs in North Carolina. In 1785 and 1786 he represented Davidson County in the North Carolina legislature. While there he sponsored the establishment of Davidson Academy (later called Cumberland College, the University of Nashville, and Peabody College) and became a member of its original board of trustees.[8]

[6] Thomas P. Abernethy, *From Frontier to Plantation in Tennessee* (Chapel Hill, 1932), 49–59.

[7] Clark (ed.), *State Records*, XIX, 697.   [8] *Ibid.*, XXIV, 751–52.

This action was no doubt prompted by both a genuine interest in education and a desire to develop the Tennessee country.

The Indians were unwilling to co-operate in this development. Upon learning of North Carolina's designs on their hunting grounds they renewed hostilities, making life miserable for surveyors and attacking settlements. If William Polk had intended to make Middle Tennessee his permanent home, Indian hostilities and thoughts of "Old Mecklenburg" changed his mind.

By 1787 he was back in Charlotte. In that same year he was chosen to represent Mecklenburg County in the legislature, a position he continued to hold until President Washington appointed him supervisor of internal revenue for North Carolina in 1791. In the meantime he married Grizel Gilchrist, daughter of Thomas Gilchrist. When Grizel died in 1799 he moved from Charlotte to Raleigh, where in 1801 he married Sarah Hawkins, daughter of Philemon Hawkins.[9]

William Polk was an ardent Federalist, as were many other men of property, especially speculators in western lands. This party loyalty was reflected in the names of his children—George Washington, Alexander Hamilton, Rufus King. He viewed with much concern the rise of Jeffersonian Republicans to power in state and nation. When the Republican legislature began reducing public support of the University of North Carolina he became much aroused. Since 1790 he had been a member of the board of trustees and was soon to serve as president of the board from 1802–1805. Again and again he sponsored schemes for giving financial relief to that struggling institution.

A century later a biographer of the university remarked that "Col. Polk was a stern, determined, strong man, physically and mentally, ready to fight any man on provocation, of commanding influence by reason of his war record, unyielding will, a mind, not

---

[9] Two sons—Thomas G. and William J.—were born to Polk's first wife. Thomas married Mary Trotter, William became a medical doctor and married Mary Long.

Nine children were born to the second marriage: Lucius J. (married Mary Easten and then Mrs. Ann Pope); Leonidas; Mary B. (married George E. Badger); Alexander H. (died unmarried); Rufus K. (married Sarah Jackson); George W. (married Sallie [Mary] Hilliard); Susan S. (married Kenneth Rayner); Andrew J. (married Rebecca Van Leer); Charles J. (died in childhood).

great but strong, vigorous and well-balanced." [10] He continued to serve the university as trustee until his death in 1834.

In politics William Polk remained a Federalist long after many of his former associates, tempted by federal patronage, were assisting in making North Carolina a Republican state. Shortly after Thomas Jefferson's election to the presidency some eager North Carolina Republicans began investigating the chances of having Polk removed from his office as an internal revenue collector. [11] But he was not proscribed and continued in office until his position was abolished in 1804.

By 1812 William Polk was still enough of a Federalist not to be enthusiastic about the efforts of the "War Hawks," even though North Carolina friends were still applying pressure. When in preparation for probable war Congress authorized a considerable addition to the army, Senator James Turner and Congressman Nathaniel Macon informed Polk that the North Carolina delegation had unanimously agreed to recommend his appointment as colonel in the new army. Polk replied that he had no desire to reenter military service; furthermore, even if he had entertained such a desire, he would have no interest in a commission as colonel.

A few weeks passed and then came another letter from Macon and Turner. The President had recommended and the Senate unanimously approved Polk's appointment as brigadier general. This action had come without pressure from North Carolina congressmen; after receiving Polk's letter they had pursued the matter no further. A few days later Polk also received official notification from Secretary of War William Eustis. Flattered, yet undecided, he requested time to think. He feared that should he decline the commission he would be charged with permitting political bias to destroy his patriotism. [12]

Polk did not accept the commission, but later, when British

[10] Kemp P. Battle, *History of the University of North Carolina* (Raleigh, 1907), I, 127–28, 198–99. Polk was also active in the effort to establish the university's claim to large amounts of Tennessee lands. See William Polk Papers (North Carolina Department of Archives) for correspondence on this subject during the 1820's.

[11] John Steele to William Polk, August 27, 1802, H. M. Wagstaff (ed.), *The Papers of John Steele* (Raleigh, 1924), I, 309.

[12] Polk to John Steele, April 4, 1812, *ibid.*, II, 672–73.

commissioners at Ghent made excessive demands of the United States as the price of peace, he rushed a letter to his brother-in-law, Governor William Hawkins, offering to serve in any capacity needed.[13]

William Polk had become a man of fortune and family. He had six children; his widely distributed land holdings were numbered in the tens of thousands of acres; and he was president of the board of the State Bank at Raleigh. Among associates he was well known for the characteristics that had made him a success. Judge John Haywood, writing in 1808 explaining the difficulties in acquiring slaves at a reasonable price, added: "Col Polk now and then picks up one and occasionally two or three . . . on much more advantageous terms: but he has the advantage of being applied to by the Sellers, as a monied man; and has moreover the additional advantage of a very general knowledge of human nature, together with that of being good at a bargain." [14]

In 1819 William Polk resigned his position with the State Bank in order to give full attention to his landed interests. He now owned 100,000 acres and was reaching for more.[15] His decision to devote full time to landed interests was a quick follow-up to the Chickasaw treaty of 1818 by which these Indians ceded to the United States all claims to the southwestern part of Middle Tennessee and all of West Tennessee. Congress immediately threw these lands open to holders of North Carolina warrants, and Tennessee passed a law creating a committee to adjudicate land claims and provided for sectioning the area into townships five miles square.[16]

With the opening of this new territory to warrant holders and with North Carolina continuing to issue warrants, a mad scramble for location was certain to follow. Polk and a few other men of wealth and standing had little difficulty in securing such warrants

[13] Copy in George W. Polk Papers (University of North Carolina, Chapel Hill, N. C.), October 17, 1814.

[14] Haywood to John Steele, January 6, 1808, Wagstaff (ed.), *Papers of John Steele*, II, 533–37.

[15] "Autobiography of Colonel William Polk," Hoyt (ed.), *Papers of Archibald D. Murphey*, II, 410.

[16] Philip M. Hamer, *Tennessee: A History, 1673–1932* (2 vols., New York, 1933), I, 246–48, 259; Henry D. Whitney (ed.), *The Land Laws of Tennessee* (Chattanooga, 1891), 200–220.

at a nominal price. By midsummer 1820 an interested observer could report: "There is [*sic*] more than 100 Surveyors in this country [West Tennessee] locating. They follow the Surveyors who are sectioning. Indeed every sectioning Surveyor has two or three Locators." A locator representing Colonel Polk, Doctor Hunter and himself had already located "2 or 300,000 acres" near the three forks of the Forked Deer River.[17]

The recipient of this report rushed off to West Tennessee to observe for himself, although he was too near bankruptcy to do more than cry over lost opportunity. This was truly a beautiful country, he wrote back to North Carolina, but the "Rich Spoil" was being "divided among a few, *very few.*" The harvest of fertile lands would be over within another six months, he concluded. "It is rich now and not more than twenty Men have their Sickles in it." [18]

In the midst of his harvesting of good Tennessee lands William Polk took enough time out to become a prominent contributor to the myth of the "Mecklenburg Declaration of Independence." A topic of discussion in the National Capital during the winter of 1818–19 was William Wirt's new biography of Patrick Henry, particularly the section which assigned to Henry credit for furnishing the impulse that set in motion the "ball of Revolution." Argument soon centered around the question of whether Massachusetts or Virginia should be considered the cradle of the Revolution. Still more argument developed when someone observed that neither deserved the honor, for the people of Mecklenburg County, North Carolina, declared themselves independent of Great Britain as early as May, 1775.

This statement created no great excitement in Washington, but Senator Nathaniel Macon and Congressman William Davidson, eager to increase the prestige of their home state, were interested in learning more about this declaration. They wrote Dr. Joseph McKnitt Alexander for any information he might be able to furnish. Alexander searched the papers of his late father John McKnitt Alexander and found just what was requested. The bulk of his father's papers had been destroyed in 1800, but the elderly gen-

[17] Herndon Haralson to Archibald D. Murphey, June 14, 1820, Hoyt (ed.), *Papers of Archibald D. Murphey,* I, 165–66.
[18] Archibald D. Murphey to Thomas Ruffin, July 21, 1822, *ibid.,* 244–49.

tleman, feeling that posterity should not be deprived of valuable information, decided to jot down from memory some notes on events in which he had been a prominent participant.

He recalled that on May 19, 1775, there was held in Charlotte a meeting of delegates representing the militia companies of Mecklenburg County for the purpose of discussing what assistance could be given to the suffering people of Boston. On this same day news of the fighting at Lexington reached Charlotte. Alexander further noted that he himself served as secretary of the meeting. He now recorded from memory (twenty-five years later) the text of the five resolutions adopted by the assembly. As he recalled it, the third resolution declared "That we do hereby declare ourselves a free and independent People, are and of right ought to be, a sovereign and self-governing Association, under the control of no power other than that of our God and the General Government of the Congress. . . ." According to the aged Alexander, this declaration, after free and extensive discussion, was unanimously adopted at 2 A.M., May 20, 1775.

When some New England newspapers questioned the authenticity of Alexander's account the editor of the Raleigh *Register* replied that if there were persons who still doubted they might be convinced by "the testimony of one of the most respectable inhabitants of this city, who was present when the declaration was resolved upon." [19] The person referred to was Colonel William Polk. Polk was already engaged in compiling information on this subject. He had recently received from Archibald D. Murphey a request that he write down everything he knew about "the Proceedings in Mecklenburg—the Declaration of Independence by the People of that county—the steps taken by them in consequence of this Declaration." Murphey also wanted information on settlements in Tennessee, John Armstrong's office, location of lands, work of surveyors, and land frauds. [20] He was collecting material for a proposed history of North Carolina.

Polk, having already resigned his position with the State Bank and now engaged in making preparations for a business trip to

[19] Raleigh *Register*, April 30, August 13, 1819; February 11, 18, May 26, 1820, cited in Hoyt, *Mecklenburg Declaration*.

[20] Murphey to Polk, July 16, 1819, Hoyt (ed.), *Papers of Archibald D. Murphey*, I, 147–48.

Tennessee, wrote a brief narrative of the action in Mecklenburg and of his own Revolutionary service. This along with a copy of the Alexander document taken from the Raleigh *Register* he forwarded to Murphey. He did not discuss the land question.[21] His account of the Mecklenburg declaration was based on the Alexander document but differed in some particulars. He denied credit to the Alexander clan and assigned it to the Polks instead, recalling that the meeting was called and chaired by Thomas Polk and that the declaration was written by Thomas Polk's son-in-law, Dr. Ephraim Brevard, who served as secretary.[22] He also recalled that delegates signed an official copy for Continental Congress. The names of fifteen of these signers he supplied from memory; he promised to furnish others after a trip to Charlotte.

Returning from Tennessee and finding the Mecklenburg story openly challenged, William Polk set to work collecting testimonies of persons who claimed to have been present on that historic occasion. Some of these testimonies he published in pamphlet form in 1822. Those who gave testimony were agreed that a declaration was made but they disagreed (or failed to remember) as to the date and most prominent participants, some taking the Alexander side and others the Polk side.[23] Not one mentioned another meeting on May 31, 1775, nor the resolutions adopted at that meeting. No one had a copy of any resolutions except those drawn up from memory by John McKnitt Alexander.[24]

[21] Hoyt (ed.), *Papers of Archibald D. Murphey*, II, 196–202; Polk to Murphey, August 18, 1819, *ibid.*, I, 153–54; Hoyt, *Mecklenburg Declaration*, 225–29.

[22] John McKnitt Alexander had assigned responsibility for these duties to Adam Alexander, Abraham Alexander, and himself. Dr. Brevard was a graduate of Princeton College. He entered the service as a surgeon early in the Revolution and was captured at the surrender of Charleston in 1780. While in prison he developed a disease that caused his death before the close of the war. William Henry Foote, *Sketches of North Carolina, Historical and Biographical* (New York, 1846), 68–70.

[23] One loyal North Carolinian, writing seventy years after the so-called declaration and depending entirely upon the testimony of old men, gave a glowing account in which he tried to make everybody happy. Thomas Polk was given credit for calling the convention, Abraham Alexander for chairing it, and Brevard and John McKnitt Alexander for serving as clerks. Wheeler, *Sketches*, 35–38.

[24] These testimonies and other documents were published by authority of the North Carolina Legislature in 1831 under the title *The Declaration of Independence by the Citizens of Mecklenburg County on the Twentieth Day of*

It was not until 1838 that any public mention was made of the Mecklenburg Resolves of May 31, 1775. Nine years later a complete copy was discovered in a 1775 newspaper. Complete or condensed copies were later found in several other newspapers, but no contemporary copy of the so-called Declaration of Independence of May 20, 1775, has ever been located. In the light of historical evidence there can be but one conclusion. The Polks, Alexanders, and their Mecklenburg associates, relying on memory rather than records, erred in both date and contents of the Mecklenburg Resolutions. There was no Declaration of Independence on May 20, 1775. But the descendants of William Polk, believing the myth, were ever proud of their ancestors' participation in such an historic event.

May, 1775. This was the work of a committee which had been appointed "to examine, collate, and arrange" all material relating to the subject. The appointment of this committee followed the publication of letters between Jefferson and Adams in which they pronounced the declaration "spurious." The committee concluded that the declaration was authentic.

(3)

Soldier in the Making

COLONEL WILLIAM POLK continued his increase in both acres and offspring. His first four children were boys. Leonidas, the fourth son, was born in Raleigh, April 10, 1806. Family papers yield no information on Leonidas' childhood activities. His first extant letter was written to his mother from Chapel Hill, March 10, 1822. Then a student at the University of North Carolina, he was eager to make a visit home, but more important, he was short on shirts and drawers.[1]

The faculty minutes reveal that he was examined by the faculty and admitted to the freshman class in May, 1821.[2] He had as roommates a cousin, Marshal T. Polk, and David L. Swain.[3] His older brother Lucius was a senior. There is no evidence that young Leonidas distinguished himself as a student. Both he and his father preferred that he be a soldier, and his stay at the university was but a period of preparation for West Point. When an appointment came through early in 1823, Colonel Polk immediately sent detailed instructions as to how his son should spend the remainder of the college year. There must be much concentration on arithmetic, he insisted, if Leonidas was to become an acceptable candidate for admission. He might, however, continue his Latin and possibly other subjects, studying arithmetic on the side.

Leonidas welcomed news of his appointment as a "messenger bearing tidings of an appointment so long wished for, an appointment which was to make so vast an alteration in my career in life." But as for his father's suggestions, "My time would not permit me

[1] Leonidas Polk Papers.
[2] University of North Carolina "Faculty Minutes," 1814–23.
[3] Swain, later president of the university from 1835 to 1868, remained a student at the university for only a short period.

to attend to all these duties at once." A glance at his daily program verifies this fact. "We rise in the morning at half past five o'clock, then until eight are engaged in chapel duties and recitation. At eight we are summoned to breakfast—there is then an hour appropriated for that purpose; from nine until twelve we are preparing for and reciting our Greek lesson; until one we have relaxation and exercise. We go to dinner at one, and commence at two to get our Latin lesson, are thus engaged until four, at which time we recite it; remain at recitation until five, then repair to the chapel, hear prayer, thence to supper. There is a vacation until eight P.M., at which time we retire to our room to prepare a geometry lesson to recite at seven the next morning. Our time is thus occupied during the week until Saturday, the evening of which we are entitled to, leaving very few spare hours to devote to exercise and reading. We have to show compositions every fortnight in the class, and they have to be written during play hours. The society duties [4] are to be attended to also weekly, which are of very great importance and require their portion of time."

Leonidas thought of several plans for improvement. Perhaps he could give up all of his regular subjects except Latin. This idea was abandoned when he learned that the faculty had never permitted such a course. He then decided to give up Latin. He had a "fair" reading knowledge of the language and reasoned that there would be little profit from the "review" planned for the remainder of the year. Surely this review would not be so important as arithmetic. But there was no course in arithmetic offered at the university; consequently, his study in that field must be on his own.

After careful self-examination Leonidas concluded that in two years of college work he had become "but imperfectly acquainted" with his studies. This he attributed not so much to lack of application as to his poor preparation for college. "The evil has shown itself, and I will avoid it henceforth." He resolved to go to West Point prepared "to stand the most scrutinous examination." Furthermore, he would not be satisfied with merely getting by the examination barrier. Some acquaintance with the French language would be most important, for many of the studies at the Academy were clothed in it. And, besides, he explained to his father, "It is a

---

[4] He was a member of the Dialectic Society.

language which is becoming very generally spoken, more particularly in the best circles of society, and it is an attainment truly desirable."

By the time Leonidas had reached this point in his thinking another plan had presented itself. Recognizing his need for good courses in arithmetic and French, neither of which could be had at the University of North Carolina during the spring term, he resolved to withdraw from the university and go to Hillsborough to study arithmetic, French, and geography under the direction of Mr. Rogers.[5] The expense would be no greater, for he had not yet paid his spring term fees at the university. And another point in favor of this new plan was that he could arrive at West Point on time. Should he remain at the university until the close of the term he would arrive at his new destination a week late. He wanted to leave North Carolina by the middle of May and stop for a short stay with his sister Mary, who was attending a girls' school in Philadelphia.[6]

Either Leonidas or his father altered the suggested plan. He did not go to study with Mr. Rogers, but he did withdraw from the university and spent the spring at his Raleigh home.[7] He left for West Point in mid-May, 1823, traveling via Washington, Philadelphia, and New York. He found Mary "altered very much indeed in her appearance & conversation & . . . with all a very *likely girl.*" She performed "prettily" on the harp and sang "handsomely." The two of them rented a gig and went for a ride, visiting Spring Grove, where Mary spent her summers.[8]

Leonidas found New York not to be compared with Philadelphia "in point of beauty, . . . for strictly speaking there is but one street in the City viz. Broadway, which 'by the by' is a most beautiful one." Although impressed by the appearance of the City Hall, greater enthusiasm was exhibited in reporting a circus, where he marveled at performers riding ten horses without the use of reins.[9]

At West Point prospective cadet Polk joined about seventy

[5] The identity of this Mr. Rogers is nowhere revealed.
[6] Leonidas Polk to William Polk, March 10, 1823, Leonidas Polk Papers. This sister, Mary Brown, later became the wife of George E. Badger.
[7] Lucius Polk to Mary B. Polk, March 24, 1823, Polk-Yeatman Papers (University of North Carolina).
[8] Leonidas Polk to Lucius Polk, June 25, 1823, Leonidas Polk Papers.
[9] *Id.* to Mrs. Sarah Polk, July 17, 1823, *ibid.*

other hopefuls. For purpose of examination they were divided into four sections. The staff questioned some boys "very closely" and even made them do problems on the blackboard. Leonidas was more fortunate; after asking him a few questions, which he answered "quite readily," the staff dismissed him without even arraying him before the board. Examinations over, the new cadets began "passing the life of a soldier 'in toto.' "

Camp Scott, near West Point, became their quarters, each man being made comfortable with two blankets. Some of the "effeminates" complained but Leonidas enjoyed the arrangement. A mess hall was provided, so they were not required to cook their own meals. Someone started a rumor that conditioning exercises would include a march all the way to Washington, but authorities soon put troubled minds at ease.[10] "I am now writing to you sitting with my paper on a stool," Leonidas concluded a letter to his brother Lucius, "& must now close as tatoo is beating & our light must be put out in five minutes." [11]

Dutiful son though he was, Cadet Polk was so much "taken up with the novelty of everything around me" that he waited six weeks before writing his parents. An understanding mother, pleased at last to learn he had been admitted to West Point, forgave his negligence and passed on the community news and gossip. The chief news from within family circles was that little sister Susan was growing rapidly. She could "say Mary very plain." Father and brother Lucius were in Tennessee. Lucius would probably remain there permanently.[12]

The West Point cadets moved into the barracks early in September and Cadet Polk expected the coming year to be a very agreeable one, "owing to my good fortune as to room-mates"— William P. Bainbridge and Albert Sidney Johnston of Kentucky and Bennett H. Henderson of North Carolina. Johnston was senior officer of the cadets and very "popular among the officers of the staff on account of his strict attention to duty and steadiness of character." [13]

Leonidas shared the general excitement among cadets over the

[10] *Id.* to Lucius Polk, June 25, 1823, *ibid.*   [11] *Ibid.*
[12] Sarah Polk to Leonidas Polk, August 8, 1823, *ibid.*
[13] Leonidas Polk to Sarah Polk, August 27, 1823; *id.* to Lucius Polk, September 13, 1823, *ibid.*

visits of "great folks" to the Point. He urged his mother to read the newspaper account of the visit of British Minister George Canning. He thought the account on the whole correct "though in places a little florid." General Winfield Scott and family had arrived by boat the previous night, he reported, and would remain a week. The cadets put on a dress parade in his honor. Major William Worth commanded and Colonel Sylvanus Thayer accompanied General Scott. As the General approached colors were lowered and the battalion ordered to present arms. Scott returned the recognition by "doffing his beaver." The cadets then went into various kinds of maneuvers. Among the spectators was Mrs. Scott, formerly "the beautiful Miss Mayo. . . . I was too military, though, to turn my head," Cadet Polk explained, "and therefore did not see her." He observed that the General was a rather large man, "larger than my father," but lacking in grace; "in truth, he is more awkward than otherwise." [14]

A few months later General Edmund P. Gaines visited the Point. Cadet Polk found him "plain and affable in manners," immediately relieving a young man "from that constraint he is put under in the presence of age, superiority of rank, etc." He was especially pleased at his own recognition by the General. When presented as Cadet Polk of North Carolina, General Gaines exclaimed " 'Oh! son of General Polk, I presume.' " Leonidas answered "Yes Sir," although, as he later gleefully related, he had never known his father was a general. Then, on second thought, he recalled that in Tennessee Colonel William Polk was often called "General." [15]

William Polk, upon his return from Tennessee, was displeased with his son's meager descriptions of life at the Military Academy. He wrote for more details; Leonidas replied in full. Cadet Polk was much impressed with the Academy's courses in philosophy, mathematics, and related subjects. There were none better. This was not just an "empty declaration of boyish enthusiasm," he explained, but was the opinion of prominent persons who examined other institutions both at home and abroad. In the days of Napoleon I the Polytechnic in France held first place, but it

[14] *Id.* to Mrs. Sarah Polk, August 27, 1823, *ibid.*
[15] *Id.* to *id.*, June 15, 1824, *ibid.*

had fallen into disrepute. "The internal organization of this academy is a pattern from that, and most of the authors we study are selected from the French, some of them translated into English, others not. The system of teaching is such here as to prevent occurrence of an *evil* prevalent in most colleges. I mean that lazy and idle habit contracted by many students which enables them to be dragged barely at the heels of their classes. At this place it is indispensably necessary that every one should study, and of course be acquainted with what he studies, as the daily examinations in the section rooms are very rigorous and such as to discover whether one knows his lesson or not. If he should be found repeatedly deficient, he is dismissed or forced to resign. Our time is so wholly engrossed in our academic duties that it is impossible to devote any to *literary attainments* privately. I should add, when I speak of literary attainments, I mean such as composition or attendance on debating societies, etc. I was under the impression before coming here that our knowledge of the French language would enable us to speak it tolerably fluent. But I find that we are only taught to read it sufficiently well to prosecute our studies in French with ease."

He had nothing but highest praise for the instructors in military science and tactics. They could certainly perform the duties assigned them and were strong on discipline, which he considered "the quintessence of a well-regulated army." [16]

When the first term examinations were over Cadet Polk was pleased to report that he stood fourth in mathematics. He was not so proud of twenty-seventh in French and a very low rank in English. But he promised to work harder. Several boys had been dismissed, and among them "North Carolina has an able representation." [17]

Leonidas corresponded frequently with his brother Lucius, now in Tennessee looking after their father's landed interests. Lucius was always "full of business," discussing plans for making money and urging Leonidas to hurry and settle near him. Neither showed much interest in politics, although the country was much aroused by the presidential campaign. Leonidas remarked late in 1823 that he had read of Henry Clay's re-election as Speaker of the House

[16] *Id.* to William Polk, November 16, 1823, *ibid.*
[17] *Id.* to *id.*, January 14, 1824, *ibid.*

of Representatives and wondered what effect it might have on the presidential race, but he added that the choice made by the people was a "matter of perfect indifference" to him. He was more interested in some "money making plans." [18]

Their father back in North Carolina was not so indifferent. He had known Andrew Jackson since youth,[19] and in recent years he had become closely acquainted with that group of Middle Tennesseans that had promoted Jackson's candidacy.[20] In North Carolina he was considered the leader of Jackson forces.[21] Writing to Willie P. Mangum, he expressed a willingness to accept either William H. Crawford or John C. Calhoun, "yet I have taken Jackson's side and will promote his election; not through *thick & thin*, but fairly and honestly." [22]

Springtime on the Hudson is always welcomed by West Point cadets. Leonidas was much impressed by the beauty of the river and countryside. On the one hand was nature's beauty set forth in the green foliage of the mountains and the bluegrass of the plains. On the other was the river "over spread" as far as the eye could see with canvas of minor crafts. As these boats passed in review they were "sometimes so thickly huddled together" that it would seem possible "to walk from deck to deck across the river." [23]

Spring quickly passed into summer and Cadet Polk was again in camp. When he arrived he was the "fairest cadet in the corps," but a few days tour on guard duty put him "quite in uniform" so great was the "influence of the sun." Then came relief in the form of an appointment to the Major's staff. "I attend to no military duty at this time whatsoever," he reported to his father, "but am attached to the adjutant's department, and do nothing

[18] *Ibid.; id.* to Lucius Polk, December 5, 1823, *ibid.*

[19] There is a family story of how William Polk and Andrew Jackson together escaped capture by Tarleton's Cavalry (Polk, *Leonidas Polk*, I, 46) but there is not sufficient evidence to authenticate this story.

[20] The William Polk Papers contain considerable political correspondence with such Jackson promoters as John H. Eaton and William B. Lewis.

[21] William S. Hoffman, *Andrew Jackson and North Carolina Politics* (Chapel Hill, 1958), 3. For a full treatment of the campaign see Albert Ray Newsome, *The Presidential Election of 1824 in North Carolina* (Chapel Hill, 1939).

[22] William Polk to Willie P. Mangum, Henry T. Shanks (ed.), *The Papers of Willie P. Mangum* (5 vols., Raleigh, 1950–56), I, 111.

[23] Leonidas Polk to Mrs. Sarah Polk, May 25, 1824, Leonidas Polk Papers.

but write." He considered his appointment quite an honor, for
the past practice had been to appoint the head of the class. His
title was staff sergeant.[24]

Leonidas' only comment on camp life was that he was "pleasantly situated." This was little different from his comment on
life in the barracks where he had been "very comfortably situated." A notable characteristic was that he rarely complained of
his lot except when he felt himself the victim of injustice. He
rarely gave evidence of despondency and often exhibited a
buoyancy that was contagious. Good humor often sparkled with
wit. He was much excited over plans to honor General Lafayette
during his visit to America. Following a great celebration in New
York's Chatham Garden, where a crowd of at least 5,000 was expected, Leonidas reported, the General was scheduled to move up
the river to the Point. From Newberg to the Point the way was
marked with "hosts of tar barrels (North Carolina will thrive)
which are to be fired as he passes upwards." At the Point the
cadets were to do the General all possible military honors—"stun
him with the roar of cannon, drill until he is tired of us, and as
a dinner will be given him, if he remains *until* night, he will
have a *levee!*" [25]

A few months later Cadet Polk was even more excited over
North Carolina's plans to honor General Lafayette. After a winter of visiting in the North the General's party set out for the
South late in February, 1825. Young Polk was particularly pleased
with the honor that was to be accorded his father and other
survivors of the Revolution as North Carolina staged its celebrations. He knew that at Raleigh there would not be such a great
military parade nor the discharge of so many pieces of artillery,
yet he hoped his home state would make up for this in "staunch
civility cordiality & hearty welcome." [26]

Down in Tennessee, Lucius Polk, sharing his brother's enthusiasm over Lafayette's visit, joined a movement to endow a Jackson
and Lafayette professorship at Nashville's Cumberland College.
The action, he explained to his father, would honor both of these

[24] *Id.* to William Polk, July 23, 1824, *ibid.*
[25] *Id.* to *id.*, September 20, 1824, *ibid.*
[26] *Id.* to *id.*, March 4, 1825, *ibid.*

patriots and be of great assistance to the college. If North Carolinians were interested in helping, Lucius would supply subscription blanks.[27] Nothing more was heard of the campaign.

Another term passed. Cadet Leonidas Polk, after a stiff test on analytical geometry, retained his fourth place in mathematics. His standing in French improved, although he was still low. He took up the study of fluxious, a subject not offered at the University of North Carolina. At first he found it difficult, "but like all other mathematics, was readily subservient to application. To the study of the works of the more learned philosophers, Newton, Gregory, etc. it is indispensable." [28]

Scholastically, some of the cadets had experienced a hard time. Most of those admitted the previous July from Kentucky and Tennessee had been dismissed. Cadet Polk had at first feared for his "fellow statesman [Daniel] McNeil" but had been wrong. Although "very odd as well as illiterate," the boy had proved a genius in mathematics. Polk concluded that the boy's "upright & honorable" principles and his desire to do right "so far as he knows," together with his mathematical ability, would no doubt "in the course of time rub off the rust of the N. Ca. swamps." [29]

A normal situation is certainly reversed when a college student complains of his mother's neglect to write. Yet on April 18, 1825, Cadet Polk complained: "I cannot refrain from telling you that I have been a long time patiently awaiting a letter from you." He had frequently heard from her indirectly, still "I wish however to see the scratch of your own pen." A welcomed note from "Pa" had recently been received. As later related to Lucius, "Pa's" notes usually said little more than "Howdy," but on at least one occasion he enclosed "a patch for old shirts" to the extent of fifty dollars, "which although *last* was by no means least." [30] Leonidas also explained to his brother Lucius that the pay of a cadet was not sufficient to meet necessary bills. Although for a time he had hesitated to write home for money, he had now resolved

[27] Lucius Polk to *id.*, May 13, 1825, George W. Polk Papers.

[28] Leonidas Polk to *id.*, January 14, March 4, 1825, Leonidas Polk Papers.

[29] *Id.* to *id.*, January 14, 1825, *ibid.* McNeil later withdrew or was dismissed. He did not graduate.

[30] *Id.* to Mrs. Sarah Polk, April 18, 1825, Leonidas Polk Papers; *id.* to Lucius Polk, July 15, 1825, *ibid.*

henceforth to "make no hesitation in drawing on my father whenever I shall need it." [31]

The fifty-dollar "patch for old shirts" got Cadet Polk into trouble. Early in October, 1825, Colonel William Polk was shocked by a letter from Colonel Sylvanus Thayer, Superintendent of the United States Military Academy. His son had violated regulations, Colonel Polk was informed, by receiving fifty dollars from home. Colonel Thayer was willing to overlook this one offense, however, in view of Cadet Polk's "general good conduct" and in the belief that the money was sent without his father's knowledge. Still he wished to stress that it was strictly against the rules for a cadet to receive extra money.[32] Colonel Polk assured Colonel Thayer it would not happen again.

Before writing Colonel Polk, Colonel Thayer had approached Cadet Polk with the blunt statement: " 'You have received money from home sir.' " Cadet Polk admitted as much, supposing that his father had written Thayer. After being lectured on the "necessity of obeying literally the Regulations," Leonidas tried to explain that additional funds were necessary to pay little bills and buy shirts.

Leonidas was furious when he learned that his father was not the informer. A brief investigation soon revealed the guilty party. ". . . the Col will not hesitate a moment to receive any information from *any source* concerning us," he wrote his father. There were "a great many individuals (of all ranks) on the Point, who act as his emissaries & whose duty it is to *spy out secretly* and report all infractions of regulations." He himself had learned too late that the postmaster was among these informers. He had indiscreetly opened his letter and exhibited his money in the postmaster's presence.

Leonidas regretted his father's promise to the Colonel, "for I am now in want of flannels & other things which money must buy." After deductions were made from his twenty-eight dollars per month allowance from the government, only six dollars were left "to pay the tailor, shoemaker and merchant for such articles as may be wanted." Like most other cadets he was already in debt to the extent of his next month's pay. This condition had

[31] *Id.* to *id.*, October 18, 1825, *ibid.*
[32] Sylvanus Thayer to William Polk, September 26, 1825, *ibid.*

existed for some time and there seemed to be no remedy. "Not even the rigid economy of the Yankees can withstand it," he had concluded. It was even rumored that the Colonel wished to keep cadets in debt so that they would have no money to spend on trifles. "For one, I should rather consult my own wishes, & sense of propriety." [33]

Cadet Polk's scholastic standing continued very satisfactory except in French. After the close of the 1825 spring term he stood seventh in merit, fourth in mathematics, ninth in drawing, and thirty-seventh in French. He confided to his brother Lucius that he had "become quite indifferent & almost disgusted" with French. "It has been a curse on me for the last two years, & has prevented my being one of the five best in my class who are distinguished by being annually placed on the army register." But he was now through with it and had "shaken it off." During the coming year his course of study would include chemistry, philosophy, and drawing "& I anticipate much pleasure in pursuing it."

Leonidas remained much impressed with West Point, even though he did fret about the restriction on spending money. He was particularly pleased by the visit of the new Secretary of War, James Barbour, and the Secretary's address in which he urged strict discipline administered with kindness and complete obedience on the part of cadets. The Board of Visitors also came to the Point about this same time. "They saw much that was calculated to please, because it was novel," Cadet Polk observed, "but I cannot but think they do praise us more than we deserve." [34]

Life at the Point was not all work. Cadet Polk found summer camp life far from "wearisome." Then there were frequent trips to New York and even attendance at dancing school. Among persons, distinguished and otherwise, who visited the Point were some of "the fair sex" whose presence, young Polk observed, "inspired a degree of gallantry which caused many a poor fellow to straiten [sic] himself until he was as stiff as a poker to appear military." Neither did the idea of returning to barracks bring any dread, for Leonidas had "no fears of being compelled to lounge out a lazy existence for the ten months intervening between this

[33] Leonidas Polk to *id.*, December 4, 1825, *ibid.*
[34] *Id.* to *id.*, June 12, 1825; *id.* to Lucius Polk, July 15, 1825, *ibid.*

& the next encampment." [35] Not even rigorous training could change his cheerful disposition. His sister Mary once reported that she had just received a letter from "Brother Cadet" and he was in the usual good spirits.[36]

Colonel William Polk was sufficiently impressed by Leonidas' reports to wish an appointment for his next son, Alexander Hamilton. This was not possible, however, since the Academy rules did not permit brothers to be enrolled at the same time. Hamilton entered the University of North Carolina. Leonidas was pleased and urged Hamilton to make a special effort to improve himself in literature and science, explaining that he hoped the third Polk would do better at Carolina than the previous two had done.[37]

Cadet Polk considered spending his 1825 summer vacation in North Carolina and probably visiting Lucius in Tennessee but decided to wait another year. Lucius continued to write of opportunities in Tennessee, where he was reported to be "respected, admired & beloved." He described himself as "a solitary inmate of Willsgrove and happy as a Lord." [38] Willsgrove was his father's place near the present Springhill.

Lucius' enthusiasm made Leonidas curious. "How many negroes have you?" he queried. "Who are your neighbors? How far to the nearest navigable stream? & those that might be made so? Is there much public spirit among you? Can they generally command much money?" [39]

The fall and early winter on the Hudson had been mild and pleasant, Cadet Polk wrote home. Examinations were approaching and "all are, as usual making vigorous preparations." Now that he was rid of French he had high hopes of better standing. However, when examinations had come and passed the results brought more grief than pleasure. Cadet Polk ranked fifth in both chemistry and philosophy but dropped to thirty-second in drawing. With a mixture of anger and humiliation, he sent his father both the report and his own explanation: "In regard to this latter,

[35] *Id.* to Hamilton Polk, September 4, 1825, *ibid.*
[36] Mary Polk to Lucius Polk, September 6, 1823, Polk-Yeatman Papers.
[37] Leonidas Polk to Mrs. Sarah Polk, April 18, 1825; *id.* to Hamilton Polk, September 4, 1825, Leonidas Polk Papers.
[38] Alfred Balch to William Polk, December 31, 1825, William Polk Papers; Lucius Polk to Mary Polk, July 10, 1825, Polk-Yeatman Papers.
[39] Leonidas Polk to Lucius Polk, October 18, 1825, Leonidas Polk Papers.

I feel it incumbent on me to state, that it is as unjust, as it is injurious to my general standing in the institution. In order that you should understand why it is of such a nature, I have thought proper to send you the accompanying copy of a letter addressed by me to the Secretary of War." [40]

At great length young Polk explained to the Secretary the alleged injustice suffered by himself and about half the members of his drawing class. Although the rules of the Academy prohibited such a practice, many cadets had traced the originals in preparing their pieces. Such a practice had long been general, and neither cadets nor professors had been concerned about the rule forbidding it. But recently there had been a sudden decision to enforce the rule. About half the class admitted violation, some others denied it, and still others, equally guilty, were not questioned by the professors. The result was that those who admitted their guilt suffered academic punishment, while other guilty ones were given top ranking in their class. Appeals to the Superintendent brought no relief, so Cadet Polk requested that his spirited protest be forwarded to Secretary of War James Barbour.

Several other cadets also wrote letters, some to the Secretary of War, others to congressmen. Few, however, expressed hope of assistance. But Cadet Polk confided to his father, "I do not despair, notwithstand[ing] the repeated assurance of the Col to the contrary, lest my letter should fail to produce the desired effect." Yet he realized that Colonel Thayer would furnish the War Department with "strong reasons to support the course he has taken, predicated I presume on the 'good of the institution.'" [41]

Colonel Polk, although concerned, did not consider the matter too serious; he sent Leonidas some sound advice on the necessity of accepting the unfavorable decision. Before this advice reached West Point, Cadet Polk received a reply from Secretary Barbour. The Secretary reviewed the complaints in order and then approved the action taken. To the cadets affected he suggested that the next examinations were only six months away. Those who applied themselves diligently would no doubt regain the standing they had lost.

[40] *Id.* to William Polk, February 8, 1826, *ibid.*
[41] *Ibid.*

"For this I was not prepared," exclaimed Cadet Polk. He had not expected a reversal of the decision of the Board of Visitors nor even a reflection upon the wisdom of the action of that body, he explained to his father, but he had hoped for a reopening of the case and possibly the questioning of each cadet involved. "This would have been a kind of compromise, would have secured to us our just rights, & allowed the board and others a fair opportunity of judging our merits." Nevertheless, this was not the Secretary's decision. Accepting his father's advice and with a realization of the fact that to pursue any other course would be folly, he "determined to abide tacitly by the decision," although not at all "shaken in my opinions in regard to the matter." Even though his immediate standing had been seriously affected, he realized that within a few years after graduation time would have "obliterated the fact of an individual's standing here or there." Consequently, he assured his father, he had now "put to rest all my cares about the affair, & I am now progressing as cheerfully as though I were first." [42]

Colonel William Polk, in semiretirement at his Raleigh home, scarcely had time to dismiss from his mind the controversy over his son's standing when another letter arrived. To an old soldier and man of business who had never given much attention to religion the opening paragraphs of this letter must have had an ominous ring:

> The feelings I now bring to the performance of a duty at all times my peculiar delight are such as constrain me before proceeding to request you to read patiently that which I shall write & value it, as the result of deliberate convictions, & not of hasty conclusions, or warmth of feeling.
>
> During the course of my life I have often been brought to reflect on that subject, which of all others to a large portion of mankind has always been either the most entirely interesting, a matter of indifference, or the most painful, when pressed in among their meditations on the pleasures of the present of the probable certainty of a future life. And like a vast number of my fellow beings, I have repeatedly put off the further consideration of such things as presented themselves, to, what I *conceived* a more favorable opportunity, designing at a future day, when less

[42] *Id.* to *id.*, April 2, 1826, *ibid.*

engaged with worldly affairs, to examine fairly into their truths, and close in with, & embrace, such conclusions, as I should be enabled to deduce, from that examination.

The Cadet was definitely having trouble getting started, but before Colonel Polk had read further he must have recognized that the subject referred to was the doctrines and duties of the Christian religion. About four weeks ago, Leonidas continued, he had decided to turn his attention to the investigation of this subject. This decision was prompted by the reading of two volumes of published letters written by Olinthus Gregory of the Royal Military Academy, Woolwich, England. These letters were written in response to a request from a friend and former associate who wished to continue their topics of conversation even while separated.

Drawing upon the best writings of several authors and piecing these excerpts together in logical sequence, Gregory presented both the evidences of Christianity and its doctrines and duties. Cadet Polk was much impressed with the evidences since Gregory "often—as in miracles—instituted comparisons between religion & the sciences, the established facts of the one with those of the other, the mysteries of the one with those of the other." Having recently acquired some knowledge of the sciences, Cadet Polk found much in these volumes that he could apply to himself. Before completing the study of this work his convictions were so "complete & thorough" that he immediately sought a conference with "our most excellent minister Mr McIlvaine." [43]

Charles Pettit McIlvaine, later Bishop of Ohio, had been at the Military Academy for about a year, and according to his own story, had conferred in private with only one student. He had found neither cadets nor faculty interested in religion. His sole conference had been with a cadet who was seeking comfort following the death of his father. To this young man he gave a tract on Christianity and requested that he place it in the barracks. It was this tract that fell into Cadet Polk's hands and attracted his attention to the evidences of Christianity. Wishing further information on the subject, Polk recalled that the Chaplain had deposited with the quartermaster a number of volumes on the

---

[43] *Id.* to *id.*, May 11, 1826, *ibid.*

Christian religion. He secured one of these works—the volumes
by Gregory.

Many years later, after Leonidas Polk had distinguished himself both as a bishop and a general, Bishop McIlvaine wrote an
account of Polk's conversion and subsequent religious activities
at West Point.[44] The main parts of the story may be trusted.

McIlvaine recalled that one Saturday afternoon a cadet appeared at the Chaplain's house and introduced himself as Polk.
He gave the appearance of being much upset and had some
difficulty in speaking. The Chaplain supposed that the boy was
in trouble with authorities, but soon getting control of himself,
young Polk told his story. "After I had given him instruction &
prayed with him, he became tranquil, & began to speak of his
circumstances." Henceforth he would be a marked man, the cadet
explained, subjected to curious observations and ridicule, for there
was no record of either a cadet or a professor at West Point ever
professing religion.

Cadet Polk wished advice. How must he conduct himself? Mc-
Ilvaine suggested that he immediately step out from the crowd
and take his stand. The next day this new convert was the first
cadet ever to kneel during services in the Academy chapel. His
influence was immediately felt. Soon a number of other cadets
were seeking conferences with Chaplain McIlvaine. Some were
introduced by Cadet Polk. The Chaplain began holding regular
prayer meetings in his home. Rapid increase in attendance soon
made it necessary to shift the services to the chapel. There, forty
days after his first conference with Cadet Polk, Chaplain Mc-
Ilvaine baptized Cadets Leonidas Polk and William B. Magruder.

The intense feeling with which Polk entered upon what he
considered a new life was well expressed in his report to the
homefolk:

> This step was my most trying one. To bring myself to re-
> nounce all of my former habits and associations, to step forth
> singly from the whole corps, acknowledging my convictions of
> the truth of the Holy religion which I had before derided, and
> was now anxious to embrace, & to be put up as it were a mark
> for the observations of others; were trials which, unaided by the
> consolations of the Bible, humble and fervent prayer, & above

[44] Charles P. McIlvaine to C. T. Quintard, December 31, 1868, *ibid.*

all the strong hand of him who is all powerful to shield & protect all such as do earnestly desire to make their peace with him, I should have sunk under, & again fallen back upon the world. By the especial favor of Divine Providence however, I was so strengthened as to continue my efforts, heedless of all opposition, & can now freely say that rather than relinquish the prospect before me, or yield aught of that hope which cheers me in every duty, I would suffer such torture for centuries, though it were increased a thousandfold. Since I have found my mind at ease, & fortified against the opinions of the world, I do not find the duties of religion of that gloomy, insipid, & austere character that those of the world conceive they possess, so far from it, that I am clearly convinced that the most happy man on earth is, he who practices most faithfully the duties of Christianity.[45]

Colonel Polk and family were much disturbed by the tone of Leonidas' letter. A practical business man himself, William Polk had no time for emotionalism. He apparently implied as much in his answer to Leonidas. His letter has not been found, but Leonidas wrote immediately after receiving it, expressing "deep regret" that he had been "the cause of uneasiness to the family. I can now realize more clearly, the feelings with which it impressed you, when read." He regretted his inability to repress the expression of his own feelings. This made it impossible for him to write "with coolness, or dispassionately." Considering this, plus "the natural warmth, & I hope, tenderness of my affection toward my parents, & the solicitude I had for them, as also for the rest of my relatives & friends, I trust, my dear Father, you will make every allowance for the overflowing of a heart thus filled with emotions of the liveliest regard."

In his previous letter Leonidas had stated that since there had been such a change in his life there must also be a change in his plans. He had intended to remain at the Academy until after graduation in 1827. Now he wished to visit home during the summer of 1826. His father sent funds and a letter to Colonel Thayer, and Leonidas made plans to arrive in North Carolina by July 1.[46]

Cadet Polk spent July and August, 1826, in North Carolina.

[45] Leonidas Polk to William Polk, May 11, 1826, *ibid.*
[46] *Id.* to *id.*, June 5, 1826, *ibid.*

This was his first visit in three years. News of the change in his life had already spread among relatives, and no doubt many were wondering what to expect. Following a visit from Leonidas one relative wrote Colonel Polk: "Leonidas has always been one of my favorites. I am gratified to think, that from all appearances exhibited, instead of a *melancholy* he only manifests the sedate appearance of riper years, chastened by much experience for one of his age, under the good discipline at West Point. In fact he is not only well informed and very correctly impressed as to men and things, but with us he is cheerful." [47]

There is no evidence that at this time Leonidas was considering entering the Christian ministry. He did apparently make it clear to the family that he had no desire to become a professional soldier. The life of a planter was more to his liking, and Colonel Polk was sufficiently impressed to divide between Leonidas and his older brother William a large tract of land in Maury County, Tennessee, on the condition that they settle thereon.[48]

On board the steamer *Constitution* returning to West Point, Leonidas got off a long letter to Lucius at Columbia, Tennessee. He supposed that by this time Lucius had learned of the change in his views and feelings:

> In relation to that information, so far as it referred to my change of views & feelings, in regard to that most important of all other subjects, Christianity, I have to observe that I hope you have been rightly informed. They have been revolutionized, & I most sincerely trust, completely so. I am aware of what are the opinions of men of the world, generally, as to that subject, and those who are its followers. I know what my own have been, & am persuaded, that I did conceive it impossible for man to be so completely blinded & ignorant of that, which it *most particularly* became him of *all* things to be thoroughly enlightened upon. I am free to declare, to the assembled world, that I firmly believe, the opinions I before entertained, were not only the most erroneous, but the most awfully dangerous; & that my course of life was equally ruinous. This is just such language you will say, as you have often heard, & from me perhaps, expected to hear. If I were situated as you are, doubtless I should, as indeed I have,

[47] Thomas D. Hawkins to *id.*, July 21, 1826, *ibid.*
[48] Leonidas Polk to Lucius Polk, August 25, 1826, *ibid.*

in a like case, said much about the same. But if I could, I would retract, & say as I have above, that man knows not, nor do they seem to care for knowing, the but too sad realities of the truth. It is not a phantom of man's imagining. No, my dear Brother, but the whole truth & thus it would be found, by all men if rightly examined. Then if the truth, what should be the course of such as do not seem to know it, but as soon as can be, to search it out with all diligence. And if properly sought after we have a *scriptural warrant*, that it shall surely be found, & farther the experience of mankind, has *never* found, that warrant to fail, to which let me again add my own & say, that *I* do no more certainly believe *any* fact than the truth of Revelation. What can I do less then, than *beseech you most tenderly*, to examine for yourself, & having now given you my own opinion, which are but remarkably insignificant, I leave the rest to you, earnestly hoping you will not procrastinate an investigation, & do assure you most affectionately, that you shall be ever remembered in my devotions, & especially it shall be my prayer, that you may arrive at, & believe, the solemn truths of which I have been speaking.

Returning to more worldly matters, Leonidas assured Lucius of his pleasure that the body of Polk lands in Maury County was large enough to support three or four plantation families. Polks could then be their own neighbors. After completing his senior year at the Academy he hoped to see Lucius in the fall of 1827. It might be possible that he would be retained in the army for one year, but he rather doubted it.[49]

Cadet Polk's senior year was spent in serious thought and study. His record in required subjects was good, but he was dissatisfied with his attainments in the fields of culture. The schools he had attended, although among the best, he observed, had given him no more than an "acquaintance" with the several branches of culture "& a very general & superficial knowledge of the whole." This might be sufficient to the needs and satisfaction of most students, but he had "an inclination to prosecute farther" some of these branches and to take up the study of others. "My classical education particularly, I am sensible is very imperfect," he explained to his father. "My knowledge of History & indeed of

[49] *Ibid.*

most other books, aside from my text books, is exceedingly limited, & I feel great unwillingness to close my eyes to all this light while effort only is wanting to its enjoyment." [50]

Colonel Polk must have been disturbed by this report on his son's self analysis. It was not the conclusion that might be expected from a potential planter or soldier. Reading further in this same letter he found other ideas of which he disapproved. Colonel Thayer had suggested to Cadet Polk that he accept a professorship of mathematics and physical sciences in a new seminary about to be opened in Massachusetts. The salary was $800 plus living expenses; the work would require only three hours per day. Leonidas was favorably impressed. It would not only give him an opportunity to earn while improving his own knowledge but he thought he might also take his younger brothers Rufus and George with him. And Colonel Thayer had suggested there would probably be no difficulty in securing relief from any obligation to the army. The Cadet urged his father to advise him what to do.[51]

Colonel Polk was not impressed by the opportunity; he had no desire to see his son become a schoolmaster. During the past summer he had observed that Leonidas' health was not good. He feared that a year of confinement in a Massachusetts schoolroom would further contribute to poor health. Furthermore, at this point in life his son should be cautious always to act in such a manner as to be worthy of himself, his family, and station in life. He implied a fear that in Massachusetts his son might fall under "some improper influence," distorting his mind from "its native vigor" and leading him into the blind "adoption of some wild or silly scheme." Besides, it was time for Leonidas to choose a profession and adopt a settled plan of life.

This advice gave Cadet Polk an opportunity for which he had no doubt been waiting for some months. He declined the offer of a professorship. The selection of a profession, he wrote his father, was a step of tremendous importance and required calm deliberation. "I have long time and often had the subject before me, & divesting myself of every bias, have repeatedly surveyed the whole field of human avocation, to find out that course through which interest and inclination should direct me to proceed, & I

[50] *Id.* to William Polk, March 31, 1827, *ibid.*   [51] *Ibid.*

am happy in being able clearly to pronounce my search has not been fruitless, as I am fully persuaded that the ministry is the profession to which I should devote myself." That he should eventually select this course he thought would be no surprise to the family. And he wished to make it clear that the choice was his own, free from undue influence of others. He had chosen the ministry because he felt "that in the exercise of its function I should find my greatest happiness."

Having made his announcement, Cadet Polk expressed a desire to travel some in the northern and eastern sections of the United States following graduation. He would be obliged if Colonel Polk would send the necessary funds. The money might be sent by his cousin Henry Hawkins, who was about to enter the Academy.[52]

Young Hawkins soon arrived bringing the funds and letters of introduction to Martin Van Buren and Churchill C. Cambreling. Cadet Polk graduated eighth in his class on July 4, 1827. Immediate orders were for him to remain with the corps during summer encampment, but within ten days he had secured a release and was off for New York City.

His father had approved the plans for travel with the hope that Leonidas' health might improve. He also hoped that association with people, at least some of whom were in positions of importance, might cause his son to become more settled in mind. And the son, ever conscious of his father's disapproval of the course he had selected, labored to demonstrate that, although he had decided to enter the ministry, he had not lost interest in the world about him. In New York he ran across a new "multiplying writing machine by means of which we are able to obtain two copies of what ever we write at once." He purchased one for his father's use in preserving copies of business letters sent to Tennessee.

At Philadelphia young Polk visited the improved water works and sent his father a detailed description. At Boston he saw a railroad which ran a distance of three and a half miles. It had been built for the purpose of hauling stone from the Quincy quarry to build the Bunker Hill monument. He furnished Colonel Polk with details of the method of railroad construction and in-

[52] *Id.* to *id.*, May 9, 1827, *ibid.*

cluded a diagram of the rails and the wheels used on the horse-drawn "wagons."

From Boston he rode out to Quincy to the house of the late President John Adams, which was now occupied by Judge Thomas Adams. Nothing was as he had expected. In his Southern aristocratic way of thinking, he had pictured the Adams home as "a fine country-seat, occupying an eminence, surrounded with groves, orchards, and woodland, with all the appurtenances of such a place." Instead he found "a plain, oblong, two-story, white house, with dormer windows, near the road, surrounded with fine shade-trees and fields for three quarters of a mile, at least." [53]

At Albany he called upon Martin Van Buren and while there met Thomas Ritchie, editor of the *Richmond Enquirer*. From Albany he went on to visit the Great Lakes and a small portion of Canada, and then headed for Tennessee via Wheeling. From Wheeling he preferred travel along the extension of the Cumberland Road rather than the river. The road was "quite unfinished and rough." In fact he found all western roads "wretched in the extreme" regardless of "however much politicians may disagree." Upon reaching the mouth of the Cumberland River he found the water too low to float steamboats to Nashville; so he traveled on to Middle Tennessee by stage.

At Willsgrove, the Polk estate in Maury County, he found Lucius well and busy.[54] He also found the Negroes generally well and not complaining, he reported to his father, although there was much fever in neighboring communities. The Negroes seemed well-contented with their new location. Crops were fine; cotton picking was well underway.[55]

[53] *Id.* to *id.*, June 22, July 14, 23, 30, August 22, 1827, *ibid.* On his way to Boston he visited Hartford and New Haven, met the president and some of the professors at Yale, and gave the college careful examination.

[54] At this time, however, Lucius must have been a bit disgusted with the uncertainties of farming. He wrote his father that there was very little money to be made in farming and he very much desired to accumulate a fortune. After looking about he had decided that the iron business offered good opportunities. He could arrange to enter this business in connection with Judge John Catron provided his father would make him a loan of $6,000 (Lucius to Father, August 25, 1827, Polk-Yeatman Papers). William Polk apparently was not interested; nothing more is recorded of Lucius' connection with the iron business.

[55] For letters describing his travels see Leonidas Polk Papers under dates August 30, September 14, October 23, 1827.

While at Willsgrove, Leonidas visited the Hermitage to dine with the Jacksons and "found the Genl. & his lady both as courteous as I could have wished." Desiring to remain longer in Tennessee and realizing he would not reach North Carolina by October 25, the date his furlough would expire, he wrote out a letter of resignation and sent it to his father to be forwarded to West Point. Colonel Polk had never given his approval of the course adopted by his son and had no doubt hoped that travel might influence Leonidas to change his mind. The letter of resignation put an end to such hope. Along with the letter Leonidas sent a personal note expressing the hope that there would be no difficulty in obtaining his father's consent to "my resignation." [56]

[56] Leonidas Polk to William Polk, October 23, 1827, *ibid.*

(4)

Minister to Planter

Leonidas returned to North Carolina late in the fall of 1827. During the next year Colonel Polk spent considerable time in Tennessee, leaving him to supervise family property and to keep his father informed as to crops, repairs on buildings and mills, the harvesting and storing of grain, and the prices that might be expected for surplus produce. He wrote Lucius bragging about his crops and offering to let his brother have a cotton stalk for a walking cane. "I am to have some of those stalks saved & hung up in a conspicuous place, to put to shame some of the exorbitant stories of Tenn. planters."

With Lucius he also discussed problems connected with the disposition of his own property. Through gift, apparently from his father, he had acquired some land and a number of slaves in North Carolina. He suggested that these slaves might be more profitable if placed on Tennessee lands.

> The truth is, I do not expect to live in Raleigh or perhaps the State & it would be as well for them to be in Tenn. as N. C. . . . I have not the smallest inclination to farm there or elsewhere in person. Land & negroes is all I have & I want to make the most of them. I don't know whether it would be more profitable to sell the negroes & land I have & live on what they would bring me or rather the interest of it, or to farm under all the inconveniences. . . . I should be satisfied with a moderate income. I can live on a little & am not desirous about having more than will support me decently & honourably, & will relieve me from apprehension and want.[1]

Before the end of the year he made an arrangement with Lucius to take the Negroes. As soon as crops were gathered they were to

[1] Leonidas Polk to Lucius Polk, August 22, 1828, Leonidas Polk Papers.

start their trek to Tennessee. Lucius would send wagons for supplies and children; the adults would walk.[2]

Leonidas would soon change his views about future financial needs, for during his stay in Raleigh he renewed a childhood acquaintance with Frances Ann Devereux. Romance quickly blossomed into a full-grown love affair. Early in July, 1828, he wrote Lucius, "I am & have been, since the middle of May, engaged to be married. To Miss D——. Of course you cannot be *surprised* at this. . . . *All parties,* on both sides, seem gratified with the arrangement." [3] A few weeks later he wrote that the wedding would probably take place in October or November.[4] But the wedding was postponed. Frances later recalled that Leonidas wished to be married immediately, but "I thought it best that our marriage should be delayed—with great reluctance he acceded to this." [5]

By early October Leonidas was in Brooklyn studying Hebrew under a master "highly recommended for the facility & dispatch with which he teaches." He had considered entering a seminary in New York but had now decided in favor of one in Alexandria, District of Columbia. He would remain in Brooklyn until after the "convention of this diocese" and then go straight to Alexandria.

In deciding in favor of the Virginia Theological Seminary at Alexandria he had been influenced by the lower cost and the "spirit of the place." [6] Also in studying in a Southern school he would become acquainted with many persons with whom he would later be associated in his chosen work. As to the possible difference in the ratings of the two schools, he was not too much concerned. "The real labour of an education in any branch devolves necessarily on the student himself," he explained to his father, "& the great advantage of any place of study depends on the course of study & manner of instruction, & the ability of the professor of the course. As to the lecture which a professor may

[2] *Id.* to *id.,* November 17, 1828, *ibid.*

[3] July 3, 1828, Gale Papers (University of North Carolina).

[4] *Id.* to *id.,* August 22, 1828, Leonidas Polk Papers.

[5] Mrs. Leonidas Polk, "Leonidas Polk, A Memoir Written by His Wife for Their Children," MS in Leonidas Polk Papers.

[6] This seminary had opened its doors in 1824 with only two professors and not more than fifteen students. The spirit was definitely evangelical.

give, all of them on any branch, could no doubt be comprised in a single volume. At this day, all that professors do say, can be found already published either in single volumes or several." The important point then was not what the professor had to say but that the student's time was properly allotted and the proper books placed in his hands. Then by associating and conversing with others engaged in the same pursuit of knowledge the student would be mentally improved. "These things, I think, forming the essence of a public education, & obtainable at Alexandria authorize me, with the other considerations to prefer it to New York." [7]

By early November Leonidas Polk had arrived at Alexandria and was "permanently fixed." He had stopped for a few days in Washington to attend a meeting of the Educational Society of the Episcopal Church. During his stay he joined two associates in a call on President John Quincy Adams at the White House. While they were waiting to be received Secretary of State Henry Clay came out of the President's office. One member of the party knew Clay and introduced the others. Young Polk thought the Secretary "a man of uncommonly imposing manners, tall, dignified, affable, & easy, & very intelligent looking." He was not so impressed with President Adams whom he thought "as awkward as Mr. Clay is easy." The President looked ill. This condition Polk attributed to the "harassing electioneering tour" which had just been completed. And the White House grounds looked as dilapidated as the President.[8]

The seminary proved to be all that Polk had expected. The building was so situated as to command an extensive view of the Potomac, Washington, Alexandria, and Georgetown. From his window he could see the Capitol, and with the use of a glass, members of Congress walking up and down the steps. When his sister Mary and her husband, George Badger, visited him they found his quarters "charming." [9]

Nevertheless, his letters home gave the impression of loneliness, or at least an eagerness for bits of news. Were his slaves ready for the trip to Tennessee? Would his father select persons to deter-

---

[7] Leonidas Polk to William Polk, October 7, 1828, Leonidas Polk Papers.
[8] *Id.* to *id.*, November 5, 1828, *ibid.*
[9] *Ibid.*; George Badger to *id.*, July 24, 1829, William Polk Papers.

mine their value? Lucius was to pay for them within three years. Would his father look after the stock and crop just as if they were his own? He had learned through Mary of the birth of a baby brother. Since the last one was named Andrew Jackson and "General Jackson is the last of the line of heroes and sages," he feared difficulty in finding a suitable name for this latest arrival. (Two previous sons had been named Alexander Hamilton and George Washington.) However, when the news came that the baby had been named Charles James for two of his uncles, Leonidas pronounced the name satisfactory. He was glad the baby was a boy, he told his father, for "there seems to be less difficulty, & risque in the education and lives of boys than girls. Nine sons too, make up a goodly number." [10] Colonel Polk was truly following a suggestion made by his father-in-law a few years earlier: ". . . it is clearly my opinion that the greater the number of children that you have the greater the blessing." [11]

Leonidas was greatly saddened by the news of the death of Mrs. Andrew Jackson. This must have been a great shock to the General, he commented to his mother, especially since he had recently "been so highly honored in defiance of the abuse heaped both on himself & her. And it must also teach him the frailty of human existence, & the necessity for being at any moment ready to resign it." There were rumors that in recent years the General had altered his views with regard to religion, Leonidas further commented. "I hope the high honours conferred on him by Providence through his life, & this sudden affliction will deepen his impression of its necessity." What a "noble spectacle" it would be to have the head of the government guided by the principles of Christianity. "For they would supply motives for his conduct, which would place him beyond the reach of either praise or censure, from the sycophant or the disappointed & we might see merit, wherever found, rewarded as it deserved." [12]

An excess of rain, snow, and cold weather and the "remains of a cold" kept Leonidas fairly close to quarters during the winter of 1828–29. He did make a few trips to Washington and to Mount

[10] Leonidas Polk to *id.*, November 5, 21, 1828, Leonidas Polk Papers.
[11] Philemon Hawkins to *id.*, July 3, 1822, Polk-Yeatman Papers.
[12] Leonidas Polk to Sarah Polk, January 10, 1829, Leonidas Polk Papers.

Vernon and reported interesting details. The beauty of Mount Vernon impressed him; so did the terrible road leading to it. In Washington he sat in on sessions of both houses of Congress. Both in and out of the Capitol he observed general satisfaction with the election of Jackson to the presidency, yet no one professed knowledge of who would compose the new cabinet.[13]

On another occasion Leonidas attended a meeting of the Colonization Society. In advance of the meeting he learned that the session would be of unusual interest since the Society had made many new friends during the past year. It was predicted that Henry Clay would be present to take advantage of a final opportunity to speak before leaving Washington. Leonidas braved a cold rain in order to be present and thoroughly enjoyed the evening. The report of the Board of Managers was particularly interesting. The African colony was said to be more flourishing than ever before. There had been an increase in both territory and immigrants, and relations with neighboring tribes were much improved. The Negroes in Liberia were "beginning to understand & practice successfully the principles of self government." Schools were flourishing, and there was considerable interest in literature on agriculture and trade. In view of all of these developments, Leonidas observed, "they seem to possess all any people could desire for personal comfort or exchange."

Speakers of the evening included Charles F. Mercer of Virginia, Henry R. Storrs of New York, and Clay. Leonidas thought Mercer "a very easy & graceful speaker & very fluent." Clay gave a sketch of the history of the Society, and stressed the interest ladies had taken in the work of the organization. Leonidas came away from the meeting with a feeling that "all that is wanting to remove not only the blacks that are free, but those that are enslaved also, is the consent of their owners & funds to transport them." He prophesied that "in the course of not many years one State after another will be willing to abolish slavery." He thought conditions in Virginia and Maryland were already such as to promote such a movement.[14] However, he made no suggestion that

[13] *Id.* to William Polk, November 21, 1828, *ibid; id.* to Sarah Polk, December 1, 1828, Gale Papers.

[14] *Id.* to *id.*, January 10, 1829; *id.* to William Polk, January 21, 1829, Leonidas Polk Papers.

the Polks consider emancipating their own slaves or make financial contributions to the work of the Society.

Probably because of his nearness to Washington and the family's friendship with President-elect Jackson, Leonidas was taking more interest in public affairs. He shared the preinauguration excitement and was pleased to learn that his father would likely be present at the ceremonies. Since a great crowd was expected, he suggested that his father either arrive early or arrange to take quarters with a friend. Travel by stage, although very "uncomfortable and rugged," would be advisable, he explained, for at that time of year ice prevented steamboats from making regular use of the Potomac.[15]

Colonel Polk did make the trip to Washington. In addition to a sincere desire to see his old friend inaugurated President, he also wished to secure a cabinet post for his son-in-law, George Badger. In June, 1828, Colonel Polk had spent three days with Jackson at the Hermitage,[16] and during the recent campaign he had rendered effective service as chairman of the Jackson Committee in North Carolina. Had he been a younger man with political ambitions he no doubt could have had an appointment himself. Badger had also been active, but he was scarcely known outside North Carolina. And even within his home state he had not done so good a job of self-promotion as had John Branch. The latter used every known method to endear himself to those who could be of service to him. He named his new son Andrew Jackson, made a special call upon John H. Eaton to congratulate him and his recent bride, "Peggy" Timberlake, and sent William Polk a small bust of George Washington with a note saying Polk's patriotic service had been much like that of Washington.[17] Branch, not Badger, became Jackson's new Secretary of the Navy.

Although perhaps a bit disappointed in politics, Colonel Polk had a pleasant time in Washington. He found Leonidas "in high

[15] *Id.* to William Polk, February 10, 1829, *ibid.*

[16] William Polk to Sarah Polk, June 12, 1828, Kenneth Rayner Papers (University of North Carolina).

[17] Archibald D. Murphey to Thomas Ruffin, February 3, 1829, J. G. de R. Hamilton (ed.), *Papers of Thomas Ruffin* (Raleigh, 1918–20), I, 468; Samuel Carson to William Polk, January 29, 1829, William Polk Papers; Hoffman, *Andrew Jackson and North Carolina Politics*, 38–39.

health." As a part of the inaugural ceremonies he marched in a procession with "a few of the Revolutionary Officers" and thought it "a grand and imposing sight." Years later Colonel Edward G. W. Butler, a ward of President Jackson, recalled having met Colonel Polk in Washington during the inaugural ceremonies. Polk explained that he had come to Washington to dance at the inaugural ball. Butler, in order to make conversation and remembering that Leonidas Polk had graduated from West Point, inquired of Colonel Polk where his son was stationed. " 'Stationed?' he replied. 'Why by thunder, sir, he's over there in Alexandria at the Seminary!' " [18] These might not have been Colonel Polk's exact words, but they no doubt expressed his feelings.

It took only a few months for Leonidas Polk to lose most of his interest in public affairs, especially in Jacksonian democracy. "I do not know how others may have been affected," he explained to his father, "but the proscription of the Genl from party consideration merely, of many of his fellow-citizens of unimpeachable character, seem hardly consistent with the generous and dignified course I expected from him. His descending to the removal of petty postmasters, in obscure parts of the country seems hardly suitable for the head of so great a nation, whose very station must furnish ample business of a more elevated & altogether more useful character. Were I a politician, I fear, that I would find in the administration thus far, enough to shake my Jackson principles." [19]

Evidence of injustice was always a matter of great concern to Leonidas Polk. One July day his cousin Henry Hawkins, whom he had assisted in entering West Point, called at his Alexandria quarters. Hawkins had been judged deficient in mathematics and dis-

[18] William Polk to Lucius Polk (n.p., n.d.), George W. Polk Papers; Polk, *Leonidas Polk*, I, 107. Lucius had also planned to go to the inauguration, but his cotton crop was so "short" he was forced to give up the trip. The best he could do was attend the big send-off ball in Nashville. He was astounded when Felix Grundy told him that Jackson received so much mail that to reply cost the General fifty dollars per week for postage. Lucius Polk to Sarah Polk, December 28, 1828, George W. Polk Papers.
[19] Leonidas Polk to William Polk, June 10, 1829, Leonidas Polk Papers. Later, in company with the Badgers, he had tea at the home of John Branch. The Inghams were also present. He observed that no excuse was given why Eaton and Berrien were absent. The President was out of the city. *Id.* to *id.*, July 25, 1829, Leonidas Polk Papers; George Badger to *id.*, July 24, 1829, William Polk Papers.

missed from the Academy. He was terribly upset, feeling that his future was ruined. He also felt that he had not received the same treatment as a number of more prominent cadets, including the sons of General Brown and Samuel Swartout, who had likewise been found deficient in one or more subjects. They had been permitted to remain and make up their deficiencies.

Leonidas took Hawkins directly to President Jackson and presented his case. Here was a very young cadet of good character and with only one deficiency, he explained. The *"established usage"* in such a case permitted another chance. Jackson referred the case to Secretary of War Eaton with the suggestion that if it be proper Cadet Hawkins be reinstated. Eaton permitted Hawkins to return and enter the next class. "So he is again a cadet," Leonidas proudly reported to his father, "with a severe lesson, which I trust & believe has so impressed him that he will never forget it." [20]

Other student problems gave Leonidas even more serious concern. His brother Hamilton had transferred from North Carolina to Yale in 1828. Leonidas saw him in New York that fall and thought he was showing improvement from study but noted that he was "somewhat thinned." A few months later Leonidas expressed to his father regret that Hamilton had not altogether altered his habits since going to Yale. Reports indicated that while he was a fairly good student he was extravagant and inclined toward "gayer company." He was also often reported ill.[21] It soon developed that Hamilton's failure to improve was a result of serious illness. In the fall of 1829 his doctor advised withdrawal from college, and by December 15 he was with Leonidas in Alexandria, suffering from a severe cough and pains in the chest.[22] When he reached North Carolina the doctors prescribed travel; so he wasted away traveling over the state seeking recovery.

Leonidas and probably other members of the family correctly diagnosed the disease. "Poor fellow I cannot but follow him with great interest," he wrote their mother:

[20] Leonidas Polk to *id.*, July 25, 1829, Leonidas Polk Papers.
[21] Denison Omsted to *id.*, May 12, January 19, May 13, 1829, Polk-Yeatman Papers.
[22] Leonidas Polk to *id.*, October 7, 1828; June 10, December 15, 1829, Leonidas Polk Papers.

& allowing his case not to be, as I trust it is not *now*, hazardous, yet he may have, and undoubtedly he has the appearance of having the seeds of our family malady sown within him.[23] A recognition of this fact, is at best painful, but I confess I do not see the wisdom of putting away from our minds, the contemplation of things as things are and must be. . . . The whole fabric is unstable, & to persuade ourselves that it is firm is to conjure up a delusion which stays & represses our alarms for a while, only to pour in upon us a double portion of affliction when the truth must come. Thus I reason with regard to all my earthly attachment, & while to enjoy them & cultivate them is one of the happiest of this world's employments, it is the highest wisdom to be familiar with the fact that both things & their objects must cease. And not only so, but to be willing & ready to relinquish them with resignation & submission. They may all go & leave us behind, or we may go and leave them, when and how we know not. The approach is like that of a thief in the night, at our hand sometimes when we little expect, & yet there is a condition in which if we live, such a visitation must be the herald of peace rather than dismay. . . . My prayer, dear Mother, is that the minds of all the members of our dear family may be disabused of the real state of things, & that we may all be eternally happy.[24]

During the winter of 1829–30 Leonidas disposed of his North Carolina land and personal property. His father supervised the sale and was a heavy purchaser. Leonidas needed the money, for he was planning to marry soon after leaving the seminary. And by February, 1830, he had revised his plans as to the time for leaving. He had concluded that in the study of theological courses a few months was of little importance. He would leave for North Carolina the latter part of April, stopping enroute at Richmond for ordination.

Knowing that the announcement of his decision to seek ordination before reaching home would be disturbing to his father, he made a conscious effort to convince the family that the step he was about to take was in strict accordance with his sense of duty.

I am moved to it by the soberest convictions of my judgment, under the guidance, as I firmly believe, of the supreme governor

[23] Several uncles had died of tuberculosis.
[24] Leonidas Polk to Sarah Polk, March 3, 1830, Leonidas Polk Papers.

of the universe, & that after again & again revolving in my mind the ground of my confidence in these opinions, I am but the more thoroughly persuaded of their truth & stability. Believing as I do, after mature deliberation, that there neither is, nor can be, any reasonable ground of hope for happiness in eternity, but in the belief & practice of the doctrines & duties of the Christian, & that all therefore who fail of this must be lost, I feel constrained by a regard for the welfare of my fellowcreatures, & in honor of our common Maker, whose worship and service we by nature so little regard, to use the time and talents allotted me on earth in unfolding and explaining the scheme of redemption, & in urging its acceptance.

This he thought to be his "obvious & unavoidable duty," and in its performance he must completely disentangle himself from everything that might interfere. He was resolved to concern himself no further with worldly affairs than was absolutely necessary.

He expressed hope that his family and friends would appreciate his motives. Relationships with them would be novel and might perhaps at times be painful, but regardless of how "allied & dear to me they may be by ties of natural affection, I could never lose sight of their relation to God, or of my obligations to be faithful to Him." [25]

The only glimpse we get of life at the seminary during Polk's stay is found in a letter to Charles P. McIlvaine. Only fifteen students were enrolled during 1829–30; all were candidates for orders; six planned to apply during the coming spring. Enjoying much "harmony and good will" among themselves, these future clergymen offered their services to neighboring communities and organized several meetings. The meeting to which Polk devoted his attention was attempting to raise funds to construct a small chapel. He found the group also much interested in missions and trying to raise a "full quota of funds" for that work.

After briefly relating these events to McIlvaine, Polk added that he himself would apply for orders in April. He had no idea where he might be stationed, but wherever he went he would "seek so to pass through things temporal as not to lose sight of things eternal, and I would strive to set forward the cause of God and the salvation of multitudes of my dying fellow creatures. In look-

[25] *Id.* to William Polk, February 3, 1830, *ibid.*

ing about me, I find the field white with the harvest in every direction, and I am only solicitous to know my appropriate station." [26]

Leonidas Polk was ordained deacon by Bishop Richard Channing Moore on April 9, 1830, and preached his first sermon the following Sunday, using as his subject John 3:16. Bishop Moore, who also served as rector of Richmond's Monumental Church, finding it necessary to be away from these duties, requested Polk to fill the pulpit the following two Sundays. He preached on Hebrews 12:14 and James 2:18. In these early sermons he was "very much fettered by my notes & could not help feeling that the congregation listened as to a *written essay*, rather than to a spirited, heartfelt appeal from the gospel. I hope time will make it otherwise & enable me to read freely," he explained to McIlvaine. "For it is dispiriting labor now & I do not feel able, in my present situation, to extemporize." [27]

Upon Bishop Moore's return Polk left for a visit in Raleigh where on May 6, 1830, he married Frances Ann Devereux, the daughter of John and Frances (Pollok) Devereux. John Devereux had been a British midshipman during the American Revolution. After the war he set sail for America and was shipwrecked off the Carolina coast, drifting in at New Bern. Subsequently he became owner of a small merchant fleet, a part of which was seized by the French during the Napoleonic wars. He then shifted from commerce to agriculture and became one of North Carolina's larger planters. His wife Frances Pollok was descended from Thomas Pollok, a prominent North Carolinian during the colonial period. Pollok's grandson, Thomas Pollok III, married a daughter of Jonathan Edwards. The new Mrs. Leonidas Polk was a descendant of this union. [28]

The Polk honeymoon was cut short by a request from the vestry of Monumental Church that he accept a position of assistant to Bishop Moore. Polk found the Monumental Church a fashionable congregation of about 130 communicants, mostly women and elderly men, and not *"decidedly & actively pious."*

[26] February 2, 1830, *ibid.*

[27] Leonidas Polk to Charles P. McIlvaine, July 21, 1830, *ibid.*

[28] See "Devereux Genealogy," *ibid.*; Katherine Polk Gale, "Recollections of Life in the Southern Confederacy, 1861–1865" (MS in Southern Collection, University of North Carolina).

He sensed a definite lack of the bonds of Christian fellowship required by the gospel. Bishop Moore was advanced in years, more kind and affectionate than progressive, and a bit cautious about inaugurating changes. Late in July he went north for the remainder of the summer, leaving Polk in charge of the congregation. The magnitude of the task "distressed & depressed" the young minister and greatly aggravated an undiagnosed malady that had plagued him for two years. He felt nervous lest he prove "inadequate to the instruction of such a congregation." He prayed that the communicants would respect St. Paul's exhortation to Timothy, " 'Let no man despise thy youth.' " He felt confident that he knew the way of salvation, he explained to McIlvaine, yet he doubted his ability to present it in such a manner as to "command attention & constrain obedience." He felt great need for a conference with his counsellor of West Point days, but McIlvaine was now traveling in Europe.[29]

Apparently Bishop Moore returned from his northern vacation late in the summer; during September Leonidas was in North Carolina at the bedside of his dying brother Hamilton. According to a family account, the young minister was in constant attendance, answering such questions as his brother wished to ask concerning preparation for the world to come and finally performing the baptismal service. And when the end came Leonidas fulfilled the last request of the deceased as he stood by the grave and read the burial service.[30]

Although his own illness was daily becoming more debilitating, Leonidas was soon back in Richmond. Within a few weeks other distressing news arrived. Baby brother Charles had died. A grief-stricken brother again tried to console a disconsolate father:

> . . . my dear father, the hand of death must sooner or later be laid upon us all however engaging or tenderly loved, [yet] every stroke which diminishes our number, does but draw those who are left the more closely to you. . . . Our children & our parents are sources of great comfort & happiness to us, but alas they are mortals, they cannot abide with us, nor we with them. And there is not, nor can be, any security or permanency in our

[29] Lonidas Polk to Charles P. McIlvaine, July 21, 1830, Leonidas Polk Papers.
[30] Polk, "Leonidas Polk, A Memoir."

union but that which is founded on a common interest in the inheritance of the real Christian beyond the grave. Should we all possess this, our separation at death must be but temporary, our sorrows at parting, the sorrows of those "who are without hope," & our reunion positive & eternal.

Although he recognized the duty of a son to receive rather than give advice, he begged his father's consideration of the fact that there could be no true peace or security save in the protection of Almighty God, secured through the "mediation of Jesus Christ."

> My dear father, bear with your son, who has no other earthly motive than your highest happiness, when he reminds you of your very protracted old age, the certainty of death, the immense & boundless eternity before you, & the absolute necessity of a Christian character in order to your happiness. And may the Great and Mighty Being, before whom we must stand, graciously assist us all.[31]

The uncertainty of life and man's helplessness in the face of death preyed heavily upon the mind of the young minister. This was reflected in the announcement of the arrival of his first baby, January 27, 1831. "He is of course the finest boy that ever was born, giving already strong indication of both eminence and usefulness," he explained to Lucius. Every indication was that he was extremely healthy and might escape the need of a physician for a long time. Then he quickly added "but we know that life tenure at such an age is extremely feeble & our brightest hopes may at any moment be nipt in the bud." [32] The baby was named Hamilton.

Leonidas' health did not improve during the winter at Richmond. In April he and his family returned to Raleigh. He further taxed his energy by attending the Diocesan Convention at Norfolk on May 31, 1831. He returned to Raleigh by way of Richmond, where he released his rented house and sold his furniture. Much reduced in strength, he now feared that he must soon follow his brother Hamilton. But an uncle "who had saved his life by care" advised travel on horseback through some pleasant section, taking care to do it leisurely. Setting out in mid-June, Polk

[31] Leonidas Polk to William Polk, November 4, 1830, Leonidas Polk Papers.
[32] *Id.* to Lucius Polk, February 10, 1831, *ibid.*

rode along the Valley of Virginia to Alexandria and thence to Philadelphia. There a doctor informed him that he had only a few months to live. Other doctors, however, were not so positive, suspecting that his "cough and night sweats" might be a result of general debility rather than a definite disease. They advised an immediate sea voyage followed by months of leisurely travel in Europe.[33]

Without returning to North Carolina to say goodbye to his family, Polk went immediately to New York and sailed for Europe on August 8, 1831. After a voyage of three weeks, at times delightful, "then wretchedly miserable," he arrived at Le Havre on August 28, very nervous and suffering from pains in the chest.

Taking passage in a "misshapen coach called by a singular misnomer, 'Diligence,'" he passed along the Seine to Rouen and Paris. This beautiful country, all under cultivation, "entirely open, without fences," impressed him greatly. It was harvest time and fields were dotted with shocks of grain. Everywhere, even along the roadside, ripe pears, peaches, strawberries, and grapes hung from trees and vines. He marveled at the apparent sense of honesty that protected this fruit from those who passed that way.

Two weeks of rest in Paris brought him relief from pain and some increase in strength. These were days of excitement in this French city. Smoldering dissatisfaction with the rise of Louis Philippe burst forth in outcry against the ministry when news arrived that Warsaw, the stronghold of the struggling Poles, had fallen. Louis's government had sent no aid to the Polish nationalists. A Paris mob, marching underneath Polk's window, made its way to the house of the Minister of Foreign Affairs. Finding it locked and barricaded, "they pelted the house with stones, broke out the windows etc." The government took immediate steps to quell the rioters, but Polk observed:

> Things are by no means settled. The Govt has not the confidence of the people. The poorer classes are in great distress. The money-holders will not invest their capital & many of the wealthy have either gone into the country or left France, so that few purchases are made beyond the articles of immediate necessity. The Liberals fear that now the affairs of Belgium are settled

[33] Polk, "Leonidas Polk, A Memoir."

and Poland fallen the Great Powers will turn their attention to France, & combine to put down the existing and restore the former Government.

Indeed, he thought conditions in the whole of Europe very critical, capable of producing a general war at any moment. All was much in contrast to the peace, quiet, and prosperity of North Carolina and Tennessee.

Polk spent several weeks in Paris, seeing the sights, consulting noted physicians, and attending religious services. At other times he rested in his room. "It is pleasant at times to be alone," he confided to his diary, "—away from the gaze and bustle of the world, above all, away from the presence of this extraordinary city." He was much relieved when the best doctors pronounced his lungs "perfectly sound" and assured him that leisurely living would cure his ills. He enjoyed communion in the Paris churches. "How blessed it is to hold sweet communion with kindred spirits around the board of one common Lord," he reflected. "Lord increase within me a deeper sense of goodness. Cleanse thou my soul from all that is impure and unholy, and breathe into me afresh the breath of spiritual life." At times, however, he was critical of the sermons he heard. "The preacher failed," he told his diary, by not applying his subject, a task difficult and often unpleasant, but a part of a minister's duty. As for the religion of the French people, he found no great revolt against the Catholic Church, but he thought the church had lost its hold upon them. "It is extremely rare to see any of the young of either sex, particularly young men, in churches," he wrote Bishop McIlvaine. "They are emphatically 'without God in the world.' " Although their minds were open to anything new, they totally disregarded the Sabbath.

On October 11 Polk left by diligence for Brussels, a Frenchman riding on either side. No one was in a talkative mood, so he had hours within which to reflect upon Paris and its people. That evening he recorded his conclusions: "If we had no souls, if this world were the only theater of our existence, and if pleasure in its most extended sense were the sole object of life, Paris is the place to find it. . . . But if this life is the place to prepare for another, and if the Scriptures are true, one had better live anywhere else."

The country between Brussels and Antwerp Polk compared to

"a great kitchengarden," but from Antwerp to the Dutch border he found the land flat and uninteresting, in places almost wholly unproductive, yet heavily populated. At the Dutch border he had his first experience with border patrols. Sentinels at Landort took him to the commandant who declared him "not contraband." Riding in a Quaker-like gig driven by a "dry, thin, queer-looking little Dutchman," he was almost out of town when again "brought to" by a customs official. Dirty fingers were soon throwing the traveler's clean linens in all directions while an inspector looked for evidence of "some dreadful Belgian plot." Nothing but some letters of introduction were found. The commandant no doubt concluded, Polk recorded, that a letter written by an American clergyman and sent by another to an English clergyman "could have very little to do with Dutch politics."

From the Low Countries Polk went to Switzerland, thence across the Alps into Italy, where he planned to spend the winter. He was much impressed by the Forum as "the place for the meeting of the Senate, for the gathering of the people, for the transaction of all business of interest under the kingdom, the republic, and the empire; here poets recited, philosophers taught, orators convened." He further reflected that here also "the Great Apostle of the Gentiles" must have preached the gospel. Still more thoughtful as he viewed the Colosseum, Polk imagined he could see the thousands of Christians as they were made "the prey of wild beasts, by the cruelty of imperial monsters who disgraced human nature."

The new year 1832 began on Sunday. Polk attended an English service and then spent the remainder of the day in his room, humble and lonely. "May the Lord assist me in consecrating my heart, during the whole of this year, exclusively to his service," he wrote. "My dear wife and child—their absence at this season I feel particularly. There are certain seasons signalized and set apart for special devotion to all our interests; this is one of them, and my heart goes back to my dear home. I commend it and them to the mercy and blessing of God."

Polk found Italy a place of uncommon beauty, "particularly for the eye of the farmer," but he recorded no appreciation of Italian art. His only comment was that there was an abundance of all kinds except the useful.

Polk returned to France via Nice and Toulon, thence to Marseilles, Lyons, and Paris. The week spent in Nice was especially enjoyable, for there his loneliness was dispelled by association with an English clergyman. Regular evening meetings with religious co-workers was to him "like an oasis in the desert." While in Nice, he also attempted to preach to a group of sailors and suffered much physical discomfort as a result. The least excess in talking "brings me to the ground again," he wrote his friend McIlvaine. There was much concern lest he never be able "to combat again the trials of our calling." Yet he felt assured that God would direct his life "as he shall think best."

Polk found southern France "decidedly more interesting, both from cultivation of soil & the manners of the people" than any other section visited. The people had "more life & animation— exceedingly spirited." He observed many wagons hauling American and Egyptian cotton, but was unable to find the Polk mark on any bales. This region was also a center of silk and grape culture. Prosperity apparently resulting from these activities caused Polk to ponder anew the old question of whether, if properly handled, silk and grapes might not be profitably produced in Carolina. For silk production, he reasoned, only an ample number of mulberry trees would be needed, and grapes should do well in the mountainous regions.

By the time Polk arrived in Paris an epidemic of cholera was raging, so he hurried on to London via Calais. England pleased him very much. "The county seats & villages & cultivations are highly beautiful," he wrote home. "London itself is better built & cleaner than I expected—though more or less enveloped in a constant cloud of smoke." At Woolwich he visited Dr. Olynthus Gregory whose writings had so greatly influenced him in West Point days. At Cambridge, "the seat of science on this island," he looked over most of the colleges.

The countryside pleased Polk most. "The cultivation around the county seats and cottages, to say nothing of the incessant succession of green fields, formed a panorama which to me, was quite as interesting as a more rugged surface would have been," he explained. "I confess I am quite charmed with the neatness of the country houses, and the manner in which the fields are arranged, hedged, and tilled; and when I think of our vast plantations, with our dirty, careless, thriftless negro population, I could and do, wish that we were thoroughly quit of them. The more I see of those who are without slaves, the more I am prepared to say that we are seriously wronging ourselves by retaining them."

With the arrival of June, 1832, a year had passed since Polk left his family in North Carolina. As he paused to reflect on the events of that year, he expressed fear that the "many providences" mingled with these events had "not received the acknowledgment of a grateful heart or obedient life." He had no excuse to offer except a "confession of unworthiness and guilt." And he begged that the Lord might "in pity forgive and restore me in my most humble and sincere supplication." As for his physical condition, he noted that he was much less fatigued.

On June 1 he rode out from London to Oxford. He attended services in New College Chapel and was impressed with its beauty, but not with the services. Much of this so-called cathedral service consisted of "chants performed by persons hired for that purpose." Although he liked music, he could "never be interested in a service which seemed designed so wholly for effect." After attending three such services in one day he still had no feeling of "the solemnity and sanctity of this holy day."

A high point in Polk's English tour was a sixty-four mile round trip by railroad from Manchester to Liverpool, traveling at an average speed of about twenty-four miles per hour. He considered this railroad a "magnificent work," and since its stock was 90 per cent above par, he classed it as a very successful enterprise. He explained to his father:

> The carriages which are built long & are very convenient, hold about 12 to 24 & are strung together sometimes so as to make a train of 200 yards in length. To stand at a distance & see this monster first begin to crawl off & then, hissing & puffing, increase its speed until it attains a swiftness equal to that with which the swallow skims the earth, almost makes one feel lost in amazement . . . we are at a loss for language sufficiently strong to express the astonishment—the admiration it excites.

He could only wish for as great a success with similar enterprises in America.

At Sheffield, the celebrated center of the manufacture of silverware and cutlery, Polk visited several factories. At Rodger's, a place famous for excellent blades, he purchased for his father two "first-rate razors." At Sheffield he also visited the Gales family. He had taken with him a letter of introduction from Joseph Gales, editor of the Washington *National Intelligencer*. At the Gales home he also met the poet James Montgomery. Three pleasant days were spent with this interesting literary figure.[34]

Polk had intended to sail for home by mid-June, but upon learning that not more than a month would be required to visit the most interesting places in Scotland and Ireland, he yielded to temptation to remain longer. He did not reach North Carolina until October, 1832. Enroute he stopped at Baltimore to purchase a pair of dark brown horses which he shipped by boat to Petersburg. He wrote ahead to his father requesting that "spare hands" be sent for them at that place. If his father had no spare hands no doubt Badger or the Devereuxs did.[35]

Polk entertained no plans for an immediate return to the active ministry. His doctors had prescribed a vigorous outdoor life; to a Polk this could mean only the life of a soldier or a planter. Although he had disposed of his lands and slaves in North Carolina, he still owned the tract in Maury County, Tennessee. During the winter of 1832–33 he and his family divided their time between the homes of the Devereuxs and the Polks. Occasionally he preached at the Episcopal Church in Raleigh.[36]

Apparently making use of his new horses, he also visited other relatives and friends of the family, including Fanny's bachelor uncle, George Pollok, and Governor John Branch. "Fanny and Hamy" proved good travelers, he reported. They found Pollok "quite alone" but busy. He had been experimenting with growing cane, and thought he might be successful at least in the production of molasses. Governor Branch was full of conversation rela-

---

[34] The account of this European tour is taken from letters to members of his family and to Charles P. McIlvaine found in the George W. Polk Papers, the Dillon-Polk Papers (University of North Carolina), and the Leonidas Polk Papers. Polk also kept a journal. The original has not been located. His wife later stated that the journal had been lost, yet excerpts from it are quoted in Polk, *Leonidas Polk*, I, 129 ff. References herein are to these excerpts.

[35] Leonidas Polk to William Polk, September 29, 1832, George W. Polk Papers.

[36] Thomas Ruffin to Catherine Ruffin, January 13, 1833, Hamilton (ed.), *Papers of Thomas Ruffin*, II, 73.

tive to affairs at Washington and politics in general, yet declared
he was tired of political life and ready to quit. He entertained
many doubts about "the expediency of the old extreme demo-
cratic principles etc." and was "willing to see things administered
on a more *federal* footing."[37]

The Devereuxs were eager for Leonidas and Fanny to settle in
North Carolina. Lucius urged them to come to Tennessee. While
Leonidas was away in Europe Lucius had married Mary Eastin, a
grandniece of Rachel Jackson and belle of the White House since
President Jackson brought her to Washington in 1829. Three
months before the wedding Jackson had thought Mary would
marry naval Captain William F. Finch.[38] Lucius Polk changed
these plans and the expensive White House wedding made a
heavy dent in the President's personal finances.[39] Jackson sent
William and Sarah Polk a note expressing regret that they were
unable to be present at the wedding of their son to "my favorite
niece." He also sent along a medal of "my likeness" for his name-
sake, Andrew Jackson Polk, with "my prayer that he may grow &
prosper" and become an ornament to society and a blessing to
his parents.[40] Lucius and Mary took up temporary residence at
Willsgrove while a group of North Carolina carpenters built
Hamilton Place, a gift from his father.

Even though John Devereux, Fanny's father, wished Leonidas
and Fanny to take over an improved North Carolina plantation,
he recognized that "the prospect of making a new establishment
. . . in his own style" was pleasing and exciting to Leonidas'
"ardent mind," yet he questioned whether or not his son-in-law
was equal to the physical strain. "I see with pride and pleasure,"
he observed, "that pecuniary considerations have no influence
upon Leonidas decision—he has higher motives—this is as it
should be, but the step he is about to take is an important one,
let him think well on it,—and may his Heavenly Father counsel
him in taking it. May he take it in wisdom."

[37] Leonidas Polk to William Polk, January 15, 1833, George W. Polk Papers.
[38] Jackson to John Coffee, January 21, 1832, John Spencer Bassett (ed.),
The Correspondence of Andrew Jackson (6 vols., Washington, 1926–31), IV,
401
[39] Marquis James, *Life of Andrew Jackson* (Indianapolis, 1938), 627.
[40] Andrew Jackson to William Polk, April 11, 1832, George W. Polk Papers.

Though expressing a willingness for Leonidas and Fanny to make their own decision, Devereux, nevertheless, had a suggestion. Should the young couple wish to remain in North Carolina he would give them his Hills Ferry plantation, including seventy slaves. This was an improved and very productive plantation, he explained, yielding an average annual income of about $4,500. A fair estimate of its value would be about $75,000. The current surplus produce for sale included 2,000 bushels of corn and 30,000 pounds of cotton. The cotton had just been sold for 11¢ a pound; he hoped to get $2.50 a bushel for the corn.

This lengthy explanation was made in a letter to William Polk. He further stated that he could not afford to give up all of this property and income without some security. He owed $21,000. Should Leonidas and Fanny decide to accept the plantation, he suggested that William Polk, by way of assistance to the children, should assume this $21,000 indebtedness. This would give them the plantation and slaves free of all debts.

Should the children decide in favor of Tennessee, Devereux would give them slaves and cash. His own debts prevented his doing all he would like to, "but something must be done by the parents of these young and inexperienced children in the ways of the world, and prevent their feeling degraded in their own situation, or lessened in the opinion of the world." Should they decide to go to Tennessee he would give them two domestic women servants [41] with two children and thirty other slaves. And since he himself could not furnish transportation for these he would give Leonidas $500 in cash "to enable him to transfer my daughter, child & servant, to where his future home is to be, as I do not wish that she should be at any expense to him from the day he received her from me, until he places her in his own house." [42]

The winter of 1832–33 was a pleasant one for Leonidas and Fanny Polk. They did not suffer long from indecision. Since he believed the Tennessee climate would be good for his health, she readily agreed to settle in Maury County.[43] As early as December

[41] One of these servants was "Mammy" Betsey, Fanny's nurse, who was later to nurse all of Fanny and Leonidas' eight children.

[42] John Devereux to William Polk, November 21, 1832, Leonidas Polk Papers.

[43] Polk, "Leonidas Polk, A Memoir."

10 Leonidas wrote his old West Point Chaplain of his plans and also sent congratulations on McIlvaine's appointment as Bishop of Ohio. "I do pray, as I verily believe, that it will be found—under the blessing of God—that the confidence of the church has been well placed." As for his own plans, he would settle near his brother Lucius about fifty miles to the south of Nashville. In this new life he expected still to have "opportunity for usefulness." [44]

Enough children still remained in the Polk family home to make life interesting during the winter months. The three older boys—William, Thomas, and Lucius—had homes of their own, and Rufus was away at the University of Virginia. Mary had married George Badger. But there were still George, Andrew, Susan, and Leonidas' own little Hamilton. Rufus was reported as doing exceptionally well at Virginia. Leonidas wrote, complimenting him, and adding "you will never regret it allow me to assure you." He also included comments of a lighter nature. Rufus had told of being at dinner with John C. Calhoun whose table manners he found shocking. Leonidas expressed surprise, for he had supposed Calhoun full of Southern chivalry. In a jocular manner he added that perhaps while the South Carolina statesman was "wielding his knife and thrusting his food in such style, he was thinking of the execution which the nullifiers would do with their bayonets and broad swords, and perhaps practicing. Poor man I dare say he will stand in need of all the skill he can acquire." [45] This was the time of the South Carolina nullification crisis.

Leonidas also told Rufus that he and Fanny would probably set out for Tennessee about March 20 and arrive the latter part of April. However, their departure was delayed and they did not arrive at Lucius' new home, Hamilton Place, until May 15, 1833. The trip proved very tiresome. Fanny was ill all of the distance; near Knoxville a baby son was stillborn. But after arrival at spacious and hospitable Hamilton Place all quickly recovered from illness and fatigue. Throughout the trip little "Hamy" had remained lively and he now shared the center of attraction with Lucius and Mary's new daughter Sarah Rachel.[46]

[44] Leonidas Polk to Charles P. McIlvaine, December 10, 1832, Leonidas Polk Papers.

[45] *Id.* to Rufus Polk, February 28, 1833, *ibid.*

[46] *Id.* to Sarah Polk, May 28, 1833, *ibid.*; Polk, "Leonidas Polk, A Memoir."

Shortly after the arrival of Leonidas and family Colonel William
Polk unexpectedly made his appearance for what was to be his
last tour of inspection and search for bargains in undeveloped
lands. The Maury County tract of land he had previously given
to Leonidas was some distance from Hamilton Place. Fearing
that Fanny might be lonely without close neighbors, he exchanged
this tract for about one-fourth of his 5,000 acre tract known as
"Rattle and Snap." Lucius had already been given a fourth of this
same tract.[47] Colonel Polk also set aside a 600-acre plantation for
his daughter, Mary Badger.

The Colonel, Lucius, and Leonidas were soon off to West Tennessee to inspect lands in Fayette and Shelby counties. A letter
from Lucius' wife saying that cholera had hit the neighboring
town of Pulaski and also Colonel Polk's Willsgrove plantation
caused Lucius and Leonidas to hurry home. Colonel Polk went
on to Bolivar and "met all my *kin.*" He was confident the boys
would check the spread of the epidemic by segregating those who
were affected.[48] The "kin" was the family of his Uncle Ezekiel
Polk, members of which had moved into the Western District as
early as 1821.

The land given to Leonidas had been leased to one Mr. Fleming, and the new planter feared he might be forced to wait a year
before beginning personal operation. However, he was able to buy
up the Fleming lease and was soon bragging that, except for Squire
Mullins, no man in the neighborhood had better corn. He
hoped for a harvest of 800 barrels. The report on his cotton was
not so promising, but he sent word to Mary that her crop should
yield 1,200 pounds per acre. Only a few weeks were required for
planter Polk to become fully employed and to realize that super-
intending so large an operation was "no small task . . . but I
came out here for an active life," he commented to his mother,
"& it is well I am not disappointed."

In addition to farming he was making preparation to build a

---

[47] *Ibid.*; Maury County *Deed Book*, Vol. 2, Bk. C, p. 84. The other half of
"Rattle and Snap" was later divided between George and Rufus. The country
homes constructed on these tracts became known as "Hamilton Place," "Ashwood," "Rattle and Snap," and "Westwood." There is an unverified story that
Colonel Polk won this tract from the governor of North Carolina in the familiar game of "rattle and snap."

[48] William Polk to Sarah Polk, July 4, 1833, George W. Polk Papers.

home. His father, having financed the construction of Hamilton Place for Lucius and Mary, wished to use the same North Carolina carpenters to build a suitable home for Leonidas and Fanny. There was already on the land a four-room house which had been occupied by Fleming. Although small, it was snug and "close built." In fact it was as nice as any structure in the neighborhood except Hamilton Place. The hospitality at Hamilton Place was all that could be desired, yet Leonidas and Fanny wished a place to themselves. Furthermore, the little house was conveniently situated both for farming operations and supervision of construction on the proposed new home. Consequently, they decided to move in as soon as needed repairs could be made.[49]

Leonidas spent the fall and winter of 1833–34 harvesting crops, hauling cotton to Nashville, clearing land, repairing the small house, making bricks for the new structure, and doing odd jobs. He reported to his mother that neighbors thought some of the things he did odd in more ways than one. This, however, he hesitated to admit, "Though in truth Ma I sometimes half suspect that I inherit from you a disposition to be pulling down & fixing things better, to be making new screws, or building railroads." His father suggested that, in order to accomplish all that was in process and planned, the rock quarry "on the knob" must be turned into a gold mine.

As a building site Leonidas selected a place on the Columbia-Mount Pleasant Road about three quarters of a mile from Hamilton Place. The elevation was not quite so great as he wished, still there was sufficient slope and plenty of shade trees. One great obstacle was that the immediate area was cut by three public roads. He immediately set to work getting these rerouted or closed. Only "Old Man McGee," who lived down the road toward Florence, gave trouble. McGee furnished some "pleasing excitement" before the Polks were finally able to overcome his objections. Closing or changing these roads also made it possible for Lucius, Leonidas, and Colonel Polk to fence their tracts of land in one body. When she should come to visit them, Leonidas informed his mother, "you may expect to see droves of fat, square

---

[49] Leonidas Polk to *id.*, August 17, 1833, Leonidas Polk Papers; Polk, "Leonidas Polk, A Memoir."

built milch cows, with distented accompaniments; & the woods teeming with young mules & their mammies." [50]

Early in February, 1834, there arrived at Hamilton Place the unexpected news that Colonel William Polk had died at his Raleigh home. During the late fall he had parted with his sons in Maury County and returned to North Carolina "well & antidyspeptic." The immediate cause of his death was not revealed, but Leonidas commented that the "characteristics of his illness seem to have been totally different from those of former days" and that he "expired like a candle."

Again the young minister attempted to console his bereaved family. "If there had been any among men who could have withstood the assaults of our last enemy, surely one combining such vigor of constitution with such energy of mind would have been among the number," he wrote his mother. "But exceptions, there are none, we are all frail & crumbling dust, at least as to the body." To his mother he also confided that for some time past he thought he detected "a marked & growing change" in his father. "It was not to be expected that any very sudden or complete revolution of feeling and character would have occurred in the case of one bred in the times and scenes which have marked his life. There was a natural severity of character, & high tone & bearing, which wd very likely attend him to the end, & any, the least evidences of an humble and subdued spirit, such as were evinced, were *much more* than I had anticipated." A loving family might "confidently leave him" to the God who had created him with such distinguishing qualities and "who *has ever vouchsafed mercy to the humble & penitant* [sic]." [51]

During the past ten years Colonel Polk had made extensive gifts in land and money to his older children. To those children not so favored he willed large tracts of real estate in North Carolina and Tennessee. To his sons Rufus King and George Washington he gave the remaining half of "Rattle and Snap," which was adjacent to the tracts given to Lucius and Leonidas in Maury County. To his youngest son, Andrew Jackson, he left the 1,500-acre Willsgrove

[50] Leonidas Polk to Sarah Polk, September 15, 1833, Leonidas Polk Papers; *id.* to William Polk, October 7, 1833, January 27, 1834, George W. Polk Papers.
[51] *Id.* to Sarah Polk, February 12, 1834, Leonidas Polk Papers.

estate, also in Maury County. On each previous gift as well as each bequest Colonel Polk placed an evaluation. The total amounted to about $300,000. The value of the gift or bequest received by each heir was to be considered in the division of all the remaining property. Since Leonidas had previously received gifts valued at $37,000, he inherited little from his father's estate.[52]

Leonidas and his family remained at Hamilton Place during the winter of 1833–34. Sufficient repairs had not been made on the small house, the new home was far from complete, and he was also needed at Hamilton Place. Lucius had made an investment in Mississippi land and during midwinter had shipped off a number of slaves to make ready for spring planting there. Since he had no overseer for them it was necessary that he go in person. Before leaving for Mississippi he and Leonidas made plans for a trip to Raleigh as soon as he returned in the spring.

Mother Polk particularly urged Leonidas and Fanny to visit North Carolina, not so much for selfish reasons as in the interest of the Devereuxs. Certainly Leonidas could take time from his many duties to accompany Fanny on a visit to her ill and aging parents.[53] But Fanny herself was ill, having lost another baby, and Lucius was late in returning from Mississippi; so the trip was postponed until fall.

Another reason for postponement was Leonidas' desire to attend the Episcopal convention which was scheduled to meet in the Columbia parish on April 25. From the time of his arrival in Tennessee he had taken an active part in the work of the church. The Reverend James Harvey Otey, rector of St. Paul's Church in Franklin, had just been made the first Bishop of Tennessee. Leonidas agreed to serve as minister to St. Peter's Church in Columbia.[54]

Lucius' Mississippi venture did not pay; he sold out, apparently at a loss, and brought his slaves back to Tennessee. Leonidas was much concerned about his brother's debts, which were so great as

[52] See Will of William Polk, Wake County *Records,* Vol. 23, pp. 46 ff. This will was probated in February, 1834.

[53] Sarah Polk to Mary Polk, May 30, 1834, Dillon-Polk Papers.

[54] William M. Green, *Memoir of the Rt. Rev. James Harvey Otey, First Bishop of Tennessee* (New York, 1885), 12.

to make him "miserable." If sufficient money could be borrowed from a single source to pay off these numerous smaller amounts, Lucius could have more peace of mind. With this in view, Leonidas suggested to their mother that she make Lucius a loan of $10,-000 from their father's estate. He himself would go security if necessary.[55]

Leonidas felt free to make such a suggestion since his mother had requested advice on family affairs, particularly business matters. He further suggested that she send to Tennessee all of the slaves not actually needed on her North Carolina lands. In Tennessee they could be cared for at less expense and consequently their labor would be more productive. She should also reduce the number of work horses to the point where the ratio to slaves would be 1:2. Two additional bridle horses might be kept for use by Rufus and George when at home. Sister Susan should be sent to a private Episcopal school in Maryland. He himself would assume management of his mother's Tennessee plantation and render full account to her.[56]

In mid-June Leonidas reported that his mother's overseer had planted 280 acres of cotton, but the stand was poor on about one-third of the acreage. "The crop therefore on the whole is neither very promising, nor is it very unpromising but what might be called '*sorter middling.*'" There was much damage from dry weather and the yield might be cut to about 100 bales. Lucius' prospects were also poor, but Badger's quite good. His own might also be classed as good. As a whole the Negroes had remained well. Births, including Rachel's eleventh child, had somewhat increased the number.

Leonidas was also pleased to report that he and his family had at last moved into the small house and were "quite snugly fixed." "It is a very cool place with a spring within a stones throw of the door. My plantation is all around me & although I say it I am quite an industrious farmer." [57]

Early in July the Leonidas Polk family visited friends at Franklin and then went on to Nashville for a ten-day stay with the

[55] Leonidas Polk to Sarah Polk, February 12, March 18, May 18, 1834, Leonidas Polk Papers.
[56] *Id.* to *id.*, March 18, 1834, *ibid.*   [57] *Id.* to *id.*, June 16, 1834, *ibid.*

Francis B. Foggs. Earlier in the year Mrs. Fogg had visited in the Columbia-Mt. Pleasant area and extended to the Polks a special invitation to Nashville. Thus began a friendship between the Polks and Foggs that was to be important two decades later in the founding of the University of the South. Leonidas, being his "own architect," cut short his Nashville visit and rushed back to the supervision of construction on his new house. Fanny, still weak from illness, remained in Nashville to visit the John Catrons and partake of more of the mineral water.

Alone and lonesome in his Maury County cabin, Leonidas wrote his mother of both his feelings and his plans. If Fanny continued to improve he thought that by the time they should reach North Carolina she would be quite able to pass inspection. "She is very domestic as you know, & though I say it is the *best wife* in this or any other country—& Hamy too, what shall I say of him? I must let you see him & then ask you, if you have ever seen a more observant, inquisitive, intelligent, sprightly or better boy at any time.—He is indeed a very clever boy & in feature partly, but more in character—*very like his daddy*." Daddy was really missing that "little chatter box."

Leonidas was also eager for his mother to know that farming was not his only interest. He sent her a copy of the *Journal* of the recent Episcopal convention in order that she might "see how we are employed." Also included was an address he had drafted for a committee on railroads, 5,000 copies of which had been distributed over the state. "I desire to make myself useful," he explained. "Our prospects of success I think good." [58] The prospects were good and a portion of the proposed railroad connection with Nashville was surveyed, but economic depression caused years of delay in construction.

Leonidas Polk's intense interest in young people was often reflected in letters to his younger brothers and sisters. He urged Andrew to write him all of the North Carolina news, particularly school news, and to study hard. He then in turn would write about things in Tennessee. At this point in the writing little "Hamy" entered his father's room. When asked what he would

[58] *Id.* to *id.*, July 28, 1834, *ibid.*

like to tell Andrew, Hamy replied he was sending a knife and would write a letter himself when he got bigger. He also wanted Andrew to know about his "bay pony, with a long tail," named Fenalla, who could kick and "wallow in the dirt." [59]

To Susan, Leonidas sent an expression of pleasure for the letter recently received from her. Only a few words were misspelled. He was pleased that she attended Sunday School and was interested in sewing societies and "fares." He himself had recently conducted a "fare" and raised more than $1,000 to furnish a church. From Sunday School she would no doubt learn many things that would be helpful when she later went out into the world. "The world you no doubt think is full of pleasure & without any pain, but let me tell you that this is a mistake. There is a great deal of pain & disappointment in the world, & if you have nothing better or stronger than yourself to rely upon whenever you are in pain and disappointment you will be very unhappy." She should learn of God's goodness and love and "how ready he is to help those who are in trouble & who go to him as the Bible says. In short you should learn to know what your Bible tells you." [60]

Both cholera and yellow fever struck Middle Tennessee in the summer of 1834. The Polk family and slaves escaped the former, but scores of slaves fell ill from fever. Thirty-five cases were reported early in September, yet owing to daily visits by a physician, there had been but one death. Through it all, however, Polk continued to push farm and construction operations in preparation for his proposed visit to North Carolina in October. He hoped to have the roof on his house by that time. His greatest farm problem was the harvesting of fifty acres of hemp. This was strenuous work since the plants must be pulled up by the roots. Finding his available labor unequal to the demand, he attempted to hire some of Lucius' slaves, offering one dollar per day. Lucius declined the offer, believing his slaves could be more profitably employed picking cotton. [61]

Leonidas' family and Lucius made the trip to North Carolina in the late fall of 1834. For a portion of the way they traveled in company with Bishop Otey who was visiting his diocese. At Nash-

[59] *Id.* to Andrew Polk, August 8, 1834, *ibid.*
[60] *Id.* to Susan Polk, September 22, 1834, *ibid.*
[61] *Id.* to Sarah Polk, September 6, 1834, *ibid.*

ville and Knoxville Leonidas assisted the Bishop, reading prayer, preaching, and baptizing.[62]

Since his family had not accompanied him, Lucius did not remain long in North Carolina; Leonidas spent the winter. There were family matters that needed attention. During Christmas week he, George, and Susan left for Washington in search of a suitable school for Susan. They found one in Philadelphia. Of greatest concern, however, was the serious illness of Mary, the wife of George Badger. "God only knows how her disease will terminate," wrote her distressed mother.[63] Mary died on March 1, 1835. Leonidas and family returned to Tennessee immediately, taking with them Mrs. Polk, Rufus, and Mary's daughters, Sally and Catherine Badger. Rufus had decided to give up education at the University of Virginia and take over his inheritance in Tennessee.

At home again, Leonidas continued to divide his time between parochial duties and the activities of a planter. Each Wednesday afternoon he rode into Columbia for evening service at St. Peter's. He would spend the night with relatives or friends and return to his plantation the following morning. Occasionally he would accompany Bishop Otey to neighboring towns and assist in efforts to build up local congregations. In his own parish he was particularly active among the Negroes. This "portion of our population," he explained to the Tennessee convention was "as fair subjects" for missionary activities as the Negroes in Africa.[64]

No doubt partly through the influence of Bishop Otey, Polk became widely known throughout the diocese. The Tennessee convention of 1835 chose him delegate to the General Convention. This proved an important event in his career, for the 1835 session of the General Convention made some important decisions relative to missionary work. Henceforth the membership of the church would constitute the missionary society, and all mission work would be under direction of a Board of Missions. Two missionary bishops—one for the northwest and the other for the southwest—were to be chosen by the House of Bishops and the House of Deputies. Appointments were made immediately, but

[62] Diocese of Tennessee, *Journal of Convention* (Nashville, 1835), 5.
[63] Frances Polk to Mary Polk (Mrs. Lucius), December 7, 1834, George W. Polk Papers; Sarah Polk to *id.*, December 29, 1834, Dillon-Polk Papers.
[64] Diocese of Tennessee, *Journal of Convention* (1835), 24.

the Reverend Francis L. Hawks of New York, the choice for the southwest post, declined to accept.[65] The position remained vacant.

There is no record of Polk's activities at the General Convention, but too much activity in too many fields proved a heavy strain on his physical strength. In March, 1836, he became seriously ill. While on one of his visits to Columbia he spent the night with his cousin James K. Polk. When he awoke the following morning one side of his body was partly paralyzed, and his speech was somewhat impaired. After brief medical treatment he was able to return home. During the following month he suffered other attacks. His family physician applied the usual treatment—several bleedings, two cuppings on the neck to relieve pressure on the brain, and a course of nux vomica, which made him deathly sick. In spite of it all, he began a slow recovery.[66]

In the meantime, Frances D. ("Little Fanny") arrived. Years later Mrs. Polk recalled that in spite of her husband's illness the winter of 1836–37 was probably the happiest period of their married life. They were still in their comfortable little house, which they called "Mount Breeze." The children were well, and their father, while making satisfactory recovery, had more time to spend with his family than he would ever have again. Long winter evenings were spent in reading. "I knew I was happy—I enjoyed it, & often said God gave us this time to prepare for the storms which must come," Mrs. Polk later explained to her children.[67]

Polk's main project now was the completion of his new home. He and his wife had spent months planning and purchasing furnishings for the interior. Susan, now in school at Philadelphia, was notified that in the new house there would be a room for her; there would also be a large library and plenty of books. And "Sister" Fanny was always ready to talk about their contents. The family news was that Rufus had begun farming in Maury

[65] *Journal of General Convention* (Philadelphia, 1835), 82. To Bishop William White, Hawks explained that he was forced to decline the appointment because adequate provisions were not made for the support of his family. Hawks to White, September 16, 23, 1835, quoted in *Historical Magazine of the Protestant Episcopal Church* (Garrison, N. Y. and Richmond, Va., 1932), IX, 91–92.

[66] Polk, "Leonidas Polk, A Memoir"; Lucius Polk to Sarah Polk, April 21, 25, 1836, Polk-Yeatman Papers.

[67] Polk, "Leonidas Polk, A Memoir."

County and gave evidence of becoming an industrious planter. George was giving a good account of himself at the University of North Carolina.[68] Lucius had a new daughter, raising the total to three. Brother Thomas and family were visiting in Maury County and would soon move on to West Tennessee. If they liked it there the plan was to make permanent settlement. Thomas' daughters Jane and Mary were fine girls. Little Hamy was fast becoming a farmer boy, and Little Fanny was about "the nicest little body you have ever seen." She was beginning to talk.[69]

Furnishings for the new home, which was to be called "Ashwood," were purchased in New York. William Samuel Johnson, a friend of the family, made the purchases. Bills for rugs, curtains, and furniture amounted to $1,763.[70] Dishes and tableware, including two sets of china with nine dozen dinner plates, cost $1,132. Also included was a silver coffee urn, $250; two tea pots, $140; a sugar bowl, $55; and one pitcher, $75.[71]

Early in the summer of 1837 Mrs. Polk took Hamy to North Carolina for a visit with her parents, leaving little Fanny in care of Mammy Betsey. While she was away Leonidas moved into the new house. He wrote his mother:

> It is very comfortably arranged, and its occupants whoever they may be hereafter cannot but appreciate its excellence in this particular. I have had great pleasure in building it, quite as much I dare say, as I shall have should my life be spared, in occupying it. My little girl enjoys it greatly. She has such ample play room compared with the confinement of Mt. Breeze. She is very well and is great company for me—her little prattle her warm reception when I come in, in the evening and general playfulness relieves the stillness of this vast house and the solitude of my meals greatly.[72]

Second in importance to the completion and furnishing of "Ashwood" was the construction of a hemp factory. Polk believed

[68] He had previously been at Columbia College but had dropped out because of scholastic difficulties. Sarah Polk to Lucius Polk, May 20, 1836, Dillon-Polk Papers.

[69] Leonidas Polk to Susan Polk, May 23, 1837, Leonidas Polk Papers.

[70] At the same time Lucius Polk made purchases amounting to $1,994.

[71] Leonidas Polk to William Samuel Johnson, January 13, 1837, Leonidas Polk Papers. See also bills marked "paid."

[72] Leonidas Polk to Sarah Polk, July 28, 1837, Leonidas Polk Papers.

that a planting community located at a distance from markets should make every effort to supply its own needs. Early in 1836 he began construction of a factory for the spinning and weaving of hemp. When he had difficulty in securing the proper types of lumber for constructing his home and factory, he set up his own sawmills. At first he planned to rely on water power but soon yielded to his wife's urging that he purchase "a puffing engine." A thirty horsepower steam engine was imported from Philadelphia at a cost of about $2,500. This also furnished sufficient power to operate a grist mill. His superintendent, a Mr. Williams, soon had the hemp factory in operation. The principal product was to be bagging for cotton.

Twelve hands, some of them "small fry," were assigned to factory work. Polk suggested to his mother that he should be compensated for training so many "fine mechanics." The greatest immediate difficulty was in securing a supply of hemp, most of which had to be shipped in from Kentucky. However, the Polk brothers had a solution to this problem. Next year they would plant 150 acres to hemp.[73]

In September, 1837, Leonidas and Little Fanny joined Mrs. Polk and Hamy at Raleigh for a general family reunion. Lucius and family and Rufus came from Tennessee; Susan from Philadelphia; and George from Chapel Hill. Andrew was already there.[74]

[73] Frances Polk to *id.*, February 5, April 2, 1836; Leonidas Polk to *id.*, April 8, 1836, George W. Polk Papers.
[74] *Id.* to Bishop James Otey, September 28, 1837, Leonidas Polk Papers.

(5)

"To a Higher Order"

IN THE FALL of 1838 there came unexpected news from the General Convention of the Episcopal church. Leonidas Polk, thirty-two, had been chosen Missionary Bishop of the Southwest. He was not in attendance at the convention and the records do not reveal the details of his selection. Since his friends Bishops McIlvaine and Otey were present, it is reasonable to suppose they promoted his interests.[1] It was a high honor for one of so limited experience, yet it should be noted that the $2,000 position to which he was called was not attractive to men of great reputation. This fact had been suggested by the Reverend Francis Hawks's decision to decline the appointment three years earlier. The call was for a man of consecration and determination. Polk met these qualifications, although there was serious question about his physical fitness.

He left no expression of his immediate reaction to this unexpected assignment. Years later his wife recalled:

. . . now came what was one of the greatest trials of my life—I was called to give up my dear husband from home . . . home and all its endearments must be given up, & I left alone to bring up my children—thank God I did not hesitate or by any word influence his decision—I told him he was God's servant & soldier, & I had no right to have even an opinion—there was no struggle in his mind he never felt any thing hard he was called to do for God, who had done so much for him—& though the acceptance involved loss of property, & abandonment of wife & children for months at a time he did not hesitate.[2]

Polk, his wife, and mother went immediately to Cincinnati, where on December 9, 1838, he was consecrated in Christ

[1] Journal of the General Convention (1838), 80.
[2] Polk, "Leonidas Polk, A Memoir."

Church. "The ante-communion service was begun by the Rt. Rev.
Bishop Meade, the Rt. Rev. Bishop McIlvaine reading the epistle
and the Rt. Rev. Bishop Smith the gospel." McIlvaine preached
the sermon. Then after recounting the story of Polk's conversion,
his subsequent battle with ill health, and his entrance into the
ministry, the Bishop concluded:

> Many years have since elapsed. The chaplain has been called to
> a higher order in the ministry, and more enlarged responsibilities
> in the church. The Cadet, meanwhile, after many vicissitudes of
> active duty and of disabling ill health, supposed he had settled
> himself for the rest of his life, as preacher and pastor to an
> humble and obscure congregation of negroes, whom he had
> collected together from neighboring plantations; to whom, living
> entirely upon his own pecuniary means, he appropriated a part
> of his own house for a church, and to whose eternal interests he
> had chosen cheerfully and happily to devote himself, as their
> spiritual father, with no emolument but their salvation. [This
> was the type of man upon whom the Church focused attention
> when it] needed a Missionary Bishop for a vast field, for great
> self-denial, for untiring patience, for courageous enterprise. . . .
> Regarding the call as of God, he has embraced the promised
> grace, and is now ready to be offered. And thus the Chaplain has
> here met the beloved Cadet again, seeing and adoring the end of
> the Lord in that remarkable beginning; and now, with unspeak-
> able thankfulness to God, for what he here witnesses, may he say
> to this candidate-elect, for labour and sacrifice, in the words of
> St. Paul to *his* beloved disciple: 'Thou therefore, my son, be
> strong in the grace that is in Jesus Christ. Endure hardness as a
> good soldier of Jesus Christ. And the things thou has heard of
> me among many witnesses, the same commit thou to faithful
> men who shall be able to teach others also.' [3]

Bishop-elect Polk was presented by Bishops McIlvaine and
Otey and consecrated by Bishops Meade, McIlvaine, Smith,
and Otey. Holy communion was then administered to bishops,
clergy, and laity present.[4]

Immediately after the consecration Bishop Polk and wife re-

[3] Charles P. McIlvaine, *The Sermon at the Consecration of The Right
Reverend Leonidas Polk, D.D., Missionary Bishop of Arkansas, in Christ
Church, Cincinnati, December 9, 1838* (Gambrier, Ohio, 1838).
[4] For account of ceremony see Leonidas Polk Papers, January, 1839.

turned to Tennessee,[5] traveling down the Ohio River to Louisville and thence to Nashville by stage. Ice in the Cumberland
River obstructed travel by water.[6] Shortly after arriving at "Ashwood," Bishop Polk received from the Foreign Committee of
the Board of Missions a request that he include the Republic of
Texas in his travels. This he readily agreed to do, explaining that
since the "growing importance of this Republic is daily becoming
more manifest and the influence for good or evil, on the future
destiny of countless multitudes of our fellow men is equally certain," he could not decline the invitation. Certainly in so vast
and largely unoccupied area the needs and responsibilities must be
great. But he hastened to warn that exploration and visitation
must be followed by assignment to service of "men of character,
sound in the faith, and full of evangelical zeal, as pioneers." Dis-
couragement would be great and no man should be sent into the
field except that "he be willing to endure hardness, and labour
with singleness of purpose." [7] Polk himself met the requirements
he outlined. Only one of sound faith and evangelical zeal would
leave the comforts of "Ashwood" and the pleasures of plantation
life among friends and relatives to enter upon months of hardships that gave no promise of material reward.

Bishop Polk left on his travels early in February, 1839, too
hurriedly even to write his mother. His wife, in explaining this
neglect, commented that she told him, "I thought he treated me
& the children badly, for he had no time to tell us his wishes excepting after the stage came to the door." She was certainly not
so resigned to the Bishop's leaving his property and family as she
later recalled.[8] "You know my dear mother I am not very san-
guine, & I will confess I have many apprehensions about the
result. I do not think Mr. Polk will be a loser, but it would be
much better, if the mills would burn down in my opinion." She
was not certain as to the advisability of the arrangement Polk
had made for supervision during his absence. All in all, she was
low in spirits. Several Negroes, including two house servants, were
ill. This meant a great deal of difficulty, for there were four

[5] His mother returned to North Carolina.
[6] Leonidas Polk to Sarah Polk, December 31, 1838, George W. Polk Papers.
[7] *Id.* to Board of Missions, January 10, 1839, copy in Leonidas Polk Papers.
[8] See p. 77.

adults and nine children to care for. "I am sometimes low spirited at the thoughts of being so much alone, & I find the reality bad enough thus far—I am sometimes ready to say it is out of the question, I cannot bear it—to be deprived of the only pleasure which I had in putting up with inconveniences, seems sometimes hard indeed, but then better thoughts come, & I feel I ought to submit to this & much more." [9]

Much of the burden of supervising the Bishop's plantation and mills fell upon his brother Lucius. About the time of Leonidas' departure Lucius returned from a trip to New Orleans where he had gone to receive some blooded horses he was importing from Europe.[10] He returned in fine spirits, bringing not only the horses but also an Englishman who had been recommended as one competent to operate the mills. The Bishop's wife was skeptical. "I hope he will do well & if watching will do Lucius (who is very kind) will keep him straight." Of course the man must be given "time to be acquainted with the working of the engine before he can do much." [11]

Bishop Polk entered the Mississippi region of his extensive territory by way of Florence and Tuscumbia, Alabama, and LaGrange, Tennessee. Deciding to leave most of that state for future study, he soon moved on to Memphis, thence down the Mississippi to the Arkansas, and up that river to Little Rock, where he arrived on March 7. There he began a careful study of the needs of the people and the opportunities of the Episcopal church, making lengthy reports to the Board of Missions. He found Little Rock a healthy community of about 2,500 people, drawn from many parts of the Union, and as a whole "a highly intelligent body." Among them were about twenty Episcopal families. The probability of further increase in population and the interest in the church prompted a group of men to offer a guarantee of $1,000 annually for the support of a minister "of good talents and earnest piety."

The Bishop had intended to visit Batesville and Fayetteville and probably Forts Gibson and Smith. These plans were changed

[9] Frances Polk to Sarah Polk, March 5, 1839, Leonidas Polk Papers.

[10] Andrew Jackson later sent mares to be bred to Lucius' imported stud. Andrew Jackson to Lucius Polk, April 11, 1839, George W. Polk Papers.

[11] Frances Polk to Sarah Polk, January 28, 1839, *ibid.; id. to id.*, March 25, 1839, Gale Papers.

when he learned of the great distance and the scarcity of settlers. These interim towns, he was informed, had only three to four hundred people, mostly Methodists and Cumberland Presbyterians. An Episcopal minister could be supported in that area only if the government carried out a proposed plan for combining Forts Gibson and Smith.

From Little Rock Bishop Polk traveled by mail stage to Washington, Arkansas. This three days' journey took him across many streams tributary to the Ouachita and over broad acres of rich and "more or less settled" country. Intervening were "high, undulating ranges of fine lands," which reminded him of Carolina. On his first night in Washington he preached to a small group congregated in the courthouse. Encouraged by the response, he preached a second sermon the following day. "On both these occasions," he reported, "I had in the performance of the service, to use selections from the prayer book—there being no persons present who were acquainted with our forms." Near Washington were the villages of Columbus and Spring Hill. A Presbyterian minister was the only religious leader in this general area. Polk quickly concluded that these three villages could form the center of an important missionary area if an Episcopal minister could be found who would "for the love of Christ, go out unto these lost sheep, and break unto them the bread of life."

Continuing his travels, Bishop Polk reached the Red River at Dooley's Ferry and took a boat for Shreveport, "a town lately created" near the "great raft which has, until recently obstructed the navigation." The boat to Shreveport hit a snag and sank. The passengers were transferred to another and were soon again on their way, arriving on March 22. Shreveport, with about 1,000 inhabitants, was the most promising town on the upper Red River, yet it was "without any religious services whatever." However, among the settlers were a few Episcopalians and a handful representing other churches, who professed an interest in religion.

About fifteen miles distance toward the Sabine River Polk found a settlement of Tennesseans. They gave him an enthusiastic reception and "pledged themselves to build a suitable edifice without delay, and to contribute liberally to the support of a minister if he could be had." In Shreveport Bishop Polk was offered a building lot without cost, and a number of gentlemen pledged aid in the construction of a church and the support of a minister. Being only a missionary bishop and having no funds at his disposal, all Polk could promise was an urgent appeal to the Board of Missions. Later, in making this appeal, he expressed both concern and hope for this frontier river town.

It is situated on the only point accessible from the interior for a hundred miles or more up and down its [the river's] course, and is supported by one of the most fertile planting districts found in all the southwest, extending as far west as to the Sabine. The state of things at present is somewhat rude, but not more so than might be expected from an active border population filled with the spirit of enterprise, and without the immediate and constant impression of Gospel influence.[12]

From Shreveport Bishop Polk continued down Red River to Natchitoches. There he was received and entertained by one Mr. Fearing, late of St. Paul's Church in Philadelphia. It was now Passion Week; services were held on both Thursday and Good Friday. Bad weather, the Bishop reported, kept the crowd small on the first day, but the Good Friday meeting was "more numerously attended." Easter services at the courthouse attracted a still larger crowd. A feeling of great humility and responsibility came over Bishop Polk: "I have seldom seen an occasion on which I was constrained to feel more thankful to God for the unspeakable gifts of his Son to perishing sinners, or on which I perceived so distinctly the elevating and soul-subduing power of the service of our Church, on the minds and hearts of the worshippers." Here was a town of about 2,500, one-third French Creole and two-thirds Protestant, yet there was not "a protestant minister of any kind connected with the place. They have no one to baptize their children, to bury their dead, or break the bread of life to the perishing living. They are to be pitied." This situation, however, could be changed, for many people expressed an eagerness to support a minister. But Polk warned the Board of Missions that these people

[12] There is a family story that there was much opposition to Polk's preaching in Shreveport; so in order to get the use of a meeting place it was necessary to post a $600 bond to take care of possible damage by mob action. This money was furnished by a friendly trader whom Polk had met on the boat down to Shreveport. On this boat also Polk had made friends with the crew. When the boat sank he had showed them how to raise it. This the crew did and then reached Shreveport just in time to protect the religious gathering from disturbance by unfriendly parties. Polk, "Leonidas Polk, A Memoir."

were highly intelligent; consequently, a minister, to be successful, must be a man of intelligence and "some weight of character." "The field is inviting to well founded, earnest intelligent missionary zeal."

On April 2, the Bishop took boat for Alexandria. This town did not impress him. Its winter population of about 800 dwindled to about half that number during the summer as residents left for the pine lands, seeking more healthful conditions. Few "friends of the Church" were found among these inhabitants. Throughout Rapides Parish, however, there were about 2,000 whites and 10,000 Negroes. If the few families at Opelousas were added to this number the assignment of a full time minister would be justified. "I have no doubt," Polk reported, ". . . that if proper efforts were made, great good could be effected among the blacks of that parish."

By April 6 Bishop Polk was at Natchez. Three weeks were spent in visiting South Mississippi churches. On May 2, accompanied by two ministers, Page of Natchez, and Fish of Woodville, he held services at St. Francisville, Louisiana, and then moved on to New Orleans, where he preached at Christ Church and in St. Paul's parish. Although this was Polk's first visit to New Orleans, he immediately recognized what he considered the responsibilities of the Episcopal church. There were no longer vacant pews in Christ Church and the congregation in St. Paul's parish was increasing rapidly. A building was already under construction. The "rapid increase of the American population upon the French," he noted, was producing an "annual increase in minds accessible chiefly to protestant influences." Lack of accommodations and ministers was depriving many person of Episcopal persuasion of the privilege of participation.

Completing his visitations in New Orleans, Bishop Polk was ready for a tour of the Republic of Texas. The Reverend Mr. Page of Natchez agreed to accompany him a portion of the way. Taking passage on the steam packet *Cuba* on May 10, they arrived at Galveston two days later. The Reverend Mr. Ranney of the Louisiana diocese was already there conducting services and leading a campaign to raise funds to build a church. Polk was impressed by both the location of Galveston and the enthusiasm for the Episcopal church. The town's location was such that it would certainly become the "place of deposit for all articles of merchandise imported into the republic, and from which their exports are shipped." The rapidly increasing population, already numbering 2,000, was "highly respectable" and compared favorably with other towns of equal size and age. A mild and pleasant climate, with the heat of the summer sun "broken by the constantly prevailing breeze," made it a pleasant place to live. All in all, the Bishop saw here "a good point for an enterprising man, of competent talents, to exert an influence in behalf of the Gospel." The present was "time for him to begin," for proprietors of undeveloped lands were eager to donate sites for churches. Polk himself was requested to choose one for a proposed Episcopal church.

From Galveston he went to Houston, traveling by way of Galveston Bay, the San Jacinto, and Buffalo Bayou. The flat country and the narrowness of the bayou impressed him. In Houston he found an "air of business." Although the capital was soon to be moved to Austin, he was convinced that Houston would remain second in importance to Galveston. Religious life in the town was centered around one Presbyterian and one Episcopal congregation. The latter had already raised $4,000 toward a new building.

At Houston Bishop Polk received a letter from the Foreign Committee requesting his reaction to a proposal to appoint a standing committee within Texas to exercise ecclesiastical authority and serve as a medium of communication with the Foreign Committee. Polk urged that "the safety of the church and the purity of religion, demanded the immediate presence of some such organization," but he also urged that the arrangement be considered only temporary. "A bishop . . . is wanted here," he explained, "and he should be sent as soon as the competent authorities can convene. His influence would be immense, and no substitute can adequately take his place."

Bishop Polk subsequently visited Columbia, Brazoria, Velasco, Quintano, and Matagorda. The oppressive heat on the open prairies caused him to abandon proposed trips to Austin and Bastrop and return to the United States via Nacogdoches and San Augustin. Instead, he returned to New Orleans by way of Galveston. After one day of rest in New Orleans he set out by stage for Florence, Alabama. There on June 22, "4th Sunday after Trinity," he preached in the unfinished church then under direction of the

Reverend Mr. Harris. At daybreak on Monday he left by stage for "Ashwood," arriving late in the afternoon.

After a few weeks' rest in the quiet of his comfortable home, Bishop Polk sat down with his notes to evaluate the needs and possibilities in the areas visited. To the Foreign Committee he made some definite recommendations relative to the Republic of Texas. He found nothing in this vast area that distinguished it from the Southwest generally. The settlers, although more widely dispersed, were much the same, following the "same pursuits and sympathies." The civil government was well organized and individual rights adequately protected. The abundance of fertile soil, especially adapted to cotton, made the Republic capable of caring for an immense population.

All of this presented to the Episcopal church a great challenge. If the church were to become firmly rooted and operate efficiently in that region then no fewer than six deacons and presbyters and a missionary bishop should be sent out immediately. Town lots suitable for building churches could be had without cost. Polk himself had secured several such lots and also a plot well situated for a college and theological seminary. Lots were cheap, but that would not be the case twenty years hence. "We have in this, an opportunity of profiting by the cautionary declaration of the Savior, 'The children of this world are wiser than the children of light.' "

Bishop Polk classed the need for ministerial labor in Texas as immediate and urgent. Galveston, Houston, and Matagorda had immediate need for missionaries and would shortly be able to support the work without financial assistance from the general church. There was also a need at Austin and Bastrop. Since these towns were only thirty miles apart they could, for the present, be served by a single missionary. The same was true of the East Texas towns of Nacogdoches and San Augustin.

Further recommendations included the formation of a missionary station composed of Sabine Town, "founded by families attached to our church," and Fort Jessup, twenty-five miles inside Louisiana, where there were several friends of the church among the military officers. The expenses of such a post could be divided between the Foreign and Domestic committees. Then there were the towns along the Brazos. This river ran through the most fertile region of Texas. The twin towns of Velasco and Quintano might be joined with Brazoria and Columbia, thirty-five miles away, to form a single missionary station. Higher up the river Washington and Nashville might form still another station.

In conclusion Bishop Polk added that until a bishop could be supplied he still favored the appointment of a committee to serve as a means of communication with the Board of Missions.

To the Board of Missions Bishop Polk reported that during his tour which required five months, he had traveled about 5,000 miles; preached forty-four sermons; baptized fourteen persons; confirmed forty-one; consecrated one church; and laid the corner-stone of another.

> The field is large, the harvest white, the laborers few indeed. We have not a single laborer west of the Mississippi and compared with the population, few in the dioceses of Mississippi and Alabama. . . . There is bread enough in the Church and to spare, if the Church could come up to the sense of its possessions, on the one hand, and its responsibilities, on the other. These destitute men are our brethren; the brethren of us all—of the Eastern man as well as the Western—of the New Yorker and the New Englander, as well as the Virginian and the Carolinian. . . .
>
> I would here take occasion to say, not by way of discouragement certainly, but of caution only, let those who may propose to enter on this field, reflect well on the nature of the enterprise before it is undertaken. . . . We honestly confess that, in inviting our brethren to share with us the toil of our work we have small wages of a pure worldly character to offer. We are constrained to believe that the Church will not deny us our food and raiment. Beyond that all that is received in this life is a gratuity of the Lord, and more than we stipulated for. Our condition of service is that "we lose our life in this world." Our recompense lies beyond. Self-denial is our vocation. A crown of righteousness is our reward. It is my earnest hope that we may speedily under God's blessing have men who shall be willing to come forth and supply "this lack of service." [13]

At home again after an absence of five months, Bishop Polk plunged into his much neglected business activities. The effects of

[13] Polk's account of his tour is found in three reports and a letter to his mother, March 18, 1839. All are in the Leonidas Polk Papers. See also *The Spirit of Missions* (New York, 1836–1939), IV, 139–42, 198–200, 306–314, 333–35.

the panic of 1837 were being seriously felt even in agricultural areas. And there were many business failures in Middle Tennessee. The Polk brothers were heavily involved as endorsers of paper of one of these unfortunate business enterprises. At the same time they had expanded their own operations by investing in Alabama and Mississippi lands.

During the summer of 1839 they also began construction of an Episcopal chapel. As a site for this structure, Bishop Polk deeded to Bishop Otey for the Diocese of Tennessee a six-acre "grove of majestic and towering oaks near Ashwood." [14] "I am very anxious to get our chapel underway before we leave," he wrote his mother.

> We begin on it next week. We shall put in hands to make brick, put them up, do the carpentry, plastering, etc.
>
> We design putting up a neat Gothic chapel, not larger than enough for our households and neighbors, yet sufficiently large to make us comfortable.
>
> It is hoped that in the making of this wilderness bud and blossom as the rose, it *would not be wholly out of place* to say to our Carolina friends *very respectfully*, that kind remembrances will not be forgotten.
>
> There are some things we cannot make, such as Bibles, Prayer Books, Baptismal fonts, organs and such sort of trimmings.
>
> We shall have a neat pretty site on the *top* of a slight eminence, midst a beautiful grove of trees.
>
> It is convenient to the road and sufficiently central. . . . [15]

In the midst of his own business and church affairs Bishop Polk also found time to advise his mother on business matters and sister Susan on love affairs. Susan had received a marriage proposal from one Mr. Dickinson. Her bishop brother opposed the match; he had reason to believe the young man would not measure up to expectations. Money was not everything, not even "the chief good," he explained, yet the total lack of an avocation was a destitution that must be regarded as "fatal to the pretentions of any man." Both happiness and respectability were dependent upon honorable employment and "it would be a hazardous enterprise to attempt life without it." The plan of things was that men should exert their energies and make themselves generally useful. He thought Susan

[14] Maury County *Deed Book*, I, Book Z, 619.
[15] Leonidas Polk to Sarah Polk, July 28, 1839, George W. Polk Papers.

too well trained and her mind too well regulated for her to be
happy if married to "a mere drone. . . . He who has nothing to do
will do worse." There was still a further consideration. The Bishop
questioned Dickinson's character. He wished his sister to marry a
man who feared "to do wrong, because to do wrong is mean, hurt-
ful to conscience, and displeasing to God." This matter of matri-
mony might not only determine her happiness on earth but also
her "lot for eternity." Consequently, he suggested that Susan
kindly but firmly inform the young man that they could never be
more than friends.[16] Susan must have followed this suggestion;
nothing more is heard of Mr. Dickinson.

Apparently a true missionary could not remain long at home
even midst such pleasant surroundings. After a visit to North
Carolina during the fall and early winter, Bishop Polk again set
out on his travels on January 29, 1840. After visiting Florence and
Tuscumbia, Alabama, he moved on to Mobile by way of Columbus, Mississippi, and numerous small towns in central Alabama,
preaching as he went but doing little in the way of organization.
At Mobile he consecrated Christ Church and at New Orleans St.
Paul's Church, which on his previous visit he had noted in the
process of construction.

A business letter from Lucius awaited him at New Orleans.
Lucius was up the river inspecting their Mississippi lands. But the
business matter most pressing on their minds was their probable
losses as endorsers of paper of the firm of Caruthers and Harris.
Back in 1833 A. D. Harris of Columbia, wishing to go into the
commission business in New Orleans with one Caruthers, was in
need of funds. A mutual friend suggested to Colonel William Polk
that he make Harris a loan of $5,000 at "bank rates" and take a
lien on some property. The Colonel was already doing business
with Caruthers and subsequently did business with Caruthers and
Harris.[17]

It is not known whether Colonel Polk made the requested loan,
but his sons Lucius and Leonidas endorsed Harris' notes for a
much larger amount. Harris was their "particular friend," Bishop

[16] *Id.* to Susan Polk, August 16, 1839, Leonidas Polk Papers.

[17] James Walker to William Polk, August 22, 1833; A. D. Harris to William
Polk, December 11, 1833, Polk-Yeatman Papers; Caruthers, Harris & Company
to *id.*, January 13, 1834, George W. Polk Papers.

Polk later explained, "one of my communicants . . . my vestry-man—my warden—my right arm in every good work. He was all that I could wish in a Christian layman." [18] Nevertheless the panic ruined Harris' business and shifted the burden of his debts to his endorsers. If he himself escaped with a loss of not more than $15,000, Bishop Polk would be thankful.

After reviewing the situation the Bishop concluded that the application of Christian principles was the only honorable course; to him such principles were also the guide for good business. He told his brother Lucius:

> I am of the opinion that the proper course obviously for all those who have been entrapped in the C&H business, is, to keep quiet & let them alone. Nothing but harm can result from either attacking them by language or action. We are bound to sustain some loss & my opinion is that this loss will be lessened by our own caution & prudence. Violence at least never yet answered any good purpose, *in any case.* He [Harris] has gone to work & promises fair, & I think the least we can do is quietly to pocket our ills, to set to & pay our liabilities as soon as we can, tell him we mean to do so, & that we do not mean to trouble him in any wise, but give him a fair chance to act the gentleman & the man of honor, always remembering that we have our eye on him & that we expect him with all due dispatch to replace the losses we are to sustain by him. This is the sensible course, & our forbearance & kindness, may strengthen his honesty. At any rate the opposite course will render him reckless & desperate, so that policy as well as Christian forbearance demands that we should obtain & keep mastery over ourselves & maintain an attitude of courtesy toward him. [19]

From New Orleans Bishop Polk went to La Fonda, Baton Rouge, St. Francisville, Natchez, and Edwards, and thence into the interior of Mississippi, returning home early in May, 1840, weary and somewhat discouraged, but in excellent health. Months of arduous travel had convinced him of the impossibility of doing effective work over so extensive an area. To make one complete

[18] Leonidas Polk to Charles P. McIlvaine, August 10, 1840, Leonidas Polk Papers.
[19] *Id.* to Lucius Polk, April 2, 1840; *id.* to Charles P. McIlvaine, August 10, 1840, *ibid.*

coverage of this territory, the surface of which was "exceedingly rough and the facilities of communication off the river wretched," he estimated, would require "*two years of incessant labour.*" The Bishop also felt very keenly the long absences from his family. Out of eighteen months in the Episcopate, he wrote Bishop McIlvaine, only four had been spent with his family. "I have often felt strongly, that a Miss. Bp ought not to have a family. He should be literally married to the church. He should have a thought for nothing else, a man of one idea, of one book, of one object." [20]

Regardless of whether he should or should not have been a family man, Polk definitely was. "My home seems more sweet than ever," he confided to his mother. "The grass is so luxuriant & the foliage of the trees so full & rich." [21] Yet there was no time to relax and enjoy these things. He was soon off to Nashville on business. While there he visited his cousin, Governor James K. Polk, and saw General Jackson. The old General, in spite of age and years of public service, looked "very well & is very spirited yet." Polk also visited Mrs. John Catron and found her well and "full of conversation." Judge Catron had recently visited "Ashwood."

Other happenings of interest during these summer months included the marriage of Rufus Polk to Sarah Jackson, daughter of the James Jacksons of near Florence. They immediately moved into their new Maury County home which they named "Westbrook." The Bishop thought Sarah "a sensible woman." George was also expected soon to join "our circle" and make Maury County his place of residence. Bishop Otey returned from a Northern tour on which he solicited funds for Columbia Institute, a school for girls which he and Polk were sponsoring. He brought with him $3,000 in cash and $5,000 in promises. The school had about 130 girls enrolled and was "very flourishing." A new organ had been added and there was quite a display of musical talent. [22]

Probably the summer task most satisfying to the Polk brothers was the completion of their chapel. By late fall all outside work was finished except a portion of the tower. The structure measured

[20] *Ibid.* For short report on tour see *Journal of General Convention* (1841), 162.

[21] Leonidas Polk to Sarah Polk, June 4, 1840, Leonidas Polk Papers.

[22] *Ibid.* For an interesting sketch of Columbia Institute see Frances M. Stephenson, "The Twilight of the Institute," in Nashville *Banner*, August 11, 1935.

sixty-five by forty-one, with a sixteen-foot vestry room in the rear
and a fifty-foot tower. Work inside was to be finished during the
winter months. The plan was to have everything complete and
ready for consecration when the Tennessee Convention should
meet in Columbia in the summer of 1841.

Farming picked up considerably during 1840. The depression
had about passed. The Bishop completed fencing his entire plantation and added many cross fences. This accomplishment, he figured, would give comfort to both himself and the livestock. He
and Lucius sent off to their Mississippi plantation thirty slaves,
including a carpenter and a blacksmith. He left behind sixteen
hands, besides servants and four blacksmiths. The Mississippi overseer predicted a crop of 150 bales of cotton. "But you know how
those prospects turn out," Bishop Polk remarked to his mother.
However there was plenty of range down there; so an ample supply
of meat should be produced.[23]

While Bishop Polk was making preparations to start again on
his travels, his brother George, recently arrived from North Carolina, married Mary (Sally) Hilliard. The newlyweds would soon
begin construction of "Rattle and Snap," another addition to the
Polk nest of fine country homes. Still another brother, Dr. William
Polk, would build "Buena Vista" on the site of the present Columbia Military Academy. The name would seem to indicate that
this home was not built until after the Mexican War.

Leaving home became increasingly unpleasant for Bishop Polk,
for he was now the father of four—Hamy and "three sweet little
girls," Frances, Katherine, and Sarah.[24] Nevertheless, he set out for
Arkansas on November 30, 1840, thus missing Christmas and the
New Year celebrations with his family. "It is a sad trial to be so
much absent from my family," he wrote his mother, "but I am
hoping it will not be so always." While in the mood he also took
stock of himself, noting his achievements and failures of the past
year. He felt as though he were standing on "top of a high hill,
up which I have been struggling from midsummer." From such a
point he could look both forward and backward. Looking backward, "I feel that I have done but too little in accomplishing the

[23] Leonidas Polk to Sarah Polk, November 26, 1840, Leonidas Polk Papers.
[24] These daughters later married Peyton Skipwith, William Dudley Gale, and
Frank Blake.

end of my creation. . . . I have meditated too little; I have
humbled myself too infrequently before the throne of God; I have
been too seldom found in prayer; I have watched against the
intrusion of a worldly spirit too little; I have thought too seldom of
death, of its inevitable certainty, of the necessity of being constantly prepared for it. I have not governed my temper as I ought;
I have not sufficiently hoarded my time and applied it to profitable
uses." However, with the grace and strength of God he was resolved to make amends during the coming year.[25]

Bishop Polk spent more than a month visiting in Arkansas. He
first tried travel by buggy. It was soon "shattered" in the ruts and
swamps. He then shifted to horses, "handsomely equipped with
saddles, bridles, martingales, and saddlebags" and a fine buffalo
rug. He had little fear of personal harm, he sent word to his brother
George, but he did fear some thief might make off with his horse
and equipment. From Arkansas he crossed into the Indian Territory, visiting both Cherokee and Choctaw countries before crossing the Red River into Texas. In Arkansas and Texas he found
several of his Hawkins kin—Henry, Ben, and William. At Springhill, Arkansas, he gave up travel by horse for the comforts of steam-
boat down the river to Shreveport. One horse had developed a bad
case of "scratches." "Folly," formerly a carriage horse, proved a
good saddle horse, but the roan was unable to keep the pace. Rain
and mud had made travel almost impossible, he explained to his
mother. His fare had been rather rough; his lodging was uncertain
and often uncomfortable. One night was passed "in a cotton-house
on the top of a pile of cotton, with dogs and negroes lying around,
and a hamper basket to hang my clothes upon." Yet his health
remained good and thanks to his buffalo robe and an ample supply
of blankets he was not too uncomfortable.[26]

Passing down Red River to Shreveport, Natchitoches, and
Alexandria, Bishop Polk noted, "I find the field quite white to the
harvest, and no laborers here. There is no portion of the whole
country so destitute, I presume, as Louisiana. She has not, so far as
I know, a single church west of the Mississippi River; and I find
few or no Presbyterians, and only now and then a wandering

[25] Leonidas Polk to Sarah Polk, January 18, 1841, quoted in Polk, *Leonidas
Polk*, I, 166–67.

[26] *Id.* to *id.*, February 2, 10, 1841, *ibid.*, 167–68.

Methodist. The Sabbath is no Sabbath here. The stores and shops are kept open just as on other days, and the planters and tradesmen look upon that day as a day set apart for laying in supplies and doing odd jobs." At Natchitoches, where he preached five times at the courthouse, it was necessary to delay Sunday services until 12:00, the hour when stores closed. Yet there was considerable interest in the services and his congregation included a number of French Catholics. "They set lightly by their religion." [27]

Lucius met the Bishop at Natchez and they took time out from missionary work to inspect some sugar plantations in Louisiana. For some time Bishop Polk had been considering a possible change of residence. His letters and reports had frequently indicated displeasure with the necessity of being away from his family for long periods. The work of a missionary and a planter could be successfully combined only if the plantation was centrally located. Middle Tennessee was even beyond the border of Polk's territory. Futhermore, both he and Lucius had about decided that sugar planting was more profitable than cotton. Consequently, both were interested in a Louisiana sugar plantation.

If they should buy a sugar plantation, Lucius reassured his wife, it would be "in the midst of good society" and near New Orleans, "where our time can be very pleasantly passed." [28] The region under inspection was along Bayou La Fourche. Bishop Polk reported they were pleased with the fine country. Many French families resided there and mong them were a few planters.[29]

If Lucius were seriously interested in a Louisiana sugar plantation he changed his mind. But before returning home Bishop Polk purchased from James Porter a large plantation known as "Leighton," situated along Bayou La Fourche near Thibodaux, for $100,000. The tract was described as twenty-one and seven-twelfths arpents fronting on the Bayou and forty arpents deep with 764 "superficial acres" of "back lands." [30]

[27] *Id.* to *id.*, April 5, 1841, *ibid.*, 169–70. For report on tour see *Journal of General Convention* (1841), 169.

[28] Lucius Polk to Mary Polk, March 27, 1841, George W. Polk Papers.

[29] Leonidas Polk to Susan Polk, April 7, 1841, Leonidas Polk Papers.

[30] Lafourche Parish, *Conveyances,* 1840–1842, Vol. R, 446–52. This was an involved transaction. To the Union Bank of Louisiana Polk gave two notes totaling $27,945 secured by a first mortgage. To Porter he made a note for $5,220 payable on demand and fourteen others for $5,313.77 each payable at

Bishop Polk probably planned an early removal to "Leighton," for back in Tennessee again, he wrote his mother, advising the employment of lawyers to look after her Tennessee business. He also spoke of plans for an autumn visit to North Carolina. He and his family would "travel by private conveyance across the mountains litterally [sic] 'Bag & Baggage' for we come with all the children little Sally, *wet nurse & all.* . . . Our style consists of our carriage & buggy . . . & a baggage wagon. 'Women & children & much cattle' (see account of the journey of the Israelites from Egypt into Canaan)." [81]

The trek was completed without unexpected hardships, and leaving the three little girls with their grandparents in Raleigh and placing Hamilton in boarding school, Bishop Polk and his wife hurried on to New York in October, 1841, to attend the General Convention.[32] While there Polk accepted an invitation to become the first bishop of the Diocese of Louisiana. The Diocese of Louisiana had been formally organized in 1838. Its first convention, meeting in January, 1839, had voted to request missionary Bishop Polk to include Louisiana in his charge. This Polk had agreed to, hence his visitations in that state. In May, 1841, the diocese framed a petition to the General Convention urging the appointment of a Bishop of Louisiana. The convention honored this petition and, upon a motion by Bishop Thomas Church Brownell of Connecticut, seconded by Bishop Otey of Tennessee, the House of Bishops nominated Polk. The nomination was quickly confirmed by the House of Deputies on October 16, 1841.[33]

If Bishop Polk had entertained any doubts about the advisability of moving from "Ashwood" to "Leighton," they were dispelled by his new appointment. There is no evidence that he had been assured of such an appointment before purchasing "Leigh-

---

specified intervals over a period of seven years. To secure these notes Porter was given a second mortgage on the property and eighty-three slaves. All of the above notes drew 10 per cent interest.

[81] Leonidas Polk to Sarah Polk, July 15, 1841, Leonidas Polk Papers. He also added that henceforth his Maury County address would be Ashwood, Tennessee, for a new post office had been established "at the turnpike gate which you know is in my lane."

[32] Polk, "Leonidas Polk, A Memoir"; Frances Polk to Mary Polk, November 18, 1841, Dillon-Polk Papers.

[33] Journal of . . . General Convention (1841), 71, 113.

ton," yet he certainly knew that the Diocese of Louisiana was petitioning for a bishop. He must also have known that he was a logical choice. At any rate, his ready acceptance indicated that he had given such an appointment serious thought.

Returning to North Carolina, Bishop Polk made preparations for taking over both his sugar plantation and his new diocese. As a sugar planter he would need additional funds and slaves. Both could be had by exercising an option granted by Mrs. Polk's father two years earlier. In April, 1839, Mrs. Polk's bachelor uncle, George Pollok, had died intestate. His extensive property in land and slaves was therefore divided between his sister, Mrs. John Devereux, and the children of a deceased sister. John Devereux and his wife, already financially independent and not wishing to assume additional responsibilities, transferred to their son John P. all the real estate (spread over seven counties) and personal property received from the Pollok estate on the condition that the said John P. would pay to his father and mother certain specified amounts, to the two children of his late brother George $22,000 each, and to Leonidas and Frances Polk $100,000. The Polks were to have until 1841 to decide whether to take the amount in installment payments or land and slaves.[34]

The Polks now decided to take one half in slaves. They received 161 slaves of varying ages valued at $50,132.[35] The Bishop collected wagons and teams and soon had his slaves on the way to Louisiana, traveling by way of Tennessee, where he apparently picked up others. Mrs. Polk and the children remained in Raleigh for the winter. Another daughter, Susan, was born in April, 1842.[36] The Bishop, after getting his Negroes off to "Leighton," made a hurried visit to Raleigh before setting out for New Orleans to

[34] For the legal documents relating to this inheritance see Devereux Papers (North Carolina Archives) and Pollok-Devereux Papers (North Carolina Archives) under dates of April and July, 1839. Under the agreement John Devereux was to receive $10,000. Mrs. Devereux was to receive $3,000 annually for life plus an additional $50,000 in cash or in investments according to her direction. Mrs. Devereux's fondness for making donations to charity was not fully appreciated by her husband. The $50,000, he explained, was to be used for charity and she was not to "call upon him for anything for that object." See Frances Polk to John P. Devereux, June 28, ?, Pollok-Devereux Papers.

[35] For papers relating to final settlement see Devereux Papers under December, 1841.

[36] She later married Joseph Jones.

attend his first meeting of the Convention of the Diocese of Louisiana. And he and all his Tennessee brothers were again in Raleigh in the early summer to attend the wedding of their sister Susan to Kenneth Rayner. All then returned to their Tennessee homes, the Bishop's family traveling overland and the others by way of Baltimore.[37]

Bishop Polk first met with the Louisiana Convention on January 20, 1842. The office to which he had been appointed was a challenge rather than a position. He was promised no salary. Five hundred dollars annually could be expected for traveling expenses. The diocese included four parishes with six clergymen and a total of 238 communicants.[38] Polk immediately began a program of development. Essential requirements of progress, he told the convention, were unity of purpose and able leadership by a native ministry. He no doubt was already dreaming of a Southern university for the training of Southern ministers. Natives alone, he would later explain, understood the South and its peculiar institution. They would understand that slavery was the fault of neither the Negroes nor the present generation of whites. Regardless of responsibility, slavery was a condition that must be recognized and every effort must be made to elevate the unfortunate blacks. There was not a single congregation of Negroes in the Diocese of Louisiana.

This was a subject to which Polk would return again and again. In 1843 he told the convention that "provision of religious instruction of the colored race" should be of "most intimate concern" to all Christians as well as the ministry. "It is one of the chiefest charms of the Gospel of Christ, that it seeks to equalize the human condition; and to compensate, by the richness of its spiritual provisions, for the disparities existing in the worldly circumstances of our race." The Gospel, therefore, was eminently "the property of the poor." Success in carrying the Gospel to people in all walks of life depended, however, upon "the countenance and hearty co-operation of our brethren and laity." But no difficulty need be feared, he believed, if all were made to understand that "our purpose is to teach all orders and degrees of men,

[37] Polk, "Leonidas Polk, A Memoir."
[38] *Correspondence of Right Rev. L. Polk with the Vestry of Trinity Church* (New Orleans, 1858).

in the language of our formularies, 'to do their duty in that state of life, in which it has pleased God to call them': that we are not political crusaders, but simple guileless teachers of that Gospel which was preached by our Savior and His Apostles, in a region whose social condition was altogether similar to our own." [39]

[39] Diocese of Louisiana, *Journal of Convention* (1842, 1843).

(6)

Life at "Leighton"

SHORTLY BEFORE BISHOP POLK moved his family from "Ash-wood" to Louisiana, St. John's Chapel was consecrated. No doubt partly due to Polk's absences from home, completion had been delayed a full year. It was finally completed, furnished, and ready for consecration by the late summer of 1842. ". . . of chaste and simple Gothic architecture" with "plain but beautiful interior" and "capable of seating, with a small gallery, about five hundred persons," it was truly a credit to its builders and donors; the Polk brothers—Lucius, Leonidas, Rufus, and George—presented the chapel and adjoining cemetery to the community free of debt. The minister, it was explained, would be supported by public contribution. No pews would be sold, but each family was urged to select one for its own use. Whites would select pews near the front, leaving those in the rear for Negroes.

The building was almost entirely "home made." The bricks were made by skilled slave labor, and the lumber was cut and sawed in the immediate vicinity. The chancel and altar railings were made from a cherry tree cut from the site on which the chapel was erected. Mother Polk and sister Susan gave the silver communion service and the marble baptismal font.[1]

On the day of consecration, September 4, 1842, the Polks, their friends, and neighbors filled the little chapel to capacity. Few among them had ever witnessed a consecration. After the whites were seated the Negroes were admitted, quickly filling the gallery, stairs, vestibule, vestry room, and door. One elderly Negro sat at "the very feet of the clergy." Consecration was by Bishop Otey. Within the chancel were also Bishop Polk, the Reverend Mr.

[1] George W. Polk, "St. John's Church," *Tennessee Historical Magazine*, VII, 147–53.

Smith, rector of Columbia Institute, and three other clergymen. Bishop Otey preached from the 122nd Psalm. Rufus and George Polk were baptized by their bishop brother. The sacrament was then administered by Bishop Otey. After the whites had been served, a few words of explanation were given to the Negroes. They then came forward in large numbers with much "reverence and devotion." In order that they might also participate in the singing of hymns and psalms, lines were read aloud two at a time, and the "loudest strains of praise came from the sable group." "Ah! could some of our friends have witnessed that scene," exclaimed a visitor from Pennsylvania, "how would it have silenced the suspicion that the slave holder values not the soul of his slave." The services lasted four and a half hours, yet "there appeared no evidence of weariness on the part of those who could not be expected to feel the interest of churchmen in the proceedings." [2]

The consecration over with, the Leonidas Polks made rapid preparation for their departure for Louisiana. "We are getting ready to go down so soon as the season will allow," the Bishop wrote his mother on September 28, 1842.[3] It was fear of the season in Louisiana that had caused the family to remain at "Ashwood" during the summer while the Bishop and the Negroes set up operation in the sugar cane country and a few household servants readied "Leighton" for occupation. Life in the Deep South was to prove quite different from that at "Ashwood." And the Bishop's frequent and continued absences from home would make adjustment more difficult.

[2] This account of the consecration was written by a visitor from Philadelphia and published in the Columbia *Guardian*, October 15, 1842. Manuscript copies are in both the George W. Polk Papers and the Leonidas Polk Papers. The first person to be buried in the quiet little churchyard to the rear of St. John's was Rufus Polk, who died in 1843. Subsequently his brothers Lucius and George were also buried there, as was Bishop Otey and many years later Bishop James M. Maxon. It also became the temporary resting place for five Confederate generals killed at the battle of Franklin. The story was told that as General Hood moved the Army of Tennessee back into the state in November, 1864, Major General Pat Cleburne's division passed along the road in front of St. John's Church. Cleburne reined in his horse and sat for a moment gazing at the ivy-covered tower, the beautiful trees, and the "calm restful loveliness of the landscape surrounding." As he rode away he remarked to a staff member, "It is almost worth dying for to be buried in such a beautiful spot." A few days later he was one of the five Confederate generals whose bodies were interred there. Polk, "St. John's Church," *loc. cit.*, 147.

[3] Leonidas Polk Papers.

"Leighton," a low spacious structure of nineteen rooms, fronted on Bayou La Fourche. "This is not a fine house nor sumptuously furnished," wrote a visitor, "comfort and convenience seem to be the object instead of pomp and show." [4] The sloping front lawn was bordered by a broad hedge of Cherokee roses. Between the hedge and the bayou ran the parish road. The plantation road approached the house from the side, separating the lawn from the cane fields and Negro quarters. On the back lawn stood the plantation office and quarters for domestic servants. A row of fig trees shut off view of the stables beyond.

The charm of "Leighton" was in its "simplicity and good-heartedness." Across the front of the building was a broad portico onto which looked the large windows of Mrs. Polk's bedroom, Bishop Polk's study, the front parlor, and the hall. On hot evenings it was the favorite place for adult relaxation and children's play. No part of the house, however, was forbidden to the older children, for as at "Ashwood," Bishop Polk insisted that they have full run of the place and constant association with adults. A relative quoted him as saying that "good manners could be taught to girls and boys, but that easy, unconscious ones must be inhaled with the air of their daily lives."

To this way of handling children Mrs. Polk gave her consent, although it was probably a departure from the life she had known in the Devereux home. Bishop Polk had little difficulty with discipline. His genial nature seemed to command obedience through respect. His return from a tour of visitation was a holiday at the Polk home, and his harassed wife was quite willing for him to take over. From boyhood he had exhibited a strong sense of justice—a trait he always observed in dealings with others. He could not tolerate deceit or misrepresentation, yet he often remarked to family and friends that man was weak and allowances must often be made. The desire to conceal the truth he considered a natural result of fear. In most cases love and patience could overcome fear and thus render deceit unnecessary.

On family affairs as well as other matters Mrs. Polk was "timid in maintaining an opinion in opposition to the bishop." This, however, was no indication of inferiority; associates thought her a

---

[4] "Mrs. I. H. Hilliard's Diary" (University of the South Archives).

person of ability and judgment, possessing "a remarkable power of finding out the resources of others, and the faculty of making them available." Although she and Bishop Polk were quite different in many respects, there is no evidence of a lack of confidence or harmony.

The Polk family led a well-ordered life, following a daily routine from which there was seldom a departure. There was time for study and time for recreation, and regular duties were performed even when visitors were present. For adults and older children the Bishop's library offered almost unlimited advantages for literary and cultural development. "What fine opportunities the Bishop's daughters have!" observed a visitor. "Such an extensive and rare library. I could linger forever over the books and prints collected in Italy!!" [5] There was usually a governess present to look after the interests of the older children. When the family moved from Tennessee they took along a Mrs. Porter, a tutoress at the Columbia Institute, "a very elegant & accomplished lady," as governess for the girls and companion to Mrs. Polk. Her salary of $350 annually was considered "a modest sum" for so valuable a service.[6] Later a Miss Beauchamp, fresh from Ireland with letters of reference from the Bishop of Cork and the Chief of the Exchequer in Dublin, served in this capacity.

Then for the little ones there was always the faithful Mammy Betsey. Coming as a wedding gift from John Devereux to his daughter Frances, she was to nurse all of the Leonidas Polk children and several of the grandchildren. Sometimes a bit fussy yet always sympathetic, she constantly lectured both the children and household servants on the importance of good manners both for their own sake and the "credit of the family." An impressed visitor at "Leighton" noted that Mrs. Polk had a "faithful negro nurse to whose care she abandons her babies entirely. Only when she has a fancy to caress them does she see them—eight children and she can not lay to their charge the loss of a single nights rest." [7]

[5] *Ibid.*

[6] Leonidas Polk to Sarah Polk, September 28, 1842, Leonidas Polk Papers.

[7] Hilliard, "Diary." Mammy Betsey lived to be almost 75, dying in New Orleans in 1874. Last rites were said at the little Prytania Street Chapel, the Reverend William T. Leacock of Christ Church, a frequent visitor in the Polk home even before removal from Tennessee, officiating. A full account of the funeral and burial was published in a New Orleans newspaper. See undated

When at home Bishop Polk devoted much time to his family.
"My wife and children are all now with me, and I am enjoying
their society greatly . . . ," he once wrote his sister Susan.

> I pass my time in the instruction of Hamilton and Fanny; my
> daughter in mathematics and the classics, Hamilton alone in the
> latter, my study hours being from nine A.M. till two P.M. I am
> highly pleased to witness their advancement, which I would fain
> believe quite as decisive as it has hitherto been under instructors
> less interested in their improvement.
>
> They *all* sing, and that pleases me. Should you hear us some-
> times accompanying the piano to "The Old North State," you
> would think we were hearty lovers of all her simplicity, her
> honesty, and her pines—as we assuredly claim to be.[8]

In the words of a brother-in-law, Polk's "family idolised him,
and well they might,—for he made every thing bright and joyous,
around him; and you know his character was well calculated to
inspire respect and regard among all who approached him." [9]
Life at "Leighton," particularly the relationship between master
and slave, was the kind that defenders of slavery liked to cite as
typical. The family and house servants began the day by assembling in the parlor before breakfast for scripture reading and prayer
by the Bishop or the chaplain. Then each Sunday afternoon the
plantation slaves assembled at the "big house" to sing hymns and
receive spiritual instructions from members of the master's family.
The governess reported, however, that in her class of "grown-up
boys" she had great difficulty in keeping the students awake "no
matter how edifying I fancied my instruction to be." These Sunday gatherings the Bishop referred to as his Sunday School. Devotions were conducted by a salaried plantation chaplain in the
largest room of the house. There was much singing and chanting.
Men and women were then divided into study groups and questioned on elementary points of the Christian religion. The Bishop
frequently passed from room to room supervising and questioning.
There was also a children's department in which the Polk daugh-

clipping in the Leonidas Polk Papers. Also see Elizabeth Polk to William
Mecklenburg Polk, October ?, 1874, *ibid.*
[8] Quoted in Polk, *Leonidas Polk*, I, 186.
[9] Kenneth Rayner to Thomas Ruffin, June 15, 1864, Hamilton (ed.), *Papers
of Thomas Ruffin*, III, 391–93.

ters had a part in the instruction. For the closing exercises all assembled in the large hall where a hymn was sung and prayer offered by the chaplain. When present the Bishop himself pronounced the apostolic benediction.

Bishop Polk stressed social and family life among his slaves, making full use of their fondness for ceremony. Weddings were particularly festive occasions when the hall of the big house was decorated with evergreens, flowers, and candles. A reward to the Polk children for good behavior was the privilege of holding aloft the silver candlesticks. Mrs. Polk furnished the wedding clothes, and the Bishop performed the ceremony. A wedding supper of many varieties of meats and sweets, which the cooks had spent days preparing, and singing and dancing to the sound of fiddle and banjo until a late hour followed the ceremony. Only in the case of a "shotgun" wedding was there no celebration. The couple was merely married in work clothes, without candles, flowers, or feasting.

The largest plantation celebration at "Leighton" was the "Rolling Ball" given at the close of the cane rolling season. Mammy Betsey supervised the preparation of the feast; Old Washington concocted the punch made of half-boiled (and probably half-fermented) cane juice flavored with green limes. This must have been a potent drink, for Washington complained of being "stupid-like" from smelling it.

In dealing with servants Bishop Polk applied the same principle as if dealing with children—kindness and sympathy backed by a certainty of punishment for wrong-doing. Sarcasm and ridicule he believed more effective than drastic punishment for minor offenses. Although kind treatment was not a guarantee against wrong-doing or absconding, Polk reported little of the former and none of the latter.

Good business as well as an interest in human welfare made protection of the health of slaves an important matter. Mrs. Polk made this her special interest. Since many women with small children were regular field hands or domestic servants, a day nursery was provided and qualified nurses assigned to care for these children. Each Monday Mrs. Polk made a regular inspection of the nursery, often taking along tea cakes for the children. A hospital building, with both male and female wards, was provided for chil-

dren and adults. Persons able to do only limited work were assigned to suitable tasks.

All clothing used by laborers was produced on the plantation.
Cotton and wool were purchased by the bale and turned over to
an experienced Negro who supervised the spinning, weaving, and
sewing, "without even troubling his master, or overseer, about the
matter." When a visiting agricultural observer questioned the
economy in home production of clothing Polk explained that the
work was done by "old people, and by mothers, just before and
after giving birth to children, and by invalids, or convalescents,
who are unable to go to the field." [10]

Except during the sugar making season, Bishop Polk made some
use of the "allotted task" method of distributing labor among his
hands. This gave the fast and efficient worker some leisure time to
cultivate a garden and raise a few chickens. They were permitted
to sell any surplus produce. Men too old for regular field work
cultivated a plantation garden and cared for poultry and livestock. [11]

For several years life at "Leighton" seemed to have moved on in
much the same fashion as other sugar plantations. In spite of
Bishop Polk's frequent absences and his inexperience in the
production of sugar there was evidence of prosperity. He produced
his first crop in 1842 even before moving his family to Louisiana.
From the beginning he was interested in large scale production. A
shortage of cash for financing growing crops was his greatest concern. To meet this need he suggested to his mother a $10,000 loan.
She was unable to oblige; Kenneth Rayner, Susan's husband, had
already found use for her surplus money. However, pressure was
soon relieved when the Bishop secured from another source a
$25,000 advance on the present crop. "My crop is by dint of the

[10] Herbert A. Kellar (ed.), *Solon Robinson, Pioneer and Agriculturist: Select
Writings* (2 vols., Indianapolis, 1936), II, 203.

[11] This account of life at Leighton is based upon reports by the Reverend
Charles Goodrich, "a relative," "a governess," and "a daughter." A manuscript
copy of the Goodrich report is in the Leonidas Polk Papers. The originals of
the other three have been lost. They were submitted to E. J. Biddle, who was
preparing an extensive account of the civilian life of Bishop Polk. He found
these reports so poorly written as to require much "editing." In revised form,
they were later published in Polk, *Leonidas Polk*, I, 186 ff. The wording was
no doubt greatly changed, but there is good reason to believe that the information therein is reliable.

most extraordinary exertion on my part a very decidedly good one," he bragged to his mother. The stand of cane was good and growing well. Eight hundred hogsheads at fifty dollars each he thought a reasonable estimate of the value of his crop. This would give him "a lift" and next year he would "pitch a still greater crop," for he would have more land and hands. "Now if Brother Rayner will manage to keep the tariff where it is, for a few years [12] I will not only not wish to borrow his change but will have some to lend him." With "good management & God's blessing" he was now in a position "to turn out something. . . . The former we have secured & will probably continue to secure, the latter we may hope, & do pray for."

During the past year Polk had been able to reduce his Tennessee debts by $16,000. If the banks would only be patient he and Lucius would soon be able to pay off the Caruthers and Harris debt. The banks had made property arrangements with some endorsers but were trying to force the Polks to pay in cash. He still had hope, however, and would try to get something settled when he returned to Tennessee for his family later in the summer.[13]

In preparation for that still greater crop in 1843 planter Polk took still more slaves with him on his return to Louisiana in the fall of 1842, increasing his field hands to 150—"not a hand too many for the capital I have in land there," he observed.[14] But instead of greater things the cane crop fell to about half the amount expected—an estimated 500,000 pounds of sugar and 25,000 gallons of molasses.[15] This decline in production might have been due partly to the fact that Polk spent much of the summer in Tennessee, where he and his brother Lucius found it necessary to sell off some West Tennessee lands and to mortgage his Maury County plantation to pay on the Caruthers and Harris debt and make adjustments in other obligations. "This operation has enabled me to sink my debt in Tennessee . . . full $15,000," the Bishop explained. This he considered "a good three months work" and as placing his business affairs "in a better condition than they have been for the past 5 years." With only fair crops, he was certain of

---

[12] Rayner was a Whig member of Congress.
[13] Leonidas Polk to Sarah Polk, June 9, 1842, Leonidas Polk Papers.
[14] *Id.* to *id.*, September 28, 1842, *ibid.*
[15] *Id.* to Lucius Polk, December 13, 1843, Polk-Brown-Ewell Papers.

meeting all of his "future engagements." [16] This note of optimism was sounded before he knew how poor his present crop actually was.

The above letters terminated the interesting and informative correspondence between Leonidas Polk and his mother; she died at her Raleigh home late in 1843. He was much bereaved over the loss of "the greatest blessing God ever gave us," yet he found comfort in the knowledge "that she died in the firm hope of salvation through the blood of her redeemer, and so sank in peace. . . . It is all I could ask of my heavenly father as a mitigation of the affliction, and my heart on hearing it bounded in praise, and I felt as though I was prompted to cast about instantly to see what my hand found to do . . . that I might do it to please him, and so prepare to follow her." [17]

There was little left of the William and Sarah Polk estate for final division among their numerous children. Bishop Polk received some stock in the Columbia Turnpike Company and a number of pieces of family silver. Mother Polk also specified that the unwilled portion of her estate be divided equally among her sons. From this division Leonidas received ten slaves and possibly a small amount of cash. More substantial inheritance, however, was soon to come from the estate of John Devereux, who died in 1844. He bequeathed to his daughter Frances Polk one hundred Negroes (to be taken by families) "free from any control of her husband— and not liable for any of his debts." [18]

With this great increase in labor force there was soon great increase in production at "Leighton." By 1847 Bishop Polk could report prospects "good, very good." He was expecting a corn crop sufficient to meet his need, and "that is saying something for me who have bought every year I have been here & who consume about 10,000 bushels," he explained to Lucius. And the cane crop was the best yet. Also it was necessary to discuss at length with

[16] *Id.* to Sarah Polk, August 31, 1843, *Ibid.; id.* to *id.*, September 23, 1843, Leonidas Polk Papers; Lucius Polk to *id.*, August 31, 1843, Leonidas Polk Papers.

[17] Leonidas Polk to Susan Polk Rayner, January 10, 1844, Leonidas Polk Papers.

[18] Wake County (North Carolina) *Record*, Vol. 25, pp. 363, 492; Leonidas Polk to Lucius Polk, June 6, 1844, George W. Polk Papers; receipt for slaves from Polk estate in Devereux Papers.

Lucius what was to be done with his abundant wheat crop in Tennessee.[19]

This last problem was a part of the larger problem of what to do with his Tennessee plantation. His plan had been to continue its operation and to use "Ashwood" as a summer home for his family, protecting them from the excessive heat and threat of disease in South Louisiana. Mrs. Polk and the children spent the summers of 1843 and 1844 in the comforts of "Ashwood" midst Maury County relatives and friends. During these two summers two more children —Elizabeth and William Mecklenburg—were born to the Polks.[20] But the use of "Ashwood" as a summer home was not satisfactory. The Bishop was either neglecting his family in Tennessee or his business interests and church work in Louisiana. Further, the distance from "Leighton" to "Ashwood" was great and travel was most difficult. Consequently, the two-home plan was abandoned after 1844 and the burden of supervising the "Ashwood" estate fell upon Lucius. Finally, in the fall of 1847, Bishop Polk sold the Tennessee estate to his sister-in-law Rebecca, wife of his brother Andrew, for $35,000 and paid off his Union Bank obligation.[21]

Relieved of responsibilities in Tennessee and able to concentrate all of his energy in Louisiana, Bishop Polk seemed on the threshold of great material and spiritual progress. When agricultural observer Solon Robinson visited "Leighton" in February, 1849, he found evidence of much progress and prosperity. Of his 2,500 arpents of land Bishop Polk now had 1,000 to 1,100 in cultivation. Six hundred had been planted to cane in 1848, of which 358 were for sugar and the remainder for planting cane. The 358 arpents had produced 510 hogsheads of sugar. The plan for 1849 was to increase the sugar acreage to 800 arpents. About 200 arpents were usually planted to corn.

The slave population, Robinson reported, numbered 370, but only about one-third were active field hands. More than seventy were children under ten. And since these slave families had been owned by the Polk and Devereux families for many years, the

---

[19] Leonidas Polk to Lucius Polk, July 15, 1847, George W. Polk Papers.

[20] Elizabeth (Lilly) married William E. Huger; William Mecklenburg, known to the family as "Meck," married Ida Lyon.

[21] Maury County *Deed Book*, II, Bk. C, pp. 86, 87.

number of aged Negroes was great—"upward of 30 entirely super-
annuated. . . . What a host to feed and clothe," observed Robinson, "and all to be looked after and provided for by the care of one
man! Quite enough to frighten a New-England farmer." [22]

Robinson was impressed with Polk's experiments with "good
tillage and manure." All plows, wagons, hoes, and spades were
made by Leighton blacksmiths. Among these implements was an
excellent "fluke plow." [23] Botner, Polk's overseer, described as a
very intelligent man, insisted that subsoil plowing did not pay,
but with this Robinson did not agree. The "Beranger plow" was in
most common use, but Botner preferred the "Jacob plow" for
tough land. He thought the "sidehill" plow the best tool for
"plowing back ditch banks." Both Polk and his overseer were
strong believers in the use of well-rotted bagasse as fertilizer, but
they believed that the difficulty in plowing under cane blades and
tops made it more economical to burn them.[24]

Bishop Polk was also experimenting with the cultivation and
grinding of cane. On seven acres he had stripped the blades from
the stalks, hoping to hasten maturity. The expense was small, for
the work was done by children. The results were not convincing,
although he did have his greatest yield on these acres. He was also
experimenting with the process of grinding. "Instead of elevating
the cane on the carrier, so as to pitch it down into the mill, he
brings it up to a level and there it is seized upon by two rollers that
feed it to the mill in a very regular manner." [25] Believing that too
much juice was lost by the regular process of grinding, Polk tried a
second grinding. From 2,300 pounds of cane he pressed 163 gallons of juice weighing 8½ pounds each. By regrinding the bagasse
he got another five gallons. In another experiment he got eighty-
seven pounds of juice from one hundred pounds of cane. "To do
this," Robinson observed, "the mill must be first rate." [26]

To cultivate this vast plantation Bishop Polk used about seventy-

---

[22] Kellar (ed.), *Solon Robinson*, II, 202.

[23] Robinson described this plow as having a beam "5½ feet long, 17 inches
high—the handles fastened to the sides of the beam, and supported by a standard down to the centre bar, which bar is 29 inches long. The moldboards are 10
inches high, and 27 inches apart behind, and are made of wrought iron." Kellar
(ed.), *Solon Robinson*, II, 202.

[24] *Ibid.*, 203.   [25] *Ibid.*, 202–203.   [26] *Ibid.*, 202.

five mules and horses in addition to many oxen. He preferred horses to mules since they cost less, could do equally as much work, and lived almost as long. He expected eventually to make his plantation entirely self-supporting. About 11,000 bushels of corn were consumed annually and it was his policy to furnish each person with one-half pound of pork daily. Solon Robinson questioned the wisdom of attempting to produce so much pork. Curing pork in so warm a climate was always uncertain, and he figured that more money could be made from planting the land to cane rather than to corn for the production of hogs.[27]

Just when prosperity seemed assured, calamity came. Cholera struck Louisiana in the spring of 1849. The Bishop himself was stricken at the home of his friend James Robb while visiting churches in the New Orleans area. Before he had time to recover the disease spread to his plantation. The first case at "Leighton" was noted on May 11, and before the close of the day five slaves were dead. Soon, of the entire population, white and black, estimated at "360 or 70," not fifty persons were free from the disease. About seventy, including twenty-five children, died. Among the dead were twenty-eight field hands. The dead also included Old Jeff, one of the cooks, and the overseer's wife. The Bishop's son Hamilton and two daughters became ill but recovered, as did the chaplain, who resided on the plantation. On a neighboring plantation sixty field hands died.[28]

The death of valuable slaves was not the only financial loss resulting from the epidemic. Weakened and disorganized, the remaining field hands were unable to give the cane crop proper attention, especially when neither Bishop Polk nor his overseer was able to supervise. The corn crop was such a complete failure that purchases had to begin early in August, and the entire plantation crop failed to pay the expenses of production, which that year amounted to $50,000. The Bishop was so broken in health and spirit that he took Hamilton and went North for two months, leaving his wife and daughters on the bayou.[29]

Later the Polk family might well have pondered the truth of the

[27] *Ibid.*, 203.
[28] Leonidas Polk to Susan Polk Rayner, July 9, 1849, Leonidas Polk Papers.
[29] Polk, "Leonidas Polk, A Memoir."

saying that trouble travels in pairs, for disaster struck again in the spring of 1850, just after the Diocesan Convention which met at Thibodaux in May. At the close of business Bishop Polk invited the delegates and a few neighbors to dinner at "Leighton." Among the guests was the Reverend Charles Goodrich of New Orleans. "I was invited with others to take dinner at the house of the Bishop," he later recorded.

The party was a large one. The day shone with all the brilliancy of a Southern spring. Seated at the table I observed through the open windows, a dark heavy cloud just risen above the horizon— Scarcely had I called the attention of a lady at my side to its threatening appearance when the air became chilled & soon the rattling of hail on the roof of the house with a violent gust of wind told that the storm was on us: The hail stones were very large. One more than an inch in diameter was brought in by the servant & passed in a plate around the table as a curiosity. Suddenly the wind changed & blew with increased violence driving the hail through the open windows like balls from a battery— flooding the floor—attempts were made to close the windows but the storm was too fierce. The guests were driven from the room. The glass and china on the deserted table were broken & swept away. In a few moments the trees and bushes around the place were stripped of their leaves—fowls great & small, exposed in the garden or fields were killed—negro cabins were overturned. The roof of a large barn or sugar-house was taken up like a balloon and lodged 60 yards from the walls—a tree near the mansion more than a foot & a half in diameter was torn up by the roots & thrown across the yard, & in the shortest possible time the face of the whole country was changed as by the wand of magic—and where before was a smiling garden & green fields with all the flowers & fruits of spring, appeared a wild scene of desolation.[30]

Mrs. Polk later recalled that the sugarhouse, stables, and several Negro cabins were completely wrecked. The damage in broken windows and china plus the destruction of buildings and crops was estimated at $100,000.[31] What a wreck of a fortune! What a

---

[30] Manuscript account written by the Reverend Charles Goodrich in 1867, Leonidas Polk Papers.

[31] Polk, "Leonidas Polk, A Memoir." Still a third account of this destruction, written by a neighbor planter, was published in Polk, *Leonidas Polk*, I, 207.

hardship upon a bishop who had never accepted a dollar in salary!

Crops that year were further damaged by an early frost and the sugarhouse was not rebuilt by the time it was badly needed; operation expenses for the year greatly exceeded the income. Nevertheless Bishop Polk left it all behind and journeyed to the General Convention in Cincinnati. "I have done all I could," he told his wife. "I must leave the future in God's hands. If he sends this trouble, it is his will. Let him do what seemeth to him good, but though he slay me, yet will I trust him." [32]

In 1851 Bishop Polk decided to mortgage his property to raise funds for paying off his outstanding debts. The person trusted with handling the funds, however, "appropriated this trust money to his own use," leaving the Bishop with double the amount of his original obligations. Polk did not prosecute; there was no hope of recovering the money and he did not wish to bring disgrace to the man's family. ". . . this put the finishing stroke to our fortune," Mrs. Polk later recalled, "& from this time forward I felt we were beggars." [33]

In 1849, before disaster struck, Polk had made a will directing that his body be buried in St. John's churchyard, Maury County, his books (after a few selections by his wife) be given his successor for use in educating young ministers, and his other property be disposed of according to the "Laws of the Land." After disaster struck he added a codicil: "Since writing the above the misfortunes which came upon me have deprived me of my property. My Library I wish disposed of as I have indicated and so of my body. To my children I leave a Father's blessing." [34]

Mrs. Devereux, mother of Mrs. Polk, died in 1852, but her estate brought little financial relief to the Polks. She bequeathed thousands of dollars to individual friends and relatives and to religious and charitable organizations. Certain lawyers suggested the possibility of "breaking" this will. Polk, however, refused to have any part in such an action. Mrs. Polk received half of the Devereux slaves (to be taken by families). Although badly needed cash could have been had from the sale of these slaves, the Polks were unwilling to see the family Negroes separated "from their kindred . . . for no fault of their own." Brother-in-law Kenneth Rayner

[32] Polk, "Leonidas Polk, A Memoir."   [33] *Ibid.*
[34] Copy in Gale Papers.

was instructed to supervise the division of the slaves and the transportation of the Polk share to Louisiana. The total value of the slaves was estimated at $20,000.[35]

As late as May, 1853, the energetic bishop was still humbled and determined. He wrote his brother Lucius:

> No man in America, I don't care who the other man is, has been more crowded for time for the last few years than I have been, & I will venture to add, that no man has had more to do, or more places to go to, or a greater variety of people & things to deal with, & yet that Kind & Ever present arm upon which it has been my happiness to lean in all my troubles has always been about me & under me & I have been enabled to bear up under all & carry my burden triumphantly & cheerfully inward. And I desire here as ever to be humbly thankful for it all.

He again felt encouraged about his financial condition. Recent arrangements, he explained, had relieved him from some pressure. His crops looked promising. Twelve hundred acres were under cultivation. "A year or two more & I think I will relieve all my friends & creditors of all solicitude on my account." [36]

Yellow fever again hit the bayou country in the fall of 1853. Bishop Polk, away at the General Convention, rushed home to his stricken people. Casualties among slaves were high. Two of his daughters became ill but recovered. Still again in 1854 "yellow jack" returned bringing death to slaves and neighbors. Polk himself became ill. As he lay on his sick bed and calculated his losses he concluded that he could no longer carry on as both bishop and planter. Creditors were pushing him, his plantation was heavily mortgaged, and during the year 1853–54 he had received only $1,308 from the Diocese. Recognizing his plight, the Louisiana Convention proposed to come to his assistance, guaranteeing an annual salary of not less than $4,000.[37] Consequently Bishop Polk decided to satisfy his creditors by giving up Leighton plantation

---

[35] Will of Frances Devereux, Wake County *Record*, XXVIII, p. 124: Leonidas Polk to John P. Devereux, February 23, 1853, Devereux Papers; *id.* to Kenneth Rayner, February 25, 1853, Rayner Papers.

[36] *Id.* to Lucius Polk, May 19, 1853, Gale Papers.

[37] Polk, "Leonidas Polk, A Memoir"; *Correspondence of the Right Rev. L. Polk with the Vestry of Trinity Church.*

and moving to New Orleans. On April 8, 1854, he sold Leighton plantation and 189 slaves to John Williams of New Orleans for $307,000. Of this huge amount, however, $245,553.86 went to pay the mortgage Williams held on the property. To Mrs. Polk went $18,060 to repay a loan from her estate, and six notes held by James Potter, from whom he bought the plantation, a New Orleans friend James Robb, and B. A. Soulé consumed all of the remainder except $34,047.81, which was the amount received by Bishop Polk.[38]

Polk used money inherited by his wife to purchase another plantation located in Bolivar County, Mississippi, sent one hundred of her slaves to cultivate it and their son Hamilton to manage them. In June, 1854, Hamilton journeyed to Hartford, Connecticut, to marry Emily Beach, whom apparently he had met during student days at Trinity College. The Mississippi plantation consisted of 2,760 acres. The total cost is not known, but the Polks gave a mortgage on the estate to secure $28,907 in eight notes covering the unpaid balance.[39]

A prominent lady who knew Polk well during his Louisiana years described him as "a grand man: a colossal nature, both physique and morale. He thought largely, he acted nobly—his instincts were all right and true. He had invention, imagination, policy, skill and valor of a high degree—but no sense of economics —no frugality. To travestie a homely proverb, if he 'had a coat to cut, he must have plenty of cloth.' . . . His was a broad, lavish hand!" [40] Truly, Polk, whether as planter or bishop, did operate on a broad scale.

Though depressed by his material loss, Bishop Polk had some feeling of accomplishment in things spiritual. He reminded the Louisiana convention of 1854 that during the past thirteen years the number of parishes had increased from four to thirty-two. To this should also be added twenty-three congregations of slaves on plantations. Twenty church buildings had been completed at a cost of $350,000, and twelve other congregations were in varying

[38] Lafourche Parish, *Conveyances*, I, 237–50.
[39] Polk, "Leonidas Polk, A Memoir." See deed of trust in Leonidas Polk Papers.
[40] Sarah A. Dorsey, *Recollections of Henry Watkins Allen* (New York, 1866) 70–71.

stages of planning and construction. During this same thirteen years the clergy had increased from six to twenty-six. Three of this number, however, had recently died of yellow fever. The number of communicants had increased from 238 to 1,421.

He was not displeased with the rate of progress, yet he urged all Christians to push forward toward still greater accomplishments. The people, he believed, were willing to furnish financial support. "Our chief want is ministerial labor. Labor that counts not its life dear unto it, that it may fill up the full measure of its calling in an unshirking selfdenial, and hearty devotion to the building up of the Kingdom of God in the souls of men." [41]

By the time the Polks moved to New Orleans yellow fever had become an annual epidemic. Scores of city dwellers were making annual summer pilgrimages to more secluded places, hoping to escape this dread disease. The Polks refused to join those leaving the city. "It is now my home," the Bishop wrote his sister, "and we shall not leave it. Our house is very large and high up town, in open space surrounded by shrubbery." [42]

In 1856 the epidemic was even more severe than the previous year. It would have equalled that of 1853, Polk reported to his friend Stephen Elliott, Bishop of Georgia, "had there been material. . . . But three years in succession has left comparatively few unacclimated. [Yet Mrs. Polk, two of the girls, and four servants had the disease.] We have made up our minds, it is to be regularly established among us, and I have therefore not removed my family but have deemed it best in every point of view, to put our trust in God, and face the danger at once. And the Lord has been thus far gracious to us and spared us." Owing to steam transportation on both land and water, he feared the spread of the disease far into the interior. "It seems to be one of God's great agencies to keep himself visible before the world's naughty heart, and to check it up in its forgetfulness, for who can pass under its hand, either as an individual or in community, without having all his memories of God in his goodness, and Christ in his fullness, and the spirit in its preciousness, freshened up, and his mind and heart deeply impressed with the utter emptiness of all else. 'It is

[41] Diocese of Louisiana, *Journal of Convention* (New Orleans, 1854), 31–32.
[42] Leonidas Polk to Susan Polk Rayner, June ?, 1855, Leonidas Polk Papers.

better to go to the house of mourning than the house of feasting.' " [43]

It was the opinion of Bishop Polk's children, expressed in later
years, that only after taking up residence in a city was the Bishop
able to make fullest use of his ability and influence. In the words
of a son, "he ought always to have lived there." It was certainly
true that, relieved of plantation worries and assured of an income
of $4,000, he could devote full energy to the work he loved. His
influence upon people in general and the clergy in particular was
attested by those who came under that influence.

Physically, Bishop Polk was attractive and impressive. In the
prime of life, standing over six feet, with broad shoulders and a
rather lean body, he had much the carriage of the soldier. A bright
piercing eye and a clear distinct voice marked him as one born to
command. Yet a kind and sympathetic facial expression made him
equally as effective as counsellor and comforter. He always thought
of himself as a soldier—in earlier years a soldier of his country, in
later years a soldier of God. "His air of command never left him,"
yet he was always aware that he himself was under command.

He disliked the puritanical approach to religion. To him to be
religious was a pleasure, not a task. A kindly smile was more effective than a stern demeanor. He was probably at his best in giving
advice to young ministers. "Above all things," he often said, "gain
your people's confidence, and see that you deserve it. Live the gospel, and you will preach the gospel." Much instruction he handed
out to laymen and clergymen alike in his fondness for what he considered religious maxims: "Faith is a charger that carries a man
into battle, but he must fight when he gets there, and then Faith
will bear him through the fight. . . . There is no pattern of human life worth following but that of Christ himself. Take no other
for your model. If you do, you may rather acquire its defects than
its excellence." One must strive to be no one else but himself. "If
the good Lord had not some use for you in the world, you would
not be here; and if he had wanted you to be any other sort of man,
you would have been a man of that sort, and not the man you are.
. . . Only try to be yourself, your ideal self. Keep yourself well in
hand. . . . When a man gives the rein to his own peculiarities of

[43] *Id.* to Stephen Elliott, October 2, 1856, *ibid.*

character, he is sure to miss the purpose of his life, and to become a caricature of the man God meant him to be."

As a visiting clergyman Bishop Polk was both systematic and diplomatic. He learned as much as he could about members of a family before he visited them. He made it his business to think of people. "Be sincerely interested in all that concerns them," he advised a young clergyman, "and let them feel that you are interested. That is the secret of pastoral influence. . . . There is nothing so good as a word in season; but there are few things more likely to do harm than good words out of season. . . . The man who seems callous to-day may be sensitive to your lightest touch to-morrow, unless in the meantime you have repelled him."

To assistants of all ranks Bishop Polk advocated giving a great amount of freedom of action. "There is a great deal of fine art in letting people alone," he explained. This might cost more than doing the job yourself, but it would be worth more when done. "Let your working-people work their own way. . . . Make yourself felt rather than seen in your people's work. Always give them credit for what is done; never take it to yourself."

Of course the Bishop realized that all workers could not be left entirely to themselves. Some would undoubtedly need assistance in order to do right. There would even be times when rebuke seemed necessary and proper. "Take care that the bishop does not have to take you in hand," one young Louisiana clergyman counseled another. "If he does, he will make you ache in every bone of your spiritual body. . . . But when you feel sorest, you will be almost angry that you cannot be angry at what he has said to you." This advice was not strictly observed and this same young man was taken "in hand" more than once. He later related that the Bishop made him feel sore enough, "But he never made me angry nor failed to send me away with a deeper reverence for himself and with a deeper longing for his approbation." He could never forget how utterly helpless he felt in the Bishop's hands.[44]

---

[44] The above discussion of Bishop Polk's philosophy is based upon accounts prepared by the Reverend John Fulton and published in Polk, *Leonidas Polk*, I, 211 ff, and in "The Church in the Confederate States," in William Stevens Perry, *The History of the American Episcopal Church*, 1587–1883 (Boston, 1885), II, 563. The quotes are Fulton's.

(7)

"For the Glory of God and the Good of Men"

AGAIN AND AGAIN, even before moving to Louisiana, Bishop Polk had referred to the urgent need for a trained Southern ministry. By this he meant native Southerners trained in the South. For at least a decade he had been collecting material on educational institutions and had made it a point to visit many college campuses. Before he moved to Louisiana the state had attempted to establish colleges at Jackson, Opelousas, and a point on the Red River. The first two of these struggling institutions were soon taken over by the Methodists and Catholics. Polk considered buying the third for the Diocese of Louisiana, but the idea was abandoned after investigation revealed that most people preferred to send their sons to a "colder climate." Then he even considered buying it himself; cholera, fever, and windstorm blasted that hope.[1]

Once comfortably situated in New Orleans and free from plantation responsibilities, Bishop Polk again turned to the subject of religious education. On July 1, 1856, he issued an open letter to the bishops of Tennessee, Georgia, Alabama, Mississippi, Florida, Arkansas, Texas, and North and South Carolina, setting forth the educational needs within their dioceses and challenging them as leaders to join in a plan to meet those needs.

Within their dioceses, Polk noted, was a total population of about 5,800,000. Regardless of the varying shades of religious opinion among these people, the Episcopal church had a grave responsibility. "Our mission is to all, as well to those who differ from, as those who agree with us, and we are bound by this conviction to concert measures, and adopt such combinations, as will enable us to fulfil this mission with adequate power and efficiency." Circumstances had placed many persons under the in-

[1] Polk, "Leonidas Polk, A Memoir."

fluence of other forms of religious opinion and left still others without any affiliation at all. There was no reason to dwell upon why this was true in the past; the future course was clear. "We have to do our work, and our whole work, in bringing men to Christ, and to be of one mind in Christ. We have not only to propagate the truth, but also the order of the Gospel; and this is the spirit of the Gospel."

These conditions and responsibilities made it imperative that the church sponsor the establishment of a system of educational training, both academic and theological, for the young men of the Southern States. Numbers of religious groups were already trying to supply such a need, and some were having considerable success. But this did not relieve the Episcopal church of its responsibility. Boys were still going North for an education "beyond the reach of our supervision or parental influence, exposed to the rigors of an unfriendly climate, to say nothing of other influences not calculated, it is to be feared, to promote their happiness or ours." A still more compelling force in favor of the proposed type of higher education was that at present there was no institution within reach where boys just out of preparatory school could be "kept under the influence of those Christian principles and that Church instruction, to which we pledged them in baptism, which we have accepted and hold as of the essence of Christ's religion, which we would transmit in their vigor to them and through them unmarred to our latest posterity."

Most of the dioceses, he believed, were too weak to offer within their borders the advantages needed. Even if they did possess the pecuniary ability their small church population and poor preparatory schools would render individual effort inexpedient. But what could not be done individually might easily be done collectively. He thought the time had arrived for the establishment of an institution "to be our common property, under our joint control, of a clear and distinctly recognized Church character, upon a scale of such breadth and comprehensiveness, as shall be equal in the liberality of its provisions for intellectual cultivation to those of the highest class at home or abroad" and meet the demands of the Southern people for the "highest educational advantages, under the supervision of the Church."

Closely connected with this need and equally pressing, Bishop

Polk explained, was the need for locally trained clergymen. It was of the greatest importance that the ministry be raised from among those they were to serve. By making a school of theology a part of the proposed academic institution this need could be met and there would also be a great advantage from the combination as opposed to the operation of two separate institutions. In what otherwise would be duplicate courses the same professor could be used, and by funneling the resources of all the dioceses into one channel the several chairs could be made financially attractive to men of the highest talents.

If it should be decided that such a university was needed and that its establishment by the dioceses was financially possible, the next question for consideration would be location. If the institution were to be common property of and to render adequate service to all of the dioceses then it should be centrally located and at an easily accessible point. Recent railroad construction, Polk explained, had made Southeastern Tennessee—the Chattanooga area—the most accessible centrally located spot in the South. From any point in the participating dioceses a prospective student could reach Chattanooga within forty-eight hours.

This region also had other attractions—fresh mountain air, pure water, freedom from epidemics such as cholera and yellow fever, and low cost of living. Furthermore, it was within "the pale of the plantation States."

The subject he was bringing to the attention of the bishops and their people was not a new one, Polk explained. Again and again it had been discussed at conventions. There was always agreement that it was a matter of paramount importance. Likewise, there had been agreement on the inability to put the proposal into operation. Consequently, it was "dismissed in silence, or consigned by the help of that convenient vehicle—a resolution—to the 'earnest consideration' of some future convention." The result was always no action and a further loss of valuable time.[2] He was conscious that there must always be "regard for the proportion which exists

---

[2] As early as 1835 Bishop Otey had called attention of the Diocese of Tennessee to the need for a college to instruct Episcopal youth in the arts and sciences and to train candidates for orders. He suggested the co-operation of Tennessee, Mississippi, and Louisiana in such an enterprise and that the college be located near the southwestern border of Tennessee. This suggestion was referred

between means and ends." Nevertheless he maintained that the means existed; all that was needed was a spirit of determination and co-operation. And this should certainly be possible in dioceses where population was homogeneous and whose pursuits, institutions, and sympathies were one.

Last but by no means least, the establishment of such a proposed institution would be a powerful force in bringing together bishops, clergymen, and laymen who were interested in developing the proficiency of children "for the glory of God and the good of men." Should the bishops take kindly to his proposal, Polk suggested a "personal conference" for further discussion at the time of the next General Convention. A decision could then be made as to whether or not to place the matter before clergy and laymen by first presenting it to convention delegates. "A cardinal principle in the whole movement," Bishop Polk concluded, "would of course be, that the institution would be declaredly out and out Episcopal, founded by the Church for the special benefit of her own children, for the advancement of learning generally, and for the propagation of the Gospel as she understands it. But that they would be freely open to all, who might desire to avail of their advantages on the terms they were dispensed to the children of the Church." [3]

------

to a committee of which Polk, then rector of St. Peter's, Columbia, was a member.

Otey returned to the subject in 1836 and it was again referred to a committee of which Polk was made chairman. This committee approved the idea and suggested that steps be taken toward raising funds. At least some work was done; a few places including Bolivar, LaGrange, Somerville, and Jackson pledged donations conditional on location of the proposed institution.

By 1837 Otey felt that the goal was within reach. The convention authorized a committee, of which he was chairman, to locate said college in Madison County, provided a suitable site and attractive terms could be had. Polk, who was ill, was not a member of this committee.

A year later Otey was able to report only that he had examined several sites in or near Jackson, Madison County. The panic had destroyed all hope of immediate success in the establishment of a college. Polk, the Reverend George Weller, and the Reverend Hamble J. Leacock were named trustees of the proposed Theological Seminary but Madison College was never opened. Diocese of Tennessee, *Journal of Convention* (1835, 1836, 1837, 1838); George R. Fairbanks, *History of the University of the South* (Jacksonville, Fla., 1905), 3–10. There is in the Otey Papers (University of North Carolina) a typed copy of a plan for a "Theological and Literary Institute" under the auspices of the Diocese of Tennessee.

[3] Leonidas Polk, *A Letter to the Right Reverend Bishops of Tennessee, Georgia, Arkansas, Texas, Mississippi, Florida, South Carolina, and North*

Bishop Polk sent printed copies of his letter to all the clergymen and many laymen in ten Southern States. Along with the copy for Bishop Stephen Elliott of Georgia he also sent a personal note. He apologized for errors in the printed copy, explaining that after submitting his draft to the printer he had left town on a visitation leaving to another the responsibility of proof reading, and "the rascal had the audacity to say he could not read my writing." To Elliott, Polk confided that if such a project was approached in a judicious, yet liberal manner, he was confident that within five years this new Episcopal university would rival Yale, Harvard, or Virginia. "I am perfectly and increasingly satisfied that nothing short of that will save us as a church, and as a Southern Church in particular." The time had come to rise above mere diocesan considerations and look to the good of the whole. "Separately we are powerless, and we can gain efficiency only by combination." [4]

Polk was particularly interested in Elliott's reaction, for Elliott was a scholarly man, a lawyer by profession before entering the ministry. And he also had had some experience in the field of education.[5]

During the summer of 1856 Bishop Polk spent a few weeks at the seashore as his health was poor. Upon his return to New Orleans the reply from Bishop Elliott was waiting. The Bishop of Georgia was enthusiastic yet cautious, questioning neither the need for nor the ability to establish and support such an institution. He was doubtful of the willingness of the church as a whole, especially men of means, to give the project proper financial support. An unfortunate experience with a similar but much less extensive project made him cautious.[6]

Polk replied at great length. He was aware of Elliott's unhappy experience and had expected to be reminded of the adage of "the

---

Carolina from the Bishop of Louisiana (New Orleans, 1856). Reprinted in Telfair Hodgson (ed.), *Reprints of the Documents and Proceedings of the Board of Trustees of the University of the South Prior to 1860* (Sewanee, 1888), 4 ff.

[4] Leonidas Polk to Stephen Elliott, July 23, 1856, Leonidas Polk Papers.

[5] Edgar L. Pennington, "Stephen Elliott, First Bishop of Georgia," *Historical Magazine of the Protestant Episcopal Church*, VII, 203 ff.

[6] An institute at Montpelier Springs, Monroe County, Georgia, sponsored by Elliott, had recently closed for lack of patronage after fourteen years of struggling existence. Pennington, "Stephen Elliott," *loc. cit.*, 210 ff.

burnt child," still he felt that Elliott's experience might prove very beneficial in their new endeavor, probably helping "to keep us off a rock or a sand-bar." He refused to admit that failure in even a dozen instances would be "conclusive against all effort to remedy a confessed evil of growing, and portentous magnitude." Even wise men and prophets were still only men and were by no means free from errors. Besides, did it not appear that good providence sometimes prevented minor success in order to prepare for still greater accomplishments?

Standing out boldly and in startling relief on the face of the situation, Bishop Polk insisted, were facts that commanded attention and demanded action "if we mean to meet what the times exact, and keep the church . . . from being swamped." A few more years of wasted time would turn a shadowy phantom into an impressive living reality. There would then be left only "bitter and unavailing reproaches, if we do not wake up to the necessity—*the stern necessity*, of providing amply for the emergency that is at the door."

The trend of feeling and events in the North, Polk believed, was such as to make a division of the states a future possibility. Should the union of states be dissolved it would be impossible to continue a union of dioceses. "Impossible, because they of the north will not desire it, because, to say nothing else, *our laity*, of the South would not tolerate it." A wall as high as the heavens was rising between the North and South, and it was time to consider what would be the position of the Southern church when the ties were severed. The North had long been the source of supply of ministers, teachers, and governesses. What would be the situation when this supply was cut off or Southern people refused to accept Northerners for these positions? True the Good Book said "sufficient for the day is the evil thereof," but it also added on the other side "a wise man, forseeth the evil, and hideth himself, and the fool passeth on and is punished."

As to the institution of slavery, Bishop Polk thought those "madcaps" in the North had no understanding of it. In the South it was the slave, not the master, who was at the top of the ladder. "We hold the negroes and they hold us. They furnish the yoke and we the necks. My own is getting sore, it is the same with those of my neighbors, in church and state." He believed that the South was becoming distrustful, afraid—afraid of the influence of Northern educational institutions upon the minds of Southern youths. The only means of escape from such a situation was to rise up and meet the emergency, shake off lethargy and provide for Southern needs.

Although in his letter Bishop Elliott had admitted that some institutions were exercising undesirable influence upon Southern youth, he still doubted the ability of the Episcopal church to correct this evil by establishing an institution of the proposed type. Polk had an answer for these apprehensions and doubts. Colleges and seminaries were here to stay, he explained. Either the church must use this means for impressing others or else its youth would be impressed by others. "We must either receive or make impressions." He was confident that Southern churchmen had the ability and, if properly approached, would provide the foundation for the type of institution so "indispensable for our security, our protection, to say nothing of prosperity."

Now was the time to launch such a movement, Polk reasoned, for youths of all denominations were being forced to return South of the Mason-Dixon line. "Right or wrong, their parents are in their own language 'done with northern colleges.' They would rather their children go half educated than send them thither." These parents would welcome and support educational advantages free from "the taint of northern fanaticism."

Bishop Polk considered the existing Southern colleges largely local in character, lacking in prestige. They could not offer advantages equal to those at Yale or Harvard. Southern people disliked this existing deficiency and felt keenly the taunt of inferiority. Many were conscious of the necessity of uniting, yet they could scarcely be united in support of any existing institution. They would be more easily attracted to something new that promised to provide what they were being forced to abandon in the North. Consequently, if the proposed movement was to be "anything" it must be "everything."

Polk felt greatly encouraged by public reaction as expressed in the New Orleans press and to him personally by people outside the Episcopal church. He quoted an intelligent Methodist as suggesting that failure of people to give sufficient support to a local enterprise did not mean they would fail to support one of great sectional promise. Polk was confident that all Episcopal leaders needed to

do was step forward and seize the "labouring oar." Love for learning and religion should be sufficient to guarantee success of the
enterprise, yet if this did not prove true there was still another
influence that could not fail. "*The negro question will do the
work*. It is an agency of tremendous power, and in our circumstances needs to be delicately managed. But it is in hand and is
great force to be used by somebody. It will be used. *It insists upon
being used*. . . . If we—churchmen—do not let it have its own
way and operate through us, it will cast us aside and avail of the
agency of others."

Regardless of the approach used, Polk recognized that the greatest task was adequate financing. But surely there must be some
Abbots or Lawrences in the South, he concluded, who would endow professorships or libraries or chapels. The only way to know
was to give people of wealth an opportunity.[7]

Two days after addressing his lengthy letter to Elliott, Bishop
Polk and his family left for Virginia Springs. Since both he and
Mrs. Polk had been ill during most of the summer all felt need of
rest. They would remain at the Springs until time for the meeting
of the General Convention at Philadelphia. Before leaving New
Orleans Polk received letters of encouragement from all the
Southern bishops except two, and these two had previously given
oral expression of approval of the project.[8]

The General Convention assembled at Philadelphia in October,
1856. At a special meeting nine Southern bishops endorsed the
plan outlined in Bishop Polk's recent public letter and requested
Bishop Otey to draft an official appeal. This address, in substance
essentially the same as Polk's letter, was issued from Philadelphia
on October 23. Included were a number of proposals relating to
the organization of the proposed university. The board of trustees
was to consist of the bishop, a clergyman, and two laymen from
each diocese. An endowment of $500,000 would be considered the
minimum necessary before beginning operation. This endowment,
however, need not necessarily be paid into a university treasury. A
part or all could be kept in the individual diocese and the interest
thereon paid to the university each year. Should the enterprise fail

---

[7] Leonidas Polk to Stephen Elliott, August 20, 1856, Leonidas Polk Papers.
[8] *Ibid.*

that portion of the endowment held in each diocese would become the property of that diocese. The senior bishop by consecration was to be chancellor of the university, which was to be located near Chattanooga "where the various Railroads traversing our dioceses converge, thus rendering access to it from every direction easy and speedy." After clergymen, laymen, and other friends of education had had time for serious reflection upon the proposal a delegated convention would be held on Lookout Mountain near Chattanooga. The date set was July 4, 1857.[9]

Bishop Polk returned to New Orleans more enthusiastic than ever, but Mrs. Polk, suffering from an eye ailment, remained in Philadelphia for treatment. Polk began an extensive correspondence with clergymen and laymen and gave particular attention to the press. Almost daily he found the interest in the movement deepening and widening and was still more thoroughly convinced that all that was needed was work in its behalf. "The parties concerned in its success," he wrote Bishop Elliott, "must put their shoulders to the wheel and shove it forward with sturdy vigor, and that without hesitation or pausing." Southern people, he had concluded, were not merely eager but were demanding the establishment of such an institution. Fortunately this Episcopal proposal had come at the flood tide of this demand and the names endorsing it were impressive from the viewpoint of position, personal character, and other qualifications.

The Episcopal church alone, Polk believed, was in position to give leadership in this great service to the South. "It would in the hands of the states be an inevitable failure. The Baptist or Methodists have not the bearing, or the social position, or prestige, requisite to command the public confidence, the Romanists in such a protestant population are of course out of the question, and the field is left to the Presbyterians and ourselves." He recognized that there were Presbyterians of sufficient distinction, but they were in no better position than Episcopalians. And the Episcopal church had the added advantage of continuous organization. The job then could be done by "no other so well [as] our heads of dioceses, officials that never die—banded together, and supported

[9] *An Address to the Members and Friends of the Protestant Episcopal Church in the Southern and South-Western States* (Philadelphia, 1856). Also reprinted in Hodgson (ed.), *Reprints*, 15 ff.

by co-laborers from the leading clergy and laity elected annually by their several committees."

People were willing to be guided by competent men, Polk further explained to Elliott; consequently, the bishops must supply the leadership. Normally, people were full of their "own particular business and fancy." If one would shift his neighbor's attention to other matters he must first persuade this neighbor to stop and listen. To be successful, then, the advocate must be able "to unfold and explain and enforce; to arouse and instruct and excite, until he gets his neighbor's mind so full of what he has to present, that if he does not become a propagandist in turn, he at least becomes an ally."

Polk was much pleased with the early financial response. Many persons had offered $1,000 each, a few $5,000, and one $25,000. From still another there was hope for $100,000. If the matter should be vigorously pushed, *"now it is warm,"* he believed any reasonable amount could be raised.[10]

Bishop Elliott, although favoring the university plan, did not share Polk's great enthusiasm. As months passed and Polk heard nothing from him, he became much concerned. Wholehearted assistance from one "so fortunate in all the gifts of birth, education, mind, and person, so gracious in his disposition, so nobly guileless in his character"[11] was badly needed. "I am very solicitious to know what you are doing in Georgia for our enterprize & the state of public feeling in regard to it," Polk wrote on April 1, 1857. He himself had received encouraging news from Mississippi and Alabama. He urged Elliott to stress everywhere possible that this enterprise was of broad scope designed to give to the whole South relief from a great want. It was not the plan to interfere with any other movement. He himself was planning to take the campaign to East Tennessee in May or June, where along with Bishop Otey he would explore that country, "seeing & hearing everybody & collecting such facts as to location as may help to simplify our work in July when we get together."[12]

Two weeks later Bishop Polk reported that Bishops George W. Freeman of Arkansas and William Mercer Green of Mississippi

[10] Leonidas Polk to Stephen Elliott, January 31, 1857, Leonidas Polk Papers.
[11] Fulton, "The Church in the Confederate States," *loc. cit.,* II, 563.
[12] Leonidas Polk to Stephen Elliott, April 1, 1857, Leonidas Polk Papers.

had been with him in New Orleans for several days. They were encouraged about the university enterprise and would have their clerical and lay delegates at Lookout Mountain on July 4. He urged Elliott to join him and Otey at Chattanooga in June. The three could no doubt spend three weeks together with pleasure and profit.[13]

Polk arrived at Chattanooga early in June and was soon viewing the surrounding country from atop Lookout Mountain. He then journeyed to Beersheba Springs on the Cumberlands, where he was met by Bishop Otey, John M. Bass, and V. K. Stevenson. All of this interesting group were guests of John Armfield. Armfield, a former associate of Isaac Franklin, had made a fortune in the slave trade. After retiring from this business he had purchased 1,000 acres of Cumberland Mountain land, including Beersheba Springs with its tavern and guest cabins. Since the late 1830's Beersheba Springs had been developed as a health resort and fashionable gathering point.

John M. Bass, a Nashville banker and son-in-law of the late Felix Grundy, had interest in Grundy County land. His son-in-law, V. K. Stevenson, was president of the Nashville and Chattanooga Railroad, which had recently pierced the mountain near Cowan and made connection with the Memphis and Charleston Railroad at a point in Alabama that was to bear his name. All of these men were good Episcopalians. They gave the Cumberland Plateau a thorough exploration.

Armfield was at least mildly interested in having the proposed university located near Beersheba. Some months earlier he had corresponded with Bishop Otey on this subject, and Otey had assured him that he would personally oppose any decision until the Beersheba area was thoroughly investigated. He also suggested that Armfield (then in New Orleans on business) confer with Bishop Polk.[14] It seems quite likely that Armfield and Polk were already friends but the origin of this friendship is uncertain.

After the group had finished their exploration Bishop Otey went into seclusion to write an address for the Lookout meeting; Polk continued to roam the mountains. "This whole mountain country

[13] *Id.* to *id.*, April 15, 1857, *ibid.*
[14] Quoted in Isabel Howell, "John Armfield of Beersheba Springs," *Tennessee Historical Quarterly* (Nashville, 1942–) III, 46 ff.

is a magnificent region," he reported to Elliott, who had been too ill to join the party. He would leave within a few days to inspect North Georgia and Eastern Tennessee, particularly Dalton, Georgia; Cleveland, Athens, Knoxville, and Greenville, Tennessee. He had been informed that the Chattanooga city council had voted to furnish conveyance for the representatives to the Lookout meeting. His own family would come up with a large delegation from New Orleans. Bishop Otey had recently visited the North Carolina Convention, where Dr. Thomas Davis Warren had promised $25,000 to the university fund.[15]

Twenty official delegates—seven of them bishops—and many onlookers assembled on Lookout Mountain July 4, 1857. All were guests of the Lookout Mountain Hotel. The mountain setting was most impressive. "Standing on its summit, the stranger drinks in a bracing air," wrote the delegate who served as secretary, "his eye wanders over a vast sea of forest and cultivated fields, until its vision is bounded by the mountains fifty miles distant. The Tennessee River winds in graceful curves beneath his feet, and is lost to view, and then the glimmer of its waters breaks out again in the far distance."

The principal address was delivered by the Right Reverend James H. Otey, Bishop of Tennessee. Mixing Fourth of July oratory with an urgent appeal for Christian education, he stressed that the American people were the most blessed on earth. The political and social edifice of the nation, he explained, rested upon the intelligence and virtue of the people. To preserve the blessings of our liberty we must supply the proper educational advantages. "The prime end aimed at in our projected University, is, then, to make the Bible the ultimate and sufficient rule and standard for the regulation of man's conduct as a rational and accountable being; to cultivate the moral affections of the young, while their intellectual powers are in process of development, thus furnishing the community with an enlightened and virtuous class of citizens; and last of all, to supply convenient facilities for the acquisition of theological learning, that a native population may be served by a native ministry." But the Bishop was quick to deny that there was anything sectional about the project. "I repel the unfounded suspi-

[15] Leonidas Polk to Stephen Elliott, June 18, 1857, Leonidas Polk Papers.

cion. . . . We affirm that our aim is eminently national and patriotic, and as such, should commend itself to every lover of his
country. . . . We contemplate no strife, save a generous rivalry
with our brethren, as to who shall furnish to this republic the truest
men, the truest Christians, and the truest patriots."

The university idea was overwhelmingly endorsed by the delegates on Lookout Mountain. A declaration of principles, almost
identical with Polk's original proposal, was issued. And upon motion of Polk several committees were appointed, chief among them
being the one on location, of which he was made chairman. These
committees were to report at the next meeting of the trustees,
which was set for November 25, 1857, at Montgomery, Alabama.[16]

Bishop Polk was encouraged by the enthusiasm and determination exhibited at the Lookout Mountain meeting. To a brother-
in-law in North Carolina he reported on "the progress of my
scheme for founding an Oxford, or a Göttingen, or a Bonn, or all
three combined." July 4 was certainly a "glorious day," and the action taken "fixed the success" of the enterprise. He endorsed everything Otey said and thought the tone of the address should give
thorough satisfaction to all Union-loving men. Although the plan
gave appearance of providing for immediate needs, he thought it
also breathed "a spirit of broad nationality." Certainly all "good
gentlemen who are accustomed to indulge in gab about *the
South*" would soon have "a chance to show their hands. We shall
see what they mean when they cry, 'down with Abolitionists & up
with Negroedom!'" Still Bishop Polk believed that rather than
promoting sectionalism, the establishment of such a university
would do more than all else attempted by Episcopalians to develop national feeling through the services of the church. Besides,
it would give to the church "a respectability and influence of more
consequence than all sectional political combinations." With determined leaders animated by a spirit of enlightenment and liberal
patriotism and not lacking in nerve there was every reason to believe that ample means could be had.[17]

[16] *Proceedings of a Convention of the Trustees of a Proposed University for
the Southern States, under the Auspices of the Protestant Episcopal Church together with a Narrative, and the Address of the Rt. Rev. James H. Otey, D.D.,
Bishop of Tennessee* (Atlanta, 1857). Also reprinted in Hodgson (ed.), Reprints, 21 ff.

[17] Leonidas Polk to Kenneth Rayner, July 30, 1857, Leonidas Polk Papers.

Immediately following the Lookout Mountain meeting Bishop
Polk returned to Beersheba Springs and began collecting information on the various sites proposed as a suitable location for the
university. Under date of July 24, 1857, he sent out "to members
of the Board of Trustees, to parties presenting sites . . . and to
the commission" printed copies of "Enquiries," requesting information on eighteen points such as elevation of proposed site, nature of the soil, available water, timber, stone, and transportation,
and accessibility.[18] Places under consideration included Huntsville,
Alabama; Atlanta, Georgia; Knoxville, Cleveland, McMinnville,
and Chattanooga, Tennessee; "& a place [in Tennessee] upon the
top of the Cumberland Table" near the point where the Nashville
and Chattanooga Railroad passed through the mountain. Polk
did not hesitate to tell friends that he had personally examined the
last mentioned locality and found it most satisfactory.[19]

As soon as those towns proposing sites had studied the inquiries
with regard to their own situation Polk planned to send a commission of engineers to make on-the-scene investigations. In the
meantime, he himself would collect from these towns statements
of what they had to offer as inducements. To head the investigating commission he secured the services of Colonel Walter Gwynn
of Anderson, South Carolina, a graduate of West Point, "late in
charge of public works in N. C. and now of those in So. Ca." Associated with Gwynn was Colonel Charles R. Barney of Baltimore,
also a West Point graduate and a friend of Bishop Polk. Although
Polk himself no doubt favored the Cumberland Mountain site, he
expressed a wish for a fair examination of each proposal.[20]

Polk met the engineers at Huntsville and started them on their
way. He then busied himself with collecting statements of inducements. By the time of the Montgomery meeting Polk had in his
possession Gwynn's report scoring each place investigated on each
of the eighteen inquiries. Also in his possession were the offers of

[18] Copy in Leonidas Polk Papers. Also reprinted in Hodgson (ed.), *Reprints*,
69.
[19] Polk to the Reverend M. A. Curtis, September 21, 1857, Leonidas Polk
Papers; *id.* to Thomas Ruffin, September 21, 1857, Hamilton (ed.), *Papers of
Thomas Ruffin*, II, 568.
[20] "I have examined it [Cumberland Plateau] thoroughly myself," he confided to Bishop Elliott, "& trust it will prove to be *the place*." Polk to Elliott,
September 27, 1857, Leonidas Polk Papers.

gifts of property, money, and materials from five localities and requests from ten other places in Alabama, Georgia, Mississippi, and Tennessee.[21]

Prior to balloting on the selection of a site the trustees agreed that voting should be by orders—the bishops constituting one order and the clergy and laity another. A two-thirds vote of each order would be required for a choice. This meant five votes from each order would be necessary. On the first ballot no site received more than two votes from either order. The Cumberland Mountain site (Sewanee) received only one bishop's vote (apparently Polk's) and two from the other order. Balloting continued until seventeen were taken. On the seventeenth Sewanee received five bishops' votes but only four from the clergy and laity. The Reverend M. A. Curtis of North Carolina then proposed that Sewanee be chosen provided a committee composed of Bishops Polk and Elliott and attorney Francis B. Fogg of Nashville could make a satisfactory arrangement with those offering inducements there and that the State of Tennessee would grant an acceptable charter. The resolution was approved. Fogg and Russell Houston (not a trustee), both of Nashville, were designated as a committee to secure a charter.

Other important actions of the Montgomery meeting were the selection of "The University of the South" as the official name and the appointment of Bishops Polk and Elliott to canvass the dioceses "for subscriptions to the funds of this University." [22]

The decision in favor of Sewanee did not meet the approval of all interested parties. A rumor was soon afloat that discontented persons in Tennessee would try to influence the Tennessee legislature to deny the desired charter. Polk rushed to Winchester, the county seat, to check with Dr. Wallace Estill and attorney Arthur

[21] For details of these offers see "Report of Committee on Location" in *Proceedings of a Convention of Trustees of the Proposed University of the South, at their Session held in Montgomery, Alabama, November 25, 1857.* Reprinted in Hodgson (ed.), *Reprints,* 58–79.

[22] *Ibid.* The Sewanee offer, made through Samuel F. Tracy, President of the Sewanee Mining Company: 5,000 acres of land, 1,000,000 feet of lumber, free transportation of 20,000 tons of building materials on its railroad, and 20,000 tons of coal over a period of ten years. To this offer the people of Franklin County, through Dr. Wallace Estill of Winchester, promised to add another 5,000 acres of land joining the Tracy tract. For deeds to all of these tracts, see Franklin County *Record Book,* Y and Z.

St. Clair Colyar. Although he found little cause for fear he observed that "those fellows about McMinnville & Chattanooga die hard." From Winchester he went to Nashville to assist Fogg and Houston in pushing the charter through the legislature. There he encountered little difficulty. The charter as passed on January 6, 1858, was "all we could wish." [23]

Although a charter had been granted and thousands of acres of mountain land had been pledged there was still a threat to change the site. It was said that disappointed persons from places that had made unsuccessful bids might join with others who had always insisted upon a lowland site to force the reopening of the question of location. Polk was concerned, noting that people from Alabama were "still harping on Huntsville." However, he believed once the trustees attended the approaching July meeting on the mountain everybody would be satisfied. [24]

Even though the question of location remained a bit unsettled, plans were made to have Colonel Barney run the lines of the property that had been pledged. Dr. Estill proposed that the people of Franklin County raise the funds to pay for such a survey. But upon checking with friends around Winchester, he found an inclination to withhold their contributions until the subject of location had been definitely settled. Estill and Colyar, however, agreed to guarantee payment of expenses and Barney began the survey in mid-June, 1858. Estill and others came to the mountain to assist in locating lines. [25]

On May 6, 1858, Bishop Otey, as president of the trustees, sent out a call for a meeting at Beersheba Springs on July 3. When the trustees assembled the subject of location became a topic for serious discussion. A recent Alabama convention had passed resolutions requesting that the trustees reopen the question of location "with a view to restore confidence in the minds of its friends who deem Sewanee an unsuitable location." [26]

[23] Leonidas Polk to Stephen Elliott, March 22, 1858, Leonidas Polk Papers.

[24] *Id.* to *id.*, June 15, 1858, *ibid.*

[25] Wallace Estill to Charles R. Barney, June 10, 11, 1858, A. S. Colyar to *id.*, June 13, 1858, *ibid.*

[26] The site on which the University was to be established was already known as Sewanee. The origin of the name is uncertain. Probably the most acceptable theory is that it came from the Shawnee word, "Shawano," meaning southern. For a brief discussion of this and other possibilities see Arthur B. Chitty, Jr., *Reconstruction at Sewanee* (Sewanee, 1954), 74 n.

A resolution to reconsider was immediately introduced. Bishop William Mercer Green of Mississippi explained that he "deemed it no more than courteous" that the trustees from Alabama should be given opportunity to express their views. Bishop Polk seconded the motion, adding that he had considered the action at Montgomery as final and therefore did not admit any right of Alabama to disturb it. Yet, wishing to remove all cause for discontent, he was "willing to waive his opinion as to the propriety of the course." [27]

It was quickly revealed, however, that the Alabama delegation was not eager for reconsideration. The Reverend Henry C. Lay of Huntsville was annoyed that Alabama had been accused of displeasure "because her merits were passed over" and that her trustees were "in opposition because Huntsville was neglected." He agreed that Alabama had preferred the plain to the mountain, but there was no more opposition to Sewanee than any other mountain location. There was sometimes a point, however, "where opposition, because useless, became vexatious and obstinate." That point had been reached, for the board of trustees had made a decision and was not disposed to change it. Bishop Nicholas Hamner Cobbs of Alabama expressed similar views: "There was in Alabama no ill-temper, no wounded jealousy, no desire to be troublesome and eccentric; her sole object had been to avert a measure in her view detrimental to the interests which we all desire to promote. . . . Since you will not come down to us from the mountain, I will climb the mountain and join you there." He moved that the resolution to reopen the question of location be tabled.[28]

Before adjourning, the trustees unanimously accepted the charter granted by the State of Tennessee, and Chancellor Otey appointed Polk chairman of a committee to prepare a constitution.

[27] Quotes are those of the secretary of the meeting.
[28] *Proceedings of the Board of Trustees of the University of the South at their Session, Held at Beersheba, Grundy County, Tennessee, July 4, 1858.* Reprinted in Hodgson (ed.), *Reprints*, 80 ff.

(8)

"For the Cultivation of True Religion, Learning and Virtue"

POLK REMAINED ON the mountain following the July, 1858, meeting of the trustees, exploring the location in company with Colonel Barney and interested persons from Winchester. George Rainsford Fairbanks, a Florida attorney, also joined him there and immediately became a thorough convert.[1] A letter from the Rev. Henry C. Lay agreed that Sewanee was the best location. When a number of Franklin County citizens expressed a desire to honor the trustees for honoring the county, Polk suggested a great picnic to which could be invited all friends of the University. Special invitations were sent to people in the unsuccessful towns of Chattanooga, McMinnville, Huntsville, Atlanta, Cleveland, and Knoxville, and to friends of the enterprise at Nashville. If disappointed people could but see the beauty of the mountains, Polk reasoned, they might be willing to "bury the hatchet in the top of Sewanee."[2]

Both Polk and the local citizenry were excited over the idea. Elliott was urged to be present; Otey would undoubtedly be there; Green was still on the mountain and would remain until after the celebration. Armfield offered to pay the expenses of some newspapermen in order to get the university idea more clearly before the public.[3]

The people of Franklin County proposed to use the Decherd-Winchester omnibus and numerous carriages to take visitors up the mountain. They planned to cut out roads connecting the more

---

[1] Fairbanks later moved to Sewanee and served the University as commissioner of buildings and lands, treasurer, instructor, and historian.
[2] Polk to Elliott, July 21, 1858, Leonidas Polk Papers.   [3] *Ibid.*

important springs and views on the mountain.[4] Tents would be provided for encampments, and the broad flat rock near Rowe's Spring would be canopied with boughs to make a pavilion for dancing. Surely the affair would be a great success and "bring the site into general notice and silence thereby all further discontent."[5]

Plans for the picnic were well publicized. A correspondent in a Nashville newspaper urged everybody to go to the picnic, for Franklin County was inviting the "whole world and the balance of mankind . . . to partake of the hospitalities." Nashvillians could leave by the morning train, "have full benefit of the good cheer, beautiful scenery there displayed, and return by tea time to the comforts of home and the stewing heat of the city."[6]

August 11 was the day. At dawn people were arriving by all roads as far as the eye could reach. Others came by train and carriages from the valley below. Among the first to arrive was the Winchester Band which "soon made the old forest echo with their stirring notes." A. S. Colyar of Winchester called the assembly to order. The purpose of this occasion, he explained, was to express the appreciation of Franklin County for having been chosen as the site for the new university. But there was no desire to express any feeling of "selfish triumph"; there was no claim to "peculiar privilege." The enterprise was one which all could promote and which demanded "unity of action and effort."

Speeches were made by Bishops Green and Polk, and the Reverend Doctor McMahan of the New York Theological Seminary. Bishop Green said he had originally opposed this site and had voted for it "as a second choice, doubtingly." After visiting the location these doubts were quickly dispelled and he was daily becoming more strongly attached to the place.[7] Bishop Polk spoke at length, "demonstrating to the crowd that the heart, mind and en-

[4] *Ibid.* This was in addition to a pledge recently made by the people of Winchester to construct two turnpikes—one from Roark's Cove and the other from Talley's Cove—to terminate on the mountain "at or conveniently near the site of the University." Barney was to make the surveys and superintend construction. James H. Otey to Charles R. Barney, July 28, 1858, Leonidas Polk Papers.

[5] Polk to Elliott, July 21, 1858, *ibid.*

[6] *Republican Banner and Nashville Whig,* August 8, 1858.

[7] Bishop Green moved his residence to Sewanee in 1867 and became very important in the life of the struggling young University.

ergies of a great man were enlisted in this great enterprise." Then came "food for the body," the most interesting feature of the occasion.[8]

By mid-July, 1858, Barney had run the lines, drawn a map of the domain as it then existed, and prepared a railroad map showing the accessibility of Sewanee. Bishop Polk immediately saw an excellent use for this map in the coming campaign for funds. He would use copies in the financial appeal he and Elliott were planning to issue. Barney had a friend in Baltimore who would arrange for printing the railroad map and lithographing the plat of the domain. Polk instructed Barney to proceed with arrangements although, owing to the press for time, Bishop Elliott had not been consulted.

The printing, done by the John Murphy Company, cost, according to figures presented later, $792.50 for 5,000 copies of each map. Polk notified Elliott of the arrangement, explaining that he felt sure Elliott would want to include the maps with the appeal for funds. He also offered suggestions for distributing the address. Someone should compile a list of all of the newspapers in the Southern states plus a few in the North known to be friendly to the enterprise. Each of these should receive a copy of the financial address. *"Let them all get it at the same time,"* Polk explained, *"& they will do us more service than one hundred times the same number of private individuals, however devotedly friendly."* Small town newspapers must not be neglected. Polk himself began the list with the names of twenty Louisiana newspapers and a suggestion that copies of the address also be sent to the Methodist Christian Advocates published in the South. "Scatter them like the leaves of the trees. We will take care of the expense. . . . Now is our chance, & this is our method." [9]

Perhaps Bishop Elliott was displeased at not having been previously consulted. At any rate, when the work on the maps was about one-third complete he suddenly ordered Murphy and Company to discontinue the work, giving as his reason that both the time required and the expense were too great. Barney was angry; Polk was concerned. Barney explained to Elliott that the terms of the contract with Murphy had been approved by Polk, who expressly as-

[8] *Republican Banner and Nashville Whig,* August 17, 1858.
[9] Polk to Elliott, July 24, 1858, Leonidas Polk Papers.

sured him that it was not necessary to consult Elliott. Nevertheless, if Elliott was determined to break the contract then Murphy should be paid for the work completed.

Elliott made no reply to Barney's explanation; neither did he reply to a letter from Murphy and Company, but Murphy completed the work. Duplicate proofs were sent to Barney to be forwarded to Elliott, but Barney refused to have further dealings with Elliott since the Georgia Bishop had not condescended to reply to his letter explaining the circumstances under which the Murphy contract had been made. Instead, Barney sent the proofs to Polk, placing the matter entirely in his hands.

Polk again wrote Elliott, forwarding the proofs and Barney's letter, although he too had not received a reply to his last letter. Polk had supposed that Elliott had plans for getting the work done cheaper, so had done nothing himself.

But my opinion is decidedly that the maps, *both*, should accompany the address. They will arrest attention & give the movement a character for thoroughness, as well as scope, which must tell in impressing itself on the public mind. It will be seen, that the men who have charge of this matter are not dealing with it, as with a petty affair to which they have no confidence & to which they have given little thought or labour. But that they have well considered their ground, have taken their position carefully, that these views are enlarged & enlightened & they have such an appreciation of the intelligence of their constituents & their right to be fully posted as to warrant their furnishing them just such information as is contained in these maps and this address.

Armfield had agreed to pay $200 of the expense. By dividing the remainder among the ten dioceses each would be responsible for only about sixty dollars. "My opinion," Polk concluded, "is that you should order 5,000 *copies of both maps at once* & let them go out with the address." [10]

Bishop Elliott was not easy to convince. He insisted that Murphy and Company had lied about the price and that as for himself he did not propose to be "used" in this manner. Polk replied:

[10] *Id.* to *id.*, September 20, 1858, *ibid*. See also Murphy to Barney, August 10, 14, September 4, 1858; Barney to Elliott, August ?, 1858; *id.* to Murphy, September 12, 1858, *ibid*.

"Suppose they did and suppose you dont. . . . Let them lie and play the sharp, we can better afford this than to do without the work." He favored discouraging lying and encouraging self-respect, but he doubted that this was the time or place to begin.[11]

On this same day Polk wrote Barney that he was eager to get started raising funds as soon as Elliott had put a finishing touch on the address. As for the maps, he had left the matter in Elliott's hands.[12] Presumably the maps were sent out with the address, for Elliott later stated that there was a quantity of printed solicitation material and maps on hand at Savannah.

The *Address of the Commissioners for Raising the Endowment of the University of the South* prepared by Elliott and Polk was full and vigorous. It began by sketching the development of the movement to establish a university, quoted extensively from Polk's letter to the bishops in 1856, incorporated the Declaration of Principles adopted at the Lookout Mountain meeting in 1857, elaborating upon each, and then discussed at length the advantages to be expected from such an enterprise.

Since endowment funds raised in each diocese were to remain in that diocese with only the interest thereon turned over to the University, there was assurance that such funds would never be put into bricks and mortar, leaving little to pay professors. Since the University was not to begin operation until the endowment reached at least $500,000 there would be a guaranteed annual income of from $30,000 to $40,000. No university in the nation, the commissioners asserted, had that much income exclusive of fees. There were plans for expansion in both plant and curriculum but such growth would be kept within available funds. Since the Episcopal church, the sponsor and owner, was perpetual, so would be the University.

It was the aim to

secure for the South a Literary center, a point at which mind may meet mind, and learning encounter learning, and the wise, and the good, and the cultivated, may receive strength and polish, and confidence, and whence shall go forth a tone that shall elevate the whole country. We, of all men, should be the most

[11] Polk to Elliott, November 27, 1858, *ibid.*
[12] Leonidas Polk Papers.

highly cultivated, because we have the most leisure. Labor is performed among us by a caste, and there is, in consequence, a large body of men, who can devote themselves to the elegance of literature, and to such a culture as shall make their homes the envy of all lands. The world is trying hard to persuade us that a slaveholding people cannot be a people of high moral and intellectual culture.

It was true, the address continued, that during the past three-quarters of a century the necessity of clearing new lands had required much time and energy to the neglect of culture, but this was not a fault of the institution of slavery. To prove such an accusation one must ignore the greatness of slaveholding Hebrews, Greeks, and Romans. "There is secured to us by the Constitution of the United States, the most perfect liberty of thought and expression; we have that division of classes which makes one a laboring and the other a dominant class—one a working and the other a thinking and governing class." Add to this the monopoly on cotton, one of the world's great agricultural staples, and the only thing lacking was an understanding of our own resources and a determination to put all differences aside in the interest of union in the development of letters and religion.

There must be no fear that the University of the South would draw students away from other private or state institutions. Only a limited number of students would ever seek the very highest scholarship. The vast majority would always be content with a lesser amount of learning. While many other institutions offered this lesser amount, the University of the South would develop such high standards as to attract those who wished to rise above the mass, many of them having already graduated from institutions of lower standards. It was expected that many persons, some of them "abounding in wealth" and "seeking for channels through which they may dispense usefully the money which God has entrusted to their care," would be eager to support just such an institution. They would not be asked to turn over to the University large amounts of cash. They could keep the principal amount and pay to the University only the interest thereon. All the University desired was regular payment of the interest and property security for the principal.

The appeal concluded:

Take this pamphlet home with you; read it in your domestic circle; weigh in the balance against money the worth of good principles and high education for your children; summon before you the isolation in which the world is attempting to place you and your institutions; recall all you have ever said that breathed of love for the South, that savored of indignation against those that were warring against her; bring to your remembrance your many resolutions for benefiting your homes, your many reproaches because your section would not vindicate herself; above all recollect that your wealth is a trust from God, for which you must account to him as well as to society and determine . . . whether you will turn your back upon this most promising conception, or come up like whole-hearted Southern and Christian men, and found an University for the South that shall be worthy of our Fathers, worthy of our children.[13]

Following the distribution of the financial appeal Elliott and Polk began an active canvass for funds. Working out of New Orleans, they concentrated on the Diocese of Louisiana. By June, 1859, Polk could report that $320,000 of the required $500,000 had been secured and "this from say about 50 persons."[14]

For months Bishop Polk had given the greater portion of his time to the university movement. His diocese, especially Trinity parish, of which he had been rector since 1855, might well have complained of neglect. Polk, however, also had complaints, especially financial. During 1858 it was rumored that the Bishop was about to move his family to their Mississippi plantation. When questioned by the Trinity vestry, Polk admitted considering such a move. And in an open letter to the vestry he related in detail the history of his financial support for the past sixteen years. He gave up a salary of $2,500 to accept a position the only income from which was $500 traveling expense. There was assurance, however, that as churches within the diocese grew and multiplied there would be hope for adequate compensation. In 1854, following the loss of his private fortune, the Louisiana Convention promised him $4,000 to $5,000 annually. On the strength of this he had moved to

[13] Copy in *ibid.* Reprinted in Hodgson (ed.), *Reprints,* 108 ff. It cannot be determined just how much of this address was written by Polk; the whole document has a distinct Polk flavor.

[14] Polk to Barney, June 18, 1859, Leonidas Polk Papers. See also James H. Otey to Thomas Ruffin, July 8, 1859, Hamilton (ed.), *Papers of Thomas Ruffin,* III, 37.

New Orleans. But only during 1855–56 had he received as much as $4,000. During the past year he had received only $1,338.95. During the past sixteen years he had received from the diocese only $18,211.49, yet the number of parishes had increased from four to forty and communicants from 238 to 1,551, not including thirty-five congregations of Negro slaves. The Trinity parish had offered some relief with a salary of $2,000, but he found it necessary to pay an assistant one-half this amount. Consequently, since moving to New Orleans he had gone into debt $5,000. He therefore felt compelled to settle his family on "their property" where they could live more cheaply.[15] Presumably Trinity Church provided the needed assistance; the Polk family did not move to Mississippi.

During the period of solicitation of funds Polk also kept in close touch with Barney on the mountain. The trustees had authorized Barney to make a complete survey of the University domain and prepare a topographical map. Barney made the survey during the spring of 1859, but was slow about preparation of the map. Polk urged him again and again to have the map ready by the next meeting of the trustees which was scheduled for August. Otey authorized Barney to draw on commissioner Polk for funds up to $500.[16] He was also instructed to build three cabins—one double and two single—for the accommodation of visitors. John Armfield had made $200 available to assist in this construction.[17]

Bishop Otey called the trustees into session at Beersheba Springs on August 10, 1859.[18] Highlights of this meeting were two reports of considerable progress. The committee on conveyance and survey

[15] *Correspondence of Right Rev. L. Polk, with the Vestry of Trinity Church, New Orleans.*

[16] Otey to Barney, April 26, 1859; Polk to *id.*, July 4, 1859, Leonidas Polk Papers.

[17] Otey to Barney, May 24, 1859, *ibid.*

[18] To one lay trustee he sent interesting instructions as to the best way to reach Beersheba: "Upon your arrival at Chattanooga remember to get on board of the Nashville *cars*, and check your baggage to Cowan—not to *McMinnville* but to Cowan. There (Cowan) you will change cars for the Train of the *Sewanee* Mining Company which will take you directly thro' the University grounds to *Tracy City* where you will be met by good four-horse coaches to take you over a good road 16 miles to *Beersheba*—" John Armfield sent word he would like to have the trustee make his house "your place of sojourn." Otey to Thomas Ruffin, July 8, 1859, Hamilton (ed.), *Papers of Thomas Ruffin*, III, 37. The good road referred to was largely the work of Armfield, who fur-

reported details of the boundaries of the University domain, enumerating the tracts (and donors) included therein. Polk and Elliott, as commissioners to raise endowment, explained that their work had been almost entirely in Louisiana. Instead of skimming the surface of all of the dioceses, they had decided to cover each one thoroughly. Although a skimming campaign would no doubt have raised the required amount, a thorough canvass would raise a vastly greater sum. At present they were able to report $363,580 in "cash, bonds, and notes, payable in available periods." Reliable parties had also pledged, but not yet secured by bonds or notes, an additional $115,000.[19]

The financial goal now seemed within reach. The enthusiastic trustees urged Polk and Elliott to continue their good work for another year. Since they would have sufficient time "only by the relinquishment for the time of their parochial charges, and must be attended, as a necessary consequence, by the sacrifice of their respective salaries," each was authorized to appropriate for his own use the sum of $5,000 from funds collected. The trustees also appointed an executive committee, of which Otey, Polk, and Elliott were members. Whenever the fund-raisers should report that the required $500,000 had been secured this committee was to make all preparation necessary for proper ceremonies in laying of the cornerstone of the University.[20]

Immediately following the trustees' meeting Polk returned to New Orleans, gave up his rented house, and prepared to send his family to Philadelphia for a year. He would be unable to be with them in New Orleans and his wife needed medical treatment for her eyes which she could get in Philadelphia. These arrangements

---

nished laborers for construction and maintenance. Armfield did not operate the Beersheba Hotel himself but leased it to others. In December, 1859, he sold it to an incorporated Beersheba Springs Company in which Lucius Polk and Bishop Polk's son Hamilton were stockholders. Elaborate plans for development of a fashionable resort were terminated by the war. Howell, "John Armfield of Beersheba Springs," *Tennessee Historical Quarterly*, III, 59.

[19] It was reported in the press, but not in the minutes of the trustees, that John Armfield had pledged $25,000 annually for life, and that Henry Johnson of Louisiana had pledged $40,000. *Republican Banner and Nashville Whig*, December 25, 1857; New Orleans *Times-Picayune*, July 3, 1859.

[20] *Proceedings of the Board of Trustees of the University of the South at their Session held at Beersheba, Grundy County, Tenn., August 10, 1859*. Reprinted in Hodgson (ed.), *Reprints*, 125 ff.

complete, he hurriedly left for an eastern tour to inspect a number of educational institutions, for in addition to his fund-raising assignment he was chairman of the committee to draft a constitution and statutes for the University. His brother Lucius met him in Raleigh and accompanied him to Chapel Hill where the two would renew old University of North Carolina acquaintances.

At Chapel Hill Bishop Polk received a letter from Bishop Elliott telling of the arrival of a batch of books from abroad. These were gifts from educators in Prussia, France, and England. "It is a valuable cargo," Polk replied. ". . . I trust . . . that when we come to their examination we shall deal with them neither in the spirit of servile copyists, nor yet with that ridiculous modern conceit which affects superiority to the lessons of experience; but that, with an eye to the peculiarities of our national and local circumstances and necessities, we will give everything its appropriate value, take what meets our own case, and leave the rest alone."

At the University of North Carolina Polk visited with his roommate of student days, David L. Swain, who for many years had been president. This was Polk's first visit to the campus since he left it for West Point. He and Swain discussed university matters in general. Several professors were also consulted. Polk found the Episcopal professors enthusiastic about the University of the South; others viewed it with respect but also with concern, fearing the effect it might have upon the University of North Carolina. Polk later related that he did his best "to allay those fears, and not without success." Swain himself, Polk reported, thought that education should be left to the state; however, he agreed that the Episcopal church was "the most compact and perfect thing that has ever been devised on this continent."

The whole discussion at Chapel Hill merely increased Polk's enthusiasm and his feeling of responsibility in directing so great an enterprise. "We have need to pray for wisdom and prudence and moderation and judgment as few men ever had," he told Bishop Elliott.[21]

[21] Polk to Elliott, September 20, 1859, quoted in Polk, *Leonidas Polk*, I, 256–57; *id.* to Daughter (Mrs. W. D. Gale), September 22, 1859, Gale Papers; David L. Swain to Thomas Ruffin, October 10, 1859, Hamilton (ed.), *Papers of Thomas Ruffin*, III, 48.

From North Carolina Polk went to Virginia, attending the Convention at Richmond and visiting the university and Virginia Military Institute. Early in September he had entered his youngest son, William Mecklenburg, known to the family as "Meck," as a student in V.M.I. Bishop Polk found this "a noble institution . . . doing a good work for the State of Virginia and the whole South." From Colonel Smith and his associates he got some "very useful hints." He made no mention of having seen Professor Thomas J. Jackson, later to become the famous General "Stonewall."

Moving on to Washington, Polk made contact with a number of former West Point associates. Colonel Robert Anderson of the army took him to examine a number of buildings being constructed under the supervision of Captain Alexander H. Bowman. He and Professor Henry of the Smithsonian Institute dined with Professor Bache of the coastal service. Upon Henry's invitation he visited the Smithsonian and found it a "very extended affair . . . accomplishing a great work." He thought some of the plans might "be appropriated by us with advantage."

Polk also visited Harvard, Brown, and West Point, having a full conference with the professors at the Point. While in the East he also visited Bishop John Henry Hopkins at Burlington, Vermont. A few years earlier Hopkins had been a guest in the Polk home in New Orleans. The University trustees had authorized the employment of a landscape architect to lay out the proposed campus. Polk was to interview a prospect in Washington but found him too ill to undertake the task. Knowing Hopkins as "a man of eminent taste & skill in everything of that sort," Polk turned to him. Hopkins certainly was a versatile man, having had experience in law and engineering, as well as preaching, and being recognized as a musician and painter. He agreed to accept the job and begin work at Sewanee in December, 1859.[22]

During his tour Bishop Polk had examined the best educational institutions and talked with men of varying opinions, yet his enthusiasm suffered no setback. "I think I see my way for carrying out all my plans for the Church & the Country on a scale to the

---

[22] Polk to Elliott, November 4, 1859; *id.* to Barney, November 30, 1859, Leonidas Polk Papers; *id.* to Daughter (Mrs. Gale), September 22, 1859, Gale Papers.

full as large as our highest conceptions," he wrote Barney.[23] Upon his return Polk stopped with Bishop Elliott at Savannah. For two weeks they discussed what should be incorporated in the constitution and statutes of the University of the South, making full use of the information collected both at home and abroad.

It was indeed fortunate for the university movement that two men such as Elliott and Polk assumed leadership. In the words of a friendly contemporary clergyman, the university idea was "Polk's own," but Elliott was his "coadjutor in the inception of the enterprise. . . . The affection between Polk and Elliott was more than that of brothers. Each was the complement of the other. Polk had the greater energy; Elliott had more deliberation. Polk's plans were magnificent; Elliott had the genius of proportion. Polk aroused enthusiasm; Elliott disarmed opposition. It was natural that Polk should take the lead, and Elliott loved to have it so; yet it may be doubted whether Polk would have attained the eminent position he held among the Southern bishops if Elliott had not stood by him and supplemented what Polk lacked." [24]

While working on the constitution and statutes Elliott and Polk were also making plans to join Bishop Hopkins on the mountain shortly before Christmas to learn his ideas relative to landscape design for the new campus, a subject in which Polk was interested. In his numerous letters to Barney during 1859 he had stressed the importance of making the approaches attractive to visitors. Among other things, he suggested that "views" be cut out so that persons could see the beautiful valley below. It was these views that so impressed Bishop Hopkins that he wrote his wife: "If Lake Champlain could be thrown in it would be absolute perfection." [25]

Clearing views, opening up roads, and assembling materials for construction of University buildings were expensive operations. Barney was constantly embarrassed for want of funds to pay for labor and supplies. Polk sent him $400 from New York and hundreds more from Savannah. Barney also wrote Bishop Otey for $1,000. Otey, unable to supply the amount, sent the request to

---

[23] November 30, 1859, Gale Papers.
[24] Fulton, "The Church in the Confederate States," *loc. cit.*, 563.
[25] [John Henry Hopkins], *Life of the Late Right Rev. John Henry Hopkins, First Bishop of Vermont and Seventh Presiding Bishop* (New York, 1873), 313–14.

banker John M. Bass, suggesting a temporary loan. In spite of the stress of it all, Polk kept his optimism. As soon as he and Elliott should reach the mountain, he wrote Barney, they would "take measures to put all further troubles at an end." [26]

When Polk and Elliott did arrive on the mountain in mid-December, 1859, Polk brought along much material, if little cash. Bishop Hopkins later related: "He brought with him to Sewannee at that time, a large box, entirely filled with the results of correspondence with the leading men in Europe and the scholastic institutions of the old world, as well as laborious and thoroughly digested plans projected for the Southern University. . . . And as he unfolded the design, and gave some idea of the vast amount of toil and work accomplished by Bishop Elliott and himself in its preparation, I was amazed and delighted at the combination of original genius, lofty enterprise, and Christian hope, with the utmost degree of practical wisdom, cautious investigation, exquisite tact, and indefatigable energy." [27]

Polk, Elliott, and Hopkins spent a pleasant Christmas on the mountain talking and planning the location of buildings and roads. Hopkins soon returned to Vermont, although he had a six-months' leave from his diocese and had used only half of it. He and Polk had an understanding that if needed he would return to Sewanee later in the year. He did not return, for he was busy establishing his own Vermont Episcopal Institute. However, by way of further encouragement, he wrote: "The more I reflect upon it the more I am convinced of the religious and moral grandeur of your plan." [28]

In January, 1860, Polk set out on a fund-raising tour through Alabama. The exchange of correspondence between him and Barney continued. Buildings and roads were an inexhaustible subject for discussion. Of particular interest to Polk was the impression people would get as they approached the campus from the railroad station. As for his success in Alabama, he was able to report from Montgomery on January 25 that he had secured an average of

[26] December 2, 1859, Leonidas Polk Papers.
[27] John H. Hopkins to Mrs. Leonidas Polk, February 14, 1867, *ibid.* In evaluating Hopkins' statement it should be noted that it was written to Mrs. Polk after the Bishop's death.
[28] Hopkins to Polk, March 26, 1860, Leonidas Polk Papers.

$8,000 per week for the past three weeks. Equal success was expected in the Selma and Mobile areas. He must then move on to New Orleans for the trustees' meeting on February 8.[29]

The New Orleans meeting was called for consideration of the proposed constitution and statutes of the University. For eighteen months a committee of eight headed by Bishop Polk had been laboring on these rules and regulations under which the University should be organized and operated. Polk's chief assistant was Bishop Elliott, with Francis B. Fogg furnishing needed legal advice. In presenting to the trustees the results of its labor the committee explained that it had examined the "programmes" and "working machinery" of "the most eminent institutions of learning in our country and in Europe," even enlisting the services of the President of the United States, who through the embassies, placed the committee in touch with the highest sources of information in England, France, and the German States. From these sources was received all of the information desired.

After several hours of discussion the board tentatively approved both the constitution and statutes with minor changes. Final approval was postponed until the next meeting. Polk was not quite satisfied with these documents; so he continued to seek opinions of prominent educators, especially as to the statutes. Among those contacted were Professors R. L. Cabell and Albert Taylor Bledsoe of the University of Virginia. Their replies were very similar, suggesting the probability of consultation. They disapproved of a number of provisions in the statutes, particularly with regard to the duties of the vice-chancellor and his relationship with the professors. They would not make him a supervisor of instruction. Instead, they would hold each professor strictly accountable to the trustees for faithful discharge of duties. No vice-chancellor, Bledsoe observed, could be an authority in so many fields. In attempting such supervision this official himself would recognize that he was "acting the part of a humbug."

Both of these Virginia professors advised against a five-year-term for professors, suggesting instead permanent tenure after two years probation. They thought the curriculum embraced too many schools (departments). "I would not elevate to the dignity of full

[29] Polk to Barney, January 25, 1860, *ibid.*

professorship any one of the living languages," Cabell explained. He thought, however, "literature, history & philosophy might constitute a curriculum of one chair." [30]

Polk's reaction to these suggestions is not a matter of record. They were not incorporated in the statutes when finally adopted. However, Polk was sufficiently impressed with Bledsoe to propose that he become a member of the first faculty of the University of the South. Bledsoe replied that if chosen he would be inclined to accept. He was sorry that he could not be present at the laying of the cornerstone, but he must use all available time in completing his book on calculus, which was due off the press in January, 1861. Much of the work for his next book, on moral philosophy, was already completed. Would it not be best to delay publication until after he joined the faculty at Sewanee? [31] Polk was much interested in the prestige that such men as Bledsoe would bring to his mountain university.

In addition to recruiting a faculty Polk was also recruiting architects. The trustees had not employed an architect for any building; neither had they approved any style of architecture. Interested architects were encouraged to submit their own ideas and plans. Polk had some ideas of his own about the more important buildings. He left no copy but he circulated his ideas among prospective architects. J. F. Wharton of New Orleans wrote that he had received Polk's sketch for a central edifice and would try to make his plans conform.[32]

Suddenly, in April, 1860, all work on cabins and landscaping was suspended. Heirs of one Thompson had produced an old grant laying claim to seventeen hundred acres of the University domain, including the site on which the campus was planned. Bishop Otey and Francis Fogg rushed to Winchester, the county seat, and found the Thompson heirs willing to settle for one dollar per acre. Otey dashed off a letter to Polk asking advice,[33] and Polk was soon on the scene. The financial report at the next meeting of the trustees made no mention of the claim. However, on May 26, John Hendley deeded to the University his claim to any and all portions of the 5,000 acre tract donated by the Sewanee Mining

---

[30] Cabell to Polk, April 18, 1860, Bledsoe to *id.*, September 11, 1860, *ibid.*
[31] *Id.* to *id.*, October 8, 1860, *ibid.*
[32] Wharton to *id.*, August 11, 1860, *ibid.*   [33] April 11, 1860, *ibid.*

Company. No money was involved. It was a gift, the deed stated, "in consideration of the benefits to be derived from the location of the University of the South in Franklin County."[34] This might have been the Thompson claim.

Although no university edifice was under construction, October 10, 1860, was set as the date for laying the cornerstone. Bishop Polk took up residence in the cabin Armfield had built for him at Beersheba Springs,[35] and Mrs. Polk and five daughters came from Philadelphia to join him.[36] The summer was spent in preparation for the cornerstone ceremonies. The twenty-five miles separating Sewanee and Beersheba made it inconvenient for Polk to continue residence at the latter. Consequently, he decided to sell his cottage at Beersheba and build at Sewanee. Construction was begun during the summer.[37]

The executive committee planned to make the laying of the cornerstone an occasion that would be long remembered. From the time Sewanee was designated as the site for the University, Polk had contended that if people would only visit the mountain their doubts would be changed to enthusiasm. The entire preparation for the cornerstone ceremonies bears unmistakable evidence of his energy and ability to organize. Many special invitations were sent out. General invitations were issued through newspapers. Thousands of people were expected to attend. Hundreds would stay over for at least one night. Temporary accommodations were provided in hastily constructed one-story cottages, some covered with canvas. A large hall equipped with benches for 3,000 was so arranged that it could be quickly converted to a dining hall with tables and seats for 500. Every possible convenience, even to a barber shop and porter service, was provided for guests.

For days before October 10, the date set for the ceremonies,

[34] Franklin County *Record Book*, Z, 354.

[35] Sometime during the past two years Armfield had built cabins for both Polk and Otey.

[36] A sixth daughter, Katherine, had married William Dudley Gale of Tennessee and Mississippi in 1858. Polk sent her $500 for a trousseau with a note saying, "I hope it may give you as much pleasure to receive it as it does me to offer it." The Bishop's only advice to his daughter who was now leaving her old home was that she always faithfully discharge her Christian duties. Polk to Katherine Polk, September 4, 1858, Gale Papers.

[37] Polk, "Leonidas Polk, A Memoir"; Mrs. Polk to John Armfield, September 24, 1860, Leonidas Polk Papers.

visitors from far and near arrived by every means of conveyance.
Some brought their own provisions and camped out. For those
who came from a distance the best means of travel was the Nashville and Chattanooga Railroad to Cowan and the railroad of the
Sewanee Mining Company up the mountain. The president of
the mining company was particularly obliging, even to borrowing
comfortable passenger coaches from the Nashville and Chattanooga. To most of the excursionists a ride up a mountain by rail
was a new and thrilling experience. "Our locomotive, the *General
Mosquera,*" one excited traveler reported, ". . . puffed like a
grampus, and screamed as if in defiance of the onerous duties it
had to perform."

Polk and Barney had extended their preparations even along the
railroad line, for as trains crawled slowly along its crooked track,
through "artificial openings" one could see "the mountain gorges,
the distant slopes, the rugged cliffs, and the sweeping plain in the
valley below, with here and there a 'clearing' and a rude cottage,
[which] presented a picture not easily to be erased from
memory." Twelve miles in the distance "the pretty little village of
Winchester, with its pointing spires" was "clearly visible in the
sunlight." [38]

The scene at the Sewanee depot was all hustle and bustle as
"vehicles of great variety of style" hauled new arrivals the one-half
mile to University Place. Hawkers of fruits and tobacco were already on the job. Horn's Silver Band of Nashville had been employed to furnish the music. As its members stepped off the cars
they struck up "Dixie's Land," and the "mountain peasantry run
wild."

A program of proceedings had been prepared in advance, giving
the order of procession, the names of participants, and the scripts
of what they were to say. The procession formed at the trustees'
office and moved to the site designated for the principal University
building. Bishop Otey, by seniority of consecration the chancellor
of the University, opened the ceremonies, "giving out" a psalm to
be sung by a choir under the direction of the Reverend Doctors

[38] *Republican Banner and Nashville Whig,* October 13, 1860. For a hundred
years Polk's advocacy of "views" has continued sound; today an attractive feature of the location of the University domain is still the "views" of the valley
below.

Charles T. Quintard and J. Freeman Young. Then the Bishop of Florida recited several passages of Scripture. The Bishop of North Carolina delivered the exhortation, and the Bishop of Alabama offered prayer. It was left to Stephen Elliott, the Bishop of Georgia, to deposit sundry items in the stone.[39]

Bishop Polk then stepped forward and read his prepared statement: "A corner-stone is that which unites the walls of a building, and may symbolize strength and stability—the union of the intellectual and spiritual natures of man—the emblem of Christ—the sure and tried corner-stone—the wisdom of God and the power of God." Striking the stone three times with a hammer, he dedicated the University of the South to "the cultivation of true Religion, learning and virtue, that thereby God may be glorified, and the happiness of man be advanced."

The ceremonies concluded, the crowd moved over to the "Oration Hall" to hear the speeches. Much care had been taken in selecting speakers. John S. Preston of South Carolina and John M. Bright of Fayetteville, Tennessee, were public figures well known for their oratory. Frederick A. P. Barnard, chancellor of the University of Mississippi, was both an educator and a religious figure. Matthew Fontaine Maury was a naval officer and a distinguished scientist. And Bishop Benjamin Bosworth Smith of Kentucky represented a diocese that might some day be induced to support the University of the South.

Preston spoke during the morning; the others in the afternoon. In between, an excellent dinner with "a profusion of everything" was served. "And thus passed off the day, harmoniously and delightfully, and to the entire satisfaction of all interested." [40]

On the day following the cornerstone ceremonies the trustees went into a two-day session. The constitution and statutes were approved. A report was received from the commissioners on endowment showing that the University had to its credit $375,000 in cash, bonds and other securities. Adding to this the value of the

[39] This huge block of marble came from the valley below. Polk had engaged I. T. Miller, one of Barney's assistants, to drag the stone up the mountain. Using thirty-four oxen, he completed the task in one day. Statement of I. T. Miller in Lily Baker, *et al.* (eds.), *Sewanee* (Sewanee, 1932), 16. During the Civil War persons reported to have been Federal soldiers blew up the rock and made off with its contents.

[40] *Republican Banner and Nashville Whig*, October 13, 1860.

domain, supplies, and services pledged, the total was estimated at
$505,000. Considering that the minimum financial requirement
had been met, the trustees authorized the executive committee to
examine plans submitted by architects and pay up to $400 for the
one most suitable. The committee was also instructed "to lay out
Public Grounds, Avenues, Streets, etc.," and to lease lots to those
persons who wished to build on the University domain.[41]

[41] *Proceedings of the Board of Trustees of the University of the South, at
their Session, Held at Sewanee, Franklin County, Tenn., Oct. 9th, 1860.* Reprinted in Hodgson (ed.), *Reprints,* 194 ff.

(9)

"It Seemed the Duty Next Me"

BISHOP POLK REMAINED at Sewanee until December 4. Then leaving his family in their newly constructed cottage he set out for his much neglected diocese to visit parishes and ponder the course of political events. He was absent from his family during Christmas, 1860, but the Elliotts, who had built a cottage nearby, were on hand to help the Polks celebrate. The Elliotts entertained with an egg-nog party on Christmas Eve and all had "a good deal of merriment" at the Polk home on the following night.[1]

By January 1, 1861, Bishop Elliott was reported to be "hot for secession";[2] Bishop Polk was probably not far behind. Some members of the Polk family, especially "Meck," now a student at V.M.I., were much excited. A year earlier, following disturbances at Harpers Ferry and Charleston, Meck had excitedly reported that the Governor of Virginia had ordered eighty V.M.I. cadets to stand ready for call to duty. They were to report to Charleston. "I am not permitted to go," he wrote his father, "because I never went to any artillery drill I would give anything on earth to go, and if they get in a fight down there, I know some of them will get killed. I have therefore determined to go, that is if they get in a fight with those rascals, even if I am dismissed because I think it is my duty both toward the south and toward my fellow cadets. I am not going to stand by and see my fellow cadets killed, and I think any man who would ought to have his head broke." Would his father please send him some money?[3]

---

[1] Charles P. Barney to George R. Fairbanks, January 2, 1861, quoted in Baker et al. (eds.), *Sewanee*, 17–18.

[2] *Ibid.*

[3] Mecklenburg Polk to Leonidas Polk, November 20, 1859, Leonidas Polk Papers.

The cadets did not march, and before the Bishop could send advice to his impetuous son, Meck had cooled down. A week later he apologized for being so excited; he "did not comprehend" what he was saying.[4] Meck's enthusiasm for a possible fight rather than for his studies gave his father much concern. Meck agreed that in the past he had been nothing but trouble and expense but resolved to do better, making a "stand" on military science and mathematics. It was too late to do much about French. The Bishop was disgusted, if not angry, and expressed himself in no uncertain terms. Meck replied "I am sorry to see that you had such a poor opinion of me. You seemed to think that I was utterly lost & good for nothing." Nevertheless, he was determined to prove "that I am not such a blockhead a[s] you might suppose." Having made this promise, he quickly returned to the exciting crisis, expressing regret that Virginia had failed to join other Southern States in secession. The state was full of "abolitionists," he charged, and thousands of Virginians would have voted for Lincoln had they not been afraid.[5]

The flesh was weak. Soon came a note from Colonel Smith, saying Meck had been dismissed "for excess of demerits." Although Colonel Smith decided to give him another chance, Meck had no heart for classes while troops were marching.[6] His father instructed him to stay where he was.

In the meantime, Bishop Polk's thinking relative to the crisis had changed from hope to despair and advocacy of secession. He spent Christmas of 1860 drafting a long letter to President James Buchanan. It was with the hope of preventing further complications, he began, that he was making this appeal. He had not the slightest doubt of the President's "integrity of purpose or patriotic devotion" to what he considered the true interests of the nation. Neither did he question the President's firmness of intention to discharge the duties of his office. He did, however, fear that a lack "of accurate and reliable information" as to the true condition of affairs in the South might result in an erroneous conception of duty.

[4] *Id.* to *id.*, November 27, 1859, *ibid.*
[5] *Id.* to id., January 16, February 4, 1861, *ibid.*
[6] *Id.* to *id.*, April 18, 1861, *ibid.*

Doubtless you are required to enforce the laws; but assuredly no sane man will say "without regard to consequences." That would be madness. A right to exercise a sound discretion necessarily accompanied the imposition and the acceptance of the oath of office. Such must be the judgment of our Christian civilization. And to assume the responsibility of exercising that right when such issues as those with which you are called to deal are impending . . . involves the highest exercise of courageous independence and the most discriminating and considerate regard to the duties of your own position and the best interests of those whose destinies are in your hands

Polk felt that he was in position to furnish the President with accurate information as to the state of mind of the Southern people. "I write to say that I am thoroughly convinced that they have deliberately and inflexibly resolved to cut themselves off from the Union. This feeling is deepening and widening every day, and no difference exists except as to the mode of effecting it. To attempt to prevent it by force of arms would instantly extinguish that difference and unite the whole population as one man." The people of the South wished to avoid the "ruthless carnage" that would no doubt accompany a resort to arms; it was up to the President to say whether or not it should be forced upon them.

The people of the South, the Bishop concluded, had resolved to stand upon their rights and resist all efforts to infringe those rights, regardless of the source. "We believe it is practicable for the two parties to separate peacefully; this we most earnestly desire." There was every wish to spare the President embarrassment. In view of the President's previous record and his known spirit of moderation, the people of the South were unable to see why peaceable separation could not be accomplished.

The pattern of developments was clear. Georgia and the Gulf States would follow South Carolina out of the Union by February 1. Within another month this group would organize a Southern Union. Other states would soon join them. Once this was accomplished there would not be the remotest possibility of reuniting the two sections as long as slave labor appeared necessary to agricultural prosperity in the Southern Confederacy.

In closing, the Bishop could but offer "my earnest prayer that you may have grace and strength given you to support you in the discharge of your trying position, and that you may decide wisely for yourself, your countrymen, and the best interests of mankind." [7]

Polk made no public expression of his views on the secession crisis, yet there can be no doubt of his belief in the right of secession. He made no public statement as to the course Louisiana should take, yet he prepared to follow his adopted state in whichever direction its representatives should lead. Had he chosen to speak out many persons would have listened eagerly, but it would be folly to suggest that, even if he had wished, he could have stemmed the tide of secession.

On December 28, 1860, President Buchanan issued a proclamation urging the people of the United States to observe a day of prayer, fasting, and humiliation. Bishop Polk immediately addressed to the clergymen of the Diocese of Louisiana a pastoral letter specifying the prayer to be used in the parish churches on this occasion:

> Oh Almighty God, the Fountain of all wisdom, and the Helper of all who call upon Thee: We, thy unworthy servants, under a deep sense of the difficulties and dangers by which we are now surrounded, turn our hearts to Thee in earnest supplication and prayer. We humble ourselves before Thee; we confess that as a nation and as individuals, we have grievously offended Thee, and that our sins have justly provoked thy wrath and indignation against us. Deal not with us, Oh Lord, according to our iniquities, but according to thy great and tender mercies, and forgive us all that is past. Turn thine anger from us, and visit us not with those evils which we have justly deserved. Guide and direct us in all our consultations; save us from all ignorance, error, pride and prejudice; and if it please thee, compose and heal the divisions which disturb us. Or else, if in thy good providence it be otherwise appointed, grant, we beseech Thee, that the spirit of wisdom and moderation may preside over our councils, that the just rights of all may be maintained and accorded, and that the blessings of peace may be preserved to us and our children throughout all generations. All which we ask through the merits and mediation of our Lord and Savior Jesus Christ.[8]

[7] December 26, 1860, quoted in Polk, *Leonidas Polk*, I, 299–301.
[8] Diocese of Louisiana, *Journal of Convention* (1861), 29.

Bishop Polk visited his family at Sewanee in January, 1861, but was back in New Orleans for services at Trinity Church on Sunday, January 27, on which occasion there was substituted a new prayer for the state government. On the previous day a Louisiana convention had passed an ordinance of secession. This action was expected and Polk had given much thought to what would be the position of the Diocese of Louisiana once the state was no longer a part of the Union. He had already reached his decision before the convention voted secession. Consequently, in Trinity Church on January 27, 1861, prayer for "the people of this State in general, and especially this Legislature, now in session" was substituted for the prayer for "the people of these United States in general, and especially for their senators and representatives in Congress assembled." And prayer was offered for "the Governor of this State" instead of "the President of the United States." Bishop Polk thought the change "made deep impression on many minds." [9]

On January 30 Bishop Polk addressed a pastoral letter to the clergy and laity of the diocese officially informing them of Louisiana's secession from the Union. This action, he explained, had severed all connection of the Diocese of Louisiana with the Protestant Episcopal Church of the United States. "We have, therefore, an Independent Diocesan existence."

The events and circumstances leading to the action taken by Louisiana were too familiar to require comment, Bishop Polk explained. He was pleased to add that to these political grievances the Episcopal Church had made no contribution. Instead, through her well-ordered organization, she had confined herself to teaching and preaching the gospel of Christ. Pressure had often been exerted from both sides, yet neither her pulpit nor presses had contributed to "the radical and unscriptural propagandism which has so degraded Christianity, and has plunged our country into its unhappy condition."

Of the justice of the Southern cause, Bishop Polk had no doubt. The wisdom of the action taken he thought might be judged by the character of Southern leaders who supported separation. "We have taken our stand we humbly trust, in the fear of God, and under a sense of the duty which we owe to mankind."

[9] Leonidas Polk, "Diary for 1861." Manuscript in Leonidas Polk Papers.

The decision to separate from the Protestant Episcopal Church of the United States was a result of the necessity of following "our Nationality. Not because there has been any difference of opinion as to Christian Doctrine or Catholic usage. Upon these points we are still one. With us, it is a separation, not division, certainly not alienation. . . . Our relations to each other hereafter will be the relations we both now hold to the men of our Mother Church of England." It was in view of this necessity that he had exercised the authority of his office in ordering the change in prayers inaugurated at Trinity Church on the previous Sunday.

Anticipating the meeting of a convention for the formation of a Southern Confederacy, Bishop Polk included in his pastoral letter a special prayer asking protection and guidance for "the Convention of this State." Should a Southern convention assemble, "and the Convention of Southern States" was to be added.[10]

There is no evidence that Bishop Polk consulted anyone while considering the course to be taken by the Diocese of Louisiana; he considered the decision his responsibility. Once he had made his decision, however, he was eager that church leaders, both North and South, should understand. He particularly desired the approval of those bishops in whom he had the greatest confidence. On January 29, 1861, he dispatched a letter to Bishop Horatio Potter of New York. The letter was an attempt to explain that the lower South had acted only after close study and calm consideration. There was no longer need to argue the question of the right of secession; the deed had been done. It was now left to the people of the North to determine "whether the interests of humanity demand the maintenance of the General Government at such a sacrifice of treasure and life as must follow an attempt, by force of arms, to prevent a separation."

Polk did not believe people of the North would support such a war, a struggle arraying one-half the nation against the other and from which there could come no adequate compensation.

> I cannot but think and hope that the good sense and Christian feeling of the North will prevail over passion and pride, and that we shall be saved from such a disaster and be permitted to go in

---

[10] *Diocese of Louisiana, Journal of Convention* (1861), 30–33.

peace. It is our very great happiness to know that the Church has stood firm, throughout all this contest, to her duty to the Constitution and the laws, and that she has not contributed in the very least to the causes which have brought these mischiefs upon us. . . . Our affection for our brethren in the North has not been shaken, therefore, in the least, and we earnestly trust that there will be no reason why it should be. If we must separate, it must be to follow our nationality, and not because we have differed on any point of Christian doctrine or religious duty, and there will be no reason why we should not continue to love each other afterward as we both now love the men of the Church of England.[11]

Although Bishop Polk had already decided that the Diocese of Louisiana now had an independent existence, he made only general mention of the course he proposed to take.

When Bishop Potter replied, he had no knowledge of Polk's pastoral letter of January 30; consequently, he made no observations as to the soundness of the position taken by the Diocese of Louisiana. His greatest concern was that the people North and South did not have a proper appreciation of the seriousness of the crisis. He offered no hope that the South would return to the Union and he was opposed to the use of force. "If nothing can heal this breach, I, for one, most earnestly hope that we may separate, if such a thing be possible, peaceably." He doubted, however, whether the Northwest would consent to the mouth of the Mississippi River passing under control of a foreign power. Neither did he consider the delight being expressed by northern abolitionists a very encouraging omen. But regardless of the crisis, "Our feeling toward you and your brethren (and we love much, though we may have said little) is not in the least changed." [12]

In private correspondence Bishop Hopkins of Vermont was sympathetic, although he disagreed. After hostilities had begun Polk wrote him in great warmth of feeling. Hopkins replied that although he had deep sympathy for the feelings of the Bishop of Louisiana, he could not agree that this was a war of subjugation. In the first place, it appeared to be a necessary defense of Washington against threatened attack. It was also the exercise of a duty to

[11] Copy in Polk, *Leonidas Polk*, I, 310–12.
[12] Horatio Potter to Leonidas Polk, February 12, 1861, Leonidas Polk Papers.

recover and protect United States property. It was likewise an act of protection of those Southerners who were alleged to have opposed secession. As for his own views of the crisis, Bishop Hopkins concluded, he recognized that the South had as much right to secede as the Thirteen Colonies had to throw off English rule. Yet at the same time he questioned the wisdom of the act. He was unable to see that the mere election of Abraham Lincoln endangered the constitutional rights of Southern people.[13]

By mid-February, 1861, South Carolina, Georgia, and all of the Gulf States had seceded, and meeting in delegated convention at Montgomery had organized the Confederate States of America. Bishop Polk found it necessary again to revise the prayer book. "The progress of affairs makes it expedient to direct further changes in the public services of the Church," he wrote the Louisiana clergy on February 20. "In the Prayer for those in civil authority, for the words 'the President of the United States,' substitute the words, 'the President of the Confederate States.'

"In the special prayer set forth in my letter the 30th ult., for the words, 'and the Convention of Southern States,' substitute the words, 'and the Congress of the Confederate states.' " The prayer for the Legislature would continue as previously directed.[14]

Bishop Polk spent the month of February quietly visiting the parishes of his diocese. On March 13, he left for Sewanee, stopping at Memphis for a visit with Bishop Otey. "Talked of the times & my position—Saw no reason for changing my ground," Polk wrote in his diary.[15] He did, however, request Otey to put his opinions in writing. Polk then left by train for Cowan, arriving on the fifteenth. After a night's rest, he walked up the mountain to Sewanee which made him "very tired." [16]

Bishop Elliott arrived on the mountain on March 20, and the two bishops spent the next day discussing the political condition of the country and its effect on the Church. Apparently Elliott agreed with Polk's views and sanctioned the action he had taken. On March 23 they decided to write a letter to other Southern bishops giving their views as to the course to be taken by the dioceses of the Confederate States.[17]

The change in civil relations, they began, had made necessary a

[13] Hopkins to Polk, May 23, 1861, *ibid.*
[14] Diocese of Louisiana, *Journal of Convention* (1861), 33.
[15] Polk, "Diary for 1861."   [16] *Ibid.*   [17] *Ibid.*

conference of the Dioceses of the Confederate States for the purpose of deciding their relationship to the Episcopal Church of the
United States. This necessity was not a result of dissension within
the Church nor any disagreement on discipline or doctrine. In
faith and purpose the Church was still united. Yet political developments had made it necessary that the Southern dioceses give
immediate attention to their ecclesiastical relations.[18] It was suggested that each diocese send three clerical and three lay delegates
to a meeting at Montgomery on July 3.

Before receiving the letter from Polk and Elliott, Bishop Otey
had put his views in writing and addressed the letter to Polk. He
disapproved of the action Polk had taken. The Church, he wrote,
was the kingdom of Christ established on earth. From its foundation "it was a kingdom in the world, but not of the world. It was a
kingdom superior to & above all other kingdoms and destined to
out last all dynasties of human origin or construction. . . . The
authority given by Christ to his ministers is single & alone & derives
not one particle of its power, its validity & its binding obligations
from the state. All ministers who claim to be ambassadors for
Christ, act in the name of the Father, Son & H. Gost. For performance of any strictly religious & ecclesiastical act they are accountable for its performance or neglect to no tribunal of human organization or origin." The state had no part in naming bishops;
therefore, no bishop was responsible to the state for performance
of his duties. There was no obligation to follow nationality.

Otey denied that the existing situation was the same as that of
the American Colonies. "The colonial church did not by any act
jointly or severally in her congregations declare her independence
of the Anglican Church. She was left to herself without help—or
Bishop or Protector save God! But you without any action on the
part of your Brethren with whom ecclesiastical relations were established, the most solemn the soul of man can realize, declare
that these ties are dissolved, that you have an independent Diocesan existence, because the State of La has by an ordinance
declared an independent sovereignty." [19] At the time of this writing
Otey's own state of Tennessee had not seceded; it had even voted
against the holding of a convention.

In reply Polk complained that Otey had misunderstood both

[18] Polk and Elliott to Dear Brother, March 23, 1861, Leonidas Polk Papers.
[19] Otey to Polk, March 18, 1861, *ibid.*

his position and his purpose and referred the Tennessee Bishop to a second pastoral letter issued March 28, 1861.[20]

Many church officials, both North and South, disapproved of the position taken by Bishop Polk. And immediately there arose the question of what was to be done with missionary funds collected if the Church in the seceding state was no longer to be a part of the national organization. Polk's pastoral letter of March 28 was an attempt at clarification. His letter of January 30, he explained, was designed to present the change of status of the Church in Louisiana, a result of which he found it necessary to alter the Book of Common Prayer as used in his diocese. Nothing more was determined by that letter. It did, however, look toward a probable union of the dioceses of all seceding states. It did not suggest that union between such an organization and that of other states would be impracticable.

A change in status Bishop Polk argued, did not necessarily lead to a breach of church unity. *"Christ hath made us free,"* and this freedom carried with it the liberty to change status when necessity dictated, provided church doctrine and order of administration remained unchanged. The organization of the Confederate States of America had been completed, Polk concluded. No doubt the dioceses within this confederacy would soon form a union. Even after this was done there would be no reason for church organizations, North and South, not to act together in matters that were above the local level. As to funds for missions, he recommended that they be forwarded in accordance with the established practice.[21]

During March and April, 1861, Bishop Polk continued visiting his parishes, while his family remained at Sewanee. As war clouds gathered he withdrew Meck from V.M.I. and instructed him to go to Sewanee. Now that hostilities had begun with an attack upon Fort Sumter, the Bishop wrote his wife, the South would soon be in need of the services of all of its young men.[22] A month later Meck was at Camp Trousdale serving as "a sort of aid de camp to General Zollicoffer." [23]

[20] Polk to Otey, April 24, 1861, *ibid.*
[21] Diocese of Louisiana, *Journal of Convention* (1861), 34–36.
[22] Polk to Wife, April 21, 1861, quoted in Polk, *Leonidas Polk*, I, 323.
[23] Mecklenburg Polk to Mother, May 28, 1861, Leonidas Polk Papers.

From his visitation in the Shreveport parish Bishop Polk returned to New Orleans by cattle boat. While at the stock-landing he dashed off a note to his family. He had enjoyed a good night's rest down the river and felt much refreshed although greatly concerned. "The whole world is in arms, in the country and in the town. All are agreed now. There are not two parties any more, and I am glad to see that we are at last to have the border States. Of the issue I have no doubt. As Tennessee is now aroused, you are, of course, in a very safe and secure place, and need have no apprehension." [24]

From the landing Polk went to his New Orleans lodging. There he found four letters from his wife and daughters telling of their plight in their place of "security." During the night of April 12 the "crude but comfortable" Polk cottage at Sewanee and the Elliotts' cottage nearby had been burned. An unknown person tossed a burning object through the window of the "company chamber" of the Polk cottage. Mrs. Polk and the girls were dragged to safety by their faithful servant Altimore. The only items of clothing saved were the garments then in the laundry. The silver plate stored in a basket and the portraits of the Devereuxs were all that escaped the flames. Among valuables lost was the entire correspondence between Polk and his wife from the days of their courtship to settlement at Sewanee. Bishop Elliott's cottage was in flames at the same time, but the Elliotts were not at home. "I think it was the work of some abolitionist," wrote Mrs. Polk.[25]

"Was there ever in all the world such a hellish proceeding?" exclaimed Bishop Polk from New Orleans. "To fire the houses of two such utterly lonely and defenseless families, composed of

[24] Polk to Wife, April 26, 1861, quoted in Polk, *Leonidas Polk*, I, 324. In his letters Meck made no mention of Professor Thomas J. Jackson, but later, after "Stonewall" Jackson had become famous, he recalled the professor as "a persevering but rather dull master" whom the cadets delighted in irritating. At the outbreak of the war the cadets demanded a speech from Jackson. He responded: " 'Soldiers make short speeches: be slow to draw the sword in civil strife, but when you draw it throw away the scabbard.' " The enthusiasm created by this short remark was "beyond description." Walter Lord (ed.), *The Fremantle Diary* . . . (Boston, 1954), 120–21.

[25] For details see Frances Polk to Leonidas Polk, April 15, 1861, Gale Papers; *id.* to Susan Rayner, April 16, 1861, Leonidas Polk Papers; Henry C. Yeatman to Mary Yeatman, April 15, 1861, Polk-Yeatman Papers; Stephen Elliott to George R. Fairbanks (n.p., n.d.), Baker *et al.* (eds.), *Sewanee*, 18–19.

women only, and in the dead of night! The spirit of hell was never more exhibited . . . such a diabolical spirit and heart I never before heard of. How I should have liked to come upon the scoundrels when they were engaged in the act! I am satisfied that it was the work of an incendiary, and that it was prompted by the spirit of Black Republican hate." [26]

Since Bishop Polk's course had met with some criticism at home as well as abroad, the 1861 meeting of the convention of the Diocese of Louisiana was of considerable importance. It assembled at St. Francisville in May. Since Louisiana had seen fit to exercise her indefeasible right to sever her connection with the United States, Bishop Polk explained to the delegates, citizens of that state had ceased to be citizens of the United States. It was the duty of churchmen to recognize this change just as the Founder of the church had urged his followers to recognize *de facto* governments. Both church and State were divine institutions. "So that whether it be Sanhedrin or Caesar, 'the Powers that be are ordained of God.' They are to be supported, not only with material aid and personal services, but by supplication and prayers." It was therefore the duty of the church under the present circumstances "to alter her formularies, so as to make them conform to the new condition of things."

But the constitution of the Protestant Episcopal Church in the United States reserved to a national convention all powers to make alterations in the Book of Common Prayer; consequently, there was a conflict between the duty of the Diocese of Louisiana "to pray for the Rulers of one Government, and the duty which we owe to the Law of Christ Himself, which required us to pray for those of another." In such a conflict he as bishop could make but one decision—the law of Christ must prevail.

Bishop Polk further explained that the Diocese of Louisiana was admitted to the Protestant Episcopal Church in the United States upon its own application. In accepting membership in this national organization, however, the diocese "did not intend to impose upon herself impossible obligations, which in any future contingency would conflict with her duties to Christ." Certain inalienable rights were reserved and were now being exercised by

[26] Leonidas Polk to Frances Polk, April 27, 1861, quoted in Polk, *Leonidas Polk*, I, 326–27.

the diocese. ". . . we have been forced, whether we would or not, into the position of Diocesan Independence."

Although the state had no control over the church, its action must always have important bearing upon church action. In Louisiana the Church "assumes what her duty to her Lord requires her to assume, that, though she be compelled to set aside her obligation to her Ecclesiastical Constitution in the United States of America, she must follow her nationality. . . . The destruction of this constitutional bond, while it may be lamented, carries not with it the destruction of the Oneness of the Body of Christ. The elements of which that consists are of a higher and more enduring nature."

Believing in the expediency of the union of dioceses, Bishop Polk concluded, he and Bishop Elliott had addressed other bishops of the Confederate States inviting them and their dioceses to participate in a convention to be held in Montgomery on July 3 for the purpose of consulting "upon such matters of interest to the Church as have arisen out of the changes in our civil affairs, with the view of securing uniformity and harmony of action." He wished to submit to his own diocese this same proposal for co-operation in the interest of uniformity and harmony.[27]

Bishop Polk's address and proposal were referred to the convention's Committee on the State of the Church. The committee's report approved the action taken by the Bishop and urged the appointment of delegates to the proposed Montgomery convention.

Of more immediate concern to Polk than even the position the church should take in the crisis was the question of defense of the Mississippi Valley against possible invasion from the North. Family background combined with West Point training to give him a soldier's viewpoint. On May 14, 1861, he wrote President Jefferson Davis at Montgomery expressing concern for the safety of the Valley. Davis assured him that there was no immediate danger. He thought the people in the North had too much dread for Southern summer heat to attempt invasion at that time. Nevertheless, precautionary steps were already being taken to meet any advancing columns. Guns were being mounted at strategic points along the Mississippi and troops assembled at Union City, Tennessee, and

[27] Diocese of Louisiana, *Journal of Convention* (1861).

Corinth, Mississippi, "to sustain the batteries on the river." In closing, the President assured the Bishop: "It would gratify me very much to see you." [28]

It is not certain that there was any special significance to this statement. Yet in the light of future developments, it would seem probable that Davis was already planning on making use of the fighting qualities of the Polk family. Polk also wrote to Leroy Pope Walker, Confederate Secretary of War, calling attention to the "defence of this portion of our border." Lincoln's aim was no longer in doubt. "His line is that of aggression & if possible conquest," Polk charged. "He has stifled Maryland & paralyzed Missouri. His next victim in order is Kentucky. What is to be done?" [29]

At the close of the session of the Louisiana Convention Bishop Polk left for Middle Tennessee to visit his family. His married daughter, Mrs. Gale, was spending the summer at the Gale estate near Nashville. Following the fire at Sewanee Mrs. Polk and her other daughters had gone to Hamilton Place. While visiting in Nashville Polk conferred with Governor Isham G. Harris. The governor solicited his assistance in completing the armament of Tennessee troops, many of whom had already moved to Virginia. Polk also wished to visit the Louisiana troops now concentrating in Virginia. Add to this the desire to confer in person with President Davis, now in Richmond, and we have the motives that prompted Bishop Polk to visit Richmond early in June, 1861.

A few days after arrival he could write his wife:

> I am quite well & have had good reason to know that my visit here has been of decided use to our cause in several important particulars. I have dined with Davis & members of his cabinet & have had two long & full conversations with him in which I discussed matters pertaining to our affairs with great freedom & fullness. He has received me with great kindness and confidence & I think the interview will not be otherwise than productive of good results. I think well of him. He is the best man we could have had & commands general confidence. We want & he wants

[28] Jefferson Davis to Leonidas Polk, May 22, 1861, quoted in Polk, *Leonidas Polk*, I, 352–53.

[29] Leonidas Polk to Leroy Pope Walker, May 27, 1861, Leonidas Polk Papers.

Genl A. S. Johnston badly. He has not yet arrived. I have had several interviews with Genl Lee. He is a highly accomplished man, but my friend Johnston is his superior. . . . Davis will take the field in person when the movement is to be made. I am doing what I can to serve Tennessee in getting field batteries. . . ."[30]

He made no mention of any plan to become an active participant.

But a week later he had more important news. President Davis had requested that he accept a commission as brigadier general in the Confederate army; military and civilian friends, some of them from New Orleans, were urging him to accept. But he declined giving an immediate answer. "No man is more deeply impressed with the paramount importance of our success in this movement and more filled with apprehension at the prospect of its failure," he explained. ". . . What my duty may be I have not yet determined. I see how things are going on around me & I see much very much on the part of persons in position which invokes sharp criticism. . . . I cannot ignore what I know. I cannot forget what I have learned, nor can I forget that I have been educated by the country for its service in certain contingencies."

In view of the great importance of his decision he would not act hastily, he assured his wife. He was leaving the following day for a visit with Bishop William Meade, president of the Virginia Theological Seminary since 1842, who resided near Millwood. Along the route he would pass Manassas Gap where important battles were expected soon. Troops from all quarters were moving into Virginia and the people appeared resolute and determined.[31] Polk traveled extensively among these troops, particularly those from Louisiana, often conducting open-air services. In addition to Manassas he visited Yorktown, Norfolk, Bethel Church, and Winchester. The twelve thousand Louisiana troops he had seen, he reported, were the flower of her youth, a group of which he felt proud.

The visit with Bishop Meade was just what Polk needed to convince him that he should accept a military commission. The two bishops discussed at length all matters relating to church and state. Polk was delighted with Father Meade, describing him as "a

[30] *Id.* to Wife, June 10, 1861, *ibid.*   [31] *Id.* to *id.,* June 19, 1861, *ibid.*

regular old Roman, . . . quite ready to be southern all through,"
eager for "a downright good fight," unwilling to sanction "half
way measures," and "very refreshing."

Meade explained that as a general rule he could not sanction a
bishop's acceptance of a military commission, but since "all rules
have exceptions & taking all things into consideration as they relate
to the condition of the country," and to Bishop Polk personally, he
could not condemn Polk's course should he accept a commission.

Meade convinced Polk, if he needed convincing, yet in relating
the details to Bishop Elliott, Polk stressed that he reserved the
decision for himself. "Under all the circumstances I cannot see
how I could stand excused in my own judgment & conscience in
declining it." By the time he returned to Richmond his mind was
made up. He accepted a commission. "I believe most solemnly,"
he confided to Bishop Elliott, "that it is for Constitutional liberty,
which seems to have fled to us for refuge, for our hearth stones and
our altars that we strike. I hope I shall be supported in the work
and have grace to do my duty." [32]

Polk explained to his wife that both before and after his conference with Bishop Meade he was urged by a deputation of gentlemen from the Mississippi Valley to accept command in that area.
For a week he thought and prayed over the matter. "I find my
mind unable to say No to this call, for it seems to be a call of
Providence. I shall, therefore, looking to God for his guidance and
blessing, say to President Davis that I will do what I can for my
country, our hearth-stones, and our altars. . . . And may the Lord
have mercy upon me, and help me to be wise, to be sagacious, to
be firm, to be merciful, and to be filled with all the knowledge and
all the graces necessary to qualify me to fill the office to his glory
and the good of men." [33]

There is no ground for doubting Bishop Polk's sincerity when he
classed the Confederate cause as a holy one. He had never sought
glory or fame. It is unlikely that anything short of what he believed
to be a call of Providence could have even temporarily pulled him
away from his Diocese and University. President Davis later recalled that "Nothing impressed me more in the interview [with
Polk] . . . than the confidence manifested by this great and holy

[32] *Id.* to Stephen Elliott, June 22, 1861, *ibid.*
[33] *Id.* to Wife, June 22, 1861, quoted in Polk, *Leonidas Polk,* I, 358–59.

man, that he had a sure correspondence with his God, and was treading in the path approved by Him." [34]

Polk received numerous letters from clergy and laity expressing surprise or astonishment at his decision to enter military service. Several writers suggested that he might have waited until the emergency became greater. Others urged him to continue as bishop even though now a general. Most of his correspondents, however, approved the course he had chosen. Bishop Elliott wisely suggested that, while he himself agreed with Bishop Meade, Bishop-General Polk must expect to be subjected to "the ordeal of all men who do unusual things—Success or failure will be made criterion of right or wrong—If you succeed, you will need no defenders; if you fail, such is the world, you will have a pack of curs at your heels, especially all those you may have had occasion to kick during your previous life." [35]

In personal appearance Leonidas Polk was as much soldier as bishop. "Of good stature and an erect military carriage, broad shouldered and deep in the chest, with a well-poised, shapely head, strong but finely-cut features, one white lock overhanging his wide forehead, clear complexion, and keen but frank and kindly blue eyes, the first glance recognized him as a man to be obeyed; a closer scrutiny revealed him as a man whom noble men might love, and meaner men might fear."

In scholarly attainments he was not so well balanced. His West Point training had included little that could be classed as literary. "Of classics he knew little," observed a close friend. The same was true of theology. "Of canon law, with the exception of our small American code, he knew nothing at all." But he possessed personal characteristics that largely overcame other weaknesses. "In conversation he was wonderfully charming. In preaching and writing he was clear and vigorous, but at times diffuse. His habit of mind was to grasp at the root-principles of things, and the clearness of his thoughts was always apparent, though his style of composition lacked the graceful facility of expression, the fertility of illustration, and the facility of arrangement which belong to the accomplished scholar." Consciousness of his own weaknesses caused him to

---

[34] Jefferson Davis to William Mecklenburg Polk, December 15, 1879, Leonidas Polk Papers.
[35] Elliott to Polk, August 6, 1861, *ibid.*

admire scholarship in others and inspired his leadership in the cause of education.[36]

Bishop Polk did not consult his diocese before making his decision to accept a military commission; he considered his decision a private matter. Neither did he suggest giving up his episcopacy. Instead, considering himself on temporary leave, he merely notified his diocese that he had entered the service of the Confederacy "because it seemed the duty next me." His prayer was for a quick termination of hostilities and an early return to his chosen work.[37] Bishops Otey and Elliott promised to give some time to the Louisiana Diocese.

The commission accepted was that of major general, not brigadier, and the command was to embrace that portion of Alabama north of the Tennessee River, that part of Tennessee south and west of the Tennessee River, the Mississippi River counties of Arkansas and Mississippi plus that portion of North Mississippi including Corinth and extending to Eastport on the Tennessee, and the Louisiana parishes north of Red River.[38]

As Bishop-General Polk descended the steps of the Virginia Capitol following his conference with President Davis a friend stepped forward to congratulate him on his promotion. " 'Pardon me,' said Polk gravely; 'I do not consider it a promotion. The highest office on earth is that of a bishop in the Church of God.' " When another friend exclaimed in surprise, " 'What! you, a bishop, throw off the gown for the sword!' " Polk replied, " 'No, sir, I buckle the sword over the gown.' " [39]

[36] The above quotations are from Fulton, "The Church in the Confederate States," *loc. cit.*, 2563. During the 1850's Fulton was a New Orleans clergyman and close personal friend of Bishop Polk.

[37] Leonidas Polk to Stephen Elliott, June 22, 1861, Leonidas Polk Papers.

[38] S. Cooper to Polk, June 25, 1861, *The War of Rebellion: A Compilation of the Official Records of the Union and Confederate Armies* (Washington, 1880–1901), Series I, LII, Pt. 2, 115. Hereafter cited as *Official Records*. All citations are to Series I unless otherwise noted.

[39] Polk, *Leonidas Polk*, I, 362.

(10)

"Not By Choice, But By Necessity"

GENERAL POLK DESIGNATED Memphis as headquarters for Department No. 2. Traveling by rail through East Tennessee to Chattanooga, thence to Nashville, he was in the Tennessee capital by July 9, 1861. President Davis had requested that he check on conditions in East Tennessee while passing through. From Nashville Polk reported that "No time is to be lost in East Tennessee." Not more than 2,000 men were available for duty there; 10,000 were needed immediately. He urged that East Tennessee be made a separate department and that Felix K. Zollicoffer of the Tennessee forces be assigned to command as "brigadier of the Provisional Army." In this he said Governor Isham G. Harris concurred.[1]

After a brief conference with Governor Harris at Nashville General Polk hurried on to Memphis where, on July 13, he issued General Orders No. 1, officially assuming command of his department. The Memphis public and press gave him an enthusiastic reception. The Memphis *Appeal* proclaimed editorially: "Bishop Polk has devoted the flower of his talent and life to the service of that God that he now draws his sword to defend. Like Jephthah, Gideon, and David, he is marshaling his legions to fight the battle of the Lord, even Israels God, the Lord of Hosts! All hail to our intrepid and wise chief, who has chosen to sanctify the western division of the Confederate army by the miter above the girdles and stars!" [2]

In assuming command of Department No. 2 Polk spoke as much as bishop as soldier. He assured his army and the general public

[1] Leonidas Polk to Jefferson Davis, July 9, 1861, *Official Records*, IV, 365–66.
[2] July 7, 1861.

that the unhappy conflict in which they were now compelled to engage was "not warranted by reason or any necessity . . . but that it is indefensible and of unparalleled atrocity." The South had asked no more than to be permitted "to repose in quietness under our own vine and . . . fig tree." It wanted no more than the right of freemen to enjoy self government, a right that only tyrants would deny. But there could be no peaceable enjoyment of these rights, for those who once pretended fraternal regard had now decreed merciless war to destroy Southern rights, fortunes, and lives. Such a war, motivated by lust or hate, although under the pretense of a restoration of the Union, could result only in ruin. "Of all the absurdities ever enacted, of all the hypocrisies ever practiced, an attempt to restore a union of minds, hearts, and wills like that which once existed in North America, by the ravages of fire and sword, are assuredly among the most prodigious." Just as sure as there was a righteous Ruler of the universe, those who instigated and prosecuted such a war must eventually suffer disaster.

Since the South's solemn protests had gone unheeded and even those persons of the North who once opposed invasion had now joined in the prosecution of this "unnatural, unchristian, and cruel war," the General explained, the people of the South were "left alone, under God, to the resources of our minds and our own hearts, to the resources of manhood." No longer was there a choice of courses. Persons of all ages and conditions must unite "in one grand and holy purpose of rolling back the desolating tide of invasion, and of restoring to the people of the South that peace, independence, and right of self-government to which they are by nature and by nature's God as justly entitled as those who seek thus ruthlessly to enslave them. . . . A cause which has for its object nothing less than the security of civil liberty and the preservation of the purity of religious truth, is the cause of Heaven, and may well challenge the homage and service of the patriot and Christian. In God is our trust." [3]

Even though impressed by the enthusiasm in the Memphis area and convinced that united resistance was the only course left to Southern people, one who had recently traveled through East

[3] *Official Records*, IV, 368–69.

Tennessee must have realized the difficulties in building Southern unity, even in resistance to probable invasion.

Two problems immediately confronted General Polk as he took command in the Mississippi Valley. First, he must receive into the Confederate service the provisional army of Tennessee, which would constitute the major portion of his forces. Next he must ascertain the location and strength of the numerous small fighting units within the department and prepare for concentration and defense of the more strategic points. Solution of the first problem would not be difficult, except for a few technicalities. The second, however, would be greatly complicated by Kentucky's declaration of neutrality and by the civil war already in progress in Missouri.

When Polk arrived in Memphis he found instructions from Adjutant General Samuel Cooper authorizing him to make preparation to receive the Tennessee troops. Enclosed was a letter to Governor Harris, setting forth the steps necessary in implementing such a transfer.[4] In anticipation of his state's official separation from the Union, Governor Harris, with legislative sanction, had organized a force of about 22,000 men and appointed a full quota of staff officers. In command of this force was Major General Gideon J. Pillow, a veteran of the Mexican War and sometime law partner of the late James K. Polk. What was to be the status of these officers once the Tennessee forces were received into Confederate service? Governor Harris urged that where possible they be given Confederate commissions of rank equal to that held in the Tennessee army. Then there was the question of the disposition of military stores collected and paid for by Tennessee. If these were to be taken over by the Confederacy, Tennessee would expect to be reimbursed.[5]

General Polk was agreeable; he needed both the military stores and the better qualified Tennessee officers. He recommended that Pillow be commissioned major general and Benjamin F. Cheatham brigadier. Both were made brigadiers, dating from July 9, 1861. Pillow reluctantly accepted the reduction in rank, but he never became reconciled to being subordinate to men of no

---

[4] Cooper to Polk, July 5, 1861, *ibid.*, 362–63.
[5] G. Gantt to Leroy P. Walker, July 23, 1861, *ibid.*, 372–73.

previous military service or those he had outranked in the Mexican
War.

Recognizing Polk's immediate need for troops, Governor Harris
made the Tennessee forces subject to Confederate command even
before details of transfer had been worked out. Thus Pillow's force
of about 6,000 men stationed in West Tennessee became the core
of Polk's army. Other units were scattered. Governor Claibourne
Jackson of Missouri arrived in Memphis on July 22 on his way to
Richmond, bringing exaggerated reports of military strength in his
state. General Benjamin McCulloch was on the Arkansas line, he
reported, with about 6,000 Confederate troops, mostly from Arkansas and Louisiana. General Sterling Price was twelve miles away
with 12,000 Missourians. And reports from General William J. Hardee's camp in Arkansas were that he had about 7,000 men at Pocahontas ready for action.[6]

Polk was optimistic; he immediately began plans for offensive action. Price and McCulloch with a combined force of about 25,000
would advance against Springfield, Missouri, where Union commander Nathaniel Lyon was reported to have only 10,000 to 12,-
000 men. Meanwhile, Pillow would move his 6,000 men into Missouri by way of New Madrid. There he would be joined by 3,000
Missourians reported to be stationed near by. By that time Polk
hoped to have two more regiments ready to join Pillow, raising his
strength to 11,000.

From New Madrid the advance would be toward Ironton where
Pillow would join forces with Hardee moving up from Pocahontas.
The combined force would then move triumphantly toward St.
Louis, isolating Lyon, seize the city and the boats on the river, and
then turn up the Missouri "raising the Missourians as they go." If
still more troops were needed Polk had promise of an additional
10,000 from Arkansas.

If all went well in Missouri, Confederate forces might cross into
Illinois and take Cairo from the rear. In view of the recent Federal
defeat at Manassas, Polk had no fear that heavy reinforcements
could be sent to the West. To provide for a possible emergency
east of the Mississippi, Governor Harris had promised to recruit
more Tennesseans. Many men could also be drawn from "neutral"

---

[6] Leonidas Polk to *id.*, July 23, 1861, *ibid.*, III, 612–13.

Kentucky. ". . . and I may add," Polk suggested to Richmond authorities, "that every man we draw out of Kentucky relieves us from drawing so much on Tennessee and the States south of us." [7] Never again was General Polk to enjoy such pleasant dreams of complete victory.

As would often be the case in this and other theaters of operation throughout the war, reliable information proved unreliable. Instead of 7,000 men at Pocahontas, Hardee reported only 2,300 effectives. And it was soon learned that Governor Jackson had reported Price and McCulloch twice as strong as they actually were. When these two generals called upon Hardee for active co-operation he declined, reporting that even when all expected units had joined him he would still have no more than 5,000 poorly equipped men "without discipline, without instruction, and without transportation." [8]

In view of revised information, Polk realized that his plan for extensive operation in Missouri must at least be delayed. Yet he urged the War Department that an active campaign be launched in Missouri before the Federals recovered from Manassas. While operating in Missouri a careful eye should also be held on neutral Kentucky. Polk ordered Pillow to move to New Madrid immediately.[9]

This Pillow did promptly without incident, and he was much impressed by the effective operation of the fleet of eight large steamers which transported his men and baggage across the river.[10]

He was so impressed with his reception at New Madrid that he designated his force the "Army of Liberation" and urged immediate advance upon Ironton. However, Hardee, who now had headquarters at Pitman's Ferry and was soon to send his advance column as far as Greenville, advised caution. Pillow should wait, he urged, until he too was in position to move with his 4,000 available men. He erroneously estimated Pillow's force at about 10,000.[11]

Polk, realizing his inability to send the re-enforcements required, restrained Pillow, and Pillow grew very impatient. "I have never

[7] *Ibid.*
[8] William J. Hardee to Leonidas Polk, July 28, 1861, *ibid.*, 618–19.
[9] Leonidas Polk to Leroy P. Walker, July 28, 1861, *ibid.*, 617–18.
[10] Gideon Pillow to Leonidas Polk, July 28, 1861, *ibid.*, 619.
[11] William J. Hardee to *id.*, July 29, 30, August 4, 1861, *ibid.*, 619, 620, 629; Gideon Pillow to *id.*, July 30, 1861, *ibid.*, 620–21.

been in favor of occupying this place [New Madrid], except as a base of operation for movements into the interior," he wrote. If such a move was not intended then he should be ordered back to a stronger position at Randolph or Fort Pillow. "I am clearly of the opinion that we should advance *promptly* or *abandon* this place." [12]

Polk was unwilling to order either advance or withdrawal. Instead he called upon Richmond for more troops. He was further disturbed by reports from Kentucky friends that as soon as the state election was over the Federals planned to disregard Kentucky neutrality. Union General B. M. Prentiss was quoted as admitting as much. [13]

Pillow, unhappy at not being sufficiently re-enforced for movement into the interior of Missouri, threatened attack upon Cape Girardeau or Bird's Point. Hardee advised against it. It was always desirable to whip the enemy but there should be no fighting without an object. What could be gained by capture of either of these points? Any base held on the Mississippi would be constantly in danger. Pillow, therefore, instead of attempting to capture more should abandon the base he had and join Hardee at Pitman's Ferry. Their combined force, Hardee explained, could then "take Ironton, march on Rolla; then abandon our base of operation, cut off Lyon from his communications, attack and rout him; then march with all our forces combined (yours, McCulloch's, Jackson's, and mine) on Saint Louis. With Saint Louis in our possession, the points you are going to attack would be turned, and must fall as a necessary consequence." [14]

Pillow was not inclined to abandon the river and join Hardee. Instead he continued to call for re-enforcements. Governor Jackson ordered Jeff Thompson's Missourians to his aid but they never arrived. Pillow confided to Polk that he expected little assistance from Missouri troops, for they were in poor condition—no discipline, no staff officers, no money, no supplies, except those seized from the civil population. [15]

[12] *Id.* to *id.*, August 5, 1861, *ibid.*, 630.
[13] C. Wickliffe to *id.*, August 6, 1861, *ibid.*, IV, 381.
[14] William J. Hardee to Gideon Pillow, August 7, 1861, *ibid.*, III, 633–34.
[15] *Id.* to Leonidas Polk, August 11, 1861, *ibid.*, 641–42; Gideon Pillow to *id.*, August 9, 1861, *ibid.*, 639–40.

Polk did not approve of Pillow's proposal to take the offensive, but he did realize the need for re-enforcements. The Federals were now reported to have 20,000 men at Cairo and a considerable force at Cape Girardeau. If promises could be relied upon, Polk saw a possibility of securing sufficient manpower from the surrounding territory. He requested permission from Richmond to enroll troops as fast as he could equip them. He hoped soon to have ammunition in abundance. Plenty of lead could be secured in Arkansas. Near Memphis there were two powder factories about ready for full production. And the cap factory would soon be producing 100,000 per day.[16]

Considering the two Confederate forces too weak to act independently, Polk ordered Pillow to join Hardee, but the junction was never effected. A Federal threat down the Mississippi caused Polk to order the fortification of Island No. 10 and the Tennessee side of the river opposite it. Examination by an experienced engineer revealed that no place above Memphis was so well situated for protection from invasion by land or water as Island No. 10.[17]

In spite of much talk and many promises, few re-enforcements arrived. Two Mississippi regiments moved up to Union City, but before Polk could send them to either Pillow or Hardee the War Department ordered him to rush them to Zollicoffer in East Tennessee. The only other regiment immediately available was the Fourth Tennessee commanded by Colonel R. P. Neely. This Polk ordered to Island No. 10, but when it arrived at New Madrid Pillow changed the order and attached it to his advance for a probable invasion of Missouri. Neely protested and reported the matter to Polk.[18]

Polk demanded an explanation and Pillow, assuming a self-righteous, injured attitude, explained that Captain A. B. Gray, the officer directing the fortification of Island No. 10, neither needed nor wanted the Fourth Tennessee. "I have no motive to gratify but to serve the country; and it seems to me that you ought to be disposed to strengthen the force all you could," he complained. "If

[16] Leonidas Polk to Leroy P. Walker, August 9, 1861, *ibid.*, LII, Pt. 2, 128–29.

[17] Report of Captain A. B. Gray, August 15, 1861, *ibid.*, III, 651–52.

[18] S. Cooper to Leonidas Polk, August 13, 1861, *ibid.*, LII, Pt. 2, 129; R. P. Neely to *id.*, August 19, 1861, *ibid.*, III, 662.

I have not your confidence, and if I am to be tied down and allowed no *discretion*, I certainly cannot but regard it unfortunate that I yielded to your wishes and accepted a command my feelings so strongly prompted me to decline. . . . If I have fitness for command you ought not to incline to cripple my energies. If I have not, and possess not your confidence, it would be better for the interest of the service that I had not been intrusted with this important command." [19]

Polk quickly assured the injured General that there was no desire to cripple his energies and that his discretion would not be curtailed unless he showed a disposition "to exceed your lawful authority." The matter would not be called to the attention of the War Department and would be given no "further notice or recollection." [20] There the matter rested but the Commanding General must have again questioned his own wisdom in selecting Pillow his second in command.

Soon came news of the battle of Wilson's Creek (August 10) in which the combined forces of Price and McCulloch met the Missouri Unionists under Lyon. The battle was at best a draw, with casualties about equal. But Lyon was killed and his forces fell back to Springfield and thence to St. Louis.[21] Pillow, seizing upon this news as evidence that Union strength in Missouri was on the decline, renewed his request for permission to invade the state. If Polk would only give him additional ordnance and subsistence stores, he urged, "I will drive everything out of my way, join Hardee in five days, and push on to Saint Louis, destroying the railroad; but for God's sake don't hold me back or cripple me. . . ." [22]

Polk was not too much impressed by Pillow's clamor, but he did wish to know what Hardee was in position to do. Hardee reported inability to move until crops had been harvested and reenforcements had arrived. In view of this continued weakness, Polk suggested that Hardee leave a portion of his small force to protect the Arkansas saltpeter mines and transfer the remainder to the

---

[19] Gideon Pillow to *id.*, August 20, 1861, *ibid.*, 664–65.

[20] Leonidas Polk to Gideon Pillow, August 23, 1861, *ibid.*, 669–70.

[21] For a detailed account of this engagement see Jay Monaghan, *Civil War on the Western Border, 1854–1865* (Boston, 1955), 170 ff.

[22] Gideon Pillow to Leonidas Polk, August 16, 1861, *Official Records*, III, 654–55.

Mississippi near Chalk Bluff or New Madrid. Pillow was instructed to pull his advance back from Benton and Sikeston and divide it for defense at New Madrid, Island No. 10, and Union City.[23]

Before receiving these instructions Pillow was considering the occupation and fortification of Columbus, Kentucky. This was really "the gateway into Tennessee," he wrote Polk, and the first truly strong point above Fort Pillow. He considered Kentucky a boiling caldron. Organized Union forces in at least five counties were threatening to move into Tennessee. Kentucky could no longer be classed as neutral. A strong point like Columbus must soon be occupied by either the Confederacy or the Union. If Union forces moved in first they could not be driven out. But if he were only given permission to move first, Pillow explained, he would be there before the enemy suspected his object. Such a movement was absolutely necessary and it was justified by Kentucky's abandonment of neutrality.[24] Engineer Gray supported Pillow with a statement that "I regard it as a military necessity to occupy and fortify that place."[25]

None of this was news to General Polk; for three months he had been collecting information on Kentucky "neutrality." When Lincoln issued his call for troops following the fall of Fort Sumter, Governor Beriah Magoffin of Kentucky had refused to furnish any. There was strong feeling throughout the state that Kentucky should take no part in the controversy between North and South and hope that as a neutral she might assist in bringing about a peaceable settlement. On May 16, 1861, the Kentucky House of Representatives passed a resolution calling for a position of strict neutrality. (A similar resolution was later passed by the senate). Four days later Governor Magoffin issued a proclamation urging all Kentuckians to guard their words and actions so as to give neither offense nor assistance to either belligerent.[26]

Reports of Federal plans to invade Tennessee through Kentucky made the question of neutrality a matter of serious concern

[23] Leonidas Polk to William J. Hardee, August 26, 1861, *ibid.*, 682–83; *id.* to Gideon Pillow, August 26, 1861, *ibid.*, 683–84.

[24] Gideon Pillow to Leonidas Polk, August 28, 1861, *ibid.*, 685–87.

[25] A. B. Gray to *id.*, August 29, 1861, *ibid.*, 687.

[26] E. Merton Coulter, *The Civil War and Readjustment in Kentucky* (Chapel Hill, 1926), 54–56.

at Polk's headquarters. The list of Kentucky concessions to Union strength continued to grow.[27] Conscious of the Federal build-up in the Mississippi Valley and the weakness of the scattered Confederate units opposing the enemy's progress, Polk urged President Davis to place all forces in the west under a single commander, giving him large discretionary powers. For this responsible position he could think of no one but his old West Point roommate Albert Sidney Johnston. "The success of our campaign in this valley may depend upon such an arrangement, and I know of no man who has the capacity to fill the position, who could be had, but General Johnston." [28]

Before this recommendation reached Richmond, Polk's command was "extended to embrace the State of Arkansas and all military operations in the State of Missouri." [29] Some such extension of command had long been needed, for Pillow's force alone was technically subject to Polk's orders. Price and Thompson commanded Missouri troops; McCulloch was on his own; and Hardee had requested Polk to remember that the "Secretary of War, in assigning me to command in Arkansas, directed me to protect the district included in my command and the counties in Missouri contiguous thereto." Although always eager to cooperate with Polk, "I must not lose sight of my instructions or my duty to Arkansas." [30]

Federal forces in Southeastern Missouri were now under the immediate command of General U. S. Grant. The occupation of Columbus was already in the mind of his superior, General John C. Fremont, if not Grant himself. When Grant was assigned to command he was informed that occupation of Columbus was a part of the plan.[31] Considering as reliable the numerous reports of Federal plans to disregard Kentucky neutrality, Polk decided to seize the initiative. On September 1, 1861, he dispatched a note to Governor Magoffin requesting full information as to the "future plans and policy of the Southern party in Kentucky" and stressing that

[27] Polk to John M. Johnston, September 9, 1861, *Official Records*, IV, 186–87, and William B. Greenlaw to Polk, September 2, 1861, *ibid.*, LII, Pt. 2, 134–35.
[28] Polk to Davis, August 29, 1861, *ibid.*, III, 687–88.
[29] Special Orders, No. 141, September 2, 1861, *ibid.*, 691.
[30] William J. Hardee to Polk, September 3, 1861, *ibid.*, 693–94.
[31] John C. Fremont to U. S. Grant, August 28, 1861, *ibid.*, 141–42.

"I should be ahead of the enemy in occupying Columbus and Paducah." [32]

Without waiting for an answer, Polk ordered Pillow to occupy Columbus. Finding that the enemy had placed cannon on the

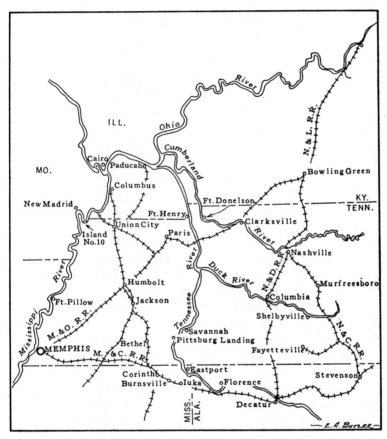

WESTERN TENNESSEE AND KENTUCKY—*Columbus to Corinth*

Missouri shore opposite Columbus, Pillow landed his troops at Hickman and continued by land. News of the movement spread rapidly. When Governor Harris at Nashville learned that Pillow's troops had reached Hickman he excitedly wired Polk: "This is un-

[32] *Ibid.*, IV, 179.

fortunate, as the President and myself are pledged to respect the neutrality of Kentucky. I hope they will be withdrawn instantly, unless their presence there is an absolute necessity." [33] On the same day came a wire from Secretary of War Leroy P. Walker: "Order their prompt withdrawal from Kentucky." Walker also wired Governor Harris that Pillow's movement was "wholly unauthorized, and you will [so] inform Governor Magoffin." [34]

Before the telegrams from Harris or Walker arrived at Polk's Union City headquarters Pillow had already occupied Columbus. Polk immediately dispatched to President Davis a brief statement of the reasons for his exercise of "the plenary power delegated to me." Davis replied: "The necessity justifies the action." [35] To Governor Harris Polk replied that he was not informed of any agreement the governor and the President had made "upon any particular course in reference to the State of Kentucky." In any case, regard for the security of Western Tennessee prohibited his concurring in the governor's views.[36]

Confederate invasion might have been unexpected by Governor Harris and Secretary Walker, but it could scarcely have been a surprise to Governor Magoffin and President Davis. In mid-August Magoffin had written Davis stating that "Since the commencement of the present unhappy difficulties . . . the people of Kentucky have indicated a steadfast desire and purpose to maintain a position of strict neutrality." But in view of the collection of Confederate troops along their southern frontier the people had become uneasy. "In order to quiet this apprehension" he wished "authorative assurance" that the Confederacy would "continue to respect and observe the position indicated as assumed by Kentucky." Davis replied that the Confederate Government had "respected most scrupulously the neutrality of Kentucky" and would continue to do so "so long as her people will maintain it themselves." [37] Both the President and the governor knew that Kentucky was not observing a policy of strict neutrality.

While local citizens were giving Confederate troops an enthusi-

---

[33] September 4, 1861, *ibid.*, 180. A similar message was sent to President Davis, *ibid.*, 188–89.

[34] *Ibid.*, IV, 180, 189.   [35] *Ibid.*, 181.   [36] September 4, 1861, *ibid.*, 180.

[37] Magoffin to Davis, August ?, 1861, *ibid.*, 378; Davis to Magoffin, August 28, 1861, *ibid.*, 396–97.

MRS. SARAH HAWKINS POLK, Mother of Leonidas Polk

WILLIAM POLK, Father of Leonidas Polk

University of the South

LEONIDAS POLK as a young clergyman

BISHOP LEONIDAS POLK

"Ashwood Hall," Leonidas Polk's Maury County Home

"LEIGHTON PLACE," Leonidas Polk's Louisiana Home

University of the South

St. John's Chapel near "Ashwood"

GENERAL LEONIDAS POLK

astic reception in Columbus, Polk thought it proper to issue a public statement of reasons and intentions. To Governor Magoffin he reported his action as a military necessity but concluded, "I am prepared to say that I will agree to withdraw the Confederate troops from Kentucky, provided that she will agree that the troops of the Federal Government be withdrawn simultaneously, with a guarantee (which I will give reciprocally for the Confederate Government) that the Federal troops shall not be allowed to enter or occupy any part of Kentucky in the future." [38]

The Kentucky Senate quickly appointed a committee to investigate both Union and Confederate violations of the state's neutrality. The chairman of this committee, however, exceeding his instructions, addressed a note to General Polk stating that the people of Kentucky were "profoundly astonished" by his actions. They had "with great unanimity determined upon a position of neutrality in the unhappy war now being waged, and which they had tried in vain to prevent, [and] had hoped that one place at least in this great nation might remain uninvaded by passion." It was further hoped by the people of Kentucky that they might in some way assist in the mitigation of the horrors of war, "or, if this were not possible, that she might be left to choose her destiny without disturbance from any quarter." Consequently, "I ask you to withdraw your forces from the soil of Kentucky." [39]

In reply Polk noted that the senate resolution creating this committee had restricted its activity to the collection of facts. He was pleased to present facts concerning both the Confederate occupation of Columbus and the numerous incidents in which Kentucky had co-operated with the Federal Government in violation of so-called neutrality. The sole Confederate violation of this neutrality, he contended, had been the occupation of Columbus and the narrow strip of territory over which troops passed in reaching that point. And this had come only after the Federal Government had, with Kentucky's knowledge, cut large quantities of timber from state forests to build boats for use against the Confederacy, and had recruited and trained Federal troops on Kentucky soil. At that very moment, Polk charged, 10,000 such troops, equipped by the Federal Government, were in training at Camp Dick Robinson in

[38] September 8, 1861, *ibid.*, 185.
[39] John M. Johnston to Leonidas Polk, September 9, 1861, *ibid.*, 185–86.

Garrard County.[40] Furthermore, Kentucky congressmen at Washington had consistently "voted supplies of men and money to carry on the war against the Confederate States." Such assistance to a belligerent, either through collusion or neglect, could scarcely be considered in keeping with a policy of neutrality.

Yet in spite of knowledge of these violations the Confederacy had "continued to respect the attitude which Kentucky had assumed as a neutral" hoping that she would force the United States to do likewise. Kentucky's failure to force this respect and knowledge that Federal commanders were planning to occupy Columbus left the Confederacy no choice but "to seize it in advance. . . . We are here, therefore, not by choice, but by necessity." [41]

As was expected, opinion both inside Kentucky and within the Confederacy was divided. Of course Union sympathizers denounced Polk's action and demanded either immediate Confederate withdrawal or all out assistance to the Union. Confederate sympathizers, on the other hand, disagreed among themselves. Although agreeing that the occupation might be supported from a military viewpoint, many thought it unfortunate, even fatal, politically. Two men, classing themselves as Southern Rights Kentuckians, protested to Polk that under the policy of neutrality Confederate sympathy in Kentucky had been gradually molded in the direction of "final union with the Southern States." But this sudden violation of Kentucky soil would check that development and give the Unionist legislature excuse to create "a force to operate against your force." The present state Guard would no doubt be disbanded and a new force under command of General Robert Anderson, probably 30,000 strong, would be charged with the suppression of Southern sentiment in central Kentucky. Southern men, without organization or equipment, would be helpless. "No matter how numerous or how brave, they will be powerless for self-protection, and may finally fix the destiny of the State." [42]

[40] The existence of this camp was definitely known to President Lincoln. On July 1, 1861, Lieutenant William Nelson was instructed by the United States War Department to recruit and arm three regiments in Southeastern Kentucky for service in Tennessee. Arms to be furnished from Cincinnati. L. Thomas to William Nelson, July 1, 1861, *Official Records*, IV, 251–52.

[41] Leonidas Polk to John M. Johnston, September 9, 1861, *ibid.*, 186–87.

[42] John L. Helm and E. M. Covington to Leonidas Polk, September 13, 1861, *ibid.*, 191–92.

From General Simon Bolivar Buckner, recently inspector general of the Kentucky State Guard and soon to become a Confederate general, came a similar warning. After conferring with prominent Kentuckians he rushed to Nashville for a conference with Governor Harris. From Nashville he wired Richmond recommending Confederate withdrawal. He was not convinced that the Federals would do likewise, but he believed Polk's withdrawal would be a positive political gain. "If a withdrawal is authorized, I can rally thousands of neutrality Union men to expel the Federals. . . . I regard a prompt withdrawal the only chance to unite the State." The telegraph line was kept open for a reply.[43]

President Davis wired Harris that Polk's action had been sanctioned as a necessity. However, if withdrawal could be carried out with safety "it would conform to my declared policy of respect for the neutrality of Kentucky." General Albert Sidney Johnston would soon arrive in Nashville with power to act.[44]

General Polk was not impressed by the gloomy views expressed by Kentuckians. ". . . they overrate the importance of the seizure on the public mind of Kentucky," he wrote Davis. The mistake was not that Columbus had been occupied but that the action had not been taken months earlier, for during recent months the Confederate cause had been steadily losing ground in Kentucky. "If we make the stand now, and do it vigorously, we shall find we have more allies in the State than we shall ever have at any future day." A few Confederate victories would dispel fear of the Federals and cause Kentuckians to "rally strongly to our support for their emancipation."[45]

Davis agreed that the Confederacy could not permit indeterminate quantities, such as political elements, to control its action in matters of military necessity. He further agreed that Polk's offer to evacuate "furnishes all that could be required of respect for the declared neutrality on the part of Kentucky." He also informed Polk that his wish to have General A. S. Johnston assigned to command the operation in the West had been fulfilled. The General was now at Nashville.[46]

[43] Buckner to S. Cooper, September 13, 1861, *ibid.*, 189–90.
[44] Davis to Harris, September 13, 1861, *ibid.*, 190.
[45] Polk to Davis, September 14, 1861, *ibid.*, 191.
[46] Davis to Polk, September 15, 1861, *ibid.*, 188.

At Nashville Johnston quickly put an end to any uncertainty that might have still existed. "The troops *will not* be withdrawn," he notified Davis. Instead, it was his plan immediately to occupy Bowling Green with 5,000 troops. The political question involved he considered as already having been settled by the Kentucky legislature.[47] Simon Bolivar Buckner, now a Confederate brigadier, was ordered to Bowling Green with all available troops. While passing through East Tennessee Johnston had already ordered General Zollicoffer to occupy Cumberland Gap on the Kentucky-Tennessee line.

Governor Magoffin had sent to the Kentucky legislature a message urging that both belligerents be required to respect Kentucky neutrality. But the legislature, dominated by Unionist sympathy, passed a resolution demanding Confederate withdrawal, taking no notice of Federal violations.[48] Magoffin vetoed this resolution, but when it was promptly passed over his veto he did issue the required proclamation, saying "Kentucky expects the Confederate or Tennessee troops to be withdrawn from her soil unconditionally." [49]

After a few days at Nashville Johnston moved on to Columbus to be greeted by his friend Polk. He quickly examined the fortifications there and pronounced them good, ordered Hardee, whom Polk had instructed to move from Pitman's Ferry to the Mississippi, to move on and join Buckner at Bowling Green, then left to establish his own headquarters at that point.

Overworked but in excellent health, General Polk felt some satisfaction over his decision and accomplishment. "I thought I saw my way as a path of duty before me," he wrote his wife, "and I could do nothing else than tread firmly in it. We are in possession of the town and are strongly posted, how long we are to be permitted to be so remains to be seen. . . . But we are increasing our force as rapidly as possible from all sources and hope to give a satisfactory account of things when the issue can no longer be avoided. The town is in the bottom land and the bluff comes up to the lines just above it. The bluff it is which constitutes the strength of the place and it is a bluff not unlike that at Memphis." The only

[47] Johnston to Davis, September 16, 1861, *ibid.*, 193–94.
[48] A resolution to require *both* to withdraw was defeated.
[49] Lewis Collins, *History of Kentucky* (2 vols., Covington, Ky., 1882), I, 93. To follow steps taken in Kentucky toward formal adherence to the Union cause see Coulter, *Civil War and Readjustment in Kentucky*, 111 ff.

enemy activity in the area was occasional light bombardment from a gunboat. He had now been joined by his son Hamilton and had sent word to his other son, Meck, that he thought best for him to join a cavalry company.[50]

When Johnston assumed command of Department No. 2, Polk became commander of the First Division of that department. His command embraced roughly that portion of Kentucky west of the Cumberland River and of Tennessee west of the north-south railroad which ran through Nashville. Johnston now had a thin line of defense extending some four hundred miles from the Mississippi River to Cumberland Gap. The middle was anchored at Bowling Green where Buckner and Hardee commanded under the personal supervision of Johnston himself. According to Polk's official report his own force consisted of four divisions at Columbus, commanded by Pillow, Cheatham, John P. McCown, and John Bowen, totaling about 16,300 present. Garrisons at Fort Henry, Trenton, Island No. 10, Fort Pillow, Memphis, and Iuka increased the total to 23,870.[51]

Polk was conscious of the inadequacy of his force in defense against possible invasion along three rivers and urgently called for re-enforcements. Johnston applied all pressure possible at Richmond and upon the governors of Georgia, Alabama, and Mississippi. President Davis felt that no troops could be spared from the eastern area, so great was the threat toward Richmond. The governors of Alabama and Georgia claimed a need of all available forces for the defense of their coasts. Governor John J. Pettus of Mississippi was willing and able to furnish a few regiments, but an order from Richmond not to accept any more twelve-months' men cut off this source of badly needed troops. Only from Tennessee was there possibility of substantial assistance. Governor Harris urged more men to enlist and bring in weapons of all descriptions. Johnston must have sensed his dependence upon Tennessee troops when he addressed a Nashville audience as "soldiers" and quickly added "I call you *soldiers*, because you all belong to the reserve corps." [52]

[50] Polk to Mrs. Polk, September 18, 1861, Leonidas Polk Papers.
[51] *Official Records*, III, 730.
[52] William Preston Johnston, *Life of Albert Sidney Johnston* (New York, 1878), 306.

Rumors of threats and intentions of the Federals along all rivers leading into his territory kept Polk in a state of uneasiness. (It later developed that Federal commanders were equally as uneasy lest they be attacked by a formidable Confederate force which rumor placed at twice its actual strength.) Of one thing Polk was certain —the Union forces being concentrated at Cairo would begin moving southward as soon as their commanders felt strong enough for offensive action. He was particularly concerned for his right, which did not make connection with Johnston's forces at Bowling Green and included the defense of both the Tennessee and Cumberland rivers. For defense of the forts on these rivers he urged the appointment of a man of experience and military efficiency, suggesting Colonel Lloyd Tilghman with advance in rank. Tilghman he thought "better informed as to the military aspects and capabilities of the country" than any other person available.[53] Tilghman, a West Point graduate, veteran of the Mexican War, and an experienced engineer, had been a resident of Paducah since 1852.

Johnston was thinking along this same line of defense and before receiving Polk's suggestion wrote him calling attention to the fact that by using the Tennessee and Cumberland rivers the enemy "may turn your right with ease and rapidity." Any force that could be spared from his left should be shifted to the right.[54]

The problems of ordnance, ammunition, and food supplies were also serious. Polk urged upon President Davis the necessity of increasing the manufacture of guns and powder in the Memphis area and the importance of securing guns through Cuba. The shortage continued, yet on October 27, Polk was able to report to Johnston: "I am glad to say, too, that I am having an increase of powder and other munitions. More heavy guns are arriving also from Richmond, and I am promised yet others." [55]

So great was Polk's fear of a shortage of food during the coming winter he resorted to the drastic step of restricting the exportation of grain and meat until the needs of the army had been satisfied. Agents were sent out to contract for wheat, corn, hay, and salt meat. He was making provisions for 50,000 men, he reported to

[53] Polk to W. W. Mackall, October 31, 1861, *Official Records*, IV, 491–92.
[54] W. W. Mackall to Polk, October 31, 1861, *ibid.*, 491.
[55] Polk to Davis, November 2, 1861, *ibid.*, 499; *id.* to Johnston, October 27, 1861, *ibid.*, III, 728–29.

Davis, and thought he would be able to save the Government $100,000. Speculators and those engaged in transportation were complaining, but not the producers.[56]

By early November so great was Johnston's concern for defense along the Tennessee and Cumberland rivers he ordered Polk to dispatch Pillow with 5,000 men to Clarksville, Tennessee, a few miles up the river from the Kentucky line. Let Pillow use the rails or march, whichever he thought best, he urged, "but be prompt and say nothing of his destination." [57] Polk warned against the possibility of "serious consequences that may follow from weakening the forces at this place," but prepared for Pillow's departure.[58]

Although there does not appear to have been any connection between Johnston's order for the transfer of Pillow's division and Polk's action, on November 6 Polk sent to President Davis his resignation from the Confederate service. Under a feeling of duty, supported by conviction that " 'resistance to tyranny is duty to God,' " he explained, he had reluctantly turned aside "from employments far more congenial to my feelings and tastes" to accept a commission in the Confederate Provisional Army. It was understood that he might be relieved from duty when his services were no longer required. The arrival of "our mutual friend" in the West had supplied distinguished leadership and rendered his own services no longer necessary.[59]

In his letter of resignation General Polk expressed some satisfaction over his accomplishments, but he gave no indication of fear of attack on his Mississippi line. However, on the very date that he penned his resignation six Federal transports, protected by two gunboats and carrying 3,000 men commanded by General Grant, steamed out of Cairo and headed down the river. On November 2, Grant had received information from department headquarters that Jeff Thompson was giving trouble in Missouri. He was instructed to send out troops to assist in driving Thompson into Arkansas. Grant quickly dispatched the forces of Colonel Richard Oglesby by way of Commerce and Sikeston and Colonel Joseph B. Plummer from Cape Girardeau toward Bloomfield. Then on the

---

[56] Id. to Davis, November 3, 1861, ibid., IV, 504–505.
[57] W. W. Mackall to Polk, November 4, 1861, ibid., 513.
[58] Polk to Johnston, November 4, 1861, ibid., 513–14.
[59] Id. to Davis, November 6, 1861, ibid., 522.

fifth came additional information that the Confederates were sending re-enforcements to Price in Southwest Missouri. Grant was to check this movement by making a demonstration toward Columbus. His forces which left Cairo on the sixth traveled to within about six miles of Columbus and then tied up for the night along the Kentucky shore. If Grant intended nothing more than a demonstration he no doubt wished Polk's scouts to learn of his presence. He later stated that he was not under orders to attack any Confederate position. His purpose was to prevent the sending of assistance to Price or any interference with the Federal forces sent in pursuit of Thompson.

At 2 A.M. on the seventh a courier brought news to Grant that Confederate troops were crossing from Columbus into Missouri to cut off Oglesby who had been sent to chase Thompson. Grant quickly decided "to attack vigorously" the small enemy force known to be stationed at Belmont across the river from Columbus. Orders were given for an advance promptly at 6 A.M. The gunboats were to lead, followed by General John A. McClernand's First Brigade. The Second Brigade, commanded by Colonel Henry Dougherty, was to bring up the rear. Captain Henry Walke, commanding the naval force, would designate the point of debarkation.

By dawn of November 7, Grant's transports were nearing Columbus-Belmont. A courier had arrived at Polk's headquarters as early as 3 A.M. with information that a strong force was moving to attack Jeff Thompson at Bloomfield and New Madrid. Shortly after daybreak another courier reported a considerable Union force landing on the Missouri side of the river some half dozen miles north of Belmont. Polk quickly concluded that the attack would be upon Belmont and dispatched this information to general officers east of the river and to Colonel James C. Tappan, commanding at Belmont. General Pillow was ordered to cross the river immediately and move four of his regiments to Tappan's support. Tappan commanded the Thirteenth Arkansas and had with him Captain Daniel Beltzhoover's Watson Battery. Fearing possible attack in the rear on the Columbus side, Polk contacted General John P. McCown whose force was situated a short distance above the fort. McCown was already on guard and moved a battery up to the bluff to play on enemy gunboats. Polk took position on the bluff and watched developments.

About 10:30 A.M. Grant's advance drove in Pillow's pickets and firing soon became fierce. The Confederates fell back "foot by foot, and from tree to tree." Pillow called for re-enforcements and more ammunition. Colonel Knox Walker's regiment was sent with the ammunition, and two field batteries commanded by Captains W. H. Jackson and Hamilton Polk (the General's son) were ordered to cross. Difficulties in landing, however, prevented these batteries arriving in time for the battle. Beltzhoover's battery ran out of ammunition while in the thick of fighting and was captured (only to be later recovered). The Federals were clearly getting the advantage. Retreating Confederates sought protection along the river banks. Then the apparent victors turned to looting the rebel camp, some laying down their arms and rummaging the tents for trophies.

From his position on the bluff Polk, noting the yielding of his columns, ordered Charles M. Carroll's Fifteenth Tennessee and S. F. Mark's Eleventh Louisiana to cross over. Next went General Benjamin F. Cheatham with his First Brigade, commanded by Colonel Preston Smith. Polk accompanied these fresh troops, leaving the east bank of the river to McCown. Major A. P. Stewart, commanding the heavy guns of the fort, opened fire on the gunboats and the Federal position across the river. Captain Melanchthon Smith's Mississippi battery also moved up to the bluff and opened fire.

Under pressure from an infantry flanking attack now directed by Polk and within range of the batteries on the bluff, Grant's forces began falling back toward their boats. The retreat increased in speed with distance. "Under this galling fire," Polk later reported, the enemy "cut his lines and retreated from the shore, many of his soldiers being driven overboard by the rush of those behind them." So rapidly did the boats push off from their landing General Grant was almost left behind. At the last moment his horse "put his fore feet over the bank . . . and with his hind feet under him, slid down the bank, and trotted aboard the boat." The fighting had covered the period from about 10:30 A.M. to 5 P.M.

"The enemy fled, and were pursued to gunboats," Polk wired

President Davis. "A complete rout—roads filled with dead, wounded, guns, ammunition, knapsacks. . . . Precipitate embarkation. . . . General Grant reported killed." Before giving to officers and men the praise and credit due them, Polk stressed, "My acknowledgments for this signal triumph of our arms and the defeat of the machinations of our enemies are due to the favoring providence of Almighty God, by which his plans were unvailed [*sic.*] and frustrated, and by which the hearts of our troops were made strong in the day of battle." Polk gave his killed, wounded, and missing as totaling 641.

Grant also claimed victory, but he recognized no assistance from Providence. "The general commanding . . . returns thanks to the troops under his command . . . ," he announced. "Such courage will insure victory wherever our flag may be borne and protected by such a class of men." Only a lack of wagons, he explained, prevented his hauling off large quantities of enemy supplies. And for the want of teams he was forced to abandon four captured guns. Nevertheless, "The victory was complete." In addition to the damage inflicted upon the enemy the re-enforcement of Price and Jeff Thompson had been prevented, and "the confidence inspired in our troops in the engagement will be of incalculable benefit to us in the future." He placed his own losses at 250 killed, wounded and missing.[60] Revised figures later showed his losses to have been well over twice this number.

Despite the celebrations and claims on both sides, the battle of Belmont was of little importance except in making veterans out of raw recruits. Belmont was not a town, merely a boat landing. Polk soon abandoned this place he had fought to hold, and Grant did not see fit to move in and occupy the place he had attempted to take. Of course he knew that Belmont was of no military importance and could not be held without first capturing Columbus. He was in error when he claimed that his attack interrupted Polk's attempt to assist Price and Thompson; no such attempt was being made. Polk was also in error when he believed this demonstration to be a part of a plan to capture Columbus. Strange indeed is the

---

[60] *Personal Memoirs of U. S. Grant* (New York, 1885), I, 262 ff; Report of General Grant, November 17, 1861, *Official Records*, III, 267–72; Report of General Polk, *ibid.*, 305–310; Orders No. ——, *ibid.*, 274; Grant to Charles F. Smith, *ibid.*, IV, 346.

reasoning that has prompted one of Grant's ardent admirers to declare the hour of his decision to attack Belmont as one "heavy with destiny for the United States." [61]

On the day following the battle Polk received a note from General Grant calling attention to the necessity of caring for the Federal wounded left on the battlefield. Under a flag of truce he was sending sixty-four prisoners whom he proposed to release unconditionally. Polk replied that he had already begun to transfer the Federal wounded to his own hospitals. It was "with pleasure" that he granted permission for Federal assistance to these unfortunates. He then added "In your note you say nothing of an exchange of prisoners." [62]

This again focused attention on a subject the discussion of which had begun three weeks earlier. On October 14 Polk had sent his son to Grant's headquarters to suggest exchange of a few prisoners taken in fighting in Missouri. Grant replied, "I recognize no Southern Confederacy myself but will communicate with higher authority for their views." [63] A week passed and then Polk received a note from General McClernand stating that the only prisoners now held were three men taken at Charleston, Missouri. These he proposed to release unconditionally. They were being sent under a flag of truce in care of Colonel Napoleon B. Buford. To Buford, McClernand gave instructions that "In your conversation with the commandant . . . you will avoid all discussion upon the rights of belligerents." Polk accepted the release. ". . . although your mode of accomplishing it waives the recognition of our claims as belligerents," he explained, "I am not disposed to insist on an unimportant technicality when the interests of humanity are at stake." [64]

This was the state of affairs relative to a policy of exchanging prisoners at the time of the battle of Belmont. In reply to Grant's note of November 8 relative to the exchange of wounded Polk stated, "My own feelings would prompt me to waive again the unimportant affectation of declining to recognize these states as belligerents," but he would refer the matter to Richmond. On this same day he wired Adjutant General Cooper that the Federals

[61] Kenneth P. Williams, *Lincoln Finds a General* (New York, 1949–59), III, 81.
[62] *Official Records*, Ser. II, I, 515–16.   [63] *Ibid.*, 511.   [64] *Ibid.*, 512–13.

had requested a return of their wounded. "Shall I give them? And on what terms shall I accept our wounded prisoners offered me?" Cooper waited two days to reply and then advised, "Make full exchange if possible; if not exchange on equal terms." On the following day Secretary of War Benjamin suggested, "Exchange your prisoners on the best terms you can get. An unconditional exchange is preferred. If you cannot exchange give up all that are seriously wounded after taking a strict parole." [65]

Within the next week Polk exchanged with Grant "all his wounded for the whole of my wounded and well" and still held 100 Federal prisoners whom he sent to Memphis for safe-keeping. A memorandum sent by Polk to Grant on December 6 showed 124 Confederates and 114 Federals had been released. A few days later Polk released ten more, evening the score.[66] And on December 22, Polk proposed to Grant an "exchange grade for grade and man for man" of any other prisoners within their districts.[67]

Negotiations for exchange of prisoners had been interrupted on November 11 by an accident that almost cost General Polk his life. While on a tour of inspection he stopped to look at the big Dahlgren gun which had done such valuable service in the recent battle. The gun had remained loaded but apparently no one knew how heavily or with what.[68] The captain in charge proposed to demonstrate the gun. Polk gave permission. The gun exploded, as did a powder magazine near by. Polk and two staff officers were blown several feet and hurled to earth. Two officers and several men were killed. Two men were hurled into the river below. "My clothes were torn to pieces, and I was literally covered with dust and fragments of the wreck," Polk wrote his wife.[69] His nerves and hearing were so impaired as to force him to take his bed and place Brigadier General Pillow temporarily in command.

While convalescing Polk went aboard a Federal boat to confer with General Grant and Colonel Napoleon B. Buford of the Twenty-seventh Illinois, an old West Point friend, relative to the proposed exchange of prisoners. The conference was satisfactory,

---

[65] *Ibid*, 515, 541.   [66] *Ibid.*, 541, 529, 530.   [67] *Ibid.*, 513.

[68] It was later revealed that fine rifle power had been used instead of coarse cannon powder.

[69] Polk to Mrs. Polk, November 12, 1861, quoted in Polk, *Leonidas Polk*, II, 44. See also statement of E. W. Rucker, *ibid.*, 45–46. For several other eyewitness accounts see *Confederate Veteran* (Nashville, March, June, 1904).

but Polk thought Grant "looked rather sad . . . like a man who was not at ease and whose thoughts were not the most agreeable. . . ." The two generals agreed in denunciation of "savagery, and vandalism, and plundering," pledging themselves to prevent such as far as within their power. "I confess I was not much impressed by him," Polk wrote his wife, "I think him rather second rate, though I dare say a good man enough." [70] Polk's son quoted this letter in the biography of his father but changed it to read: "I was favorably impressed with him; he is undoubtedly a man of much force." [71]

Polk found Colonel Buford much as he had been in West Point days, "as good a fellow as ever lived and most devotedly my friend, a true Christian and a true soldier, and a gentleman every inch of him." The two "hob-knobed it for several hours" and steamed up the river almost to Cairo. "So you see how much we have done toward ameliorating the severities of this unfortunate and wretched state of thing on this line," Polk wrote his wife. "How strange too that such men should have yesterday been engaged in pouring into each others lines most murderous fire and today so agreable [*sic*.] and amiable and tomorrow ready to resort to the same work of wholesale and sweeping destruction." [72]

While convalescing Polk also had time to reconsider his decision to resign. Two days after the battle at Belmont he sent to General Johnston a copy of the letter of resignation recently forwarded to President Davis with the explanation that "I am on many accounts strongly tempted to remain and continue to support you, and if my services were essential to the success of the army, I should feel my position one of extreme embarrassment; but, that not being by any means the case, I must claim the privilege of being guided by that sense of duty in retiring from the military service which influenced me in accepting it." [73]

But Davis had already decided not to accept Polk's resignation. On November 12 he wrote: "You are master of the subjects in-

[70] Polk to Mrs. Polk, November 15, 1861, Leonidas Polk Papers.
[71] Polk, *Leonidas Polk*, II, 48. A recent military historian and admirer of Grant, accepting this revision rather than checking the original, has assumed that Grant's opponents recognized his greatness even this early in the conflict. (Williams, *Lincoln Finds a General*, III, 100).
[72] Polk to Mrs. Polk, November 15, 1861, Leonidas Polk Papers.
[73] Quoted in Polk, *Leonidas Polk*, I, 372–73.

volved in defense of the Mississippi and its contiguous territory. You have just won a victory, which gives you fresh claim to the affection and confidence of your troops. How should I hope to replace you without injury to the cause which you beautifully and reverently described to me when you resolved to enter the military service as equally that of our altars and our firesides?" [74]

Davis permitted Secretary of Treasury C. G. Memminger to read both Polk's letter of resignation and his own in reply. Memminger then added his pressure. He agreed with Davis, he wrote, that Polk's services could not be spared at that time. "Permit me as a brother in the Lord to say that I think both you and I are as much *called and ordained* to the posts we occupy as the presbyter upon whom your hands are laid. The President is, in his high office, the minister of God for the State; and when, in the discharge of his office, he calls upon you as best qualified to defend the altar of God and the homes of your people, it seems to me to become an indication of Providence." [75]

Meanwhile aged Bishop Meade, ill and despondent, feeling that his "days of labor must soon be numbered," was thinking along the same line. He had heard of Polk's "late victory." and rejoiced that his friend had "been preserved alive and unhurt," but he knew nothing of Polk's intention to retire from military service. However, while in Richmond during October he had conferred at length with President Davis and put to the President the direct question whether Bishop Polk might not soon be relieved and returned to his diocese. Davis had emphatically replied in the negative. And Bishop Meade agreed that as long as Polk's military service was required he himself could not urge his retirement. This, Meade explained to Polk, was also what he said to the clergy and bishops recently assembled at Columbia. [76]

The greatest pressure came from Bishop Otey, although it is not certain that his letter arrived in time to influence Polk's decision. Otey had received copies of Polk's letter to Davis and Davis' and

[74] *Official Records,* IV, 539.

[75] Memminger to Polk, November 12, 1861, quoted in Polk, *Leonidas Polk,* I, 374–75.

[76] Meade to Polk, November 15, 1861, quoted in *ibid.,* 375–77. The trustees of the University of the South, including eight bishops, had met in Trinity Church, Columbia, on October 15 to decide what might be done about university affairs during the conflict.

Memminger's replies, but it is not known who furnished them. "If a doubt lingered in your mind as to the propriety of retaining the position, into which you have been called by the wise providence of God," he wrote Polk, "it seems to me that it should be removed by the statements & reasonings of those letters." Polk's own letter to Davis he thought would "triumphantly indicate the purity of your motives & the high and noble considerations which have influenced your course." If there were still persons who doubted that a bishop should become a soldier let them look into the Holy Writ. Many times had the God of Israel sent forth his leaders into battle. Samuel, "the prophet & priest of the Lord," seized the sword with his own hand and " 'hewed Agag,' the king of Amalek, 'in pieces before the Lord.' "

"If ever man drew the sword in the cause of righteousness & justice, in defense of the dearest & most sacred rights of man, I think you have done so. . . . The approval of your own conscience, which I fully believe you have, is of more worth & comfort to you than all the words of man's approbation & sympathy." [77]

On December 8, Polk dispatched to Davis a note of three sentences, closing with: "I have concluded to waive the pressing of my application for a release from further service, and have determined to retain my office so long as I may be of service to our cause." [78]

[77] Otey to Polk, December 4, 1861, Leonidas Polk Papers.
[78] *Official Records*, VII, 746.

(11)

Columbus to Corinth

GENERAL JOHNSTON CONSIDERED that the battle of Belmont had relieved the pressure at Columbus but not in the Tennessee-Cumberland area, where he feared a thrust to turn Polk's right. "The necessity for General Pillow's force at Clarksville is greater now than when ordered," wrote Johnston's adjutant general; consequently, there should be no delay in the transfer. Polk protested, urging that undoubted intelligence of impending danger made it necessary that Pillow remain where he was and even be reenforced.[1]

Johnston continued to insist. Polk wired that he was confronted by 20,000 to 25,000 Federal troops at Cairo. Should Pillow's force be transferred not more than 6,000 men would be left to defend Columbus. Johnston finally yielded and cancelled the order.[2] Reporting to Richmond from Bowling Green, he explained that there was a strong probability of either defeat at Columbus or a successful enemy advance on his left. He had decided to risk the latter. "The first would be a great misfortune, scarcely reparable for a long time; the latter may be prevented." [3]

The defense of Columbus was not Polk's only concern. Memphis citizens were becoming uneasy lest gunboats run the fort and continue down river. They already sensed the inability of shore batteries to destroy gunboats and they envisioned a three-pronged movement—two by land and one by water—that would bypass Columbus and head toward Memphis. The only hope, it was urged, was to destroy the gunboats by the use of submarine batteries. At a meeting of Memphis citizens financial aid

---

[1] *Official Records*, IV, 532, 550, 553, 554.   [2] *Ibid.*, 553, 554.
[3] Johnston to Judah P. Benjamin, November 15, 1861, *ibid.*, 553.

was pledged for the construction of 500 to 1,000 such batteries. If a few gunboats could be destroyed by batteries placed in the river north of Columbus, it was reasoned, the fear of further destruction might cause the enemy to change tactics. But should Columbus be bypassed and cut off from the south by water and New Madrid seized, Memphis would be open to attack both from the river and by land.[4]

Polk was already aware of the need for this type of defense. As early as October 10 he had urged Secretary of War Benjamin to send him a man familiar with submarine batteries, and he had placed orders for such batteries with both public and private producers. From Richmond Mathew F. Maury wrote on December 4 that six batteries were ready for shipment. Twenty-five more were under way, "all of which, if, in spite of the drift-wood and other habits of the Mississippi, they can be made to answer for that river, are at your service." If possible he would come in person to supervise the planting of them.[5]

From Memphis came a report from A. L. Saunders that nineteen improved submarine batteries of his own invention had been forwarded to Columbus by rail. The remainder of Polk's order of fifty would soon be ready. Instructions for submerging this type of battery were also being sent.[6]

Still other suggestions for defense of the Mississippi came from Colonel Edward Fontaine, who had been sent to examine the fortification at Vicksburg and to suggest means of strengthening defenses on the lower Mississippi. Batteries along the shore, he suggested to Polk, would not be effective unless erected on both sides. And it would also be necessary to obstruct the main channel in order to check the speed of gunboats, giving the shore batteries time to play upon them. This could best be accomplished by driving piles in the river and lodging tree trunks against them thus making a succession of obstructions the width of the river beneath the guns of the fort. Should this be accomplished the defense of

[4] J. T. Trezevant to Polk, November 21, 1861, *ibid.*, LII, Pt. 2, 214–16. Trezevant, ordnance officer at Memphis, had presided at this meeting of citizens.

[5] Maury to *id.*, December 4, 1861, *ibid.*, 227.

[6] Saunders to *id.*, December 5, 1861, *ibid.*, 230.

Vicksburg and New Orleans might be made successfully at Columbus.[7]

Polk considered carefully these suggestions and at least made a beginning in implementing some of them. In one of his more optimistic moments he wrote his wife, "I am paving the bottom of the river with submarine batteries which will take good care of themselves and Mr. Lincoln's Gun Boats to say nothing of a tremendous heavy chain across the river. . . . I am planting . . . mines out in the roads also so that if they make their appearance we will not fail to give them a warm reception."[8] Even confident claims like these were poor defense; these very gunboats would soon prove the Confederacy's undoing.

Polk did not resume active command of his division until December 4, 1861.[9] In the meantime, the impatient Pillow, never lacking in courage but often in wisdom, was plotting aggressive action deep into the enemy's territory. If left to his own judgment, he informed Polk, he was determined to make an early advance against the enemy's position. With the co-operation of Commodore George N. Hollins' fleet of gunboats, he had no doubt of his ability to destroy the enemy's fleet and capture Bird's Point, Fort Holt, and probably Cairo. He could "conceive of no movement so important, no victory so pregnant with great results to the cause . . . as . . . the capture of Cairo. . . . I ask your approval of the movement."[10]

At least two brigade commanders filed written objections to Pillow's proposal. All agreed that destruction of the enemy fleet and capture of his base at Cairo would be highly desirable. But there was the important question of how this could be accomplished by 12,000 men against 35,000. If the attempt failed would it not also result in the loss of Columbus, with its valuable equipment and supplies, and leave the lower Mississippi open to invasion? Would not even an attempt brand the Confederacy as the aggressor and bind together those Northern elements now so widely separated in plans and opinions? Yankees were "troublesome customers" under any circumstances, "but flushed with victory and led on by bold,

[7] Fontaine to *id.*, November 28, 1861, *ibid.*, VII, 708–709.
[8] Polk to Wife, January 6, 1862, Leonidas Polk Papers.
[9] General Orders, No. 21, *Official Records*, VII, 736.
[10] Pillow to Polk, December 2, 1861, *ibid.*, 731.

bad men, God only knows where their course down the valley of the Mississippi would or could be stopped."[11] Polk considered these possibilities, disapproved the proposed advance, and hastened to resume active command.

It was plans for defense, not an offensive campaign, which demanded Polk's attention. Johnston warned him of a probable three-pronged Federal advance on his front. In the process, the enemy might attempt to reduce the fortifications at Columbus or possibly bypass it and seek to cut off supplies from below.[12] Yet in spite of this threat Johnston requested Polk to send 5,000 to Bowling Green.

Problems continued to multiply. General Mansfield Lovell at New Orleans urged Polk to return a Louisiana regiment recently sent him on loan. McCulloch, instead of making threats or demonstrations in Missouri, put his troops in winter quarters in Arkansas. Polk renewed his call upon Southern governors for all troops that could be spared. Governor Pettus of Mississippi ordered up 3,000 men, but they proved to be six- and twelve-months' men with little discipline or equipment. In keeping with instructions, Confederate commissary and ordnance officers refused to supply them. Polk petitioned Richmond for a suspension of the rule but Secretary of War Benjamin replied: "We have a plenty of men who could be sent you, and for whom we have no arms. Pray cease accepting unarmed twelve-months' men, who are immensely expensive and utterly useless."[13] Thus the situation stood as the year 1861 came to a close.

For Bishop-General Polk, as for most other soldiers, Christmas 1861 was scarcely a festive season. He was suffering from a "heavily pressed and bruised" leg, an injury received when his horse slipped and fell on the frozen ground, pinning the General's leg beneath. To discomfort was added depression resulting from absence from his wife and daughters, although Hamilton and Meck were present as members of his staff. Mrs. Polk had visited her husband during his recent illness and left him with "a sweet memory." She returned to Nashville early in December where she had taken a house for

[11] S. F. Marks to *id.*, December 2, 1861; J. Trudeau to *id.*, December 2, 1861, *ibid.*, LII, Pt. 2, 224–26.
[12] W. W. Mackall to *id.*, December 10, 1861, *ibid.*, VII, 752.
[13] *Ibid.*, 733, 757, 771, 798, 807, 823.

the next year. Polk rejoiced that his family was so comfortably situated. By the close of another year, he told his daughter, he had hope that this unnatural war would have been terminated.[14]

During the Christmas holidays Polk tried to substitute thankfulness for loneliness and disillusionment. "It is Christmas day!" he wrote his wife. "A day on which angels sang 'Glory to God in the highest *peace on earth* & good will toward men,' and oh how my heart yearns to join the same song if those wretched fanatics would let us. Indeed I may say with truth I can and do feel the full force of the sentiment of the song toward them notwithstanding the warlike purposes in their hearts. I feel no unkindness toward them or toward any living being and would bless and pray for them all if they would let me. But we trust now as ever that the Lord would and will deliver us out of their hands, and that with a great deliverance and give them a better mind." [15]

General Polk's private correspondence was not always gloomy; at times there was a note of encouragement bordering on satisfaction. "We are still quiet here," he told his wife on January 6, 1862. "I am employed in making more & more difficult the task to take this place and feel I am in a good measure accomplishing it." He had mounted 150 cannon of varied caliber and planted numerous submarine and land mines.[16]

General Polk's report for December, 1861, showed an aggregate of 842 officers and 16,020 men present for duty at Columbus, but by mid-January, 1862, illness had reduced his effective force to about 12,000. The December report also showed an additional 8,919 officers and men present in six scattered posts, including Fort Pillow (on the Mississippi) and Fort Henry (on the Tennessee). Several regiments, however, had few if any arms. All were hard hit by measles, and the term of the three regiments of sixty-days' men from Mississippi (now located at Union City) was about to expire.[17]

---

[14] Polk to Daughter (Fanny), November 29, 1861, Leonidas Polk Papers.

[15] Polk to Wife, December 25, 1861, *ibid.*

[16] Polk to *id.*, January 6, 1862, *ibid.* He added a note of praise of his sons Hamilton and Meck. The former was a great comfort, "amiable and obliging and capable." And Meck was a fine fellow and taking well to his work. "I have much reason to be proud of my boys as well as thankful."

[17] Polk to Albert Sidney Johnston, January 11, 1862, *Official Records*, VII, 825–26.

Along with the December report and mid-January observations
Polk sent personal letters to General Johnston and President
Davis. "The time for the enemy's attack on this post . . . is at
hand," he began. The build up had been accomplished. A flotilla
of gunboats and mortar boats would support a land force of 30,-
000 to 50,000 men. Reliable reports indicated the points of attack
would be New Madrid, Columbus, and Union City. In the flotilla
there were said to be thirty-eight mortar boats and twelve gunboats, each armed with fifteen "32 and 48 pounders." [18]

To meet this mighty force Polk had nowhere to turn for assistance. Price had withdrawn from Missouri to Arkansas, releasing
the pressure on Union forces. McCulloch was in winter quarters
near Fort Smith, Arkansas. Jeff Thompson's men had disbanded
and gone home. Appeals to the governors had failed to bring units
ready to fight. And fear of Federal movements up the Cumberland prevented Johnston from sending re-enforcements from the
vicinity of Bowling Green. "We shall, however, make the best defense our circumstances will allow," Polk reported to Davis.[19]

On the eve of this impending crisis Brigadier General Gideon J.
Pillow, second in command at Columbus, submitted his resignation and returned to his home at Columbia, Tennessee. Secretary
of War Benjamin requested an explanation and this gave the dis-
gruntled Pillow an opportunity to set forth his complaints and
reasons for distrusting the leadership of General Polk. Most of the
complaints were too petty to merit serious consideration. Only
one reflected upon Polk's fitness to command.

On the morning of the battle of Belmont, Pillow related,
General Polk sent him across the river with four regiments. Immediately confronted by superior forces, he sent back an urgent
request for re-enforcements. None came. Again and again he renewed his request. Still none came. Ammunition ran low, but calls
for a fresh supply met with no response. "I had nothing left me
but the bayonet." Three times his weary forces charged; three
times they pushed the enemy back but could not hold. After fighting four hours against a force three times as great as his own, it became necessary for him to order his battered regiments to fall back
to the river. There he met Colonel J. Knox Walker's regiment,

[18] January 12, 1862, *ibid.*, 828, 829.   [19] *Ibid.*, 828–29.

the first assistance to be sent him. All the while, on the opposite shore, an army of 10,000 well-disciplined and well-armed men stood watching the unequal struggle. In view of the circumstances, Pillow explained, "I trust I shall be pardoned for *distrusting* the *efficiency* of the commanding general of that army, and for expressing apprehension that a like occurence [*sic.*] or even greater calamity awaits his want of fitness to command." [20] On the basis of this account it would seem that either Pillow should have been branded as a liar and dismissed for insubordination or Polk should have been dismissed for incompetence and probably shot for treason! Yet the affair was not quite this serious.

In concluding his letter to Benjamin, Pillow remarked that "inasmuch as I knew General Polk possessed the full confidence of the President, and as I had never, as I felt, been recognized by the Government, I felt it my duty to *silently retire*." He did not wish a transfer to another command. "If I were transferred to another field of duty I would be *overshadowed* and ranked by the very staff who earned their reputation under me as their chief in the Mexican war, and who are now nearly all distinguished general officers." [21] This was the crux of the matter. Brigadier General Pillow had never become reconciled to his demotion from major general and his subordination to others of less military experience. When neither glory nor advancement came his way, he had no desire to remain in the service. Injustices, real or imaginary, were but a pretext.

When Pillow's resignation reached Richmond President Davis wired Polk for the reasons. Polk replied that "the reason assigned by him to me was that the Government had not recognized his claims to such higher rank as in his opinion his services warranted." [22] When Pillow's letter to Benjamin came to the President's attention he endorsed thereon that the reasons given by Pillow were not the same as those reported by Polk and ordered a copy of the letter sent to Polk. This was January 30, 1862.[23]

[20] Gideon Pillow to Judah P. Benjamin, January 16, 1862, *ibid.*, III, 313–16.
[21] *Ibid.* In retirement, Pillow's wrath increased with reception of news that Polk had quashed a soldier's petition to the President in his behalf. "This last act of his," he exclaimed, "is a deeper wrong and has done more to shake my confidence in the sense of justice of General Polk than all that had preceded it."
[22] *Ibid.*, 317.   [23] *Ibid.*

Polk made no reply to Pillow's charges of injustice until July 22, although in the meantime he had collected from commanding officers a mass of evidence which branded Pillow's account of Belmont a great exaggeration, if not outright prevarication. One by one, Polk denied the other charges of harshness and injustice, citing proof, and showing that the rights insisted upon by himself were only those legally conferred upon a commanding general.[24] By this time, however, several important battles had been fought; Pillow, after re-entering the service, had been disgraced by his flight from Fort Donelson, and no one was longer interested in an old controversy between him and his former commanding general.

Although General Polk continued to stress the danger of a many-pronged movement down the Mississippi, the greatest Federal build-up proved to be for advance up the Tennessee and the Cumberland. The danger to the Tennessee country along this line had been recognized from the beginning of the war, yet little had been done to provide adequate defenses. Soon after Tennessee voted separation, Governor Harris sensed the importance of these rivers, and sent Daniel S. Donelson to select the most suitable points for defense within the border of Tennessee. Donelson designated a place on the Cumberland between the town of Dover and the Kentucky line. There Fort Donelson was begun. A dozen miles west on the Tennessee was built Fort Henry. No first-rate engineer ever claimed great strength for either position and the progress of construction was never vigorously pushed.

When General Polk was assigned to Department No. 2 his command was limited to the south and west bank of the Tennessee; consequently, neither of these forts was within his jurisdiction. It was not until Johnston assumed command in the west that Polk was given responsibility for the forts and then his powers were nominal. Upon his recommendation Colonel Lloyd Tilghman was promoted to brigadier and assigned to command at both Henry and Donelson in November, 1861.[25]

Tilghman made regular reports to Polk, explaining the progress being made and also his great need for more men and arms. Polk, under daily threat from three sides, could spare no troops for Henry or Donelson. On January 17, 1862, Tilghman wired that

[24] *Ibid.*, 317–24.   [25] Polk to Johnston, April 1, 1862, *ibid.*, VII, 923.

Federal gunboats were on the river just below Fort Henry. A few hours later three opened fire on the fort, but were not within range. Tilghman did not return the fire.[26]

Polk suspected that this demonstration was part of a plan to "draw out so much of my command as they may induce to leave my defenses." The Federal attack would then be on the fort at Columbus. He refused to take the bait, resolving instead, he informed Johnston, to stand a siege, and to look to the Commanding General and the War Department for such aid as could be afforded. He had provisions sufficient for 25,000 men for 120 days.[27]

Polk looked in all directions for assistance in preventing or raising a possible siege. He must have an additional 30,000 men if the Kentucky line was to be successfully defended, he wrote Governor Pettus of Mississippi. The South, the whole South, must put forth its greatest efforts in Kentucky.[28] He also urged Johnston that an addition of 40,000 men must be placed between Columbus and the Tennessee River. Immediate action was required. Both the men and resources were available, and no time should be lost in getting them into position.[29] Polk then sent a special messenger to Richmond to explain "certain facts with regard to the condition of the defenses of that part of our frontier." Mixing complaint with hope, he wrote Secretary of War Benjamin of how his many efforts to impress the Government with "the inadequacy of the force at my disposal . . . have been met by occasional spasmodic efforts, which have fallen far short of our necessities." If the Mississippi Valley was to be defended and his flank toward the Tennessee made secure, more forces were absolutely necessary.[30]

Benjamin had no substantial re-enforcements to rush to Polk but he did send General Pierre G. T. Beauregard, hero of Sumter and Manassas, and idol of the Army of Northern Virginia. Who originated the idea of sending Beauregard to the West is uncertain. And it appears that he was somewhat reluctant to agree to the shift. But he assured political and military friends that he would

[26] Tilghman to George Williamson, January 17, 1862 (two telegrams), *ibid.*, 835.
[27] Polk to W. W. Mackall, January 17, 1862, *ibid.*, 837.
[28] January 22, 1862, *ibid.*, 846.
[29] Polk to W. W. Mackall, January 24, 1862, *ibid.*, 847.
[30] *Id.* to Benjamin, January 28, 1862, *ibid.*, 850.

return to Virginia as soon as he had rescued the Mississippi Valley. He arrived at Albert Sidney Johnston's headquarters at Bowling Green on February 4.[31]

A quick survey of the numbers and locations of forces presented a picture that must have chilled Beauregard's optimism. There was no longer a semblance of Confederate defense east of Bowling Green. In mid-January General George H. Thomas had severely defeated the forces of Generals George B. Crittenden and Zollicoffer at the battle of Fishing Creek (Mill Springs). Zollicoffer was killed, and the Confederates hastily retreated into East Tennessee, leaving to the enemy most of their artillery and supplies—even the body of Zollicoffer.

This defeat in eastern Kentucky left Bowling Green as the eastern terminus of the Confederate line. There General Johnston had established his headquarters, even though the position had no advantages either as a defensive site or a center for directing operations. At Bowling Green Johnston had about 14,000 troops, commanded by Hardee and Buckner, and at nearby towns were another 10,000 to 11,000 mostly under John B. Floyd and Gideon J. Pillow, who had come out or retirement and been placed in command at Clarksville. From Bowling Green the Confederate line swung southward to Forts Donelson and Henry and then northward to Columbus, a distance of some 150 miles. The forts on the Tennessee and Cumberland rivers had garrisons totaling about 5,500. Polk had reported in mid-January that he had only 12,000 effectives at Columbus. Including those who had probably recovered from illness and the small forces in a few other posts under his command, Polk possibly had 16,000 to 17,000 men. All told, Johnston had fewer than 50,000 men to defend the whole Tennessee front. The troops west of the Mississippi, now under command of Earl Van Dorn, though subject to Johnston's command, were of no immediate use.

Poised ready to strike this thin line were two strong, well-equipped Federal forces. At Paducah Grant had some 20,000 and could depend upon support from Andrew H. Foote's gunboats.

[31] For a discussion of possible reasons for the transfer of Beauregard to the West, see T. Harry Williams, *P. G. T. Beauregard, Napoleon in Gray* (Baton Rouge, 1954), 114–15.

Don Carlos Buell with his base at Louisville had possibly 60,000 along the railroad north of Bowling Green.

When Polk learned that Beauregard was coming west he confided to his wife: "That suits me very very well as it will furnish the ground of my insisting on Davis' allowing me now to retire. Which I have done by letter by Hamilton & sent it to Richmond. *But this is a secret*." He was confident Davis would no longer have good reason to decline.[32]

Again Davis discussed the request with mutual friends and Polk soon received urgent letters from John Perkins, Jr., Confederate congressman from Louisiana, and Albert Taylor Bledsoe, now assistant secretary of war. Polk must not resign, Perkins urged. "Indeed, my dear general, as a member of Congress, I feel I have almost the right to protest against your permitting the public to know that you ever thought of taking such a step." Bledsoe, whose friendship dated back to West Point days, could be more intimate. "Turn not back, I implore you, but hold right on in spite of all opposition of all kinds. . . . We feel as if we could not spare you." [33]

And again came a letter from Bishop Otey. He knew nothing of Polk's renewed attempt to resign but was despondent and bitter, having just returned from Nashville, where he had attended the burial of General Zollicoffer and Major Henry Fogg. Surely just and certain punishment awaited those responsible for this inhuman conflict, he exclaimed. But as long as the conflict should last and Polk's services were needed he would with pleasure be "the messenger of your love to your people." [34]

Fort Henry had fallen before Davis got around to replying to Polk's request. If he had been inclined to grant it the news of this disaster would no doubt have changed his mind. As the clouds of war became darker, he explained, need for the General's services increased. As a personal friend and in the interest of public good, he must urge that all thought of resigning be abandoned for the present. Recognizing that Polk was overworked, Davis concluded, he was furnishing some relief by assigning General Beaure-

[32] Polk to Wife, January 31, 1862, Leonidas Polk Papers.
[33] Perkins to Polk, February 1, 1862, quoted in Polk, *Leonidas Polk*, I, 381–82; Bledsoe to *id.*, February 3, 1862, *ibid.*, 383.
[34] Otey to *id.*, February 6, 1862, Leonidas Polk Papers.

gard to command at Columbus. "He will, it is hoped, divide your troubles and multiply your means to resist them." [35]

The reference to Beauregard touched upon a subject that might have influenced Polk in his second attempt to resign. Of his sincere desire to retire there can be no doubt, but the need for the services of efficient officers had increased rather than decreased since he last agreed to remain on duty. Yet if his own services merited the praise received from both the President and Congress then why should a superior officer be sent to Columbus? Polk's reactions, however, must remain a matter for speculation; if he resented Beauregard's coming he kept his thoughts to himself. "I am ready to turn over my stewardship to Genl Beauregard," he wrote his wife, "and hope he may take as good care of it in the future as I have in the past. I shall of course give him my frank & generous support." [36]

Polk did not retire; neither did Beauregard reach Columbus. While the latter was still at Bowling Green news arrived that Fort Henry had been surrendered. With 17,000 men aboard transports and escorted by Foote's gunboats, Grant had set out from Cairo on February 2. Four days later he was in possession of Fort Henry. The infantry, though landed on both sides of the river, never really got into the fight. The gunboats did the work. Tilghman and fewer than 100 men surrendered; the main garrison escaped overland to Donelson.

The fall of Henry raised new problems. Should Fort Donelson be re-enforced and held if possible or should it be evacuated and a stand made elsewhere? If Donelson was lost, either as a result of evacuation or attack, what should be done about Columbus? Beauregard later claimed that he favored concentrating all available forces at Donelson, defeating Grant and then turning on Buell. Johnston disagreed, insisting that the defense of Nashville required that Hardee fall back to that point.

The plan finally adopted defies explanation. There was to be no effective concentration at Donelson. Pillow, Buckner, and Floyd were ordered there, raising the total to about 15,000 men. Hardee, however, was to evacuate Bowling Green and fall back upon Nashville. Had Hardee's 14,000 men been added to the defense at

[35] Davis to *id.*, February 7, 1862, quoted in Polk, *Leonidas Polk*, I, 384.
[36] February 15, 1862, copy in Leonidas Polk Papers.

Donelson, Grant might have been defeated. Buell then would certainly not have rushed for Nashville leaving his only supply line in enemy possession. If Johnston and Beauregard had decided that Fort Donelson was either untenable or unworthy of concentrated effort (and the records show they had) [37] it was poor generalship to send in thousands of men to be crushed or captured by twice their number.

Following the fall of Fort Henry, Federal gunboats cruised up the Tennessee, striking terror as they went. A small landing party seized the telegraph station at Florence, Alabama, and began intercepting Confederate messages. A wedge had been driven between Johnston at Bowling Green and Polk at Columbus. Having no troops to send to Polk's assistance and fearing an assault upon Polk's right from the Tennessee River, Johnston ordered him to destroy all railroad bridges and trestles between the river and Humboldt. [38]

At Bowling Green Johnston and Beauregard had decided that Polk must evacuate Columbus and withdraw to Humboldt or possibly farther south. Island No. 10 and Fort Pillow, however, were to be defended. This much Johnston informed Secretary of War Benjamin on February 8. [39] On February 14 Beauregard left to take command at Columbus. Before departing he put his views in writing in the form of a letter to General Johnston. "Columbus must either be left to be defended to the last extremity . . . or abandoned altogether," he asserted, ". . . I am clearly of the opinion that to attempt at present to hold so advanced a position as Columbus, with the movable army under General Polk, when its communications can be so readily cut off . . . would be to jeopardize, not only the safety of that army, but, necessarily, of the whole Mississippi valley." Johnston approved the proposed evacuation of Columbus, provided it was first cleared with the War Department. [40]

By February 16 Beauregard was in Corinth where he received a telegram from Johnston telling of the fall of Fort Donelson. Some

---

[37] Alfred Roman, *Military Operations of General Beauregard* (New York, 1884), I, 219.

[38] February 7, 8, 1862, *Official Records*, VII, 861, 864; W. P. Johnston to Polk, February 9, 1862, *ibid.*, 867.

[39] *Ibid.*, 130–31, 861–62.   [40] Roman, *Beauregard*, I, 221–23.

members of his staff had preceded him and were already in Columbus.[41] On the morning of the seventeenth a special train took him on his way toward Columbus but illness forced him to stop at Jackson, Tennessee. On the eighteenth he received a wire from Johnston at Nashville: "You must now act as seems best to you. The separation of our armies is for the present complete." [42] Beauregard immediately wired Richmond: "Columbus, with present defensive resources, must meet the fate of Fort Donelson, with loss of entire army, as all ways of retreat by rail and river can be cut off by the enemy's superior forces from Tennessee River; a hazard contrary to art of war. Therefore should now decide whether to hold Columbus to the last extremity, with its garrison (say 3,500 men), withdrawing other forces for subsequent use, or the evacuation of the place and new defensive positions taken. My health is too feeble to authorize me to assume command, but I shall advise with General Polk." Secretary Benjamin (with the President's approval) replied: "Evacuation decided on. Select defensive position below. Look to safety of artillery and munitions. A fleet of boats should promptly be sent from Memphis or other point to aid the movement." [43]

Meanwhile at Columbus, General Polk had not been informed either of the impending sacrifice of troops at Fort Donelson or the plan to evacuate Columbus. On February 15, he hopefully wrote his wife that there was news of heavy fighting at Donelson but "our troops have held their own thus far very decisively. This is cause of great congratulation certainly & I hope Johnston may be able to give that column all the aid needed." In spite of miserable weather, tomorrow he himself would send out a strong column under General Cheatham to threaten Paducah, with the hope of checking re-enforcements to Grant at Donelson. Before completing this letter on the following day, however, Polk received a dispatch from Johnston ordering cancellation of the proposed movement.[44]

On this same day came news that Fort Donelson had been surrendered and Buckner and thousands of troops were prisoners.

---

[41] Polk to Mrs. Polk, February 16, 1862, Leonidas Polk Papers.
[42] Quoted in Roman, *Beauregard*, I, 233.
[43] *Official Records*, VII, 890, 892.
[44] Polk to Wife, February 15, 16, 1862, Leonidas Polk Papers.

Floyd and Pillow had escaped. The advance column of Johnston's troops from Bowling Green had arrived at Nashville. "On reflection," Polk wrote his wife, he thought she and the girls should go to the home of Lucius in Maury County. Her heavier less valuable possessions might be locked in the house; articles of considerable value should be deposited in John Kirkman's bank. Lighter things such as bed clothing might be taken with her.[45]

General Johnston, traveling in advance of Hardee's division, had reached Nashville on the fifteenth. News of Donelson's fall came on the following day. Nashville was panic stricken as wild rumors circulated freely. As Hardee's troops, ill and straggling, moved through the city, the worst element of a stunned and disgusted population gave full vent to baser desires. Cursing, screaming, denouncing, they filled the streets, threatening safety of lives and property. Soon streets and roads leading southward were jammed with all sorts of vehicles as families sought safety for person and property. Governor Harris increased the panic by urging women and children to flee the city before Federal bombardment began.[46]

Within the fleeing crowd was the family of General Polk. Fortunately his son Hamilton, returning from presenting his father's resignation to President Davis, had been granted permission to stop for a few days with the family. Confederate military authorities in Nashville notified Mrs. Polk that regardless of who else remained the family of General Polk must seek safety elsewhere. Hamilton got his mother and sisters aboard a special train on the night of the sixteenth. Nothing but clothing was saved.[47] On the following day Hamilton wired his father from Corinth. They were on their way to either Jackson, Mississippi, or New Orleans, he said.[48] Later Mrs. Polk wrote from New Orleans: "I felt that I wish to be among friends & nothing can exceed the kindness of mine— Lucia & I are at the Adams—Fanny & Lilly at Henry Rodewald's— Susan & Sally at Mr. Huger's." [49]

General Johnston made no attempt to defend Nashville. Charging General Floyd with the responsibility of restoring order in

---

[45] *Id.* to *id.*, February 16, 1862, copy in *ibid.*
[46] Stanley Horn, *The Army of Tennessee* (Indianapolis, 1941), 99–102.
[47] Mrs. Fanny Polk to Susan Rayner, March 20, 1862, Leonidas Polk Papers.
[48] February 17, 1862, *ibid.*
[49] Mrs. Fanny Polk to Susan Rayner, March 20, 1862, *ibid.*

Nashville, he retired with Hardee's division to Murfreesboro. Floyd shifted the responsibility to Nathan Bedford Forrest and his cavalry, which group galloped out of town as Buell's advance guard entered. The state capital was moved to Memphis. Irate citizens denounced General Johnston in no uncertain terms.[50]

For days Johnston was out of connection with his generals to the West. Polk heard that he had fallen back to Chattanooga. Beauregard lay ill at Jackson. Brigadier General Daniel Ruggles, recently ordered up from New Orleans with 5,000 men, arrived at Corinth. His instructions were to go to Nashville. Polk ordered him to Columbus. Ruggles replied that unless Johnston covered the Tennessee River the enemy would gain possession of the Memphis and Charleston Railroad. "Shall I intrench here and defend the crossings at Florence and Decatur or join you at once?" [51]

On February 19, Polk was summoned to Jackson for conference with Beauregard. David B. Harris and Thomas Jordan of Beauregard's staff had visited Columbus and surveyed the strength of that salient. They reported that the fortification was defective in location, its lines were too extended, requiring too large a garrison, and the defensive forces were imperfectly organized. The officers, though brave and zealous, were without training or experience. This last criticism was scarcely justified; of the general officers at Columbus John P. McCown was both a graduate of West Point and a veteran of the Mexican War; A. P. Stewart and Lucius Marshall Walker were graduates of West Point; and Benjamin F. Cheatham was a veteran of the Mexican War.

General Polk, however, with "unbounded confidence in the strength of Columbus, which he termed the 'Gibraltar of the West,'" and with "characteristic gallantry" insisted that he could hold the fort against any force as long as his supplies should last. Yet, according to Beauregard, after a discussion of the weaknesses of the position he "concurred in the opinion that it could not long withstand a determined attack." [52] This veiled criticism of Polk's work at Columbus was not written until after the death of Polk had removed all possibility of a rebuttal.

Years later General Polk's son and biographer was critical of

---

[50] Horn, *Army of Tennessee*, 102–105.

[51] Polk to Ruggles, February 17, 1862, *Official Records*, VII, 889; Ruggles to Polk, February 18, 1862, *ibid.*, 890–91.   [52] Roman, *Beauregard*, I, 233–34.

Beauregard's hasty action in ordering the evacuation of Columbus. He contended that the real reason for transferring Beauregard to the West was to give that region the benefit of his engineering ability. Yet Beauregard condemned the fortification at Columbus without seeing it, even though it had been approved by Colonel Jeremy F. Gilmer, chief engineer of the department and a man of much more experience than Captain Harris. It was further explained that Polk "was not disposed to yield a ready assent" to all of Beauregard's plans. Any weaknesses that might exist in the fortifications at Columbus, Polk insisted, could be corrected in less time than would be required to construct works on Island No. 10. If Beauregard would "give some occupation" to the enemy force along the Tennessee, he would defend Columbus with 6,000 or 7,000 men.

Polk's biographer-son further claimed that his father did not give his assent until after returning to Columbus, and then it was more through willingness to give "effective and hearty support" to his superior than from conviction that Beauregard's views were correct. Furthermore, nothing was later done at Island No. 10 that could not have been done better at Columbus. In short, according to William Mecklenburg Polk, "Good or bad, Columbus should have been held." [53]

There is no evidence in the records that General Polk insisted upon this, although he did express fear of the effect the loss of another fort would have upon Confederate morale. It is understandable that he would be reluctant to see the results of six months of hard labor demolished and abandoned, yet he was too good a soldier not to understand the fate that awaited Columbus. He knew that Beauregard could scarcely muster 10,000 men for immediate action against Grant along the Tennessee.

Preparation for the evacuation of Columbus began immediately.[54] Within five days the accumulation of six months—quartermaster, commissary, and ordnance stores, including 140 pieces of

[53] Polk, *Leonidas Polk*, II, 75–80.

[54] As he prepared to fall back from his advanced position Polk addressed a note to his friend in blue, Colonel N. B. Buford (February 23, 1862, Leonidas Polk Papers). He of course made no mention of any plans, but he wished to express definitely and finally his sincere convictions: "I have said, and now say, if the guarantees of the Constitution had been secured to the South she would have acquiesced in its provisions; and, notwithstanding events had demonstrated

artillery—had been moved and the buildings burned. About 7,000 troops were sent to Humboldt. On March 2, Polk wired Secretary of War Benjamin: "The work is done. Columbus gone. Self and staff in half an hour. Everything secured." [55] To his wife he confided: "This is my last day and hour in Columbus; the evacuation has been complete, and all are gone except myself and staff. Never was anything done with greater celerity, or so completely; for we left virtually nothing to our enemy but the works. Those I sadly regret."

Polk felt that Columbus had served its mission. Military necessity had prompted him to occupy that point; military necessity and orders from the Secretary of War now caused him to abandon it.[56]

A week later, apparently in an effort to boost his own sagging spirits as well as those of his family, Polk explained to a daughter that the surrender of Forts Henry and Donelson and the abandonment of Bowling Green made the evacuation of Columbus a necessity. "I felt in leaving it as if I was leaving home." But the fortifications now being completed on Island No. 10 would make the river as safe as ever. He thought there would be many a long day before enemy gunboats steamed down as far as New Orleans. "They are now (the enemy) just beginning to have their trials and

---

the connexion in many respects fatally injurious to her, she would have maintained it in the strictest good faith.

"This was not done, and she took the only remedy into her own hands. That being done the way was open to right all of her wrongs and to assume such an attitude as would secure for her all she desired politically, socially & commercially.

"She is profoundly impressed with the conviction that her very existence in all that makes life desirable is involved in a dissolution of her connexion with the northern states. This is the sentiment of the Southern people, it is my sentiment, *it is my profound conviction*. And altho there are many persons at the north for whose principles and personal character I have the highest respect and regard, yet they are an inappreciable minority, so small as to be unfelt in the action of the mass.

"My persuasion is that the interest and happiness of the Southern States is to be found in a total and final separation. That is my position, and painful as it is to be separated from many valued friends, my position has been carefully taken & will be firmly maintained to the end. . . . And I beg leave to add that at no time has the determination of the Southern people to free themselves from their connexion with the north been more firm and unflinching than at the present moment."

[55] *Official Records*, VII, 437–38.
[56] March 2, 1862, quoted in Polk, *Leonidas Polk*, II, 80–81.

I do not think they will end shortly. We shall teach them many a lesson before they get back to their homes again."

He urged his family to be cheerful and hopeful, never allowing "an anxious temper of mind" to control them. "Dismiss all such feelings from your hearts and drive them far away. Our cause is just and all are contending for what God has given us, so we need not be ashamed nor yet afraid. We may have some reverses, but what of that. We must quit ourselves like men if we expect the blessings of God and you women must hold up our hands and strengthen our hearts by cheering us on and praying for us." [57]

Shortly before Polk evacuated Columbus, General McCown was placed in charge of the defenses of both New Madrid and Island No. 10. When joined by A. P. Stewart's brigade the command totaled about 7,000 men. Beauregard was still ill at Jackson and did not assume command until March 5. Meanwhile, orders were issued through Polk while he busied himself with the formulation of a plan for a grand offensive. The left of his line now rested on Island No. 10 and New Madrid. This point was all important and

---

[57] Polk to Daughter, March 9, 1862, Leonidas Polk Papers. The type of support for which Polk was pleading was expressed in a letter from Sarah A. Dorsey (February 20, 1862, Leonidas Polk Papers). She was sending him a banner fashioned in imitation of the first Christian banner unfurled by Constantine the Great and which never witnessed defeat, she explained. "Recognizing the holiness of our cause I have not feared to use the sacred Christian symbol especially as I designed to put it in the hands of a Christian Apostle. Believing as I do that we are fighting the Battle of the Cross against modern Barbarians who would rob a Christian people of Country, Liberty and Life. Reverses we have met—we may meet, but even in this dark hour *defeat* is a word banished from our thoughts and from our language. We may be destroyed if it be God's will . . . —never defeated—annihilated—never conquered. While a single Southern heart beats in the breast of a man, woman or child—there will live defiance and resistance to those who would tread us beneath their feet. And our prayers go up consistently to the King of Kings that he may protect and deliver us from the hands so strong and so deadly set against us. And we beseech you our defenders upon the borders who have taken up the sword in our behalf to remember that women and children are behind you for whom your noble hearts must make a living shield. When the land is conquered it will be time for us to die. . . . The whole work was done in your own Diocese & I offer it as a token to our Beloved Father in God that his people are not unmindful nor ungrateful for the efforts he is making in their behalf. If it be possible for you to use this as your own personal banner I should be pleased and after you lay down your arms let it be deposited as a memorial in one of the Churches in New Orleans."

should "be watched and held at all cost," he told Polk.[58] He
called upon Southern governors to send him enough men to raise
his field force to 40,000. With this force he would seize the
mouths of the Tennessee and Cumberland rivers and possibly
Cairo and St. Louis.[59] On this same date he rushed off a letter to
General Van Dorn at Pocahontas, Arkansas. He had 15,000 men
ready for the field, he explained, and had called upon four governors for a total of 20,000 more. If Van Dorn could come with another 10,000 the combined force could seize the rivers, St. Louis,
and Cairo. "What say you to this brilliant programme which I
know is fully practicable, if we can get the forces? At all events, we
must do something or die in the attempt, otherwise, all will be
shortly lost." [60] Apparently Beauregard expected no immediate assistance from Johnston, although he did suggest that Johnston halt his retreat toward Chattanooga and turn toward Corinth.[61]

Although Polk conferred freely with Beauregard both before and
after falling back to Humbolt, his reaction to this plan of offense
is unknown. It is certain, however, that he greatly feared the effect
upon Confederate morale which would result from continued retreat. The fickleness of public opinion had been clearly demonstrated by the denunciation of his friend Johnston following the
evacuation of Bowling Green and Nashville. But regardless of who
approved or disapproved of Beauregard's plan, the one condition
upon which success must rest was never met. He did not "get the
forces."

After Polk fell back to Humboldt the Confederate line extended
from Island No. 10 down across western Tennessee to Corinth.
In between these two extremes were small forces at Fort Pillow,
Union City, Paris, and Jackson.[62] The main army under Polk was
at Humboldt. Within this Confederate line lay not only the Mississippi River below Island No. 10 but also sections of the Memphis and Charleston, Louisville and Memphis, and Mobile and

[58] February 26, 1862, *Official Records*, VIII, 757.
[59] For a copy of this appeal addressed to Governor Thomas O. Moore of
Louisiana see Roman, *Beauregard*, I, 240–42.
[60] Quoted in *ibid.*, 242.   [61] March 2, 1862, quoted in *ibid.*, 248.
[62] Beauregard Memorandums, March 3, 1862, *Official Records*, VII, 915.

Ohio railroads. All were of immense importance in the transportation of supplies and the shifting of troops.

The governors gave little assistance but the War Department acted with unaccustomed vigor. Ruggles had already been ordered up from New Orleans with about 5,000 men. Major General Braxton Bragg, upon the request of Beauregard and with his own approval, was ordered up from Pensacola with another 10,000. But by the second week in March Beauregard had abandoned his plan for an immediate offensive and decided upon concentration in the vicinity of Corinth. He now styled his command the Army of the Mississippi. It was divided into two grand divisions. The First Division was commanded by Major General Polk; the Second Division by Major General Bragg. After the three generals had conferred for a number of days at Jackson "arranging a program for our approaching campaign" it was decided that Bragg would rush his force up from Pensacola and Polk his forces down from Humboldt. Concentration would be near Bethel, on the Mobile and Ohio Railroad. "We are in good spirits, and feel confident of the final issue," Polk wrote his wife.[63]

By March 14, Polk's troops were on their way to Bethel and Corinth and he was "about the last man left." All extra baggage of officers and men had been shipped back home and everything cut to the minimum of future needs. All would be ready for the spring campaign. As for himself, he told his wife, "I do not feel downhearted in the least. I think there will be a way found by which we can carry our point." [64]

Meanwhile, Johnston's force, under Hardee and Crittenden, was on the way to join the combination at Corinth. Whether Johnston's decision to move to Corinth was his own or a result of Beauregard's urging is not worth an argument. The facts were that Johnston could accomplish nothing in the Chattanooga area, concentration was the only way to stop Grant's advance up the Tennessee, and Corinth was the logical place for such a concentration. At any rate, Johnston left the Nashville and Chattanooga Railroad and moved across country by way of Shelbyville and Fayette-

---

[63] March 10, 1862, quoted in Polk, *Leonidas Polk*, II, 83–84.

[64] March 14, 1862, quoted in *ibid.*, 84–85. He urged his wife to be "most rigidly economical. . . . You can set a good example in that respect to our people, and so be doing a high religious duty."

ville to Decatur, thence along the Memphis and Charleston Railroad to Corinth, where he arrived in person on March 22.

Hardee's division was at Corinth by March 27; Crittenden stopped at Burnsville and Iuka. Since Cheatham's division of Polk's command was at Bethel on the Mobile and Ohio the Confederate force extended from Iuka through Corinth to Bethel. Beauregard later recalled that upon arrival Johnston seemed sad and despondent, apparently a reaction to public criticism following the surrender of Fort Donelson and the evacuation of Nashville. Since Johnston feared that he had lost the confidence of the people and possibly the army, he showed little desire for active leadership in the campaign ahead. He even considered establishing departmental headquarters at Memphis, leaving Beauregard in command of the field forces. This, he explained, might restore public confidence since Beauregard was still the hero of Sumter and Bull Run.[65]

In "a spirit of disinterestedness and generosity which equalled that of General Johnston," Beauregard's authorized biographer later recorded, Beauregard declined the command, insisting that he came West to assist Johnston, "not to supersede him." Johnston, very much moved by this expression of loyalty and confidence, then exclaimed " 'We two together will do our best to secure success.' " Johnston thus showed a reluctance to capitalize on the efficient preparation Beauregard had made, and Beauregard was equally as reluctant to deprive Johnston of an opportunity to win the great victory that would restore him to public favor.[66] This account, written twenty years later under Beauregard's close supervision, may not be entirely accurate, but it correctly portrays Johnston's lack of aggressive leadership and Beauregard's egotism, tempered by a sense of loyalty.

[65] Roman, *Beauregard*, I, 266.   [66] *Ibid.*

(12)

Shiloh—"A Magnificent Affair"

A QUICK SURVEY of available Confederate forces at Corinth and the probable strength and intentions of the enemy convinced both Johnston and Beauregard that they should assume the offensive before more Federal re-enforcements arrived. Following the fall of Fort Donelson the Federal forces had moved with unnecessary caution. General Henry W. Halleck, commander of the department with headquarters at St. Louis, had neither understanding of the situation nor confidence in his district commander, Major General Grant. Instead of developing an aggressive program he spent valuable time and demonstrated his own lack of leadership in trying to discipline Grant for alleged military irregularities.[1] And Grant and Buell, not responsible to a common superior, showed little inclination to co-operate in an effort to drive the Confederate forces from Central and Western Tennessee. This jealousy and wrangling among Federal generals gave Johnston and Beauregard time to concentrate at Corinth.

When Federal forces were ready to advance up the Tennessee, Grant was in such bad standing with Halleck that he was ordered to remain at Fort Henry while Major General C. F. Smith commanded the expedition. The object of the expedition was the destruction of Confederate railroad connections. But Halleck warned that care must be taken not to bring on a general engagement. If successful in his raids Smith was to make camp at Savannah.[2] On the eve of Smith's departure Grant reported his total strength as infantry 35,147; cavalry, 3,169; artillery, 1,231 men and

---

[1] For a well balanced discussion of this controversy see Bruce Catton, *Grant Moves South* (Boston, 1960), 179 ff.

[2] Halleck to Grant, March, 4, 5, 1862, *Official Records*, X, Pt. 2, 3, 7.

fifty-four pieces. Smith would take with him 25,206 infantry and all of the artillery.[3]

Smith began moving up the river on March 10. Brigadier General William T. Sherman's division had led the way with instructions to proceed to the vicinity of Eastport and destroy the Memphis and Charleston Railroad. Smith established his headquarters at Savannah and sent Major General Lew Wallace's division to Crump's Landing to guard against a possible Confederate attack from the Mobile and Ohio Railroad to the west. Floodwaters prevented Sherman from reaching his objective; so he tied up with the intention of occupying a position on high ground near Pittsburgh Landing. Grant, having improved his standing with Halleck, resumed command of his army on March 13 and moved up to Savannah. Leaving Lew Wallace at Crump's Landing, he soon concentrated the divisions of General Sherman, Brigadier General S. A. Hurlbut, Major General J. A. McClernand, Brigadier General B. M. Prentiss, and Major General C. F. Smith at Pittsburg Landing. As a result of Smith's illness his division was now commanded by Brigadier General W. H. L. Wallace.[4]

Pittsburg Landing, about nine miles up the Tennessee from Savannah, was located about midway between the mouths of Snake Creek on the north and Lick Creek on the south. The main tributary of Snake Creek was Owl Creek, which rising several miles inland flowed almost parallel with Lick Creek, the distance between varying from three to five miles. Backwater from the Tennessee made these creeks into small rivers. Between these streams was heavily timbered high ground cut by numerous ravines, with small clearings here and there. The landing on the Tennessee was beneath a high bank down which ran a dirt road. The principal road from the landing led to Corinth about twenty-five miles away.

Although including few veterans, Grant's well equipped force was capable of immediate offensive action. But Halleck continued to urge caution. ". . . my instructions not to advance so as to bring on an engagement must be strictly obeyed," he warned Grant. Under no circumstance was he to strike a blow "until we are strong enough to admit no doubt of the result." And a few

[3] Grant to Halleck, March 9, 1862, *ibid.*, 21.
[4] General Orders No. 33, 43, *ibid.*, 87–88.

days later: "Don't let the enemy draw you into an engagement now. Wait till you are properly fortified and receive orders." [5] This excessive caution did not meet Grant's approval but he did not, probably dared not, choose wilfully to violate the order. He told Halleck, however, that Corinth could probably be taken with as much ease as Fort Donelson had been. Yet he confided to General Smith that the Confederates were no doubt increasing their strength at Corinth as fast as the Federals were on the Tennessee.[6]

In the meantime, Buell with an army of about 25,000 had slowly moved out of Nashville but with no intention of giving hot pursuit to the retreating forces of Sidney Johnston. Neither had he taken precaution to protect the route along which he was to travel. At Columbia he found the bridge destroyed and the Duck River at flood stage. Days were spent in rebuilding the bridge before he could resume his march toward Savannah and junction with Grant.[7] Buell appeared in no hurry to join Grant and thus become subordinated to him. There was no evidence of immediate danger and Halleck had wired his intention soon to arrive on the Tennessee and take command of the combined forces.[8]

On March 29, 1862, General Albert Sidney Johnston ordered the organization of his Army of the Mississippi into corps. Beauregard was to serve as second in command and Bragg as chief of staff. The First Corps, commanded by Major General Polk, was composed of two divisions under Brigadier General Charles Clark and Major General B. F. Cheatham. Each division was composed of two brigades. Brigade commanders were Colonel R. M. Russell, Brigadier Generals A. P. Stewart and B. R. Johnson, and Colonel W. H. Stephens. Except for two Kentucky regiments and

[5] Halleck to Grant, March 16, 20, 1862, *ibid.*, 41, 51.

[6] Grant to Halleck, March 21, 1862, *ibid.*, 55; *id.* to Smith, March 23, 1862, *ibid.*, 62.

[7] As Federal soldiers approached little St. John's Chapel on the Columbia-Mt. Pleasant road some stopped to enter but not to worship. They wrecked the organ and carried away the pipes as souvenirs (George W. Polk, "St. John's Church, Maury County, Tennessee," *Tennessee Historical Magazine,* VII, 147). But there is no evidence that they knew of General Polk's connection with this chapel. They did no damage to his beloved "Ashwood Hall" which stood across the road within sight of the chapel.

[8] For Buell's account of his march and subsequent participation in the battle at Shiloh see "Shiloh Reviewed," in Robert U. Johnson and Clarence C. Buel (eds.), *Battles and Leaders of the Civil War* (New York, 1887), I, 487 ff.

one regiment each from Louisiana and Mississippi, Polk's command was composed of Tennesseans. Official returns later filed by the adjutant general showed the total effectives of the First Corps to be 9,136.

The Second Corps, commanded by Major General Braxton Bragg, was composed principally of troops recently arrived from New Orleans, Mobile, and Pensacola. The two divisions were commanded by Brigadier Generals Daniel Ruggles and J. M. Withers and totaled 13,589 men.[9] Major General Hardee's command, recently arrived from Middle Tennessee, composed the Third Corps. This corps was not organized into divisions. The three brigades were commanded by Brigadier Generals T. C. Hindman, P. R. Cleburne, and S. A. M. Woods and totaled 6,789. All remaining forces constituted a reserve corps to be commanded by Brigadier General John C. Breckinridge, who succeeded Crittenden. The three brigades, totaling 6,439 effectives, were commanded by Brigadier General J. S. Bowen and Colonels R. P. Trabue and W. S. Statham. Calvary units of the army, commanded by Brigadier General F. Gardner, totaled 4,382.[10]

Organization of the Army of the Mississippi into corps was to serve a two-fold purpose, Beauregard later revealed. Inexperienced senior officers would be better able to handle their raw recruits, and it was hoped such an organization would deceive the enemy, who would likely believe a corps to contain at least 20,000 men.[11] Beauregard claimed credit for this plan of organization.[12] If credit for its strength was due him, then he was also responsible for its weakness. The plan definitely had strength. Of the corps commanders, Bragg, Hardee, and Polk were trained soldiers. The first two were veterans of the Mexican War. Breckinridge alone was

[9] Brigade commanders were Brigadier Generals Patton Anderson, A. H. Gladden, J. R. Chalmers, and J. K. Jackson, and Colonels R. L. Gibson and Preston Pond.

[10] The above figures were furnished by Assistant Adjutant General Thomas Jordan, dated April 21, 1862 (*Official Records*, X, Pt. 1, 396). On June 30, 1862, General Bragg, having succeeded to the position of commanding general, submitted a detailed report which gave total effectives as Polk, 9,024; Bragg, 14,868; Hardee, 4,545; and Breckinridge, 6,290. Artillery and cavalry were placed at 1,973 and 2,073 respectively (*Ibid.*, 398, 399).

[11] Roman, *Beauregard*, I, 268.

[12] P. G. T. Beauregard, "The Campaign at Shiloh," in *Battles and Leaders*, I, 579.

neither a trained soldier nor a veteran. But the organization also had its weakness. There was no acceptable reason for giving Bragg a command made up almost entirely of raw recruits and numbering twice that of Hardee and a third more than Polk's. Hardee's and Polk's corps were at least experienced in marching, even if they had seen little action. But according to Bragg, few regiments of his corps "had ever made a day's march," and a "large proportion of the rank and file had never performed a day's labor." [13] Organization within Bragg's Second Corps was to prove much too loose in the rain and mud leading to Shiloh.

Polk's First Corps was divided. Clark's division was stationed near Corinth. Cheatham's division was at Bethel protecting the Mobile and Ohio Railroad from a feared Federal attack from the vicinity of Crump's Landing. On the night of April 2 Cheatham (at Bethel) notified Polk that he was being threatened by a strong force believed to be the command of Lew Wallace, operating from Crump's Landing. Polk relayed the news to Beauregard, who immediately concluded that Grant had divided his forces, probably intending an attack upon Memphis. " 'Now is the moment to advance, and strike the enemy at Pittsburg Landing,' " he endorsed on the telegram, and forwarded it to General Johnston's Corinth headquarters by Adjutant Thomas Jordan. The Commanding General wished to consult Bragg before making a decision; so he and Jordan crossed the street to Bragg's headquarters and aroused him from bed. To the two generals Jordan explained Beauregard's views, which, in brief, were that the enemy was now in a cul-de-sac, wedged in between two creeks with the Tennessee River to his back. The nature of the country between Corinth and the enemy position made a surprise attack possible. It was not believed that Grant's forces had entrenched themselves. [14]

Bragg approved and Johnston was convinced. Seated at a table in Bragg's room, Jordan began drafting a circular order to the corps commanders. All troops were to be ready to move forward by 6 A.M. [15] Couriers delivered the order to Polk and Hardee about 1:30 A.M. It was telegraphed to Breckinridge. Meanwhile, in his

[13] *Official Records*, X, Pt. 1, 463.
[14] Roman, *Beauregard*, I, 270–71; Thomas Jordan, "Notes of a Confederate Staff Officer at Shiloh," in *Battles and Leaders*, I, 594–95.
[15] *Official Records*, X, Pt. 2, 383.

own quarters Beauregard was feverishly scribbling directions for the order of march and battle. These he placed in Jordan's hands early on the morning of April 3 with instructions to frame a final draft with copies for corps commanders.

Johnston and Bragg and then shortly Hardee and Polk arrived at Beauregard's headquarters in the early morning hours. Beauregard immediately launched a detailed discussion of his plans. Johnston approved and there is no evidence of objections from the corps commanders. Adjutant Jordan explained that considerable time would be required to prepare the written orders. Consequently, it was decided to begin the march on oral orders with written ones to be delivered later in the day. The major generals then returned to their commands.[16] General Johnston wired President Davis: "General Buell is in motion, 30,000 strong, rapidly from Columbia by Clifton to Savannah; Mitchel behind him with 10,000. Confederate forces, 40,000, ordered forward to offer battle near Pittsburg. Division from Bethel, main body from Corinth, reserve from Burnsville converge to-morrow near Monterey. On Pittsburg, Beauregard second in command; Polk, left; Hardee, center; Bragg, right wing; Breckinridge, reserve. Hope engagement before Buell can form junction." [17] Unfortunately, we do not know the time of day at which this telegram was sent. On this same day a memorandum over Jordan's signature went out to corps commanders explaining that in the attack the plan would be to drive in the enemy's left forcing him away from his line of retreat and protecting gunboats on the river and throwing him back upon Owl Creek "where he will be obliged to surrender." [18]

Two roads led from Corinth in the direction of Pittsburg Landing, a distance of about twenty-five miles. On the left was the Ridge Road running north and then east. After it passed an intersection with a north-south road between Monterey and Savannah at a point known as Mickey's, it became the Bark Road. The right hand road leading from Corinth went in a northeasterly direction to Monterey then joined the Bark Road about four miles from the Landing. From Monterey two roads led to the north. The one to

[16] Roman, *Beauregard*, I, 271–72; Jordan, "Notes of a Confederate Staff Officer at Shiloh," *loc. cit.*, 595.
[17] Johnston to Davis, April 3, 1862, *Official Records*, X, Pt. 2, 387.
[18] *Ibid.*, Pt. 1, 397.

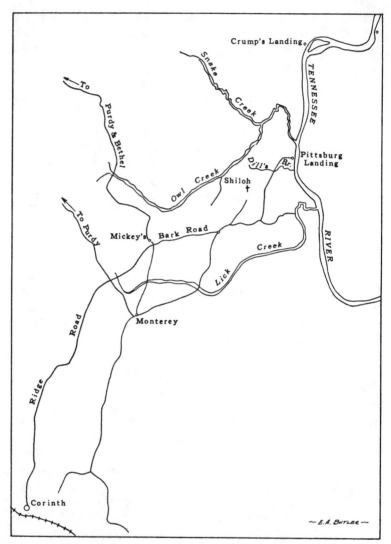

CORINTH TO PITTSBURG LANDING

Savannah intersected the Ridge Road at Mickey's. The one to Purdy intersected the same road a short distance to the west of Mickey's.

From information available to the Confederate generals it was supposed that the main enemy force was at Shiloh Church about the center of the area between the creeks and three miles from the Landing with its right resting on Owl Creek and its left on Lick Creek. The swollen condition of these creeks made flanking movements impossible. And the dense woods and undergrowth rendered cavalry almost useless. An attack, if made, must be frontal, surprising, and in force. This was truly the hard route to victory. According to the written instructions delivered sometime on April 3, Hardee's Third Corps was to advance along the Ridge Road as soon as practicable and if possible bivouac for the night near Mickey's. At 3 A.M. the following morning his corps would continue along the Bark Road to the vicinity of the enemy's advance position and then deploy in line of battle with its left on Owl Creek and its right extended toward Lick Creek. If the extreme right did not reach Lick Creek the remaining space was to be filled by units from Bragg's corps.

Bragg was to assemble his Second Corps at Monterey and as early as practicable move his right wing by the Monterey-Savannah road, the advance reaching Mickey's before sunset. The left wing was to move by the Monterey-Purdy road, arriving at the intersection with Ridge Road by nightfall. On the following morning both divisions were to fall in behind Hardee's corps, deploying in a second line of battle one thousand yards behind Hardee's line.

Clark's division of Polk's First Corps was to follow Hardee along Ridge Road and bivouac for the night just short of the intersection with the Monterey-Purdy road. On the morning of the fourth, after permitting Bragg to move into Ridge Road it would continue until it reached Mickey's and form a reserve line on the Bark Road. Cheatham's division at Bethel and Purdy was to look to its own defense if the threat in its front resulted in attack. Otherwise it was to move by the Purdy-Monterey road and join Polk.

As soon as Bragg's corps should have cleared Monterey the reserve brigades of Breckinridge, Bowen, and Statham were to assemble there and move to the battle front by the best available route. Breckinridge would command this reserve corps.[19]

Morning hours of April 3 slipped away and no troops departed for the proposed battle front. Verbal orders had proved insufficient.

[19] Special Orders No. 8, April 3, 1862, *ibid.*, 392–95.

Beauregard later placed the blame on Polk, who "instead of moving forward upon full verbal instructions . . . held his corps under arms and with its trains blocked the way of other troops." Upon learning the cause of delay, Beauregard said, he ordered the way cleared at once, but the delay had been such that it was almost dark before the last column marched out of Corinth.[20] The truth of this charge is open to question. Polk had only one division at Corinth and it was stationed two miles out of town. His troops could not move forward under "verbal instructions" until Hardee led the way. According to Polk's son, who was present, the First Corps did not come into the road until the Third had passed.[21] It is more likely that the fault was in the failure to give Hardee definite instructions. Bragg, as chief of staff and acting in the name of Johnston, had supplemented Hardee's verbal instructions with a written order to move when practicable.[22] It was not until three o'clock that he received definite instructions. The most recent biographer of Beauregard probably has the answer to the cause of this confusion—Hardee failed to move because he had received no definite orders to do so.[23]

Regardless of the responsibility for the failure to get moving it was necessary to revise the time schedule. Beauregard probably originally planned to move near enough to the enemy position on April 3 to make possible an attack on the fourth. This might have been done had the march begun early on the morning of the third. But it was midafternoon before Hardee got moving and almost night before the last of Polk's troops were on the march. Owing to the delay, the time schedule given in the written orders being prepared by Adjutant Jordan was made to provide for attack on the fifth. On the morning of the fourth Hardee reached Mickey's. Polk was some distance behind, having been delayed at the Purdy intersection awaiting Bragg's division from Monterey that was to come into the Ridge Road at that point.

Bragg had had his troubles. The road from Corinth to Monterey was extremely bad. Not until 11 A.M. on the fourth was he able to complete concentration. For three hours Polk had waited at the Purdy crossing. Then came a message from Bragg that owing to delay in concentrating at Monterey he had decided to send his

[20] Roman, *Beauregard*, I, 275–76.   [21] Polk, *Leonidas Polk*, II, 92–93 n.
[22] *Official Records*, X, Pt. 2, 387.   [23] Williams, *Beauregard*, 129.

entire corps forward along the Savannah road to Mickey's.[24] Polk
then moved ahead and bivouacked for the night just short of
Mickey's crossroads. The advance of Bragg's corps moved into the
same vicinity along the Savannah road. This was about four miles
from the proposed battle line.

Orders were for all columns to be ready to move into battle line
by 3 A.M., April 5. But during the night the rains came and continued. Hardee was unable to move before dawn. By 10 A.M. he
was deploying in battle line about one and a half miles east of
Shiloh Church with his left wing resting upon Owl Creek. Polk
was delayed until Bragg's corps could file into Bark Road. Bragg's
advanced division began moving about 7 A.M. but the other was
far to the rear. Some of Polk's brigades, thinking all of Bragg's
troops had passed, moved in and blocked the intersection. Johnston was on the scene by 8 A.M. Two hours later, having grown
impatient, he went in person in search of Bragg's "lost" division.
It was 2 P.M. before the intersection had been cleared and the last
of Bragg's troops had moved on to Bark Road. They deployed in a
second line behind that of Hardee. Since Hardee's right did not
extend to Lick Creek it was necessary to fill the gap with Gladden's
brigade of Bragg's corps. The delay had given time for Cheatham's
division to arrive from Bethel along the Purdy road. Polk then
moved his entire First Corps in to the rear of Bragg's and to the
left of Bark Road. It was then about 4 P.M. Breckinridge would
soon move in to form a reserve to the rear of Bragg and on the
right side of the road.[25]

As Polk was moving his troops into position a courier arrived with
a message that Beauregard wished to see him at once. He found
the second in command and the chief of staff standing in the road
engaged in heated conversation. Quickly turning to Polk, Beauregard remarked " 'I am very much disappointed at the delay which
has occurred in getting the troops into position.' " Polk, sensing a
criticism of himself, replied " 'So am I, sir; but so far as I am concerned my orders are to form on another line, and that line must
first be established before I can form upon it.' " Beauregard then
explained that success had depended upon surprising the enemy.
Owing to the great delay and to noisy demonstrations by un-

[24] *Official Records*, X, Pt. 2, 390.
[25] Reports of Bragg, Hardee, and Polk, *ibid.*, Pt. 1, 405 ff, 463 ff, 566 ff.

disciplined troops it was unlikely that Federal commanders were unaware of the Confederate approach and they would be entrenched "to their eyes." Consequently, the plan to attack must be abandoned, and the troops returned to Corinth after a "reconnaissance in force."

At this point Johnston came up. Beauregard made the same explanation to him. Johnston disagreed and was supported by Bragg and Polk. He believed surprise still possible. At any rate, after so long and difficult a march the army should not return to Corinth without a fight. " 'Gentlemen, we shall attack at daylight tomorrow,' " he concluded. As he walked away he remarked to a staff officer: " 'I would fight them if they were a million. They can present no greater front between these two creeks than we can, and the more they crowd in there the worse we can make it for them. Polk is a true soldier and a friend.' " [26] One gets the impression that Johnston might have resented Beauregard's tendency to dictate. At least he showed more aggressiveness than had been his custom since taking command in the West. Beauregard later stated that the "opinions of the corps commanders . . . were neither asked nor given." [27] Quite likely Beauregard did not ask for opinions, but it seems likely that Johnston would want the opinions of experienced officers like Bragg and Hardee and of his good friend Polk.

Beauregard later complained that the tardiness in beginning the march plus "unwarrantable tardiness in the general conduct of the march" delayed the attack by twenty-four hours. This tardiness, he charged, was due only in part to rain and mud; the "rawness of the troops" and inexperience of officers, "including some of superior rank," were also factors. All of these factors combined to give Buell time to join Grant. Otherwise Grant would have been defeated and "forced to retire from middle Tennessee." [28] Beauregard's explanation failed to take into consideration the fact that it was not Buell's troops that saved Grant on the first day of Shiloh. Neither did it make allowance for faultiness in his own strategy.

Johnston's plan was to attack in columns of corps, he wired Davis on April 3, with Polk on the left, Bragg in the center, Hardee

[26] Polk's report, *ibid.*, 407; William Preston Johnston, "Albert Sidney Johnston at Shiloh," *Battles and Leaders*, I, 555; Roman, *Beauregard*, I, 278–79.
[27] P. G. T. Beauregard, "The Shiloh Campaign," *loc. cit.*, 583.
[28] Roman, *Beauregard*, I, 276.

on the right, and Breckinridge in reserve. This was not the order written out by Jordan and delivered to the corps commanders. Whether Johnston agreed to the change or Beauregard disregarded Johnston and went his own way is not a matter of record, but the latter seems more likely. With Beauregard's written orders in the hands of the commanders and troops on the march perhaps it was too late to insist upon the original plans, even if Johnston had wished to do so. But in view of the confusion that followed it might have been wise to have insisted. Years later Bragg recalled that General Johnston's plan was admirable. The first he himself heard of Beauregard's modification was when he received a copy of Order No. 8 over Jordan's signature. The "elaboration" made by Beauregard, Bragg denounced as "simply execrable." [29]

As the Confederate forces slept on their arms in battle formation tensely awaiting the call to combat at daybreak, April 6, their Federal opponents were merely camping. On the previous day a member of the Third Iowa, drinking in the beauty of the sea of tents stretched out through the Tennessee forest, thought it all had the appearance of "a gigantic picnic." The rain had gone, and here and there undisciplined soldiers kept firing off muskets to test the dryness of the powder. On one of the river boats a steam calliope filled the air with patriotic music.[30]

Along the high ground between Owl and Lick creeks Grant had about 37,000 men. On the right was Sherman in the vicinity of Shiloh Church, his right resting on Owl Creek. To his rear was McClernand and then W. H. L. Wallace. On the left front was Prentiss with Hurlbut in reserve. Lew Wallace's 7,500 men were still at Crump's Landing four miles away. The Federal position between Owl and Lick creeks with the Tennessee to their backs was one of great defensive strength. Had Grant chosen to entrench himself it would have been almost impregnable. But entrenchments are for defense only; Grant no doubt intended to move toward Corinth as soon as he was joined by Buell.

Whether or not the Confederate attack on April 6 took Grant's army by surprise has long been a subject of debate. Both Grant and Sherman later argued vigorously that it did not, but contemporary

[29] Bragg to William Preston Johnston, December 16, 1874, *Battles and Leaders*, I, 553.
[30] Catton, *Grant Moves South*, 220–21.

evidence greatly weakens their argument. Grant still had his headquarters at Savannah. Upon hearing from Sherman and McClernand that there were enemy activities on the outposts, he visited
the Landing on April 4, but finding "all quiet" he returned to
Savannah that evening. On the following day he informed Halleck
"I have scarcely the faintest idea of an attack (general one) being
made upon us, but will be prepared should such a thing take
place." [31]

About 3 P.M. that day Grant visited the advance of Buell's army
that had arrived at Savannah about noon. He talked with General
William Nelson and an old acquaintance, Colonel Jacob Ammen.
There was no necessity for rushing tired troops on to Pittsburg
Landing, he advised. Let the men make themselves comfortable
and he would send boats for them " 'Monday or Tuesday, or some
time early in the week. There will be no fight at Pittsburg Landing;
we will have to go to Corinth, where the rebels are fortified.' "
However, if they should attack he would whip them, for " 'I have
more than twice as many troops as I had at Fort Donelson.' " [32]

Had Sherman's scouting been efficient he would have learned
of the Confederate approach in force not later than April 4. But he
appears to have shared Grant's views. When uneasy outpost officers
warned that some enemy infantry had been sighted, Sherman
discounted the report and added that he was under positive orders
" 'to do nothing that will have a tendency to bring on a general
engagement until Buell arrives.' " By this he could have meant that
he was determined not to attack any Confederate force, regardless
of how much he was tempted. But when a nervous Ohio colonel
formed his regiment in combat line and reported that the Rebels
were at hand, Sherman impatiently exclaimed " 'Take your damn
regiment back to Ohio. There is no enemy nearer than
Corinth.' " [33]

By 5 A.M., April 6, Hardee's battle line had begun to advance.
Firing began almost immediately, for in addition to regular Federal outposts both Prentiss and Sherman had sent out early morning reconnaissance units. It was these units that opened fire on the
advancing gray line and thus began the battle of Shiloh. Feeling

[31] *Official Records*, X, Pt. 1, 89.
[32] Extract from the Diary of Jacob Ammen, *ibid.*, 331.
[33] Quoted in Catton, *Grant Moves South*, 219.

the full weight of Hardee's infantry they soon fell back upon the main commands of Sherman and Prentiss. Soon the Fifty-third Ohio, which Sherman had on the previous day advised to return to its home state, was in flight in that direction. Johnston and Beauregard were pleased with the beginning. The former hurried off to the front leaving the latter to direct the movement of the reserves.

Polk's corps, in columns of brigades, was massed behind Bragg's left. As Hardee and then Bragg became heavily engaged reserve brigades were promptly moved to their assistance. Before leaving for the front Johnston directed Polk to send a brigade to the support of Bragg's right. A. P. Stewart's brigade was sent, Johnston leading it in person to the point of need. Beauregard then ordered Polk to send a brigade to the left. Cheatham went in person with his Second Brigade, but remained there only a half hour before being shifted to Bragg's extreme right. For the remainder of the day he fought beside the forces of Bragg and Breckinridge. The other two brigades of Polk's corps were not long in reserve before being thrown in to support the center. By this time fighting had become general along the entire line, and charging, retiring, shifting units quickly lost their organization. The weak points of Beauregard's plan of attack by line of corps were already in evidence. With each corps commander responsible for a badly mingled command distributed along the entire battle front there could be no effective direction anywhere. Sensing this weakness, Bragg and Polk agreed the one to assume command on the right and the other in the center. Hardee was already on the left.

Although the Confederate commands were confused, their massed strength had power. The attack was head-on through brush and ravine, clearings and heavy timber. The Federals gave ground, but with stubborn resistance. Sherman and Prentiss fell back upon McClernand and Hurlbut. By midmorning Grant had arrived from his Savannah headquarters and was passing from brigade to brigade, encouraging and directing. As Prentiss' command fell back it took position in an abandoned roadbed, which with its banks and trees gave needed protection. This was the "Hornets' Nest," the defense of which saved the Federals from much greater disaster. Grant instructed Prentiss to hold this position at all hazards, and this he did during six hours of fierce fighting.

At most points the Federals continued to fall back, yet the battle was not being fought according to Confederate plan. Either too much Confederate pressure or unexpected Federal weakness on the left and not enough on the right was driving the retreating Federals back upon the Landing and their gunboats rather than away from the river and back upon Owl and Snake creeks. And a dozen charges against the Hornets' Nest resulted only in repulses and heavy losses. For hours it remained a salient jutting far into Confederate territory as the Federal line folded back on either side. Here again Confederate strategy proved faulty. Had this strong position been bypassed by Polk's command on the left and Bragg's on the right and left as a blue island in a sea of gray it must soon have surrendered with much less bloodshed. In the meantime the Confederate attack could have kept rolling. Perhaps Prentiss, by his dogged defense of the Hornets' Nest, saved Grant's army on the first day of Shiloh.

Polk, in the center, with the two brigades of Clark's division and Johnson's brigade of Cheatham's, aided Hardee in driving back Sherman and McClernand and hurled repeated attacks at the Hornets' Nest. Three times Polk's men fought over the same ground as they charged and were driven back. Losses were heavy, including Colonel A. K. Blythe killed and Generals Clark and Johnson wounded. Marshall T. Polk of Polk's Battery lost a leg. And then came news of the greatest loss of all. General Albert Sidney Johnston had fallen while directing activities on the right front.

Although assaulted from one side by Bragg and Breckinridge and by Polk on the other, Prentiss refused to yield. W. H. L. Wallace, who had given him some support, fell back and was soon killed. His troops scattered to join other commands or seek safety along the river. Federal disorganization was great; Confederate not much less. Raw, hungry, tired troops fled, floated, straggled, and looted, but on each side there remained a hard core of brave determined men who continued the battle.

Not until about 5 P.M. did Prentiss finally raise the white flag, surrendering 2,200 men. He handed his sword to Colonel R. M. Russell who passed it on to General Polk. Aide-de-camp Lieutenant W. B. Richmond and a detachment of cavalry escorted the prisoners to the rear. Once the Hornets' Nest was passed it was then possible for the Confederate center and right to close ranks. But valuable time had been lost; the sun was fast approaching the western horizon. Federal gunboats opened fire. The noise was terrific; the damage slight. High river banks forced gunners to arch their shells so much as to pass over the heads of Confederates moving parallel with the river. More serious was the arrival of Nelson's division of Buell's army. After a hard march from Savannah it had begun ferrying the river by midafternoon. Buell had also arrived on the scene for a conference with Grant and the remainder of his army was not far away. Further, the 7,500 men of Lew Wallace's command, after spending a part of the day awaiting definite orders and the remainder marching on the wrong road, were at last approaching the bridge across Owl Creek. But the most immediate menace to Confederate advance was Grant's artillery.

For the past few hours, as the Federals slowly backed into the loop formed by Snake Creek and the Tennessee River, Colonel J. D. Webster of Grant's staff had been collecting all available siege guns and artillery, stationing them along the high ground behind Dill's Branch. When Nelson's troops moved up to the support of these fifty guns, Confederate chances for a complete victory on the first day of Shiloh were at an end. Troops that had been fighting since dawn were not capable of so great an assignment; there were no fresh reserves. Grant was justified in his statement to persons near by: " 'They can't break our lines tonight— it is too late. Tomorrow we shall attack them with fresh troops and drive them, of course.' " [34]

Beauregard knew nothing of the approach of fresh troops that would double the size of Grant's army, but he was too good a soldier not to realize what would be the fate of exhausted troops in the face of well placed artillery as twilight turned to darkness. Shortly after 6 P.M. he ordered an end to the advance and retirement to suitable camp sites for the night. In view of knowledge which he did not have, his decision was wise, yet it is significant that it was made at his headquarters near Shiloh Church, two miles from the fighting front, and without consultation with his corps commanders. There is no evidence, however, that at the moment they disapproved of his decision. In his report, written three weeks

[34] Quoted in *ibid.*, 238.

later, Bragg almost complainingly stated that just as his men were beginning a new assault "with every prospect of success" they were ordered to abandon the field. But he also recognized that in his front was a heavy battery and that the gunboats on the river "seemed determined to dispute every inch of ground." His exhausted troops "responded to the order with alacrity."

Hardee explained the failure to win a complete victory as a result of the death of General Johnston, which "caused a lull in the attack on the right" and a loss of "precious hours." Neither Bragg nor Breckinridge, who were on the Confederate right near Johnston, made any such observation. As to Beauregard's order to halt the attack, Hardee merely stated that the order came when "the advance divisions were within a few hundred yards of Pittsburg, where the enemy were huddled in confusion." Yet he added that Confederate troops "Exhausted by fasting and the toils of the day, scattered and disordered by a continued combat of twelve hours," began straggling "to find food amid the profuse stores of the enemy or shelter in the forest." To this we might add a further observation that Hardee was on the Confederate left and, consequently, not near the scene he described. And his report was not written until ten months after the battle.

Polk's first recorded comments after the battle were written to his wife: "The enemy was badly whipped the first day, and we ought, from the advantage gained, to have captured his whole force. We would have done so if we had had an hour more of daylight." He offered no criticism of Beauregard's decision; neither did he mention Johnston's death.[35] However, when he wrote his report five months later he felt very keenly the loss of his friend and commander, "cut off when victory seemed hastening to perch upon his standard," yet he stopped short of blaming failure upon this tragedy: "It was an event which deprived the army of his clear, practical judgment and determined character, and himself of an opportunity which he had coveted for vindicating his claims to the confidence of his countrymen against the inconsiderate and unjust reproaches which had been heaped upon him. The moral influence of his presence had, nevertheless, been already impressed upon the army and an impulse given to its action, which the news of his

[35] April 10, 1862, quoted in Polk, *Leonidas Polk*, II, 115.

death increased instead of abated. . . . He was a true soldier, high-toned, eminently honorable, and just. Considerate of the rights and feelings of others, magnanimous, and brave. His military capacity was also of a high order, and his devotion to the South unsurpassed. . . . I knew him well from boyhood—none knew him better—and I take pleasure in laying on his tomb, as a parting offering, this testimony of my appreciation of his character as a soldier, a patriot, and a man."

As to the situation at the close of the first day of Shiloh, Polk, after months of reflection, concluded: "We had one hour or more of daylight still left; were within from 150 to 400 yards of the enemy's position, and nothing seemed wanting to complete the most brilliant victory of the war but to press forward and make a vigorous assault on the demoralized remnant of his forces." Nevertheless, "Here the impression arose that our forces were waging an unequal contest; that they were exhausted and suffering from a murderous fire, and by order from the commanding general they were withdrawn from the field." Polk mentioned the ineffective bombardment from the gunboats, but he had apparently forgotten the fifty guns that bristled along the heights beyond Dill's Branch.

Beauregard's adjutant general staunchly defended him in his decision to halt the attack and placed upon the corps commanders the blame for failure to gain a complete victory. When the combat was most furious, he explained, the superior officers were at the front leading their troops and no doubt accomplishing a great deal "by their personal example," but in the rear "masses of their respective commands" were "without direction." This resulted in "piecemeal onsets" rather than mass employment, making it possible for Federals to take "several obstinate, powerful stands," thus prolonging the battle. "Had the corps been held well in hand, massed and pressed continuously upon the tottering demoralized foe; had general officers attended to the swing and direction of the great war-engine at their disposition, rather than, as it were, becoming so many heads or battering-rams of that machine, the battle assuredly would have closed at latest by mid-day." [36] Adjutant General Jordan failed to say how corps commanders could both lead and drive at the same time. Neither did he make

[36] Thomas Jordan and J. P. Pryor, *The Campaigns of Lieut. Gen. N. B. Forrest* (New Orleans, 1868), 151.

allowance for his hero's faulty battle plan nor the fact that Johnston left Beauregard in the rear to organize and direct.

No doubt Beauregard and his generals thought the Federals whipped at the time he called an end to the day of fighting. Tomorrow would be devoted to mopping up what did not escape down the river during the night. Confederate troops fell back to the vicinity occupied by the Federals the previous night, making full use of abandoned camp equipment. Beauregard occupied Sherman's tent. With nightfall came a driving rain, sweeping across the torn country over which was strewn thousands of dead and wounded. It was a terrible night even for those who had escaped bullets and bayonets. And all through the night intermittent firing of Federal guns made restful sleep impossible.

During the evening the corps commanders assembled in Beauregard's tent to take stock of the day's events and to plan for tomorrow. If anyone was pessimistic he kept it to himself. They even believed false reports that Buell was headed for Alabama rather than a junction with Grant. And Beauregard foolishly wired President Davis: "We this morning attacked the enemy in strong position in front of Pittsburg, and after a severe battle of ten hours, thanks be to the Almighty, gained a complete victory, driving the enemy from every position." [37] No one except Colonel Nathan Bedford Forrest seemed much concerned about possible Federal re-enforcements. Twice during the night his men, clad in captured blue uniforms, filtered through the Federal lines and returned with reports of the arrival of fresh troops. Twice he notified superiors of what he had learned but no one took him seriously.[38]

In spite of Confederate optimism, a check of brigades must have revealed that probably fewer than 20,000 men would be available for the next day of fighting. And fresh Federal troops almost equal that number were ferrying the Tennessee to join Grant. A force that might have been sufficient to handle Grant's exhausted army was woefully insufficient to handle his fresh one. What at sundown July 6 appeared to be a cowering foe driven to its final refuge in the loop of Snake Creek and the Tennessee River would by sunrise July 7 be an aggressive army confident of sweeping its opponent from the field.

[37] *Official Records*, X, Pt. 1, 384.
[38] Jordan and Pryor, *Campaigns of Forrest*, 136–37.

During the night Clark's division of Polk's corps camped near Bragg and Hardee. Cheatham, feeling a great need for reorganization, led his division back to the site of his own camp of the previous night. Polk followed to assist in bringing the division up for the early morning offensive. Permitting Cheatham to bivouac so far to the rear was evidence of the lack of Confederate planning. Tired troops merely camped for the night. They formed no defensive battle line; they expected to be the attackers, not the attacked, on Monday morning.

Meanwhile, Grant and Buell were preparing for an early morning offensive. On the sector next to the river was Buell's army under Nelson, Alexander McD. McCook and Thomas L. Crittenden. Next came Grant's veterans of the previous day under Hurlbut, McClernand, and Sherman. On the extreme right was Lew Wallace. This Federal line began moving at dawn. On this second day of battle it was the Confederates who were surprised, and before they could recover their balance and form a strong line of defense they had lost most of the ground gained on the previous day. For some unexplained reason Bragg and Hardee had exchanged positions along the battle line, but two of Bragg's brigades remained on the right, passing under command of Hardee. Breckinridge lined up next to Hardee. Clark's division of Polk's corps moved up beside Bragg and under his command. Cheatham's division was far to the rear when the fighting began. Polk arrived with this division about 8 A.M., and after a temporary halt at the rear of Shiloh Church, threw it into line between Breckinridge and Bragg. But Beauregard later recalled that having heard nothing from Polk by 9:30 he sent him a "rather imperative" order to hurry back to the battle front and "hurry back he did. Dashing forward, with drawn sword, at the head of Cheatham's fine division, he soon formed his line of battle at the point where his presence was so much needed, and, with unsurpassed vigor, moved on, against a force at least double his own, making one of the most brilliant charges of infantry made on either day of the battle." [39]

For six hours the battle raged, with the Confederates offering fierce resistance, even at times counterattacking, but gradually giving up their captured ground. Beauregard's army was not only tired but stunned by the fact that its hard earned gains of the

[39] Roman, *Beauregard*, I, 313.

previous day were being so quickly snatched away. Observers detected a definite lack of dash, spirit, and determination. About 2 P.M. Beauregard, realizing that his best efforts were not enough and that there was danger of being crushed by superior numbers, issued a general order to fall back upon Corinth. Although it would seem that Buell, if not Grant, was capable of spirited pursuit, the Federals permitted the Confederates to retire in order.

It was a worn and discouraged army that slushed its way through the mud on the return to the Corinth base it had so hopefully left less than a week before. On the Shiloh battlefield lay 1,728 Confederate dead. Another 8,012 had been wounded. Still another 959 were missing. Polk's effective strength had been reduced by 2,357; that of the entire army by 10,699.[40]

From his Corinth headquarters Polk reported to his wife on April 10:

> I am thankful to say that the protecting hand of God was over me and around me, and I experienced no harm during either of the two days of battle, although I was in the thickest of the storm during both days. All glory and honor be unto His holy Name for my protection and defense, for it was He who did it. It was He who "covered my head in the day of battle."
>
> I cannot describe the field. It was one of great carnage, and as it was the second battle I had been in—the other being a bloody one also—I felt somewhat more accustomed to it. This one was on a larger scale, and a magnificent affair. I believe from what I know and hear, you will have no reason to be ashamed of your husband or your sons.

Only the lack of daylight hours, he thought, prevented a complete victory on the first day. The second day he classed as a draw. "We left them, and they did not follow us. . . . The army is now refreshing itself for another attack, and we think on the next occasion our troops will behave better than on the last.[41]

---

[40] *Official Records*, X, Pt. 1, 396. This account of the battle of Shiloh is taken largely from the reports of Beauregard, Bragg, Hardee and Polk, *ibid.*, 384 ff, 405 ff, 463 ff, 566 ff.

[41] Quoted in Polk, *Leonidas Polk*, II, 114–15. Both of Polk's sons were in the battle of Shiloh. Hamilton served as captain and aide-de-camp and Meck, a lieutenant, was with Bankhead's Battery of light artillery.

(13)

Perryville—Advance and Retreat

As BEAUREGARD'S ARMY began its return march from Shiloh to Corinth the garrison at Island No. 10 was marching out under a white flag of surrender; another 7,000 men had been lost to the Confederacy. As long as Polk was at Humboldt he was in close touch with affairs on the Island and at New Madrid, often relaying instructions from the ailing Beauregard to General John P. McCown. But as Grant concentrated his troops along the Tennessee a similar Federal force under General John Pope was moving down the west side of the Mississippi. By March 3 it was before New Madrid. After more than a week of light skirmishing Pope began an all out attack, and during the night of March 13 McCown ordered evacuation. The withdrawal was less than orderly. McCown pronounced it "unsatisfactory" for "want of discipline." Meck Polk was among the fleeing Confederates; he escaped with only a blanket. Many threw all of their equipment into the river.[1] Some stopped at Island No. 10; others went down the river on the Tennessee side. Meck Polk was among the latter, and before the battle of Shiloh he joined his father at Corinth.

After the evacuation of New Madrid Polk and Beauregard went into conference at Jackson to decide what should be done for McCown at Island No. 10. Beauregard had recently ordered all infantry to be sent down to Fort Pillow, but the generals now decided to leave to McCown the decision as to what reduction might be made in the garrison. McCown, pessimistic and timorous, continuously expressed grave doubts as to his ability to hold the Island. Beauregard was displeased. "What does McCown mean by his doubts?" he inquired of Polk. On March 20, from Beauregard's

[1] McCown to Polk, March 14, 1862, *Official Records*, VIII, 780; Mecklenburg Polk to Sister, March 29, 1862, Leonidas Polk Papers.

headquarters, Polk wrote McCown "I again repeat my conviction that it is of the highest importance to hold Island 10 and Madrid Bend to the last extremity. It is the key of the Mississippi Valley." Beauregard, however, had lost confidence in McCown and on March 26 he directed Polk to place Brigadier General W. W. Mackall in command at Island No. 10.[2]

After Beauregard and Polk moved to Corinth to begin preparation for the campaign against Grant, Mackall was left on his own. There would be no re-enforcements. As long as the river below was open he had a chance, but when Federal gunboats ran the island guns and began protecting Pope's troops in crossing the river below, there was no longer any hope. Bombarded from the river and cut off by land the garrison on Island No. 10 had no choice but surrender.

The fall of Island No. 10 cleared the Mississippi for Federal boats as far south as Fort Pillow. Halleck now directed Pope to abandon the Mississippi and join Grant and Buell. And during the second week in April he himself arrived at Pittsburg Landing to assume command of the three armies. Halleck was a cautious fighter; he had no intention of allowing himself to be surprised as he apparently believed Grant had been at Shiloh. Indeed, he was too cautious for he spent a month crawling and digging when he might have moved his superior numbers against Corinth with every expectation of success. But such criticism appears a bit unfair when it is noted that Halleck greatly overestimated Beauregard's strength; Beauregard had not received the heavy re-enforcements reported. Furthermore, time was required to forge three Federal armies into one.

By the close of April the Federal force had been organized. On the left was Pope's Army of the Mississippi. Then came Buell's Army of the Ohio. On the right was the Army of the Tennessee, which was to be commanded by George H. Thomas. Grant was given the meaningless title of second in command to Halleck. Throughout the month of May this mighty army of 125,000 crawled toward Corinth digging in each night as protection against a surprise attack.

[2] Polk to McCown, March 15, 20, 1862, *Official Records*, VIII, 781, 793; Beauregard to *id.*, March 17, 1862, *ibid.*, 786; *id.* to Polk, March 17, 26, 1862, *ibid.*, 786, 803.

In the meantime Beauregard's army was arranged in line about three miles in front of Corinth, extending from the Memphis and Charleston Railroad on the right to the Mobile and Ohio on the left. Hardee was on the right with Van Dorn, who had recently arrived from Arkansas, in his rear. To the left of Hardee was Bragg. Then came Polk, with Breckinridge held in general reserve. Light skirmishing occurred almost daily, but neither opponent was eager to make an all out attack. Although the Confederate position had defensive strength general conditions in the vicinity of Corinth were such that the army could not remain in this position indefinitely. The town was crowded with sick and wounded. Food was short. The water soon became contaminated. Disease was taking a terrible toll.

On May 25 Beauregard called his generals into conference. What the others had to say was not recorded but Hardee put his observation in writing. He saw three possibilities—attack, wait to be attacked, or withdraw. To attack a foe greatly superior in numbers and well entrenched, he explained, "would probably inflict on us and the Confederacy a fatal blow." If the enemy would make the attack the Confederates could possibly repel it, but "it is manifest no attack is meditated." Instead there would likely be heavy and continuous enemy bombardment with the hope of encouraging "sorties against his intrenched position" and of making orderly withdrawal extremely difficult. In view of these probabilities, Hardee thought eventual evacuation inevitable, and that it should be carried out before heavy shelling began. "It should be done in good order, so as not to discourage our friends or give a pretext for the triumph of our enemies. . . . If we resolve to evacuate, every hour of delay only serves to augment our difficulties." [3] Beauregard endorsed on this note "I concur fully," and there is no evidence of disagreement among the other generals.

Plans quickly took form and wagon trains began moving out toward Tupelo about 11 P.M., May 29. Two hours later troops were falling into line—Van Dorn, Bragg, Hardee, Polk, with Breckinridge's reserves bringing up the rear. Federal General Pope, completely deceived by Confederate activities, notified Halleck that heavy re-enforcements were arriving in his front and "from

[3] Quoted in Roman, *Beauregard*, I, 578–79.

all appearances . . . I shall be attacked in heavy force at day-light."⁴ But daylight brought no attack and Federal scouts soon returned with the news that Corinth had been completely evacu-ated.⁵

After brief stops behind the Tuscumbia River and again at Booneville, to await possible Federal pursuit, Beauregard moved his army on to Baldwin, some thirty miles to the south of Corinth. When Halleck showed no inclination to move deeper into enemy territory the Confederates moved on to Tupelo.⁶ From Baldwin General Polk wrote his daughter, Mrs. Gale, now residing at "Poverty Hall" near Jackson. The Gales had been forced to flee "Holly Bend," their Yazoo estate, following destruction of the Mississippi levees.⁷ He was sending Meck for a visit, Polk said, "as well for your sake as for his [Meck was among those who had become ill at Corinth]. He will tell you all the news of the army and of me. We have deemed it advisable, after having kept the enemy employed six weeks in digging and embanking all the way from the Tennessee River to Corinth, and just when he had spent millions of dollars, and lost thousands of men by the climate and water, and when he had just got ready to open his heavy batteries —to bid him good-morning and invite him down a little farther South.

"How he likes it we have not heard. We like the change very much, as it gives us a delightful woodland for our camps and fine, pure, spring freestone water and plenty of fresh beef. I have a delightful camp myself, and wish you could look in on me and see how comfortable I am. My health is, thank our Heavenly Father, very good, and, except that I am separated from my family and grieved with the disturbed state of the country, I am as happy as I generally am, and you know that is not miserable." ⁸

Exhausted and ill Confederates found conditions at Tupelo even more pleasant than those at Baldwin. And in the absence of any threat of an attack a spirit of relaxation pervaded the entire camp. Beauregard (and apparently his generals) was pleased with

---

⁴ Quoted in *ibid.*, 390.
⁵ For an interesting description of the methods of deception used by re-tiring Confederates see Horn, *Army of Tennessee,* 151.
⁶ For Beauregard's account of the withdrawal and copies of orders pertain-ing thereto, see *Official Records,* X, Pt. 1, 762 ff.
⁷ Gale, "Recollections."   ⁸ Quoted in Polk, *Leonidas Polk,* II, 118.

the withdrawal. On June 13 he reported to Adjutant General Cooper: "I feel authorized to say by the evacuation the plan of campaign of the enemy was utterly foiled—his delay of seven weeks and vast expenditures were of little value, and he has reached Corinth to find it a barren locality, which he must abandon as wholly worthless for his purposes." [9] That this was a well executed withdrawal there can be no doubt; however, Richmond authorities were not interested in further retreat into the deep South. Without waiting for a report from Beauregard, President Davis wired for an explanation. Then without waiting for a reply to his telegram he dispatched Colonel William Preston Johnston (son of the late General Albert Sidney Johnston) with a list of pointed questions to be answered by Beauregard. [10]

Meanwhile, Beauregard, still suffering from the throat ailment that had plagued him since before transfer to the West, arranged to turn over his command to General Bragg and retire to Bladon Springs for a much needed rest. News that the commanding general had left his post without approval from Richmond gave Davis the excuse he needed. Bragg was made permanent commander. He had already been promoted to general shortly after the battle of Shiloh.

It is easy to understand how the almost constant withdrawal of the army in the West deeper and deeper into Confederate territory would be of much concern to Richmond authorities and the general public. Yet it is difficult to see what else this army could have done. According to Beauregard, when he began withdrawal from Corinth he had about 47,000 effectives. Halleck had 125,000 in the same area. An all out attempt to hold the Corinth line might have proved an heroic stand but it could not have failed to result in disaster. The Memphis and Charleston Railroad to the east had already been seized at Huntsville by General Ormsby Mitchel who moved down from Middle Tennessee. To the west of Corinth this same line would soon fall under enemy control when Memphis surrendered on June 6. Already suffering from insanitary surroundings and facing a shortage of food and military supplies, what could have been gained by waiting to be cut off on both flanks and eventually crushed?

[9] *Official Records*, X, Pt. 1, 765.
[10] For questions and answers see *ibid.*, 774–77.

In Confederate hands Corinth was of great importance as long as the Memphis and Charleston Railroad could be kept open, but Beauregard was correct when he stated that the enemy would find it "wholly worthless for his purposes." Halleck and Washington authorities soon realized that 125,000 men sitting astride the railroad in northern Mississippi and not daring to penetrate deeper into that state were making small contribution to the Union cause.

Following Federal occupation of Corinth and Memphis the Mississippi River was open as far south as Vicksburg. Below that point New Orleans was also in Federal hands. An immediate move on Vicksburg was considered but the idea was abandoned for the present. One wonders what might have been the result had Halleck dared relentless pursuit of the Confederate army. He had the men, and with open river and rail lines of communication how could he have failed to crush his opponent?

If this Confederate army was not to be pursued then the most important point in the West was Chattanooga, a rail center of great importance on the lifeline of the Confederacy. From Corinth Halleck had direct railroad connection with Chattanooga through Huntsville and Stevenson, Alabama. But unfortunately General Mitchel had not been satisfied with seizing the Memphis and Charleston at Huntsville; he had torn up the tracks both to the east and west and destroyed some bridges. Confederate raiders destroyed others. Mitchel had moved eastward to the vicinity of Bridgeport, Alabama, from which point he was a threat to Chattanooga.

Having decided not to pursue the retiring Confederates deeper into Mississippi, Halleck broke up the organization of his large army into its component parts, restoring Grant and Buell to independent commands. Major General Pope was called to duty in Northern Virginia. His Army of the Mississippi passed under command of Brigadier General William S. Rosecrans and was subsequently assigned to Grant's department. On July 11 Halleck himself was ordered to Washington to become General in Chief of the Armies of the United States. Meanwhile, on June 9, Halleck had notified Buell to begin movement along the Memphis and Charleston toward East Tennessee, repairing the railroad as he went and guarding it as his principal supply line. Crossing the

Tennessee by ferries at Florence and a crude bridge at Decatur, Buell was at Huntsville by the last of June.[11]

From the beginning of the war East Tennessee had been a prize much desired by the Federal Government. Strong Union sentiment in that area had resulted in the addition of several regiments to the Union armies, and many who remained behind constantly begged for protection against what they classed as unbearable Confederate oppression. This situation was of much concern to President Lincoln. But of still greater importance was the railroad through East Tennessee connecting Virginia with the Deep South. From the Confederate view this railroad must be protected against both local enemies and organized Federal forces.

In March, 1862, President Davis assigned Major General Edmund Kirby Smith, a hero of Manassas, to command in this strategic department. Defense of the East Tennessee mountains and valleys from the Kentucky-Virginia line on the north to the Alabama-Georgia line on the south with the small force at his command required Kirby Smith to look in all directions at the same time and to rush troops from one extremity to the other to meet Federal threats.[12]

Two days before Buell began his movement eastward a roving Federal force commanded by Brigadier General James S. Negley, which had moved over the mountains from Winchester, Tennessee, began shelling Chattanooga from across the Tennessee River. No attempt was made to cross over and the damage was slight, but the boldness of such an assault was alarming to the Confederate commander. After two days of intermittent bombardment Negley withdrew and recrossed the mountains into Middle Tennessee. He reported that the lack of pontoons made it impossible to cross the Tennessee River; however, the taking of Chattanooga would not be "very difficult or hazardous" if proper preparation were made.[13]

[11] Don Carlos Buell, "East Tennessee and the Campaign of Perryville," *Battles and Leaders*, III, 35.

[12] For details of Kirby Smith's problems in East Tennessee see Joseph H. Parks, *General Edmund Kirby Smith, C.S.A.* (Baton Rouge, 1954), 155 ff.

[13] Edmund Kirby Smith to Wife, June 11 (?), 1862, Kirby Smith Papers (University of North Carolina); *id.* to W. H. Taylor, June 10, 1862, and J. S. Negley to O. M. Mitchel, June 8, 1862, *Official Records*, X, Pt. 1, 922, 920.

The withdrawal of Negley brought only temporary relief, for Federal Brigadier General George W. Morgan was closing in on Cumberland Gap at the other extremity of Kirby Smith's department. As Kirby Smith was preparing to rush all available troops to the defense of the Gap a wire from Chattanooga reported Mitchel had moved up to Stevenson and Jasper and was crossing the river. Somewhat bewildered, Kirby Smith reported to Richmond that "General Buell seems to be directing the movement against this department." He was correct; on June 11 Buell had ordered Mitchel: "General Morgan is advancing on Cumberland Gap. Endeavor as much as possible to keep your force in an attitude to threaten Chattanooga and occupy the attention of Kirby Smith." [14]

Kirby Smith quickly realized that he could not defend Cumberland Gap and Chattanooga simultaneously. He decided to abandon the Gap and concentrate on Chattanooga. Cumberland Gap was evacuated on June 18 and its garrison, under command of Brigadier General Carter L. Stevenson, was withdrawn to a position on the railroad where it could either check Morgan, if he attempted to move deeper into East Tennessee, or rush to the defense of Chattanooga. On June 18 Bragg wired from Tupelo that he might be able to send aid as soon as he could learn the enemy's intentions.[15]

A week passed and the threat to Chattanooga continued to grow more serious. In spite of supply problems resulting from Confederate raids on the Memphis and Charleston and the Nashville and Decatur railroads, Buell was moving closer. On June 27 Kirby Smith wired Bragg: "Buell is reported crossing the river at Decatur and daily sending a regiment by rail toward Chattanooga. I have no force to repel such an attack." [16] Bragg was still at Tupelo organizing and disciplining his army, but undecided as to plans for carrying the fight to the enemy. Even after the departure of Buell from the Corinth area he felt that only small re-enforcements might be sent to Kirby Smith. Probably his most important assistance was the sending of Colonel Nathan Bedford Forrest to Kirby Smith at Chattanooga in mid-June for the purpose of welding together cavalry units in that area. Forrest was to win much of his

[14] Kirby Smith to S. Cooper, June 15, 1862, *ibid.*, XVI, Pt. 2, 684–85; Buell to Mitchel, June 11, 1862, *ibid.*, X, Pt. 1, 54.
[15] *Ibid.*, XVII, Pt. 2, 610.   [16] *Ibid.*, XVI, Pt. 2, 709.

fame during the next few months by his daring raids in Middle Tennessee, particularly along the Nashville and Chattanooga Railroad, Buell's chief supply line. Also, on July 3, there arrived in Chattanooga Major General John P. McCown with a division of 3,000 men from Bragg's department.

Buell continued to move toward Chattanooga. A month had passed since Bragg had promised to move on Buell's rear, but he was still at Tupelo. On July 19, Kirby Smith wired that Buell was concentrating in the Stevenson-Bridgeport area. "The successful holding of Chattanooga depends upon your co-operation." On the following day he again urged "Your co-operation is much needed. It is your time to strike at Middle Tennessee." [17] Bragg replied that he could do no more than "menace and harass the enemy," yet he urged that Kirby Smith make every effort to retard Buell in crossing the Tennessee. Kirby Smith continued to urge. Why not leave a small force to watch the Mississippi, he suggested, "and, shifting the main body to this department, take command in person?" He would "cheerfully place my command under you subject to your orders." [18] Bragg was already on the way when he received this last appeal.

At Tupelo Bragg had had his problems. Upon taking formal command on June 27 he had told the army "A few more days of needful preparation and organization and I shall give your banners to the breeze—shall lead you to emulate the soldiers of the Confederacy in the East, and with the confident trust that you will gain additional honors to those you have already won on other fields. But be prepared to undergo privation and labor with cheerfulness and alacrity." Two days later he complained to the War Department of a shortage of supplies and very inadequate transportation facilities. But most of all he complained of a lack of "proper commanders." Of his major generals, Van Dorn, Breckinridge, and Hindman had been transferred to other posts. Polk was relieved as corps commander and made second in command. This left only Hardee "as a suitable commander of that grade." [19]

It was already known to the new Commanding General that improvement in discipline and better organization were a necessity. However, this was the phase of military operation in which

[17] *Ibid.*, 730–31 [18] *Ibid.*, XVII, Pt. 2, 651; *ibid.*, XVI, Pt. 2, 734–35.
[19] *Ibid.*, XVII, Pt. 2, 626, 627–28.

Bragg excelled; consequently, he did the job well in spite of wide-spread grumbling and discontent. General Polk, according to his son, "fully shared" the feeling that gradually spread over the army that Bragg's sternness was in preparation for vigorous action against the enemy within the near future.[20]

On July 2 Bragg ordered a reorganization of his forces in the vicinity of Tupelo. Corps were redesignated as divisions. As Polk was named second in command, Hardee was designated a com-mander of the Army of the Mississippi.[21] When he moved to the aid of Kirby Smith he would leave Van Dorn with 16,000 effectives to "hold the line of the Mississippi." Price with a similar number was to remain in the vicinity of Tupelo. Hardee with 35,000 men would move immediately to Chattanooga. The artillery and trains were to move overland; infantry divisions would go by rail via Mobile, Montgomery, and Atlanta.[22] There seems to be no doubt but that Bragg intended an invasion of Middle Tennessee. Before leaving Corinth he wrote Cooper that he planned "to strike an effective blow through Middle Tennessee, gaining the enemy's rear, cutting off his supplies and dividing his forces so as to en-counter him in detail."[23]

Hardee's advance guard was in Chattanooga by July 27. Bragg arrived two days later, and Kirby Smith met him there; the two went into conference on July 31. To his wife Kirby Smith confided that he found Bragg "a grim old fellow, but a true soldier," a man much feared and respected, but not loved.[24] Bragg's failure to make a show of authority as result of his rank put Kirby Smith at ease. And he subsequently promoted confidence by his suggestion that since neither had any object other than "success of our cause," there should be "no misunderstanding" as a result of the "necessary union of our forces."[25] The two commanders agreed that Bragg should enter Middle Tennessee, where Forrest was already paving the way for his approach. Kirby Smith, re-enforced by Pat Cleburne's division from Bragg's army, would move on

[20] Polk, *Leonidas Polk*, II, 121.   [21] Official Records, XVII, Pt. 2, 636.
[22] Bragg to S. Cooper, July 23, 1862, *ibid.*, 655–56; Special Orders No. 4, *ibid.*, 656–57.
[23] *Ibid.*, 655–56.
[24] Kirby Smith to Wife, August 1, 1862, Kirby Smith Papers.
[25] Bragg to Kirby Smith, August 8, 1862, *Official Records*, XVI, Pt. 2, 745–46.

Cumberland Gap. Should the Gap be taken he would unite with Bragg for a joint invasion of Middle Tennessee.[26]

In preparation for the proposed campaign Bragg resumed personal command of the Army of the Mississippi. The army was organized into two wings of two divisions each. Polk was to command the right wing composed of the divisions of Major General B. F. Cheatham and Major General J. M. Withers; Hardee's left wing was composed of Major General Samuel Jones' and Brigadier General S. A. M. Wood's divisions. However the subsequent arrival of Major General S. B. Buckner and a decision to leave Jones in East Tennessee resulted in assignment of Buckner to command under Hardee.[27]

Kirby Smith immediately returned to Knoxville to prepare for his campaign against Cumberland Gap, but within a few days he was toying with the idea of bypassing the Gap and heading for central Kentucky. He suggested that Bragg might find the route by way of Sparta "one of your natural lines of operation into Middle Tennessee." Bragg replied that it would be another week before he was ready to move and in the meantime he would decide whether to move on Nashville or Lexington, Kentucky. "My inclination now is for the latter." He suggested that Kirby Smith be cautious about moving deep into Kentucky until he himself had engaged Buell. He was urging Van Dorn and Price to move across West Tennessee and trusted "we may all unite in Ohio." [28]

Kirby Smith moved with speed. He decided to bypass the Gap, leaving General C. L. Stevenson with 9,000 men to watch General George Morgan. Taking with him the divisions of Generals Pat Cleburne and Thomas J. Churchill, totaling 6,000 men, he passed through Roger's Gap into Kentucky. Brigadier Generals Henry Heth and Danville Leadbetter, with another 3,000, passed through Big Creek Gap and by August 22 all were at Barboursville, Kentucky. Throwing his cavalry out in front to clear the way toward Richmond, Kirby Smith was again on the march by August 25. No spirited opposition was encountered until he descended Big Hill

[26] Kirby Smith to J. Stoddard Johnston, October 3, 1866, Kirby Smith Papers; Bragg to Samuel Cooper, August 1, 1862, *Official Records,* XVI, Pt. 2, 741.

[27] *Official Records,* XVI, Pt. 2, 759, 764, 766.

[28] Kirby Smith to Bragg, August 9, 1862, *ibid.,* 748; Bragg to Kirby Smith, August 10, 1862, *ibid.,* 748–49.

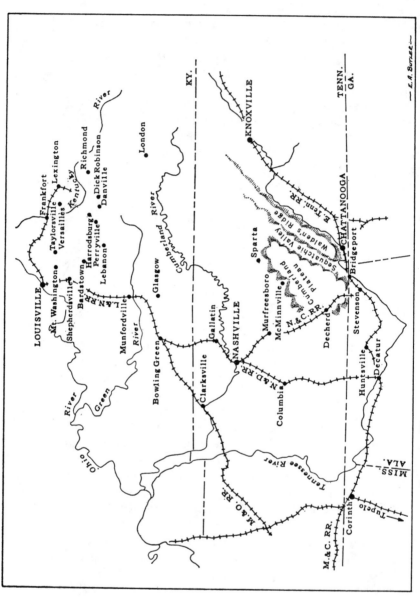

CENTRAL TENNESSEE AND KENTUCKY—To Perryville and Return

into the bluegrass country. By August 30 he was at Richmond. After a full day of small engagements Federal opposition was crushed; 4,000 men, including Brigadier General Mahlon D. Manson, had been made prisoners. Confederate losses were 78 killed and 372 wounded.

After a day of rest and thanks to God "to whose mercy and goodness these victories are due," Kirby Smith moved on Lexington. He rode into town unopposed on September 2, and a day later was joined by the cavalry of John Hunt Morgan, which had been dealing misery to the Federals in central Tennessee and Kentucky, especially along their rail connections with Louisville. "We come not as invaders but as liberators," Kirby Smith publicly announced to all Kentuckians. To his wife he described his entrance into the bluegrass country as "a perfect ovation." Louisville and Cincinnati became panic stricken. General Lew Wallace declared martial law in Cincinnati and ordered all business houses closed as citizens assembled to work on fortifications.[29]

In high spirits Kirby Smith now urged Bragg to effect "a junction with my command and holding Buell's communications, to give battle to him with superior forces and with certainty of success." But Bragg was far behind. The arrival of troops and trains had required more time than had been anticipated. Meanwhile, Buell, his line extending in a semicircle from Stevenson, Alabama, through Decherd, Tennessee, to McMinnville and with the mountains and the river between him and Bragg, had been waiting and watching.

On August 7, reporting from Huntsville, he had estimated Confederate forces in East Tennessee at about 60,000. His own forces numbered about 46,000, but when deductions were made for the protection of Nashville and the railroads, he could depend upon only 31,000 marching troops. Nevertheless, it was his intention to "march upon Chattanooga at the earliest possible day, unless I ascertain certainly that the enemy's strength renders it imprudent." Should Bragg cross the river "I shall attack him, and I do not doubt that we shall defeat him."[30]

Buell did not march on Chattanooga; neither did he attack

[29] For details of Kirby Smith's Kentucky campaign see Parks, *Kirby Smith*, 200 ff.
[30] Buell to Halleck, August 7, 1862, *Official Records*, XVI, Pt. 2, 278–79.

when Bragg began crossing the river. On August 22 General
McCook reported that Cheatham's division of Polk's corps had begun crossing a week earlier and had subsequently been joined by
Withers. Hardee was there also and was crossing. Cheatham's advance was said to have reached the top of Walden's Ridge. "The
enemy intend marching upon McMinnville." [31] Buell promptly
moved his headquarters to Decherd and sent Thomas to McMinnville. Thomas urged concentration at that point but Buell disagreed. He thought that "We must concentrate in advance and assume the offensive or fall back at last to Murfreesborough." Since
the road from Chattanooga to McMinnville passed through Altamont he ordered Thomas to the top of the mountain at that point
where he would be joined by Crittendon and McCook.[32]

Cheatham's division of Polk's wing began crossing the Tennessee
River on August 17. Since little was known of enemy location or
intention, Polk warned Cheatham "to reconnoiter thoroughly the
ground in your front" and note the best defensive positions. No attack was expected, "yet it appears the enemy is in motion in considerable force at no great distance." [33]

Withers' division followed immediately, traveling about one
day's march behind Cheatham. Polk left Chattanooga on August 28, and after one night with Withers moved on to the front
with Cheatham.[34] Hardee's divisions under Buckner and Anderson
were across by the twenty-ninth, and Bragg had established headquarters at Dunlap.[35] Before leaving Chattanooga Bragg issued to
his troops a message of courage and determination.

"The enemy is before us, devastating our fair country, imprison-
ing our old and venerable men (even the ministers of God), in-
sulting our women, and desecrating our altars. It is our proud lot
to be assigned the duty of punishing and driving forth these deluded men, led by desperate adventurers and goaded on by Abolition demagogues and demons. Let us but deserve success and an
offended Diety will certainly assure it. Should we be opposed, we

[31] A. M. McCook to Buell, August 22, 1862, *ibid.*, 389.
[32] Buell to Thomas, August 23, 1862, *ibid.*, 399–400; *id.* to Halleck, August 24, 1862, *ibid.*, 406–407.
[33] George Williamson, assistant adjutant general, to Cheatham, August 17,
22, 1862, *ibid.*, 761, 770.
[34] Polk to Bragg, August 29, 1862, *ibid.*, 786.
[35] George G. Garner, assistant adjutant general, to Polk, August 29, 1862,
ibid., 787.

must fight at any odds and conquer at any sacrifice. Should the foe retire, we must follow him rapidly to his own territory and make him taste the bitters of invasion. . . . It is for you to decide whether our brothers and sisters of Tennessee and Kentucky shall remain bondmen and bondwomen of the Abolition tyrant or be restored to the freedom inherited from their fathers." [36]

Bragg reported his effective strength at 27,320, about equally divided between Hardee and Polk.[37]

By August 30 Polk could report his advance atop Walden's Ridge and ready to drop down into Sequatchie Valley. Buell had been completely wrong when he suspected a Confederate advance into Middle Tennessee across the Cumberland Plateau by way of Altamont. Instead, Polk turned up the Sequatchie to Pikeville. After a short delay Bragg instructed him to cross over to Sparta.

Buell quickly learned of the Confederate route of advance, and fearing an attempt to cut him off from his Nashville base, he fell back to Murfreesboro and then to Nashville. There was only a short delay at Sparta; on September 5 Bragg ordered Polk to resume the march. Buckner's and Anderson's divisions would soon follow and Bragg himself would be between them. Forrest, he told Polk, reported the enemy rapidly evacuating Nashville. ". . . we must push to head him off. . . . Arouse the people to join us as you progress." [38]

Polk was moving rapidly but Bragg urged him to even greater speed; Buell was evacuating Nashville, he wrote on September 9. About one-half of the Federal force had already gone toward Bowling Green and the other would soon follow. "We cannot possibly overtake him, but must head him off from General Kirby Smith." Bragg was writing Kirby Smith and requested that Polk do likewise. "Tell of Buell's movements and say General Bragg wishes him if too hard pressed to fall back in our direction. Combined we can thrash them all." Polk was to move by way of Tompkinsville to Glasgow. Hardee would join him at that point. Speed was important but it should be remembered that Hardee was two days behind.[39] The movements of both Buell and Bragg were greatly stimulated by the news of Kirby Smith's recent victories.

Leading Bragg's advance, Polk was in Tompkinsville, Kentucky,

[36] General Orders No. 124, *ibid.*, 779. [37] Field Return, *ibid.*, 784.
[38] Bragg to Polk, September 5, 7, 1862, *ibid.*, 796, 799–800.
[39] George G. Garner to Polk, September 9, 1862, *ibid.*, 804.

by September 10. As he moved into uncertain country he became a
bit more cautious. Cheatham was instructed to picket each road
with at least a battalion and to maintain the strictest discipline. On
September 11 Cheatham's division of Polk's wing moved on toward Glasgow. On this same day Polk received notice from Bragg
that as soon as the army was concentrated at that point he would
strike a blow at Bowling Green. Polk was expected to reach Glasgow before Buell reached Bowling Green and to seize the railroad
beyond Bowling Green. At the same time he was to collect all
available supplies from the surrounding country.[40]

Polk reached Glasgow on September 12. Buckner's division of
Hardee's wing was now within thirty miles of Glasgow and Anderson's ten miles to the rear. Bragg arrived at Glasgow on the thirteenth and immediately issued a proclamation to the people of
Kentucky. His army had entered Kentucky "to restore to you the
liberties of which you have been deprived by a cruel and relentless
foe," he explained. He would see that their persons and property
were protected. He solicited the assistance of their smiles, cheers
and willing hands.[41]

Buell arrived in Bowling Green the day after Bragg's arrival at
Glasgow. Whatever idea Bragg had entertained of attacking Bowling Green was quickly abandoned, even though he had captured
important Federal mail that indicated Buell's army was "greatly
demoralized, disheartened, and deceived; utterly in the dark as to
our movements." [42] Buell could scarcely have been "in the dark"
after Bragg crossed into Kentucky, but prior to that time he definitely had expected an attack upon Nashville. With Bragg now
across his supply line from Louisville he was dependent upon
Nashville, yet by moving into the fortifications at Bowling Green,
constructed by the Confederates themselves earlier in the year, he
was well protected from attack by Bragg.

Upon reaching Glasgow, Brigadier General James R. Chalmers'
brigade, Withers' division, Polk's wing, was ordered to proceed to
Cave City and take control of the railroad and telegraph at that
point. The order was executed about midnight September 12.
Reconnaissance on the following day revealed a considerable

<hr />

[40] George Williams to Cheatham, September 10, 1862, *ibid.*, 808–809;
George Garner to Polk, September 10, 1862, *ibid.*, 806.
[41] *Ibid.*, 822.   [42] Bragg to Polk, September 11, 1862, *ibid.*, 811.

quantity of wheat stored at nearby Horse Cave. This Chalmers took over for food. Later in the day he intercepted a telegraphic dispatch from Louisville saying that re-enforcements were being sent to Munfordville. This town at the railroad crossing of Green River already had a small Federal garrison. From Colonel John Scott, whose cavalry had done excellent services in Kirby Smith's capture of Richmond, Chalmers learned that this garrison was weak and that Scott proposed to attack it on the morning of the fourteenth if he could get some infantry support. Chalmers decided to strike even though he had no orders to make an attack. Much to his surprise he found the enemy of superior strength and well entrenched. The attack was repulsed with embarrassing losses, including three colonels.[43]

Bragg, "Unwilling to allow the impression of disaster to rest on the minds of my men," decided to attack Munfordville in force. He first ordered Polk to send Withers' division to carry the position. Then, quickly revising his plan, he directed Polk to lead the attack in person after ordering Cheatham to stand by at Cave City. Before these orders could be executed Bragg learned that the fortifications were strong in front but weak in the rear. Polk was now directed to cross Green River a few miles up stream and invest the position from the rear. Hardee would move up from the front.[44]

By midafternoon September 16 Bragg reported Hardee in position in front of the fortifications south of the river. He directed Polk to drive in the pickets north of the river and place his guns in position but not to open fire. As soon as all was ready he wished a conference "to consult on plan of attack and arrange details for the morning." But no attack was made the next morning. Apparently upon Buckner's suggestion it was decided to offer the Federal garrison an opportunity to surrender before opening fire. Munfordville was Buckner's home town and he naturally wished to save it from bombardment. Colonel John T. Wilder commanded about 4,000 men within the fortification; only a very unwise leader would permit so small a garrison to be crushed by Bragg's army. After some unusual and even humorous negotiations Wilder decided to

[43] See Chalmers' reports dated September 15, 19, 1862, *ibid.*, XVI, Pt. 1, 971–80.
[44] George Garner to Polk, September 15, 1862 (two dispatches), *ibid.*, Pt. 2, 825; Bragg to *id.*, September 15, 1862, *ibid.*

surrender. Bragg directed Buckner to receive the surrender, and Polk was invited to recross the river and be present at the ceremony.[45]

Bragg immediately issued orders congratulating his troops on this "crowning success" of an "extraordinary campaign" and urging them to spend the following day in rest and "thanksgiving and prayer to Almighty God . . . [in] gratitude for a bloodless victory instead of success purchased with the destruction of life and property." [46] To Richmond authorities he announced: "My junction with Kirby Smith is complete. Buell still at Bowling Green." And later in the day, in a second dispatch giving more details, he explained: "My position must be exceedingly embarrassing to Buell and his army. They dare not attack me, and yet no other escape seems to be open to them." [47]

Bragg's statements were much in error. No doubt Buell was embarrassed by the Confederate position across his supply line, but he was not still at Bowling Green. And Bragg himself must have known that Kirby Smith was at least seventy-five miles away. Buell had moved out of Bowling Green on September 17. He later claimed that his intention was to attack the Confederate army at Glasgow but upon learning that Bragg had moved on to Munfordville he directed his march in that direction. By the afternoon of the seventeenth he was within fifteen miles of Bragg's position. Along the way he had wired General C. C. Gilbert at Louisville, reporting the surrender of Wilder and warning that Bragg might be headed straight for Louisville. He suspected, however, that the Confederates would make a stand at either Green River or Muldraugh's Hill, "probably the former." In any case, he urged Gilbert to be prepared to fight. "I expect to be at Green River early to-morrow." [48]

Buell was not at Munfordville on the following day, but Bragg, hearing of the Federal arrival at Cave City, made rapid preparation to withstand an attack. Buell's whole force was moving in for an attack, he informed Polk. Polk then ordered Cheatham's ad-

[45] *Id.* to *id.*, September 16, 17, 1862, *ibid.*, 833, 837; Arndt M. Stickles, *Simon Bolivar Buckner* (Chapel Hill, 1940), 201–202.
[46] General Orders No. 6, *Official Records*, XVI, Pt. 2, 841–42.
[47] *Ibid.*, Pt. 1, 968.
[48] Buell, "East Tennessee and the Campaign of Perryville," *loc. cit.*, 41–42; Buell to Gilbert, September 17 (?), 1862, *Official Records*, XVI, Pt. 2, 527.

vance division to return immediately to Munfordville. Promptness was of utmost importance. Polk also rushed a courier to General Forrest: "General Bragg has made up his mind definitely that it is the enemy's intention to attack us at this place." Forrest must return immediately and also send a copy of this dispatch to John H. Morgan, who was reported to be at Elizabethtown.[49]

Buell did not attack. Bragg later claimed that he made every effort to get Buell to attack, even to "maneuvering a division in his front," but to no avail. To this claim Buell replied: "No doubt he was willing to fight on his own terms at more than one point. But the General who offers battle is he who stays to give or receive it." [50] Bragg did not wait for long. On September 20 Polk's wing took up the march toward Bardstown via Nolin and New Haven. Polk sent a courier to Forrest instructing him to tear up the railroad between Lebanon and Louisville and between Louisville and Elizabethtown and to report the degree of his success. Everything was well on the road by 6 A.M., September 21. Bragg sent ahead a note: "Do not push your troops to-day." There was no sign of enemy pressure.[51] Bragg had left Buell and the railroad, surrendering without a fight the advantage he had gained by weeks of hard marching. He had abandoned all intention of attacking either Buell or Louisville. Why? This is a question that has been argued by historians and military men for a hundred years. No one has come up with the answer, for it was buried in the mind of General Bragg. For weeks he had expressed an optimism and determination that had inspired his officers and men along hundreds of miles of hot dusty travel. Now, almost suddenly it would seem, optimism turned to uncertainty and depression. Hardee, Polk, and Buckner were later very critical of Bragg, but there is no record of their opinions at the time.

After months of meditation seasoned by other important events Bragg offered a very unsatisfactory explanation of his course: [52]

---

[49] Bragg to Polk, September 19, 1862 (1 A.M.), *Official Records*, XVI, Pt. 2, 848; Polk to Cheatham, September 19, 1862, *ibid.*; *id.* to Forrest, September 19, 1862, *ibid.*, 848–49.

[50] Bragg's report dated May 20, 1863, *ibid.*, Pt. 1, 1088 ff; Buell, "East Tennessee and the Campaign of Perryville, *loc. cit.*, 42 n.

[51] George Williamson to Forrest, September 20, 1862, *Official Records*, XVI, Pt. 2, 856; Bragg to Polk, September 21, 1862, *ibid.*, 859.

[52] Report of Bragg, May 20, 1863, *ibid.*, Pt. 1, 1088 ff.

With my effective force present, reduced by sickness, exhaustion, and the recent affair before the intrenchments at Munfordville, to half that of the enemy, I could not prudently afford to attack him there in his selected position. Should I pursue him farther toward Bowling Green he might fall back to that place behind his fortifications. Reduced at the end of four days to three days' rations, and in a hostile country, utterly destitute of supplies, a serious engagement brought on anywhere in that direction could not fail (whatever its results) to materially cripple me. The loss of a battle would be eminently disastrous. I was well aware also that he had a practicable route by way of Morgantown or Brownsville to the Ohio River and thence to Louisville. We were therefore compelled to give up the object and seek for subsistence.

Were these conditions unexpected? If so, what had he expected from his campaign? Did he expect a battle to last more than three days? The mark of incompetence is stamped on this weak attempt at explanation.

That Bragg had failed miserably is beyond question. But this does not explain what might have been done to save a campaign which thus far had been so efficiently executed. The fault was with Bragg and Kirby Smith, not with their wing, division, or brigade commanders nor the fighting quality of their men. The first weakness to become evident was the misjudgment of central Kentuckians. Both commanders had expected to secure more recruits than could be armed. Both were disappointed. Kirby Smith at first reported Kentuckians were "rising *en masse*." If he had the arms he could raise 20,000 recruits within a few days. But it was soon evident that the supply of arms was far greater than the number of recruits. To his wife Kirby Smith confided that those who had been undecided were still unconvinced. Response was slower than he had anticipated, "but when I see their magnificent estates their fat cattle & fine stock I can understand their fears & hesitancy —they have so much to lose." To Bragg he reported "Their hearts are evidently with us, but their blue-grass and fat cattle are against us." [53] Bragg had also made an appeal to Kentucky patriotism, but

[53] John Pegram to J. P. McCown, September 5, 1862, *ibid.*, Pt. 2, 797; Kirby Smith to Wife, September 16, 1862, Kirby Smith Papers; *id.* to Bragg, September 18, 1862, *Official Records*, XVI, Pt. 2, 845–46. In the printed

had received few, if any, recruits.

A second mistake was the failure to maintain efficient communications between the two armies. The success of this campaign depended upon close co-operation, yet neither was kept well informed of the intentions and movements of the other. A daily express between them would have required the services of but few men and horses. The original plan was for the two armies eventually to unite against Buell, yet no effort had been made at concentration. Kirby Smith had willingly and voluntarily placed himself subject to Bragg's orders. Bragg should have selected a point of concentration and ordered Kirby Smith to meet him there, bringing with him all available supplies.

When Kirby Smith heard of Wilder's surrender he sent to Bragg congratulations and "thirty wagons of flour and hard bread," and placed his entire force subject to Bragg's command. Cleburne's and Preston Smith's brigades, on loan from Bragg, were sent to Shelbyville, a position from which they could be used in a march on Louisville. The remainder of his command Kirby Smith concentrated at Frankfurt, Georgetown, and Paris from which points units could be moved toward either Louisville or Cincinnati. He informed Bragg that he was ready if needed, but he suggested that it would be unwise to leave the Lexington area exposed.[54]

But Bragg did not order Kirby Smith to join him even at this late moment. Instead he sent notice of his abandonment of all intention to attack either Buell or Louisville. With much surprise and concern, Kirby Smith replied: "I regard the defeat of Buell before he effects a junction with the force at Louisville as a military necessity, for Buell's army has always been the great bugbear to these people, and until defeated we cannot hope for much addition to our ranks from Kentucky." His infantry and artillery totaling 11,-000 were ready. "With regard to supplies, I have large quantities at Danville and am also collecting them at Frankfort." All available wagons had already been loaded and started toward Bardstown.[55]

---

copy of this last dispatch "fat grass" was used in the place of "fat cattle." This obvious error has been corrected.

[54] Kirby Smith to Bragg, September 18, 19, 1862, *Official Records*, XVI, Pt. 2, 845–46; John Pegram to Henry Heth, September 18, 1862, *ibid.*, 844.

[55] Kirby Smith to Bragg, September 21, 23, 1862, *ibid.*, 861, 866.

It was too late. Bragg no longer blocked Buell's advance and the Federal army was on its way to Louisville where an abundance of supplies and re-enforcements were waiting. But Kirby Smith, if not Bragg, had apparently come to realize that true victory was in the destruction of opposing armies, not in the temporary occupation of territory. And now the only hope of victory was in the concentration of all available Confederate troops to meet Buell's refreshed and strengthened force when it should move out of Louisville.

But Bragg had other immediate, and apparently more pressing plans. George W. Johnson, the "Confederate" governor of Kentucky, who like Governor Harris of Tennessee had joined Albert Sidney Johnston's army, had been killed at Shiloh.[56] If Kentucky was to be redeemed as a Confederate state, Bragg reasoned, then there must be a Confederate state government ready to take over. Richard Hawes, lieutenant governor, was next in line. Traveling at a safe distance in the rear of the invading armies, he had recently arrived at Bragg's headquarters.

On September 28 Bragg turned over to Polk the command of his Army of the Mississippi with the general instructions to attack if the enemy approached in moderate force. If the force was too great, he was to fall back upon Harrodsburg. Then ordering General Kirby Smith to assemble his troops at Frankfort, General Bragg prepared for a morale boosting inaugural ceremony for Governor Hawes. However, on his way to Frankfort he confided to Polk that "enthusiasm is unbounded, but recruiting at a discount." [57] As Bragg penned this observation and announced his plan to arrive at Frankfort on October 3, Buell's army was marching out of Louisville. Kirby Smith later claimed that both he and Buckner tried to persuade Bragg to give up the inaugural ceremony and begin concentrating all available forces for an all out engagement with Buell. But Bragg expressed confidence that his

[56] Johnson had been elected governor by a secessionist convention made up of delegates from sixty-five counties meeting in Russellville in November, 1861. This convention declared Kentucky independent of its existing government, passed an ordinance of secession from the Union, and set up a new government. The Confederate Congress, upon the recommendation of President Davis, admitted Kentucky to the Confederacy and gave her a star in the flag. For a full discussion see Coulter, *The Civil War and Readjustment in Kentucky,* 137–39.

[57] *Official Records,* XVI, Pt. 2, 895.

army at Bardstown, now commanded by Polk, could take care of Buell. The inaugural ceremony would be held.[58]

Buell's army, now totaling about 60,000 men, moved in four columns. Brigadier General Joshua W. Sill marched eastward toward Frankfort. In a southeasterly direction moved McCook, Crittenden, and Gilbert along separate roads leading to Taylorsville, Mt. Washington, and Shepherdsville. These roads converged upon Bardstown. Buell later explained that the "plan of my movement was to force the enemy's left back and compel him to concentrate as far as possible from a convenient line of retreat, while at the same time making a strong demonstration against his right, so as to mislead him as to the real point of attack, and prevent him from moving upon my left flank and rear." [59] This might have been an afterthought.

During the first day of marching the Federals on each of these roads encountered the pickets of Colonel John A. Wharton's cavalry. Polk instructed Wharton to fall back toward Bardstown, and at 3 A.M., October 2, Hardee ordered Colonel Joe Wheeler to keep in constant touch with Wharton and "conform your movement to the exigencies of the occasion." [60]

At 10 A.M. on the same day Polk sent Bragg a lengthy report. The enemy was advancing along each of the three roads from Louisville toward Bardstown. Wharton was keeping a close watch, falling back when hard pressed, but not yet heavily attacked. Polk was keeping the entire movement under close observation. "If an opportunity presents itself I will strike." If there was no such opportunity and should he be pressed he would fall back toward Harrodsburg and Danville along roads recently suggested by Bragg and hope to "concentrate with Gen. E. K. Smith, Stevenson, &c. It seems to me we are too much scattered." The approach of the enemy would mean the loss of provisions furnished by a number of mills in that area; consequently, Polk suggested that if there be a place where provisions were abundant then the Confederate forces should be concentrated at that point.

Before completing this report Polk received a dispatch from Pat

---

[58] Kirby Smith to J. Stoddard Johnston, October 31, 1866, Kirby Smith Papers. See also Kirby Smith's article on Perryville, *ibid.*

[59] Buell, "East Tennessee and the Campaign of Perryville," *loc. cit.*, 47.

[60] Hardee to Wheeler, *Official Records*, XVI, Pt. 2, 897.

Cleburne at Shelbyville. The enemy was approaching Shelbyville, which was on the route to Frankfort.[61] Polk now knew that the enemy was moving along four routes but he knew nothing of the comparative strength of these forces. Bragg, now at Lexington, before receiving Polk's report, received a wire from Frankfort informing him of the Federal approach to Shelbyville. "It may be a reconnaissance," he immediately explained to Polk, "but should it be a real attack we have them. . . . With Smith in front and our gallant army on the flank I see no hope for Buell if he is rash enough to come out. I only fear it is not true." (Again Bragg was riding the crest of optimism.) Polk was instructed to hold his army in readiness and should he learn of a heavy advance on Frankfort he was to strike without further orders.[62] Polk alerted his wing commanders, ordering them to be ready to move on a moment's notice.[63]

At 1 P.M. Bragg wrote again from Lexington. "The enemy is certainly advancing on Frankfort," he told Polk. "Put your whole available force in motion by Bloomfield and strike him in front and rear." [64] Just when Polk received this order is not known, but he spent the next twenty-four hours in watchful waiting. At noon October 3 Colonel Wharton reported the enemy at Taylorsville and Shepherdsville. ". . . everything indicates an advance of the enemy to give you battle." [65] Polk now reasoned that in view of the heavy enemy concentration along the Louisville roads there could not be a heavy concentration in front of Frankfort. He summoned his wing and division commanders into conference and explained the situation. He believed that the bulk of Buell's army was approaching Bardstown. If he should move from Bardstown to strike the column at Shelbyville he would expose his flank to four columns while attacking one. The supply bases at Bryantsville and Lexington and even communications with Cumberland Gap would be left exposed. As for Bragg's order, it was not a positive one. It had said to move "available" forces toward Shelbyville but left it to the major general commanding to decide what forces were

---

[61] Polk to Bragg, *ibid.*, 898.

[62] Bragg to Polk, October 2, 1862, *ibid.*, 896–97.

[63] Circular, October 2, 1862, *ibid.*, 896.

[64] Bragg to Polk, October 2, 1862, *ibid.*, 897.

[65] Wharton to *id*, October 3, 1862, *ibid.*, 900.

available. In view of the rapid Federal build-up before him, Polk concluded that he had no forces "available for the execution of such an order." His generals agreed.[66]

At 3 P.M. October 3, Polk wrote Bragg: "The last twenty-four hours have developed a condition of things on my front and left flank which I shadowed forth in my last note to you, which makes compliance with this order not only eminently inexpedient but impracticable. I have called a council of wing and division commanders to whom I have submitted the matter, and find that they unanimously indorse my views of what is demanded. I shall therefore pursue a different course, assured that when facts are submitted to you you will justify my decision." He would begin movement of his troops in accordance with previous general instructions.[67]

That Bragg intended for Polk to move toward Frankfort all of the troops in the Bardstown area seems beyond question. Polk's decision that he had no troops "available" for such a move might have been an unjustified play upon words, but it probably saved Bragg's army from disaster. With his principal supply bases destroyed and the supply line recently opened by way of East Tennessee severed, Bragg would have been much embarrassed and possibly at the mercy of Buell. But this does not answer the question of whether or not a subordinate is justified in refusing to obey orders of his superior, even when he is confident that they are faulty.

At 7 P.M. October 3, Colonel Wharton reported to Polk that it was highly probable that the enemy forces at Taylorsville and Shepherdsville were about to join their columns.[68] Polk began falling back toward Harrodsburg and a junction with Kirby Smith.[69]

In the meantime, Bragg, still at Lexington, was calling upon Kirby Smith for information. If the enemy were still advancing on Frankfort Kirby Smith must send another courier to Polk. "Our whole force must be brought to bear at the same time," Bragg urged. Kirby Smith forwarded this dispatch to Polk, adding that his own cavalry had reported no advance beyond Shelbyville, but did report the enemy in possession of Taylorsville. However, regardless

[66] Polk to Hardee, April 17, 1863, *ibid.*, Pt. 1, 1101–1103.
[67] *Id.* to Bragg, *ibid.*, Pt. 2, 901.   [68] Wharton to Polk, *ibid.*, 902–903.
[69] See Polk's Report, November ?, 1862, *ibid.*, Pt. 1, 1109.

of the point of advance, he observed, "our commands . . . are too far apart and beyond supporting distance." [70] There was certainly general agreement that a concentration was necessary, but no one seemed to know where.

At 8 P.M. October 3, Bragg wrote Polk from Frankfort that the Federal move on that place had "proved to be only a feint." Polk would therefore act accordingly, but he suggested preparation for a concentration and that in the meantime one flank be extended to Taylorsville. (He was too late; Taylorsville was already in Federal hands.) The forces of Cleburne and Preston Smith would soon join Polk. Recruiting was "slow, but improving." The inauguration of Governor Hawes would be held the following day.[71]

"I have your dispatch of yesterday," he wrote again at 7 A.M. October 4. If he were displeased with Polk's change of orders he made no mention of it. Instead, he ordered Polk to do what he was already in the process of doing—"Concentrate your forces in front of Harrodsburg. . . . Keep the men in heart by assuring them it is not a retreat, but a concentration for a fight." [72]

Later in the morning of October 4 Bragg wrote Polk that "We shall put our Governor in power soon and then I propose to seek the enemy." But before the ceremony was concluded a courier announced that the enemy was at hand. Bragg hurriedly added a postscript to his note: "Shall destory bridges and retire on Harrodsburg for concentration and then strike. Reach that point as soon as possible." [73]

Early in the morning of October 5 Polk was at Springfield. His advance under General Daniel Donelson was well beyond that point and headed for Danville. Bragg, now at Harrodsburg, ordered the column to change direction and concentrate on Harrodsburg as rapidly as possible. By the following day Polk was also at Harrodsburg. Hardee was at Perryville and Patton Anderson had been ordered to join him there. "I have directed General Hardee to ascertain, if possible, the strength of the enemy which may be

---

[70] Bragg to Kirby Smith, October 3, 1862, *ibid.*, XVI, Pt. 2, 901; Kirby Smith to Polk, October 3, 1862, *ibid.*

[71] Bragg to *id.*, October 3, 1862, *ibid.*, 903–904.

[72] *Id.* to *id.*, October 4, 1862, *ibid.*, 904–905.

[73] *Id.* to *id.*, October 4, 1862, *ibid.*, 905.

covered by his advance, I cannot think it large," Polk reported to Bragg.[74]

It is not clear what Polk meant by his conclusion "I cannot think it large." Was he referring to the advance column or the entire force of the enemy? His biographer son later claimed the former. But Bragg, six months and two battles later, wishing to saddle Polk with much of the blame for failure, explained that he was deceived by Polk's estimate that the strength of the enemy force was not great. Regardless of what Polk meant to say, he did actually refer to "the strength of the enemy which may be covered by his [the enemy's] advance." Yet be that as it may, Bragg and Polk held a long conference in Harrodsburg and certainly must have discussed the probable enemy strength.[75]

Wharton's reports of the Federal advance upon Bardstown were correct. The town was occupied shortly after Polk's rear guard withdrew. Buell, accompanying Gilbert's corps, ordered immediate forward movement. By October 7 Gilbert was approaching Perryville; McCook's corps was at Mackville; Crittenden's corps, accompanied by Thomas, was between Lebanon and Perryville; and Sill had been ordered to move toward Perryville, if the Confederates had left Frankfort.[76]

Bragg considered a Federal movement against Lexington by way of Frankfort so logical he refused to believe reports of great strength in the Perryville area. Sometime during the day of October 7 he issued a circular addressed to Polk and directing specific movements of troops. On the following day Cheatham's and Withers' divisions would move to Versailles by way of Lawrenceburg and join Kirby Smith. In the meantime Kirby Smith would concentrate his forces at Versailles. Hardee, now at Perryville, would follow "as circumstances allow." [77]

It apparently never occurred to Bragg that he was moving away from Buell's main force; neither did Polk show unusual concern. During the day he wrote his wife: "We have come here to concen-

[74] Polk to Bragg, October 6, 1862, 11 P.M., *ibid.*, Pt. 1, 1095.
[75] Polk, *Leonidas Polk*, II, 149; Bragg's Report, May 20, 1863, *Official Records*, XVI, Pt. 1, 1091–92.
[76] Williams, *Lincoln Finds a General*, IV, 123.
[77] *Official Records*, XVI, Pt. 1, 1095–96.

trate our army with that of E. Kirby Smith. It has been done and now we shall give the enemy battle wherever he presents himself. The Lord be with us and bless our arms!" [78]

The divisions did not march to Versailles as ordered, for Hardee sent in a report that he was being hard pressed by Gilbert near Perryville. At 5:40 P.M. Bragg wrote Polk: "In view of the news from Hardee you had better move with Cheatham's division to his support and give the enemy battle immediately: rout him, and then move to our support at Versailles." Withers' division was not to go to Perryville but was to set out that evening to join Kirby Smith at Versailles. "No time should be lost in these movements." [79] It would soon be revealed that the affair at Perryville was not a matter to be so lightly treated.

Cheatham, with Donelson's and Anderson's divisions, immediately set out for Perryville. Polk arrived in person during the night. He urged Bragg to permit him to take Withers' division also but Bragg clung to his idea of concentration at Versailles.[80] At Perryville Hardee had already been hotly engaged late in the afternoon and on into the night. Upon Gilbert's approach Hardee had taken position on a ridge beyond Doctor's Creek. This creek was dry except for pools here and there, and the battle of October 7 was for possession of these precious sources of water. After hours of stiff fighting by sunlight and then moonlight, Hardee still controlled the water supply.

As the troops from Harrodsburg arrived he sent them into battle line, although firing had probably ceased. Buckner occupied the extreme right, then Anderson, with Cheatham on the extreme left. The right and left flanks were covered by the cavalry of Wharton and Wheeler. Since Polk arrived late at night he was unable to reconnoiter the battle line until early on the morning of October 8. He later estimated that the line contained not more than 15,-000 Confederate troops. Although Polk and Hardee were not conscious of this fact, within striking distance of this line were the corps of Crittenden, McCook, and Gilbert, 58,000 strong.

It was late afternoon of the seventh when Hardee saw Bragg's

[78] Leonidas Polk Papers.
[79] Bragg to Polk, October 7, 1862, 5:40 P.M., *Official Records*, XVI, Pt. 1, 1096.
[80] Polk's Report, November ?, 1862, *ibid.*, 1109–1110.

circular issued earlier in the day, setting forth details for the movement of troops toward Versailles, and also his subsequent order to Polk for Withers to move as instructed and for Cheatham's divisions to move to Perryville, rout the enemy, and rush on to Versailles. Military student that he was, Hardee could not refrain from making a mild protest. "Permit me, from the friendly relations so long existing between us, to write you plainly," he wrote Bragg. "Do not scatter your forces. There is one rule in our profession which should never be forgotten; it is to throw the masses of your troops on the fractions of the enemy. The movement last proposed will divide your army and each may be defeated, whereas by keeping them united success is certain. If it be your policy to strike the enemy at Versailles, take your whole force with you and make the blow effective; if, on the contrary, you should decide to strike the army in front of me, first let that be done with a force which will make success certain. Strike with your whole strength first to the right then to the left. I could not sleep quietly to-night without giving expression to these views." In a postscript Hardee added "If you wish my opinion, it is that in view of the position of your depots you ought to strike this force first." [81]

Bragg's orders to Polk, issued at 5:30 P.M., had been to "give the enemy battle immediately." Again there was an opportunity for playing upon words. What was the exact meaning of "immediately"? Did it mean a night attack or an early morning attack? Was it a positive order or did it leave room for the exercise of judgment? At daybreak on the morning of the eighth Polk called a conference of his commanders. It was agreed that, in view of what appeared to be a heavy concentration in their front, the best policy would be a "defensive-offensive" one, giving the enemy time and opportunity to show his hand. Liddell's brigade of Buckner's division was thrown forward to feel out the enemy, and skirmishing began immediately. [82]

At 6 A.M. Polk wrote Bragg: "The enemy seem disposed to press this morning. Their pickets commenced firing at daylight. Understanding it to be your wish to give them battle we shall do so vigorously. Should we succeed we will pass to the right, with the view of joining General Kirby Smith. If it should become neces-

[81] Hardee to Bragg, October 7, 1862, 7:30 P.M., *ibid.*, 1099.
[82] Polk's Report, *ibid.*, 1110.

sary to fall back we will do so on Danville and Bryantsville, with a view of uniting with General Smith at that point." [83]

Polk's line was along the east bank of Chaplin River with its left resting upon Perryville. To the west, almost paralleling Chaplin until it joined that stream about two miles below Perryville, was Doctor's Creek. It was along the high ground on either side of this creek that the battle of Perryville would be fought. Liddell's brigade continued light skirmishing with the enemy until mid-morning and then, when firing became heavy, fell back upon the general line. Polk, seeing that his line was not extended far enough to the right, ordered Cheatham to move around from the extreme left to the right and hold his command in columns of brigades ready to move in any direction. With the aid of Wharton's cavalry he now overreached the enemy's left, and his position was well concealed by wooded hills.

By this time Bragg had arrived on the field. He later explained that having ordered an immediate attack and still not hearing the sound of guns he rushed to the scene to find out why. No one has yet solved the mystery of why the noise of the "shelling of the woods" that had been going on since dawn had failed to reach Bragg's ears. To Bragg's displeasure, he found that Polk had adopted a "defensive-offensive" plan. He now ordered the attack to begin at once,[84] although he had no idea of the strength of the forces he was attacking.

About 1 P.M. Wharton drove in McCook's left flank. The brigades of Donelson, Maney, and Stewart of Cheatham's division followed, scaling the banks of Chaplin River and driving along Doctor's Creek. McCook was not present when the Confederate attack began and General Lovell H. Rousseau, next in command, was caught poorly organized for defense. The heaviest Confederate attack was upon Generals James S. Jackson and William R. Terrill. Jackson was killed immediately. Terrill's force held temporarily, doing heavy damage, but eventually broke and fell back in disorder. Terrill was killed.[85] When McCook arrived on the scene he found great confusion. A call upon Gilbert brought little as-

[83] Polk to Bragg, October 8, 1862, 6 A.M., *ibid.*, 1096.
[84] Bragg's Report, *ibid.*, 1092.
[85] Polk later declared this charge of Cheatham's division "one of the most heroic and brilliant movements of the war." Report, *ibid.*, 1111.

sistance, for Gilbert too was heavily engaged by Hardee. There was a gap along the creek between McCook and Gilbert. Into this gap drove Buckner, slashing at both McCook's right and Gilbert's left. Patton Anderson moved against Phil Sheridan in Gilbert's center, was checked, but continued to keep that portion of the Federal line from sending assistance elsewhere. The Federal forces under Crittenden never actually got into the fight. Joe Wheeler's cavalry scattered the cavalry of Colonel Edward McCook and spent the remainder of the day terrorizing Crittenden, with the latter showing no inclination to test the strength of Confederate forces before him. Wheeler's cavalry was all that stood between him and the Confederate left flank.

The close of the day found McCook's and a portion of Gilbert's command more than a mile behind the positions occupied at midday. The field, including most of the water holes, was in Confederate possession. Dusk increased the confusion and nightfall ended the bloody struggle. Buell's losses were later reported as 2,851 wounded and 845 killed. Another 515 were captured or missing. Confederate losses were 2,635 wounded, 510 killed, and 251 captured or missing.[86]

General Polk narrowly missed being among the casualties. At twilight Liddell's brigade, changing battle positions, moved up on the left of Polk's point of observation. A regiment a short distance away opened fire on Liddell. Polk, quickly deciding that this was a case of mistaken identity, causing Confederates to fire upon Confederates, looked about for one of his aides. Finding none at hand, he himself galloped off to the scene of the firing. In an angry tone he demanded of the colonel the reason for firing upon his friends. The colonel replied that he was convinced they were enemies. " 'Enemy!' " Polk shouted, " ' why, I have only just left them myself.' " He ordered "Cease firing!" and then demanded of the colonel his name. The colonel, commanding an Indiana regiment, asked Polk the same question.

The Commander of the Army of the Mississippi then suddenly realized that he was in the rear of a Federal regiment. His only hope was "to brazen it out." Darkness and a dark blouse saved him. " 'I'll soon show you who I am, sir; cease firing, sir, at once,' "

[86] These figures are from the reports of Buell and Polk, written a month after Perryville. *Ibid.*, 1036, 1108.

he exclaimed. Beginning a slow canter back toward the Confederate lines, he continued to yell to the Indiana regiment to "cease
firing." Not until reaching the protection of some trees did he put
spur to his horse and move at full speed.

Months later, he could smilingly recount this experience, but he
confessed that as he rode away from that Indiana regiment he experienced a sensation up his spine and calculated " 'how many
bullets would be between my shoulders.' " Upon his return to the
Confederate line he could truthfully say " 'I have reconnoitered
those fellows pretty closely' " and was certain that they were the
enemy.[87]

Where was Buell during the battle of Perryville? Like Bragg on
this same day, he suffered from defective hearing. The claim by
some historians that the acoustics of the region deadened the
sound of the guns is not convincing. Not until 4 P.M. did Buell
realize that there was hard fighting at the front. He had no important part in the battle, for by the time he arrived on the scene it
was too late in the day. Probably in no other battle during the war
did the opposing commanders know so little about each other's
strength. Bragg thought he was opposed by a small portion of
Buell's army; Buell thought he was confronted by Bragg's full
strength. Both were wrong. And both demonstrated poor leadership by their failure to ascertain facts. But thanks to competent
assistants, neither suffered very serious damage.

Bragg was not inclined to attempt to hold what he had won on
October 8. Early in the evening the Confederate forces recrossed
Chaplin River to the position they had occupied the previous
night. A few days later Bragg wrote a short report of "the severest
and most desperately contested engagement within my knowledge." He gave the highest of praise to Major General Polk, "commanding the forces," to Major General Hardee, wing commander,
and to Major Generals Cheatham, Buckner, and Anderson, commanders of divisions. To them was "mainly due the brilliant
achievements on this memorable field. Nobler troops were never

---

[87] Walter Lord (ed.), *The Fremantle Diary*, 132–33. Polk's son Hamilton
should properly be listed among the casualties, for during the battle he
suffered a stroke (the family later referred to it as a sun stroke) which rendered him totally disabled.

more gallantly led. The country owes them a debt of gratitude which will I am sure be acknowledged." [88]

Six months later Bragg wrote a more detailed account of his Kentucky campaign. In the meantime, he had turned sour on most of those generals he had complimented so highly immediately following the battle of Perryville. He now accused Polk of disobedience at both Bardstown and Perryville. At Bardstown, he charged, Polk had failed to move toward Frankfort as ordered; at Perryville he had adopted a "defensive-offensive" policy instead of obeying an order to attack immediately. The other generals Bragg inferentially accused of guilt through association and collaboration. Polk denied both charges. At Bardstown, he explained, he had been ordered to move his "available" forces toward Frankfort. It was left to him to determine availability; he found that he had no forces "available" for such a move. At Perryville he considered Bragg's "order" as a suggestion rather than a positive order. Since the suggestion was based upon information Bragg had received from Hardee, Polk thought it necessary immediately to put himself in communication with Hardee. This he did, and in council it was agreed that lack of knowledge of the enemy's strength made the adoption of a "defensive-offensive" policy the wisest course. Since he had not been ordered to "attack" but to "give battle immediately" and since "immediately" was not clearly defined, he disobeyed no order.[89]

Early on the morning of October 9, 1862, Bragg's army began the march from Perryville to Harrodsburg. The enemy was thus left expecting a renewed attack which did not come. Kirby Smith arrived the next day and at last the Army of the Mississippi and the Army of Kentucky were united. But Bragg had already started a portion of his army toward Camp Dick Robertson. Whether or not Hardee and Polk approved this further withdrawal is not a matter of record, but judging from their past record and future attitude they must have joined Kirby Smith in urging a fight. That a seasoned army of 60,000 men should withdraw from Kentucky without fight-

[88] Bragg to Adjutant General, October 12, 1862, *Official Records*, XVI, Pt. 1, 1087–88.

[89] Bragg's Report, May 20, 1863, *ibid.*, 1088 ff; Polk to Hardee, April 17, 1863, *ibid.*, 1101–1103.

ing a decisive battle must have seemed incredible. Bragg yielded to Kirby Smith's urging and decided to make a stand at Harrodsburg. The afternoon of October 10 was spent in fortifying a position just outside the town. Bragg inspected the works late in the afternoon and then returned to his Harrodsburg headquarters for the night. Kirby Smith and Polk slept with their armies. About 3 A.M. Bragg sent for Kirby Smith. He had changed his mind. The two generals argued until dawn. "I disagreed with him & combatted his objections," Kirby Smith later explained, "contending that we had supplies & provisions and should risk an engagement before evacuating the country. But Bragg replied that he could not afford to risk the destruction of his army." [90]

After two days at Camp Dick Robertson the two armies under command of Kirby Smith and Polk began the long march back to Tennessee. When 60,000 seasoned troops turn their backs on the enemy and march away there is evidence of poor leadership. Bragg was convinced that his decision to abandon Kentucky was a wise one. "The necessary concentration of my forces rendered accumulations from the small mills impracticable, and our supply was reduced to only four days' rations," he wrote six months later. "To attack and rout an enemy largely superior in numbers (for simply to cripple him would not suffice) or to evacuate the country in which we could no longer subsist became now an imperative necessity. . . . The season of autumnal rains was approaching; the rough and uneven roads leading over the stupendous mountains of Eastern Tennessee and Kentucky to and through Cumberland Gap would then become utterly impassable to an army. Should I remain till then and meet a reverse the army would be lost." [91] This in no way explains how his army got in such a situation.

Polk moved by way of Mount Vernon and Crab Orchard, Kirby Smith by way of Big Hill. Wheeler was placed in command of all cavalry and assigned the important task of protecting the flanks of the retreating columns. To the fatigue from much marching was now added the realization of the fact that there would be no vic-

---

[90] Kirby Smith to J. Stoddard Johnston, October 31, 1866, Kirby Smith Papers. See also Kirby Smith's manuscript article on the Kentucky campaign, *ibid.*

[91] Bragg's report, May 20, 1863, *Official Records*, XVI, Pt. 1, 1093.

tory; soldiers straggled badly. Again if Buell had been an aggressive leader he would have dealt out much punishment to these divided columns. Polk and Kirby Smith feared it. On October 17 Kirby Smith, into whose column both trains had been placed, notified Polk that there was little hope of saving the trains and he feared that much of the artillery might be lost.[92]

Much irritated by Bragg's decision to burden him with the trains in order that the Army of the Mississippi might move more rapidly and convinced that this movement would leave his flanks exposed, Kirby Smith rushed a second note to Polk this same day. "I have marched by a circuitous route, while he [Bragg] has taken the direct one," he complained. "His trains have been turned off on my line, delaying me two days, my command working day and night pulling them up Big Hill. I gave his wagons the preference, when I would have secured the safety of my columns had I not been encumbered with them and might have done it by moving on with my train alone. . . . Cannot we unite and end this disastrous retreat by a glorious victory?"[93] Polk would not assume responsibility for an engagement, but he did order his army to halt for twenty-four hours. Cheatham's wing at Big Laurel and Hardee's at Barboursville were instructed to lend support to Kirby Smith's efforts to save the trains.[94]

There was no serious Federal threat. Crittenden's corps followed, but at a safe distance, and was under constant sting from Wheeler's cavalry. On October 17 Bragg left the army at London and hurried on to Knoxville. Two days later Polk arrived at Cumberland Ford. On this same day he received two dispatches from Kirby Smith, forwarding reports from McCown and Stevenson. "This is the worst road I have ever traveled," Kirby Smith complained, "in some places impassable, so that a new one has to be made. My command, from exhaustion in drawing wagons and artillery up the hills and not having had sleep for some nights, are very much scattered along the road." Could not Polk delay a portion of his command at Flat Lick "to aid mine?"[95]

By midnight October 19 Polk could report to Bragg "everything

---

[92] Kirby Smith to Polk, October 17, 1862, *ibid.*, Pt. 2, 958.
[93] *Id.* to *id.*, *ibid.*, 959.   [94] Polk to Bragg, October 19, 1862, *ibid.*, 963.
[95] Kirby Smith to Polk, *ibid.*, 966–67.

has been well secured and is moving forward satisfactorily." By the
following night Hardee should be at Cumberland Gap. Cheatham
had already reached Cumberland Ford. The supply of forage and
rations had been sufficient and the Army of the Mississippi would
be able to drive 1,500 to 2,000 head of cattle through the Gap.
Kirby Smith, Polk added, had suffered some inconveniences but
had had sufficient forage and beef. Now that all was secure, Polk
concluded, he himself would ride rapidly to the front and should
be in Knoxville by the morning of the twenty-first.[96]

Kirby Smith, with his Army of Kentucky now following the
trail over which the Army of the Mississippi had just passed, did
not find supplies as adequate as Polk had pictured. From Cumberland Gap he complained to Bragg that "all along my route reports
reach me of the provisions left for my men being seized by the
Army of the Mississippi." Cheatham had taken all of the provisions that had been previously collected at Cumberland Ford
"excepting 40 barrels. . . . My men have suffered on this march
everything excepting actual starvation." No fewer than 10,000 were
now "scattered through the country trying to find something upon
which to live." Unless some arrangement was made to collect food
in advance along the route still another 6,000 must join the search
for food.[97]

Polk apparently reached Knoxville on schedule. Somewhere
along the march to Kentucky and back he had received welcomed, if disturbing, news from church associates. Bishop Otey,
broken in health and much depressed in spirit, had fled occupied
Memphis and was now residing near Jackson, Mississippi. He had
sought in vain, he wrote Polk, for the answer to why God had
placed such a burden upon the South. "With the Psalmist I have
found these things too hard for me. I feel confused and the future
is all darkness while no light sheds its cheering beams over the surrounding gloom. 'The Lord reigneth' and this being so, why
should 20 millions of people feel impelled to make war upon half
that number of their brethren who have never done them harm,
and ask only to be let alone to fulfil the destiny to which God may
appoint, even as others of his intelligent creatures? Surely, surely

---

[96] Polk to Bragg, October 19, 1862, *ibid.*, 963–64.
[97] Kirby Smith to Bragg, October 22, 1862, *ibid.*, 975.

there awaits a heavy reckoning somewhere & at some time, for the authors of all the misery & suffering & anguish which have filled up our cup for the last year." [98]

And from occupied New Orleans came the news that on September 29 General G. F. Shepley, Federal military governor of Louisiana, had served upon the Episcopal clergy his Special Order No. 33: "The omission in the service of the Protestant Episcopal Church in New Orleans of the prayer for the President of the United States and others in authority, will be considered as evidence of hostility to the Government of the United States." [99]

This followed an earlier order which forbade use of the prayer prescribed by Polk substituting the "President of the Confederacy" for the "President of the United States." The clergy had then omitted the prayer from the service. To the new order the clergy replied, "There being no connection between church and state, we can recognize no interference on the part of either civil or military authority in ecclesiastical matters. The only alternative left us is to use or to omit such services as contain the Prayer which you have held offensive. . . . Your order No. 33 conflicts with our canonical obligation and therefore we cannot obey it. But we solemnly protest against our disobedience being regarded as 'evidence of hostility to the government of the United States.'" They could not, they insisted, use a prayer "not in our Liturgy. We cannot use the Liturgy of a church to which we do not belong." [100] Polk himself could not have expressed his views more clearly than had his loyal clergy.[101]

Shortly after arriving in Knoxville Polk also learned that his wife and daughters had fled New Orleans and were now with the Gales

[98] Otey to Polk, July 15, 1862, Leonidas Polk Papers.

[99] Copy in Leonidas Polk Papers.

[100] Copy in *ibid.*, under date October 2, 1862.

[101] When Federal General Benjamin F. Butler ordered: "'Read the prayer for the President, omit the silent act of devotion [for the President of the Confederacy], or leave New Orleans prisoners of state for Fort La Fayette,'" three of Polk's close friends and associates—William T. Leacock, Charles Goodrich, and John Fulton—refused to act without directions from their Bishop and were shipped off to New York. There they were paroled and returned to New Orleans. They never landed, however, for when offered the oath of allegiance to the United States they refused and were sent back to New York. Hodding and Betty Carter, *So Great a Good, A History of the Episcopal Church in Louisiana and of Christ Church Cathedral* (Sewanee, 1955), 134–35.

near Jackson, Mississippi. Escape was not difficult, for they
brought with them Mammy Betsey, her daughter-in-law, Winny
(Winny's husband Altimore was with General Polk), a cook, and
"a huge but delicate negro named Josh." "Laud Deo! Laud
Deo!" exclaimed Polk when he learned that "the Lord had led you
out! Forever be his Holy name blessed & praised." Hamilton, suffering from some "congestion of the brain," was being sent to join
the family. He would relate all of the news, Polk told his wife.
"Thank God I was never in better health. . . . I believe too I
have been of some use to the Republic." [102]

[102] Gale, "Recollections"; Polk to Wife, October 24, 1862, Leonidas Polk
Papers.

(14)

Stone's River—
"He Had Better Be Transferred"

ON OCTOBER 23 the War Department summoned General Bragg to Richmond for a personal interview. Leaving the army under Polk's command and with instructions to put it en route toward Murfreesboro, he left for Richmond the following day. On the thirtieth Polk started the artillery and train on another long march. "Cross Clinch River at the ford above Kingston," he instructed, "thence down the Tennessee River Valley to Smith's Cross Roads; thence across Walden's Ridge via Foster's into Sequatchie Valley; thence to Jasper; thence via Winchester or Pelham, as hereafter ordered, to Tullahoma." Wheeler's cavalry would furnish protection.[1]

Before Bragg was called to Richmond, Kirby Smith had already sent a trusted staff officer to the capital with a special report to President Davis. Soon Davis would wire Kirby Smith to come in person. And when Bragg returned to Knoxville he brought a summons for Polk to come to Richmond for a full discussion of conditions within Department No. 2.[2] Polk decided to take some of his family along; so his departure was delayed until November 7. On this same day Bragg resumed command of the army and announced its reorganization. Polk would command the First Corps; Hardee the Second. Wheeler's cavalry would be attached to Polk; Wharton's to Hardee.[3]

General Polk left no record of his conference with Richmond officials. Years later, his son stated that "Many plain questions were asked and as plainly answered, the situation demanded the ut-

---

[1] Special Orders No. 24, *Official Records*, XVI, Pt. 2, 982–83.
[2] Special Orders No. 29, November 4, 1862, *ibid.*, XX, Pt. 2, 388.
[3] General Orders No. 143, *ibid.*, 393.

most candor. General Polk stated, with all respect to General
Bragg's great abilities in the direction of organization and discipline, that he had been wanting in the higher elements of generalship in the conduct of the campaign; and that, in view of the admitted possibilities of the campaign, he considered it a failure—
an opinion, he said, he believed Generals Smith and Hardee
shared with him. He further said that General Bragg had lost the
confidence of his generals, and in answer to a suggestion from the
President of a change of commanders, requested that General
Joseph E. Johnston should be assigned to the command of the
army, if a change were made." [4]

This account so closely parallels Polk's known views a year later
it seems probable that his son merely surmised what was said at
Richmond. It is quite in keeping, however, with what Polk told his
brother-in-law, Kenneth Rayner. From Richmond Polk and his
family went to Raleigh to visit the Rayners. Shortly after they left,
Rayner wrote an interesting letter to a mutual friend, Thomas
Ruffin, relating what Polk had said about the Kentucky campaign:

> . . . I will say to you *in confidence,* that if Polk had been in
> chief command, the strategy of the campaign would have been
> very different—and the practical operation, as to tactics would
> have been very different. He was in favor of a more rapid and
> energetic campaign. Instead of the long detour of 400 miles
> around by Chattanooga, he was for a more direct and vigorous
> plan of falling first on one corps of the enemy, and then on an-
> other and thus destroying them in detail. Instead of marching on
> a line, nearly parallel with that of Buell, he was in favor of a
> cross march, and falling on his flank and crushing him before he
> could get to the relief of Louisville. And instead of fighting the
> battle of Perryville with divided forces, he was in favor of con-
> centrating our forces then falling on one corps of the enemy,
> and after crushing that, then crossing Green River and crushing
> the other corps—all of which he insisted could have been easily
> done. As it was he was ordered to fight the battle of Perryville
> with less than 15,000 men against 60,000 of the enemy. He did
> fight, and drive the enemy for three miles, like sheep, covering
> the ground with their dead. Still, the victory was barren of re-
> sults. Bragg may be a good disciplinarian, but you may rely on it,

[4] Polk, *Leonidas Polk,* II, 165.

that his forte is in organizing, but not in operating and fighting armies. . . .[5]

Before returning to active duty Polk decided to locate his family at the peaceful village of Asheville high atop the mountains of western North Carolina. Aide-de-camp Lieutenant W. B. Richmond was sent to assist the family in becoming established. Hamilton brought the servants, his own wife and children, and his sisters from Jackson to join their mother at Asheville. Polk also arranged for the transfer of "some twenty excellent negro men & their families" from Mississippi to Asheville. Hamilton was instructed to hire them to neighbors and collect the wages in "supplies of Bacon, wheat, flour, potatoes etc." General Polk was overjoyed when he learned of how comfortably his family was situated. "Truly we have been blessed my beloved above, and so very (much) above what we might for our unworthiness have expected or for our sinfulness have deserved," he wrote his wife. "Really it were worth all the discomfiture & trials to which we have been subjected, to have had the opportunity of proving the Lord, that we might see how good & how full of loving kindness & tender mercy he is to us & ours. . . . I shall be very easy & very happy in thinking of you all in your own 'hired house' and such a house! Truly the finger of God seems to have pointed to it and led you all there." [6]

The appearance of Bragg, Kirby Smith, and Polk at Richmond gave Davis an opportunity to examine the Kentucky campaign from all angles. It also placed him in a position of uneasy responsibility; all three of these generals were his personal friends. There was no doubt that Kirby Smith and Polk had lost confidence in Bragg. Although they agreed to continue to serve under him if duty demanded it, they were definitely not happy with the arrangement. Davis did not appoint Joe Johnston to supersede Bragg, as had no doubt been suggested by both Kirby Smith and Polk, but instead he made Johnston department commander with general supervision over both Bragg and Kirby Smith.

Polk assumed command of his corps at Murfreesboro on Novem-

[5] Kenneth Rayner to Thomas Ruffin, November 23, 1862, Hamilton (ed.), *Papers of Thomas Ruffin*, III, 270–71.
[6] Gale, "Recollections"; Polk to Wife, December 23, 24, 1862, Leonidas Polk Papers.

ber 26, 1862. Like Kirby Smith and Hardee, he had been promoted
to lieutenant general. The Federal army was now concentrated
about Nashville. William S. Rosecrans had succeeded Buell in
command. The Confederates knew little of Rosecrans' style of
fighting, but on November 27 Bragg ordered his corps commanders to be ready for action, "as the enemy seems to be advancing in
force." [7]

On December 10 President Davis arrived in Murfreesboro. He
and General Johnston, who had recently established his headquarters in Chattanooga, were already in disagreement. Davis was insisting that a portion of Bragg's force in Middle Tennessee, now
known as the Army of Tennessee, be sent to the aid of General
John C. Pemberton in Mississippi. Johnston hesitated, insisting
that Bragg had no troops to spare. Davis came to see for himself.
Kirby Smith had also arrived from East Tennessee. McCown's and
Stevenson's divisions of his army had joined Bragg.

Polk was pleased by Davis' visit if not with his decision to send
Stevenson's division to Mississippi. "We have had a royal visit,
from a royal visitor," Polk wrote his wife. "The President himself
has been with us. He arrived on Friday, reviewed my corps of
three divisions on Saturday, dined with a party of general officers
at Bragg's, and left on Sunday. The review was a great affair; everything went off admirably, and he was highly gratified with the result—said they were the best-appearing troops he had seen, well
appointed and well clad. The sight was very imposing, and, as it
was my corps, very gratifying to me, as you may suppose. . . . We
had a great wedding the other day, as you also will see by the
accompanying notice. It was no other than the redoubtable John
Morgan. He was married, as you see, by a lieutenant-general, a
select company present—Generals Bragg, Hardee, Breckinridge,
Cheatham, etc. It was an historical event." [8] The marriage of the
dashing cavalry leader to Miss Martha Ready was indeed an historical event. The wedding was solemnized at the Ready home just
off the public square in Murfreesboro. Bishop-General Polk, wear-
ing a bishop's robe draped over his uniform, performed the ceremony. One of Morgan's young officers later recalled: "I thought

[7] George W. Brent to Polk, November 27, 1862, *Official Records*, XX, Pt.
2, 428.
[8] Polk to Wife, December 17, 1862, quoted in Polk, *Leonidas Polk*, II, 177.

him [Polk] one of the noblest looking men I had ever seen, and was impressed, as I always was, with his grand and benignant manner. He was one of the finest specimens of the ante-bellum gentleman I ever saw." [9]

A reception and dinner followed, at which was served " 'all the delicacies and good dishes of a Southern kitchen.' " George St. Leger Grenfell, itinerant British veteran of the Crimean War, entertained with Moorish songs, and Dr. David W. Yandell presented humorous impersonations, including one of General Bragg, who entered the room just in time to catch him in the act.[10]

The Army of Tennessee liked Middle Tennessee. To many officers and men it was home. An abundant harvest had made supplies plentiful, and an aggressive Confederate cavalry kept Yankee foraging limited to the immediate vicinity of Nashville. He would send her "flour, hams, lard and possibly candles," Polk wrote his wife. ". . . I get flour very fine here for $11 per bbl & other things in proportion. . . . I will add rice also, if I can, potatoes and apples you seem to have in abundance." The supplies would go by rail to Greeneville, East Tennessee, thence by wagon to Asheville. He supposed she had hens enough for eggs, if not meat. "Tell Lilly to try her hand on the chickens." [11]

Although the Yankees were only thirty miles away, Christmas, 1862, was a gala occasion in Murfreesboro, as young officers waltzed with southern belles to the strains of sweet music. For those of coarser tastes there were horse races and games of chance. And there were drinks for those who wished to bolster their sagging spirits. None of this appealed to Polk. "I have had rather a plain day to-day," he wrote his wife on Christmas Day. "We have had no clergyman at the church here therefore have had no service wh I have regretted." [12]

A grand ball was planned for December 26, but the invitations were cancelled by news that Rosecrans' army, 46,000 strong, was moving out of Nashville toward Murfreesboro. Officers hurried to their commands and Bragg began to pull in his extended lines.

[9] Basil W. Duke to (?) Steele, April 26, 1893, Leonidas Polk Papers.
[10] Cecil Fletcher Holland, *Morgan and His Raiders* (New York, 1942), 176–77.
[11] December 25, 1862, Leonidas Polk Papers.
[12] Polk to Wife, December 25, 1862, *ibid.*

Polk's corps was already centered on Murfreesboro. To his right, extending to Readyville, was McCown's command; on his left Hardee's corps reached to Eagleville and Triune. For some weeks the infantry had been stationary in these positions, but the cavalry had been very active; and Forrest and Morgan were now away on raids into West Tennessee and Kentucky striking crippling blows at the railroads upon which Federal forces depended for many of their supplies.

As soon as he received the news from Nashville Bragg ordered his corps commanders to prepare for immediate movement. Polk passed the word on to his division commanders Cheatham and Withers.[13] On the following day Bragg sent out more detailed instructions. The cavalry units of Wheeler, Wharton, and Pegram would "fall back before the enemy to-morrow." In the meantime, as soon as breakfast was finished, all troops would move into their assigned positions. Hardee's corps would form on the right, his left resting on the Nashville road, with Breckinridge's division in front and Cleburne's 800 to 1,000 yards to the rear. Polk would occupy the left, with Withers' division in front and Cheatham's in the rear.[14] McCown would form a reserve. Wheeler's cavalry would protect the right flank; Wharton's the left. For the present Pegram would remain in reserve.[15] In forwarding these instructions to Cheatham and Withers, Polk added that he would expect the troops to be in position by 9 A.M., but he wished to meet the generals themselves at the junction of the Nashville road and Stone's River "punctually at 7:30 A.M. to-morrow, that we may reconnoiter the ground."[16] On this same day Polk reported his effective force—infantry, artillery, cavalry—at 16,210.[17] Bragg's total strength, including cavalry, was slightly less than 38,000.

The field on which Bragg chose to meet Rosecrans was about

[13] *Official Records*, XX, Pt. 2, 462.

[14] When Polk filed his report of the battle he stated that he placed Withers in front because his division had seen no action since Shiloh. Before forwarding this report to Richmond, Bragg, now a bit peevish, added a note that he himself was responsible for placing Withers in front. Regardless of who originated the idea the statement of reason was unfortunate, for two brigades that had recently joined Withers' division had seen action at Munfordville and Perryville.

[15] George W. Brent to Polk, December 27, 1862, 9 P.M., *Official Records*, XX, Pt. 2, 464.

[16] *Ibid.*   [17] *Ibid.*, 465.

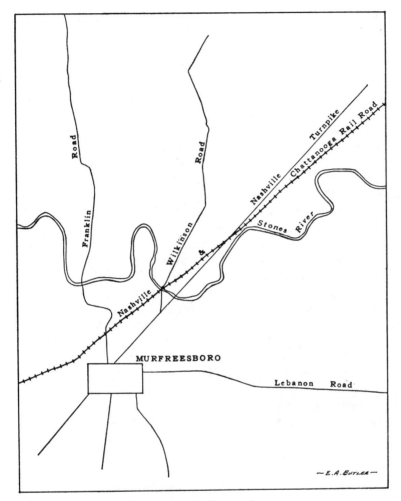

THE STONE'S RIVER AREA

two miles northwest of Murfreesboro. It was rolling country, with cleared fields here and there, abounding in limestone rocks and cedar glades. Through the area passed the Nashville, Wilkinson, and Franklin roads (often called turnpikes), and the Nashville and Chattanooga Railroad. It was also divided by the meandering Stone's River. According to Bragg's plan of battle the river divided

Hardee's and Polk's corps, with Hardee on the east and Polk on the west.

Rosecrans' three corps, commanded by McCook, Thomas, and Crittenden, moved out of Nashville by three different roads, but by making use of cross roads their routes would converge before reaching Murfreesboro. The Confederate cavalry had been so effective that Rosecrans' scouts had been unable to bring in much information as to Bragg's position. They did learn, however, that Stevenson's division had gone to Mississippi and that Forrest and Morgan were away on extended raids. This news might have influenced Rosecrans' decision to move on Bragg at this particular time. By December 30 the Federal army was close enough to Murfreesboro to make it possible for Wheeler to ride completely around it. Taking off along the Lebanon Road leading from Hardee's right, then turning to his left he crossed the other roads leading to Murfreesboro, falling upon supply trains with great devastation. Early on the thirty-first he appeared on Polk's left.

Throughout December 30th there was considerable artillery fire along the front as the Federals moved in cautiously, probing for weak points in the Confederate line. During the afternoon Polk's left became engaged but no major attack developed. This brisk activity, however, was sufficient to cause a change of plans. That evening General Bragg called Generals Hardee and Polk to his Murfreesboro headquarters. The day's activities, he explained, had convinced him that Rosecrans was massing troops for an attack upon the Confederate left. Polk must therefore be re-enforced. McCown was to move from his reserve position into the front line on Withers' left. Cleburne would move from the right, where he was in the rear of Breckinridge, and take position in the rear of McCown. Hardee would take command of these two divisions on the left.[18] An attack was ordered for daybreak December 31. Chalmers' brigade on Polk's extreme right would serve as a pivot. McCown (supported by Cleburne) on the extreme left would open the attack, and the entire Confederate line would then swing around as the hand of a clock.[19]

Bragg's diagnosis of Federal intentions was entirely wrong. Rose-

[18] David Urquhart, "Bragg's Advance and Retreat," *Battles and Leaders*, III, 606.

[19] Polk's report, February 28, 1863, *Official Records*, XX, Pt. 1, 686.

crans was planning an early morning attack but not at the point where Bragg expected. His battle line had formed with Critten-den's corps on the left next to the river, Thomas' in the center, and McCook's on the right. The activity against the Confederate left was but a feint to cover up the massing of troops opposite the Confederate right. The plan for December 31 was for McCook and Thomas to keep the Confederate left and center well engaged while Crittenden crossed Van Cleve's and Wood's divisions over the river and struck Breckinridge in front and flank. Breckinridge must then fall back as the Federals headed for Murfreesboro and a swing around to the rear of Hardee and Polk.[20] This plan could not possibly succeed unless Thomas and McCook were able to hold Polk and Hardee. This they did not do.

Hardee opened the attack at daybreak December 31, throwing McCown and then Cleburne against McCook's right. Federal division commanders R. W. Johnson and J. C. Davis, caught some-what unprepared, fought desperately but were forced back. Polk next moved in, hurling Withers against Phil Sheridan, command-ing McCook's left. All involved soon realized that a field so cov-ered with boulders, ledges, and cedars put the offense at a great disadvantage. Colonel J. Q. Loomis' brigade attacked first. He was wounded and succeeded by Colonel J. G. Coltart. The charge, though gallant, was thrown back by the brigades of Sheridan's right. Colonel A. J. Vaughn's brigade of Cheatham's division moved in and was also repulsed. Reforming, the two brigades made a concerted drive and Sheridan's right was dislodged. Meanwhile, Colonel A. M. Manigault's brigade was operating against Sheri-dan's left. Again and again it was thrown back. Not until the guns from one of General George Maney's brigades were brought into action did Sheridan's left join the retreat of the remainder of McCook's corps. A battery of four of Sheridan's guns was Maney's reward.

Next in the Confederate line was Patton Anderson's brigade. As the clockwise movement continued it was thrown against the right of Thomas' corps manned by General J. S. Negley's division, sup-ported by that of General L. H. Rousseau. Like Sheridan, Negley and Rousseau also had the protection of a "dense cedar brake."

[20] G. C. Kniffin (of Crittenden's staff), "The Battle of Stone's River," *Battles and Leaders*, III, 617.

And with open spaces in front of the brake, Anderson's men were perfect targets. The slaughter was terrific, but with Manigault's assistance and the arrival of A. P. Stewart's brigade, Thomas' right was also driven back.

The last of the Confederate front line units to become engaged was Chalmers' brigade, which held the pivot position. To its rear was D. S. Donelson's brigade. In its front was an open field well covered by enemy guns. For forty-eight hours the men of Donelson's brigade lay in their shallow rifle pits, wet and cold. Across the field they could get glimpses of J. M. Palmer's division of Crittenden's corps. It was 10 A.M. before the clockwise movement extended to the pivot brigade, and the Federals were falling back all along the line "as one half-shuts a knife-blade." The distance Chalmers was expected to travel was not great, but the going would be rough.

So fierce was the Confederate attack that Rosecrans quickly abandoned his own offensive plan. Van Cleve had crossed his brigade over the river in accordance with the original plan and Wood was preparing to follow when Rosecrans ordered them back to bolster the sagging Federal defense. Breckinridge's four brigades were left east of the river with no part in the fight.

Just as at Shiloh, as the Federal line bent back, one strong point refused to yield. On the field at Stone's River the "Round Forest" became another "Hornets Nest." Three or four acres in size, heavily timbered, and resting astride the railroad, the Round Forest was to be the scene of the greatest slaughter of the day. Chalmers' brigade was the first to test the strength of this strong point. Donelson moved to his support. "The slaughter was teriffic on both sides," but the Round Forest held. The Sixteenth Tennessee, Colonel John H. Savage commanding, lost 207 men out of its 402; the Eighth Tennessee under Colonel W. L. Moore lost 306 out of 425, including the Colonel.

The Federals had now been driven east of the Nashville-Murfreesboro road. Only the Round Forest appeared to be between them and destruction. But fresh troops were available. And as at Shiloh, Bragg had no large body of reserves with which to clinch a victory. The only fresh troops available were Breckinridge's four brigades east of the river. Bragg, finally deciding that Breckinridge was in no danger in his present position, ordered his brigades to cross over to Polk's assistance. They came but not in time. It was two hours after Donelson's bloody repulse before the two brigades under J. K. Jackson and D. W. Adams arrived. Another hour passed before the brigades of William Preston and J. B. Palmer (now commanded by Gideon J. Pillow) were on the scene. Piecemeal attacks merely added to the slaughter of the attackers. "Could they have been thrown upon the enemy's left immediately following Chalmers' and Donelson's assault in quick succession," Polk later contended, "the extraordinary strength of his [the enemy] position would have availed him nothing. That point would have been carried, and his left, driven back on his panic-stricken right, would have completed his confusion and insured an utter rout."

When the day closed Round Forest was still in Federal possession, but Rosecrans' army was pretty thoroughly beaten. "The enemy has yielded his strong position and is falling back," Bragg wired Richmond. "We occupy the whole field and shall follow him. . . . God has granted us a happy New Year." [21]

The night that followed was bitter cold, adding to the misery of the thousands of wounded scattered over the field. If Bragg had any idea what to do with the victory he thought God had given him he gave no indication of it; during the night he made no preparation for the next day other than to send Breckinridge's battered brigades back to their original position east of the river. He expected Rosecrans to withdraw during the night, but except for some reforming of lines and the evacuation of Round Forest the Federals remained in position; Rosecrans had no plan either. Neither commander gave any indication of a desire to renew the fighting on New Year's Day.

The only Confederate activity on January 1, 1863, was Polk's occupation of Round Forest, which had been abandoned by Crittenden's corps. The Federals limited their activities to sending Van Cleve's division east of the river to occupy an important elevated position a mile in advance of Breckinridge. Bragg should have thought of this himself if he had any intention of renewing

[21] Reports of Bragg, Hardee, Polk, and Breckinridge, *Official Records*, XX, Pt. 1, 663 ff, 771 ff, 685 ff, 781 ff.

the attack or even holding what he had gained, for guns on this high ground would be in easy reach of the Federal position west of the river.

During the morning of January 2, while Polk was exchanging light artillery fire with the enemy, Bragg suddenly thought of assisting Polk by artillery fire from across the river. He hurriedly dispatched an artillery officer to select the best position for Breckinridge's guns, but when the officer returned he reported that the best position was already in possession of the Federals. This was the position that Van Cleve's division had occupied the previous day. Bragg decided to storm the position and drive the Federals off. Breckinridge opposed the plan, pointing out the danger from Federal guns west of the river. Polk also disapproved, insisting that his safety did not depend upon such an attack. But Bragg was determined.

Breckinridge was instructed to be ready for a forward movement by 4 P.M. Polk was to open fire both as a signal to Breckinridge and to occupy the enemy's attention. Polk's fire brought not only return fire but also an enemy advance against Round Forest, which he was unable to repel. When night came the Federals were again in possession of this coveted position. In the meantime, Breckinridge had suffered terrible slaughter. His 4,500 men had moved according to schedule. But, on the west side of the river, Crittenden had diagnosed the situation before the attack started, and had quickly put his guns in position. For a brief period the Confederate assault was most successful, driving Van Cleve's division (now commanded by Colonel Samuel Beatty) from its position and to the river beyond. So hot was the pursuit that some Confederates even crossed the river. But now having moved into the lower ground along the river they were within range of fifty-eight Federal guns commanded by Major John Mendenhall. Within moments the whole area was all but pulverized. Beatty's reformed infantry launched a counter attack and what was left of Breckinridge's brigades fell back in great disorder. Casualties totaled 1,700 killed or wounded.[22]

About the time Breckinridge began his attack Bragg had or-

[22] Reports of Breckinridge, Polk, Beatty, and Mendenhall, *ibid.*, 786–87, 691, 575–78, 455–56; Polk, *Leonidas Polk*, II, 194; Horn, *Army of Tennessee*, 207–208.

dered Patton Anderson to cross over from the west and lend assistance, but "darkness had separated the combatants" before he arrived on the scene. Later in the night Bragg, fearing a renewed
attack upon his right the following morning, ordered Hardee to
transfer McCown's and Cleburne's divisions east of the river. This
left only Polk's corps (Cheatham's and Withers' divisions) west
of the river. News of Breckinridge's disaster quickly cast a gloom
over the entire army and chilled the enthusiasm generated by victory on the previous day. Sending Breckinridge's brigades within
range of massed Federal artillery was a great blunder; for the Confederate army to remain in its present divided position might
prove an even greater one.

At 12:15 A.M., January 3, Generals Cheatham and Withers
drafted a note to General Bragg: "We deem it our duty to say
to you frankly that, in our judgment, this army should be promptly
put in retreat. You have but three brigades [divisions] that are
at all reliable, and even some of these are more or less demoralized
from having some brigade commanders who do not possess the
confidence of their commands. Such is our opinion, and we deem
it a solemn duty to express it to you. We do fear great disaster
from the condition of things now existing, and think it should be
averted if possible."

This note was sent to General Polk for transmittal. Polk included
a note of his own: "I send you the inclosed paper, as requested,
and I am compelled to add that after seeing the effect of the operations of today, added to that produced upon the troops by the
battle of the 31st, I very greatly fear the consequences of another
engagement at this place in the ensuing day. We could now, perhaps, get off with some safety and some credit, if the affair is well
managed. Should we fail in the meditated attack, the consequences
might be very disastrous."

Polk handed the notes to aide-de-camp Lieutenant W. B. Richmond and sent him to Bragg's headquarters immediately. It was
2 A.M. when he arrived. Arousing from his sleep Bragg glanced
at the notes, but before completing a reading he turned to Richmond and said "Say to the general we shall maintain our position
at every hazard."

At 3 A.M. Polk forwarded Hardee copies of these notes and
Bragg's reply, commenting "I think the decision of the general

unwise . . . in a high degree." He would nevertheless obey orders and do his duty. He and his division commanders expected "the conflict will be renewed in the morning." [23]

There is no evidence that Bragg intended offensive action on January 3, but Polk reasoned that if his position was to be held he must have possession of the Round Forest. At daybreak he again opened fire, soon retaking Round Forest, and then spending the remainder of the day defending what he had gained.[24] He probably did not realize that during the day Rosecrans' entire army was concentrating in his front. A steady rain that had begun the previous night was causing Stone's River to rise toward flood stage. Rosecrans was too smart to allow his forces to be divided by a flooded river.

About 10 A.M., while Polk's troops were guarding against Federal threats to retake the Round Forest, Polk and Hardee were called to Bragg's Murfreesboro headquarters. Bragg had changed his mind. General McCook's papers had been captured, he informed his corps commanders, and they revealed Federal strength to be greater than was thought. It was also reported that Rosecrans was receiving re-enforcements. To Bragg these facts "suggested the necessity of retreat." Hardee and Polk agreed. At another meeting about 7 P.M. the details of withdrawal were agreed upon.[25]

Withdrawal began that evening, Polk falling back to Shelbyville and Hardee moving toward Tullahoma by way of the Manchester road. For the third time the Army of the West had won a definite advantage on the first day of battle, and then either lost it on the second or marched away leaving the task unfinished. A critical press and public would soon want to know the reason. Casualties had been high at Murfreesboro. Polk's two divisions lost 4,462 killed, wounded, or missing out of a total of 14,133. The total loss for the army was about 10,000. Of this number 1,236 were killed.[26]

Bragg hurried ahead to Winchester with the intention of making a stand along the line of Elk River if Rosecrans continued to push.

[23] *Official Records*, XX, Pt. 1, 700–701.   [24] Polk's report, *ibid.*, 691–92.
[25] Hardee to Bragg, January 12, 1863, *ibid.*, 683; Breckinridge to *id.*, January 12, 1863, *ibid.*, 682.
[26] *Official Records*, XX, Pt. 1, 693, 676–81.

Rosecrans did not give spirited pursuit; so Polk was ordered to stop at Shelbyville and Hardee took position at Wartrace on the Nashville and Chattanooga Railroad. Bragg returned to Tullahoma and established his headquarters. Polk, reasoning that there would be no immediate emergency, took a short leave of absence to visit his family at Asheville.

Shortly after his arrival in the North Carolina mountains Polk received from Bragg a copy of a letter being sent to all corps and division commanders. Bragg was much concerned over public criticism of his retreat from Murfreesboro, especially since he was accused of acting contrary to the advice of his commanders. Finding himself assailed in public and private by newspapers, officers, and citizens, he began, "it becomes necessary for me to save my fair name, if I cannot stop the deluge of abuse, which will destroy my usefulness and demoralize this army." Some of the criticism was reportedly being voiced by staff officers of "my generals," who were claiming that the withdrawal "was made against the opinion and advice of their chiefs." His corps and division commanders were the only ones who knew the facts, and since they were unanimous "in council in verbally advising a retrograde movement, I cannot doubt that you will cheerfully attest the same in writing."

Had Bragg stopped at this point his course would have been commendable, for the facts were on his side. But his next request was both unwise and in bad taste: "I desire that you will consult your subordinate commanders and be candid with me, as I have always endeavored to prove myself with you. If I have misunderstood your advice, and acted against your opinions, let me know it, in justice to yourself. If, on the contrary, I am the victim of unjust accusations, say so, and unite with me in staying the malignant slanders being propagated by men who have felt the sting of discipline." He understood that Kirby Smith had been called to Richmond, supposedly "with a view to supersede me. I shall retire without a regret if I find I have lost the good opinion of my generals, upon whom I have ever relied as upon a foundation of rock." [27]

When Polk's division commanders Cheatham and Withers re-

[27] Bragg to Polk, January 11, 1863, *ibid.*, 699.

ceived Bragg's request they hesitated to answer without first consulting their commanding general. However, Cheatham did send a short note assuring Bragg that he himself was "one of the first to suggest the movement [retreat], and fully indorsed it." [28]

Hardee did just what Bragg requested. "You will readily appreciate the delicate character of the inquiries you institute," he wrote, "but I feel, under the circumstances, that it is my duty to reply with the candor you solicit, not only from personal respect to yourself, but from the magnitude of the public interest involved." He first heard of the proposed retreat when he received the notes from Polk early on January 3. He did, however, confer with Bragg and Polk about 10 A.M. that day and fully concurred in the decision to retreat.

As to Bragg's second request, Hardee reported that he had conferred with his division commanders, Breckinridge and Cleburne, "and I feel that frankness compels me to say that . . . [they] are unanimous in the opinion that a change in the command of this army is necessary. In this opinion I concur." All had the highest respect for Bragg's purity of motives, energy, and personal character, yet they were convinced that "the peril of the country is superior to all personal considerations." [29]

Cleburne consulted his brigade commanders and reported great appreciation for Bragg's gallantry, patriotism and capacity for organization, yet all regretfully agreed that he did "not possess the confidence of the army in other respects in that degree necessary to secure success." Breckinridge found his subordinates of a similar opinion. "They . . . request me to say that while they entertain the highest respect for your patriotism, it is their opinion that you do not possess the confidence of the army to an extent which will enable you to be useful as its commander." [30]

Polk made no reply to Bragg's inquiries until he returned from Asheville on January 30; his reply was in the form of a question. His interpretation of Bragg's circular letter was that two inquiries were made, but he found that General Cheatham and some others had not so construed it when they made their replies. In order

[28] January 13, 1863, *ibid.*, 684.
[29] Hardee to Bragg, January 12, 1863, *ibid.*, 683.
[30] Cleburne to Bragg, January 13, 1863, *ibid.*, 684; Breckinridge to *id.*, January 12, 1863, *ibid.*, 682.

not to be "placed in a false position," he requested Bragg to clarify his letter.

Having already received several very frank replies, Bragg apparently wished no more. His circular "contained but one point of inquiry," he informed Polk. All that he wished was a statement in writing of that which "had transpired between us in regard to the retreat." Polk then sent a brief reply, citing the notes of January 3 already in Bragg's possession.[31] Since he was at Tullahoma when he wrote his notes of January 30 and 31, it is probable that he had not conferred with Hardee at Wartrace. Yet it appears that he had consulted with Cheatham at Shelbyville. The confusing question is why he asked Bragg for a clarification. Perhaps Cheatham requested it. Were he and Cheatham ignorant of the frank replies made by Hardee, Breckinridge, and Cleburne? Polk's actions gave the impression that he wished to avoid being "candid" with Bragg. General Joe Johnston's sudden arrival on the scene on January 30 might also have influenced the Bishop-General. At any rate, whether intentionally or not, Polk left his fellow officers of Hardee's corps in an unenviable position. And since they knew his opinion of Bragg as a commander they quickly made known their feeling that Polk had deserted them.

Hearing of the discontent among Bragg's generals and his unwise inquiries, President Davis wired General Johnston to go immediately to Tullahoma. He followed his telegram with a letter dated January 22. Bragg was under considerable criticism, he explained to Johnston, and had called upon his generals for their opinion. "The answers, I am informed, have been but partially given, but are so far indicative of a want of confidence, such as is essential to success. Why General Bragg should have selected that tribunal, and have invited its judgment upon him, is to me unexplained." Although his own confidence in Bragg remained "unshaken," Davis concluded, there was no doubt that if the General was "distrusted by his officers and troops, a disaster might result which, but for that cause, would have been avoided." [32]

Johnston was in Mobile when he received Davis' telegram; the letter was forwarded to him at Tullahoma. After conferring with

[31] Polk to *id.*, January 30, 31, 1863, *ibid.*, 701, 702; Bragg to Polk, January 30, 1863, *ibid.*, 701.

[32] *Official Records*, XXIII, Pt. 2, 613–14.

Generals Bragg, Hardee, and Polk, and Governor Isham G. Harris, Johnston reported to Davis on February 3. Bragg and Harris, he explained, agreed that there was some "feeling," but they thought it of a factious nature and largely a result of the Kentucky campaign. Both believed the feeling was declining. Polk, having been away from his corps for more than two weeks, could not be certain about the attitude of his officers, but Hardee said his generals lacked confidence in Bragg. Governor Harris reported that Cheatham had stated that "he would never go into battle under General Bragg again." However, the Governor had hope that he could bring his fellow Tennessean "to his senses."

Johnston expressed pleasure that Davis still had confidence in Bragg. "My own is confirmed by his recent operations, which, in my opinion, evince great vigor and skill." To remove such a commander he thought would be unfortunate; however, should this be decided upon "no one in this army or engaged in this investigation ought to be his successor." [33]

The next day after Johnston wrote his report Polk also wrote directly to President Davis, enclosing copies of all correspondence between the generals of his corps and General Bragg. Regardless of what his motives were a few days earlier, he now had definite convictions. In order to clear up a difference in interpretation of Bragg's request of January 11, he explained, he had asked Bragg to clarify. In reply Bragg stated that he had submitted but one question. This made Polk's "final answer plain and easy." Since General Bragg had received the opinions of some officers of "the highest grade" Polk thought the Commanding General should have been interested in hearing from the others, "but, as I have said, it was declined." This being the case, he felt it his duty to impress upon the President "that had I and my division commanders been asked to answer, our replies would have coincided with those of the officers of the other corps."

As things now stood, Polk was convinced that even if Bragg were a Napoleon or a Frederick the Great "he could serve our cause at some other points better than here. My opinion is he had better be transferred." Polk recalled that on a previous occasion Davis had said of Bragg " 'I can make good use of him here in Rich-

[33] *Ibid.*, 624.

mond.' " This seemed an opportune time to make the transfer, Polk suggested; Bragg's "capacity for organization and discipline . . . could be used by you at headquarters with infinite advantage to the whole army."

The logical successor to Bragg, Polk thought, would be Joseph E. Johnston. "He will cure all discontent and inspire the army with new life and confidence. He is here on the spot, and I am sure will be content to take it." If General Robert E. Lee could command both a department and the principal army therein, Polk could see no reason why Johnston could not do so. "I have, therefore, as a general officer of this army, speaking in behalf of my associates, to ask, respectfully, that this appointment be made, and I beg to be permitted to do this urgently. The state of this army demands immediate attention, and its position before the enemy, as well as the mind of its troops and commanders, could find relief in no way so readily as by the appointment of General Joseph E. Johnston." [34]

Of particular interest are Polk's statements that he spoke for his associates and that he felt certain Johnston would be "content" to accept such an appointment. It would seem unlikely that he would have made such statements without consulting both Johnston and the principal generals of the army, yet Johnston's subsequent actions indicate otherwise. After another week of investigation Johnston reported to Davis that he had "positive evidence of General Bragg's capacity to command." The very effective fighting in the recent battles had evinced "skill in the commander and courage in the troops." Many absentees had returned to their units and the army was now stronger than at the time of the recent battle. The troops were "well clothed, healthy and in good spirits." Throughout the investigation it had been his object "to ascertain if the confidence of the troops in the ability of the army to beat the enemy is at all impaired." He had not found it so. And although advised by Polk that the general officers lacked confidence in Bragg, he did not believe this had greatly diminished the General's value; therefore, he did not believe Bragg should be removed. But in any event, he himself should not be considered as a possible successor. [35] One can understand why, under the cir-

[34] *Ibid.*, XX, Pt. 1, 698–99.   [35] *Ibid.*, XXIII, Pt. 2, 632–33.

cumstances, Johnston did not wish to replace Bragg, but he cast a serious reflection upon his own military judgment when he wrote Senator Louis T. Wigfall: "Bragg has done wonders, I think— no body of troops have done more in proportion to numbers in the same time." [36]

This rather queer reasoning was not convincing to President Davis. He thought it unlikely, he replied to Johnston, that in view of the lack of confidence of the generals, Bragg could "possess the requisite confidence of the troops." It would be more likely that the opinions of the generals would be reflected by their staff officers and soon spread throughout the army. He was pleased with Johnston's words of commendation for Bragg, yet he recognized that "It is not given to all men of ability to excite enthusiasm and to win affection of their troops, and it is only the few who are thus endowed who can overcome the distrust and alienation of their principal officers."

Davis all but begged Johnston to reconsider, pointing out that he had had no part in the discontent and being already department commander could not be considered as having any personal interest in Bragg's removal. He did not wish, however, to urge upon Johnston any course that "would wound your sensibility or views of professional propriety." Still should it be necessary to find a successor to Bragg, Johnston, by eliminating himself and all generals attached to this army, had left a very limited field in which to find a general with rank superior to the lieutenant generals of the Army of Tennessee.[37]

After three weeks with the army in Middle Tennessee Johnston returned to Mobile, no doubt expecting the tempest to subside without serious damage. President Davis, on the other hand, was not satisfied. On March 9 he ordered Johnston to return to Tennessee, assume command of the army, and send Bragg to Richmond. When Johnston arrived at Tullahoma he found Bragg much concerned over the serious illness of his wife. Johnston assumed command and sent Bragg to the bedside of his wife at Winchester instead of to Richmond. By the time Mrs. Bragg had made sufficient recovery to permit her husband to return to active duty,

[36] Quoted in Gilbert E. Govan and James W. Livingood, *A Different Valor, The Story of Joseph E. Johnston, C.S.A.* (Indianapolis, 1956), 179.
[37] February 19, 1863, *Official Records*, XXIII, Pt. 2, 640–41.

Johnston himself was ill. On April 10 he notified Davis that he was too ill for field command; consequently, Bragg was restored to the position.[38]

During the period of Johnston's temporary command the generals made still another effort to rid themselves of Bragg's leadership and secure Johnston's permanent appointment. Late in March President Davis sent his aide, Colonel William Preston Johnston, to make a thorough inspection of the Army of Tennessee and no doubt, incidentally, to check on the discontent that was known to be prevalent. Colonel Johnston made his report on April 15, 1863,[39] but did not discuss in writing what he had learned from Polk and others relative to the dissention. But on March 30 Polk again wrote directly to Davis. He had conversed freely and frankly with Colonel Johnston, and his own views were "matured and clear." He was convinced that even if General Bragg were "entirely acceptable" to the Army of Tennessee, the General could be of greater service to the Confederacy in some other field where his great talent for organization and discipline "could find more ample scope." The exercise of such a talent was not always agreeable or welcomed, Polk commented, yet there were few armies that would not benefit from it. If placed in the proper position General Bragg could no doubt be of great service to all armies of the Confederacy. He might well be called to Richmond, Polk suggested, and assigned the duties of Inspector General. From that position the "whole family of idlers, drones, and shirks, of high or low degree, far and near, would feel his searching hand, and be made to take their places and do their duty." And if Bragg could be made to see how his peculiar talent could best be used in this manner, Polk had no doubt but that the General would be pleased with a transfer from the field to Richmond.

Once this was agreed upon then there would be no reason why General Johnston could not be assigned to command the Army of Tennessee. Polk had discussed the whole matter with Johnston and although he found him hesitant, was convinced that the Department Commander considered himself but partly employed and preferred a field command. "Whether General J. is the best man for the place or not is not the question," Polk concluded.

[38] *Ibid.,* 745–46.   [39] *Ibid.,* 757–61.

"The army and the West believe so, and both would be satisfied with the appointment, and I believe it the best that could be made." [40] That Polk preferred Johnston is quite clear, yet he wished the removal of Bragg to give something of the appearance of a promotion. It was ever the policy of the Bishop-General to lead by offering suggestions rather than to drive over opposition.

Polk's suggestion could easily have been more advice than Davis wished. It certainly did not result in the shift of Bragg to Richmond. Personally more favorably inclined toward Bragg, reenforced by strong recommendations from Johnston, and having no one to appoint in Bragg's place, Davis retained him, even though the general officers of the Army of Tennessee were unanimous in their lack of confidence in his leadership. For this serious mistake Johnston must share the responsibility.

Bragg knew the attitude of his corps and division commanders, yet he did not carry out his promise to "retire without regret" should he no longer have their confidence. Instead, he launched upon a course that could result only in the substitution of bitter hostility for conscientious lack of confidence. On March 31 General Breckinridge addressed a letter of protest to Adjutant General Cooper at Richmond. He had just read Bragg's report of the recent battles on Stone's River. "By direct statement, and by unmistakable innuendo, it is throughout a reflection upon my capacity and conduct." [41] This was but a part of the campaign of Breckinridge and his supporters to defend the Kentuckian against what they considered unjust criticism. The controversy had already reached Richmond and resulted in the Confederate Senate delaying action on a House resolution commending Bragg and his army for their action at Murfreesboro. There was also a threat, said to have been sponsored by the Kentucky delegation, to order an official investigation of the Kentucky campaign. [42]

This was the type of an attack that a wise general might well have permitted to wear itself out and fail for lack of support. But again Bragg reacted in a manner unworthy of one in his position. He sought to place to the credit of General Polk the blame for whatever failure there was at Perryville. On April 13 he addressed

[40] *Ibid.*, 729–30.   [41] *Ibid.*, XX, Pt. 1, 790–91.
[42] J. B. Sale to Bragg, March 5, 1863, quoted in Don C. Seitz, *Braxton Bragg, General of the Confederacy* (Columbia, 1924), 284–86.

to all wing and division commanders at Perryville (except Polk) a letter citing Polk's note from Bardstown, October 3, 1862, and a section of his report of the battle of Perryville. In both instances, Bragg stressed, Polk had admitted "disobedience to my orders" after a conference with his fellow officers. The purpose of this letter, therefore, was to put the facts before the officers concerned and to inquire "to what extent you sustained the general in his acknowledged disobedience." [43]

Hardee immediately sent to Polk his copy of the letter, indorsing thereon that, fearing Bragg was planning a court martial, he was inclined not to reply. To reopen the Kentucky campaign would open up controversy that could be ill afforded at the present. However, "If you choose to rip up the Kentucky campaign," he assured Polk, "you can tear Bragg into tatters." [44] To Bragg, Hardee replied "I do not consider it proper . . . to enter into details of what occurred on the occasions referred to." [45]

Cheatham explained that "My sense of duty at least for the present, compels me to decline to answer what part I took in the councils referred to." [46] Stewart had not been present at either conference.[47] Anderson gave a lengthy reply. Polk, he said, had explained at Bardstown that when Bragg issued his order he could not have had before him the "lights" now available to his generals; therefore, the order should not be executed if contrary to their better judgment. All present then agreed that if there were no definite order the safe course would be to fall back as Polk had suggested.[48]

Buckner, now stationed at Mobile, explained to Bragg that it had never been his policy either to seek responsibility or to shirk it, "but I cannot, consistently with my sense of propriety and self-respect and my regard for the public interest, reply to your questions." He then gave reasons why he thought a reply improper. All generals made errors, he concluded, and must "expect the legitimate criticism of the public and of military men." Although there were essential differences of opinion between him and his generals regarding the Kentucky campaign, he believed Bragg was sustained in his authority by "the whole weight of their character,"

[43] Bragg to Hardee, April 13, 1863, *Official Records*, XVI, Pt. 1, 1097–98.
[44] *Ibid.*, 1098.   [45] *Ibid.*, 1101.   [46] *Ibid.*, 1107.   [47] *Ibid.*, 1105.
[48] *Ibid.*, 1099–1100.

and could "still secure their earnest co-operation and support."
"You have been sustained in your position . . . by the Government. You therefore better than any one else can afford to abide
the judgment which history may pronounce on your actions." The
"expense of little personal pride on either part" could result in
"great public good." [49] This was excellent advice from a good soldier and sound citizen, but there is no evidence that either Bragg
or his generals took it seriously. Honest disagreement was fast
changing to personal enmity.

When on May 20 Bragg filed a revised report of his Kentucky
campaign he charged Polk with disobedience both at Bardstown
and Perryville and also with furnishing misleading information
as to the enemy strength.[50] Polk, expecting to be arrested and probably brought to trial, lined up the generals in his defense. All sent
to him copies of their replies to Bragg. With some he had personal
conferences, no doubt refreshing their memories as to just what
took place at Bardstown and Perryville. After such a conference
Anderson made some revisions in his written reply to Bragg. In
correspondence with Hardee, Polk stressed that what transpired
in a military conference was secret; no officer was free to divulge
what he or others suggested. Likewise, reports were not for public
examination until officially released by the government. "I note
what you say of the campaign," he concluded. "There is a time
for all things, and I agree with you the time for dealing with that
has not arrived." [51] But there was no arrest; no court martial.

Although the generals lacked confidence in their commander
and the commander charged his generals with collusion in disobedience, there was general agreement that every effort must be
made to prepare the Army of Tennessee to meet the inevitable
approach of Rosecrans. The Confederate line roughly paralleled
the Duck River. Polk's corps was centered upon Shelbyville, his
left, with the benefit of cavalry, extending to Columbia. Hardee
covered the Wartrace-Tullahoma area, with his right extending to
Manchester. Cavalry forces extended the line to McMinnville. For
almost six months this general position was maintained with little
change. Scouts made daily reports on Federal strength and movements in various localities and now and then there was small scale

[49] *Ibid.*, 1105–1107.   [50] *Ibid.*, 1088 ff.
[51] Polk to Hardee, April 17, 1863, *ibid.*, 1101–1103.

skirmishing,[52] but no major threat disturbed the beauty and calm of Middle Tennessee springtime.

These were important months for the Army of Tennessee, which not only needed to recuperate from its battles before Murfreesboro but also to recruit and train additional troops. And in spite of bickering and bad feeling, General Bragg made good use of his ability as organizer and disciplinarian. Late in March President Davis' aide, William Preston Johnston, found the army "in a high state of efficiency, well clad and armed, and marked with every evidence of good discipline, high courage, and capacity for endurance." [53] And returns for April 1 showed a total increase of 9,414 men over that of January 20.[54]

"I have to-day had a review of my whole corps for the benefit of President Davis, in the person of his aide-de-camp, Colonel W. Preston Johnston," Polk wrote his wife on March 30. "It was a fine affair, and all things went off satisfactorily. The troops looked very well, and I never saw them march so well. My corps was never in better condition, and is now about 20,000 strong. I confess I felt proud of the fellows as they marched by me to-day. In their hearts is embodied as large and as intense an amount of rebellion as was ever concentrated in the same number of men. It is a pleasure to command such men. Johnston was highly pleased and very complimentary." [55]

A few days later Polk went to Tullahoma to join Generals Johnston and Bragg in a review of Hardee's corps. It was a gala affair. Hardee, "the beau of the army," sent out special invitations

[52] In reporting to Polk's sister Van Dorn's capture of 1,700 Indiana, Wisconsin, and Michigan troops, Aide-de-Camp Richmond made an interesting observation, which was probably a reflection of Polk's opinion. "The difference in Sentiment, and conduct of the troops of the enemy, from the different sections of their country, is quite remarkable. For instance—the Indiana, and Illinois troops fight well, behave well on the field, and in conversation with them, after their capture, they are found to be as cordial haters of the abolitionists, as the warmest fire eater. The Michigan and Wisconsin soldiers decendants of the genuine Puritan—are unadulterated negro worshippers— they are literally Yankees and that covers their case. The Indiana troops, give up all thought of conquering us with the sword, and wish to quit,—the others desire to continue the contest. Most of the Michigan & Wisconsin troops ran, or Van Dorn would have captured three times as many." W. B. Richmond to Mrs. Kenneth Rayner, March 9, 1863, Leonidas Polk Papers.
[53] Johnston to Davis, April 15, 1863, *Official Records*, XXIII, Pt. 2, 758.
[54] *Ibid.*, 733.   [55] Quoted in Polk, *Leonidas Polk*, II, 211–12.

to the ladies of the neighboring towns. Breckinridge put the 14,000 men through the exercises. After the review Hardee then staged a tournament and a horse race. "I am to reciprocate the civility next week," Polk informed his wife; "the horse-race I shall turn over to General Cheatham." [56]

Bragg reviewed Polk's troops at Shelbyville on April 15 and 16, and dined with Polk and his division commanders—Cheatham, Withers, and Stewart. He was reported to be highly pleased with what he saw. Polk was apparently even better pleased. "Our transportation is in fine condition," he recorded, "horses and mules all fat, and battery horses and batteries in fine condition. The troops have plenty of clothes and are now all well shod. We have plenty of food also, and as far as the fields before us are any indication, there never was such a wheat harvest." [57]

Among those who visited the Confederate camp during this period was English Lieutenant Colonel Arthur Fremantle of the Coldstream Guard. A keen observer of all things military, especially personnel, he recorded his impression of Bragg and a number of his generals. He found Bragg "in appearance the least prepossessing" of the generals, thin, stooped, with a "sickly, cadaverous, haggard appearance, rather plain features, bushy black eyebrows which unite in a tuft on the top of his nose, and a stubby iron-gray beard; but his eyes are bright and piercing."

Hardee, "a fine soldierlike man, broad-shouldered and tall," had much the appearance of a French officer. Cheatham, "a stout, rather rough-looking man," was said to be a great fighter. It was also rumored that this division commander did "all the necessary swearing" for Polk's corps "which General Polk's clerical character incapacitates him from performing."

Fremantle found Bishop-General Polk most impressive of all,

---

[56] Polk to Wife, April 11, 1863, quoted in *ibid.*, 212–13.

[57] *Id.* to *id.*, April 16, 1863, quoted in *ibid.*, 213. While the army was at Shelbyville and Tullahoma one Colonel James C. Malone proposed to Polk a plan for kidnapping General Rosecrans at Murfreesboro. Polk approved but warned that there must be no violence to the General's person. "Bold and daring enterprises are in our line, and become those who are struggling against the bitterest persecution and the most merciless warfare. Take him, therefore, and his adjutant general's papers with him, if you can, and I believe you can." (Polk to Malone, March 16, 1863, *Official Records*, XXIII, Pt. 2, 701; Malone to Polk, March 17, 1863, *ibid.*) Nothing more was heard of the plan.

"a good-looking gentleman-like man with all the manners and affability of a 'grand seigneur.'" Fifty-seven, tall and erect, he had more the appearance of the soldier than a clergyman. "He is much beloved by the soldiers on account of his great personal courage and agreeable manners." Even before visiting this Confederate camp Fremantle had heard the Bishop-General spoken of in terms of "affection and admiration." He also learned that Polk was extremely wealthy, the owner of seven hundred slaves. (This might have been near the truth before disaster struck at "Leighton," but it was now far from it.)

While in Shelbyville, Fremantle stayed at Polk's headquarters. The Reverend Charles T. Quintard conducted prayers both morning and evening, and there was singing in which General Polk joined "with much zeal." At mealtime Fremantle found Polk rather talkative. The Bishop-General hoped that English churchmen would understand his conduct, he suggested to his visitor. As soon as the war was over he would return to his "episcopal avocations," but now he was in the position of one, who "finding his house on fire, would use every means in his power to extinguish the flame, and would then resume his ordinary pursuits." [58]

Bishop Elliott was also a visitor at camp while Colonel Fremantle was there. Shortly after the battle at Murfreesboro he had written Polk:

> Most heartily do I thank God for the glorious victory, for the gallantry which distinguished you, and for your personal safety. . . . We have been in a state of great tumult for the last week over this battle and yourself. All send you their warmest love and admiration. . . . And now, my more than brother, may God have you in his holy care and keeping; may he watch over and guard you and yours, and preserve you unharmed through this cruel war; and may we often meet over peaceful firesides to recall the honors of this period, and to thank God for all of his mercies toward us. I have come to this new year, and so have you, with an unbroken circle, and we of all men should be most thankful, for we had representatives upon almost every battlefield.[59]

[58] Lord (ed.), *Fremantle Diary*, 110–118.
[59] January 9, 1863, quoted in Polk, *Leonidas Polk*, I, 368.

When the army had become well-established and there appeared to be little chance for either an immediate fight or withdrawal, Polk wrote Elliott:

> Can you not come and see me? My feet are fast in the stocks, and I cannot get to see you! I think, too, you might do great good by coming. Come up and preach for us, and visit us, and administer the communion to us, and confirm our young people and old. You cannot spend a week or so more profitably. Come and bring Wilmer [60] with you and "refresh our bowels"; for we many times feel greatly the need of such refreshing.
>
> Something should be done for the children of the Church in the army; very little or nothing is being done. Can you not send us some clergymen? I am amazed that so few are found willing to labor in such a cause. What higher or holier could they ask?
>
> I fear our brother Otey is approaching his last days. I hear he is in bed and cannot well get out again. But I had rather talk with you than write you, so come and let us see you face to face.
>
> I think you and Wilmer, who are both so near us, might come and see "how we do." [61]

[60] Richard Hooker Wilmer, who in March, 1862, had succeeded Nicholas Hammer Cobbs as Bishop of Alabama.

[61] May 4, 1863, quoted in Polk, *Leonidas Polk*, I, 364. The matter of religion in camp was of much concern to Polk. In a letter to his wife on June 14, 1863, after referring to a sermon preached in the Shelbyville Presbyterian Church by the Reverend Doctor Palmer of New Orleans he added, "He is to spend some time with the army, as well to aid in placing chaplains with regiments not supplied as to preach himself. A great and highly commendable effort is now being made by the religious bodies of the country to supply the spiritual wants of the army, and I hope the best results will follow from their effort. It is one in which I take great interest, and which I foster in every way in my power. Indeed, I think on the judicious application of the means of imparting religious instructions to the army very much depends the future condition of our people when it shall please God to relieve us from the pressure of this scourging war and restore us to peace. If we should allow our troops to give vent to their natural feeling and passions in retaliating on the enemy, we should train them up to a condition of mind totally unfitting them to fall into a well-disciplined and chastened civilization when the war shall have closed. To us this is especially important, since literally now the country is the army; for all the men of all classes are in the army. It is therefore of the highest importance that its moral condition should be well watched, and its spiritual condition cared for and elevated. It is important, too, that, as the army is made up of all classes of religion, all classes should be represented in their teachers, and the best specimens of their teachers should be employed to act upon them." Quoted in *ibid.*, II, 214–15.

Elliott came, and Fremantle found him to be "a nice old man of venerable appearance and very courteous manners. . . . He speaks English exactly like an English Gentleman. So, in fact, does General Polk and all the wellbred Southerners, much more so than the ladies, whose American accent can always be detected." [62]

In company with Quintard, Bishop Elliott preached many times to officers and soldiers. On May 31 he preached in the Presbyterian Church at Shelbyville. Afterward he confirmed about twenty persons, including William Dudley Gale and Meck Polk. That afternoon at 5 P.M. he was at Wartrace where he preached to 3,000 including Generals Bragg, Hardee, Polk, Cleburne, and Withers. On June 2 he baptized and confirmed General Bragg. Bragg's staff, Polk and his staff, and Fremantle were the only ones present. Fremantle observed that most of the officers of the Army of Tennessee were Episcopalians but the soldiers were "Methodist, Baptist, etc." [63]

Shortly after taking leave of the Army of Tennessee, Fremantle wrote in his diary that Polk's "kindness and hospitality have exceeded anything I could have expected. . . . I shall never think of him without admiration for his character as a sincere patriot, a gallant soldier, and a perfect gentleman." He was also high in his praise of Polk's staff officers, Richmond and Yeatman.[64]

Henry C. Yeatman was the stepson of John Bell, and he was Lucius Polk's son-in-law. Meck Polk was also now at his father's headquarters. Although a lieutenant of artillery, General Polk had brought him to headquarters where he could "keep an eye on him." [65] While Polk was at Shelbyville his son-in-law, William Dudley Gale, also joined his staff as voluntary aide, and for the first time each had an opportunity to know the other. Gale confided to his wife that he found her father "a grand and noble man," Polk repaid the compliment in the same private manner. Her son-in-law was "really one of the most estimable and gentlemanly men I have ever known," he told his wife.[66] This, however, was not just

---

[62] Lord (ed.), *Fremantle Diary*, 111.　　[63] *Ibid.*, 121, 123, 129.
[64] *Ibid.*, June 3, 1863, p. 136.
[65] Polk to Wife, March 26, 1863, Gale Papers.
[66] Gale to Wife, February 21, 1863, *ibid.*; Polk to Wife, March 26, 1863, *ibid.*

an isolated compliment, for Polk had great respect for and confidence in his entire staff. He found these men "all I could desire.
They are as attentive and respectful as they could be and all so
gentlemanly." [67]

Polk made his Shelbyville headquarters at the home of a prominent businessman, an Englishman by birth who had resided in
France and was now a manufacturer of cotton goods at Shelbyville. He and his family were suspected of having Unionist sympathies, but were "very nice quiet people." Here in a first floor
room Polk and Gale had their living quarters and here also was
transacted all First Corps business. [68] As reports of the Kentucky
and Murfreesboro campaigns were completed and the feud between Bragg and his generals somewhat subsided, officers found
life a bit less strenuous. On March 26 Polk had written his wife
that his work was so heavy he often found it necessary to sit up
until 2 A.M. Three months later he sent her word that "I get to
bed always before eleven and last night shortly before nine." He
had "slept more in the last month than in any 4 months before,"
and he always "slept between sheets" and had "a table cloth and
napkins." Food, including fresh milk, was plentiful; he had
brought a milk cow back from Kentucky. [69]

Six months of inactivity gave opportunity for much speculation
and wishful thinking. Polk did his part. It is not possible to separate what he actually believed from what he said for the purpose
of bolstering the sagging spirits of his family. Late in June he
predicted that Grant would fail to take Vicksburg and would in
the attempt so weaken himself as to make it possible for Johnston
to fall upon him and "crush him out root and branch." He also
thought that Port Hudson would hold. There would then be no
other course for the enemy but "to give up the war." As for Rosecrans, it appeared he scarcely knew what to do. However, should
he decide to come on the Army of Tennessee would be "pleased
to see him here. . . . But we have no particular anxiety to see him
any where only that he should leave and go back the way he came.
He is rather an indifferent speciman and we have small respect for
him." [70]

[67] Polk to Wife, March 26, 1863, *ibid.*
[68] Gale to Wife, February 21, 1863, *ibid.*
[69] Polk to Daughter, June 25, 1863, Leonidas Polk Papers.   [70] *Ibid.*

(15)

Chickamauga—"We Should Have Made More Out of It"

"Is it your intention to make an immediate movement forward? A definite answer, yes or no, is required," Halleck wired Rosecrans on June 16, 1863. Rosecrans replied: ". . . if immediate means to-night or to-morrow, no. If it means as soon as all things are ready, say five days, yes." [1] This might be interpreted as a final demand for action.

For almost six months Rosecrans' Army of the Cumberland had camped comfortably in the vicinity of Murfreesboro; authorities at Washington were growing impatient. Lincoln had wired on May 28: "I would not push you to any rashness, but I am very anxious that you do your utmost, short of rashness, to keep Bragg from getting off to help Johnston against Grant." To this Halleck added on June 3 "If you cannot hurt the enemy now, he will soon hurt you." Rosecrans had replied to Lincoln, "I will attend to it." [2]

Between the Confederate lines north of Duck River and Rosecrans' position at Murfreesboro was a range of rugged hills cut by a few passes or gaps. Through Hoover's Gap ran the road from Murfreesboro to Manchester. Branching off of this road and passing through Liberty Gap was a road to Bellbuckle, thence to Wartrace. In front of Shelbyville was Guy's Gap, through which passed the Murfreesboro-Shelbyville road. These gaps were strong positions in the first line of Confederate defense, but Bragg had not seen fit to have them strongly fortified. Light fortifications were constructed at Shelbyville, however, and more extensive ones at Tullahoma.

Bragg gave no evidence of even contemplating an offensive

---

[1] *Official Records*, XXIII, Pt. 1, 10.   [2] *Ibid.*, Pt. 2, 369, 383.

against Rosecrans. He organized and trained a good army, but he
had no plans for its use unless attacked. Some idea of what was
expected of Rosecrans can be gathered from Colonel William
Preston Johnston's report to President Davis on April 15: "It is
not the intention or expectation of Generals Johnston and Bragg
to await attack there [Tullahoma] unless made in front, and this
they do not expect. They believe that Rosecrans will attempt to

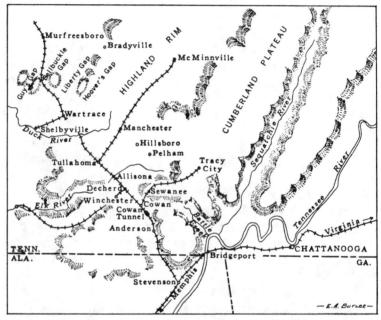

FROM MURFREESBORO TO CHATTANOOGA

pass our flank, most probably our right flank; in which case we
would go out and attack him." [3]

As early as February 25, in a letter to Johnston, Polk had recorded his speculations as to Rosecrans' possible intentions. If reports of recent re-enforcements were true, the Army of the Cumberland must number possibly 70,000. He believed Rosecrans
would move this army in two columns, the left going directly
from Murfreesboro to McMinnville and seizing the mountain

[3] *Ibid.*, 760.

passes between Sparta and Decherd, possibly including the Cowan tunnel. A force of 10,000 could then be thrown across the mountain to seize the East Tennessee Railroad and possibly Chattanooga. In the meantime, the other column would be used to protect the line of communications. He thought there was also a possibility of a third column skirting the Confederate left by way of Huntsville, Stevenson and Bridgeport, Alabama.[4] These possibilities must have been brought to Bragg's attention, even discussed with him, yet he did little to protect against a flanking attack and the destruction of the railroad in his rear. And that was exactly what Rosecrans planned.

On June 23 he ordered a spirited cavalry attack upon Polk's left by way of Eagleville, hoping to create the impression of a mass movement upon Shelbyville, thus concealing his intention to move on Manchester instead. The attack was a complete failure; after light skirmishing around Rover and Unionville the Federal cavalry fell back. But in spite of this minor reversal, Rosecrans wired Washington at 2:10 A.M. June 24 that his army would begin to move "at 3 o'clock this morning." [5] Now 70,000 strong, including 10,000 cavalry,[6] he was prepared to take the offensive, yet he clearly preferred maneuvering to hard fighting.

The Federal advance toward Manchester was led by a brigade of mounted infantry commanded by Colonel J. T. Wilder of Munfordville fame. The route led through Hoover's Gap, which was almost without fortification and weakly defended. By nightfall this gap was in Federal possession. The same was true of Liberty Gap, and still another Federal force had moved along the Shelbyville road as far as Christiana.

At 6:15 P.M. Bragg, learning of some activity but without knowledge of its strength or purpose, made a weak gesture at defense by ordering Polk to send Wharton with two regiments of cavalry toward Manchester and to strengthen his own front on the Murfreesboro pike with another regiment of infantry. At 10:15 that evening Polk ordered Cheatham and Withers to stand ready "for any movement." Troops that had been sent out to cut wheat were to be recalled.[7]

Heavy rains that had begun to fall on the twenty-fourth con-

---

[4] *Ibid.,* 649–50.   [5] *Ibid.,* Pt. 1, 10.   [6] *Ibid.,* 411.
[7] *Ibid.,* Pt. 2, 883, 884.

tinued throughout the twenty-fifth (and almost daily for another two weeks), greatly retarding progress. Not until the following day did the Federal advance pass through Matt's Hollow and reach the highland rim on which Manchester was located. On the twenty-sixth Bragg called Polk to headquarters for a conference. Since no attack had been made upon Guy's Gap in Polk's front and Hardee was being hard pressed at Liberty Gap, Bragg wished Polk to pass through Guy's Gap and strike the enemy in flank and rear while Hardee struck from the front. "Owing to the character of the country, the heavy cedar growth, and the peculiar topography," Polk objected. He considered the position into which he was asked to move "nothing short of a man-trap." [8] But Bragg insisted and the movement was ordered for daylight on the twenty-seventh.

At 4 P.M. Bragg, now at Shelbyville, canceled the order and an hour later sent Polk his reason. He had learned that a large enemy force was operating against Stewart between Fairfield and Hoover's Gap; consequently, he wished Polk's opinion "as to whether it be possible to hold a line this side of Tullahoma, to strike the enemy successfully this side Tullahoma, or is retreat to Tullahoma a necessity?" [9]

What Polk advised at the moment is not recorded, but at 11 P.M. came news that Stewart's right had been turned, so Polk immediately ordered Cheatham's and Withers' divisions to fall back upon Tullahoma early on the twenty-seventh, marching by Shofner Bridge and Flat Creek roads respectively. Mud, more rain, and general congestion from moving so large a number of men and their supplies retarded progress; it was 4 P.M. before Polk's corps reached Tullahoma.

The Federal force that had turned Stewart's right was McCook's corps which had abandoned Liberty Gap and swung to the left headed for Manchester, which was reached on the twenty-seventh. Wilder's cavalry had arrived early that morning, and Thomas' and Crittenden's corps would begin streaming in before night. Crittenden had moved by the roundabout way of Bradyville and Pocahontas.

On the morning of the twenty-eight Wilder's cavalry took off

[8] Notes of Lieutenant W. B. Richmond, *ibid.*, Pt. 1, 618.
[9] W. W. Mackall to Polk, June 26, 1863, 5 P.M., *ibid.*

again through the rain and mud, this time no doubt seeking revenge for his humiliation at Munfordville. Galloping by way of Hillsboro to Pelham and thence across to Decherd, Wilder was soon completely in the rear of Bragg's position at Tullahoma. At Decherd he tore up the Nashville and Chattanooga Railroad, destroyed the water tanks, and burned the trestle between Decherd and Winchester, over which ran the track of the spur line to Fayetteville, before retiring to the vicinity of Pelham for the night.

On the morning of the twenty-ninth Wilder's men climbed the mountain to Sewanee, the site of Polk's beloved University of the South, which had not yet opened its doors to students. Apparently for practice, they tore up the railroad leading to the Tracy coal mines, and then descended the south side of the mountain, intending to cut the Nashville and Chattanooga again between the Cowan tunnel and Stevenson. But reports of the presence of trainloads of Confederate infantry at Anderson caused them to recross the mountain to Pelham. Strangely enough, Wilder did not destroy the Cowan tunnel. Here a few kegs of powder could have rendered the railroad useless for months. But perhaps the Federals themselves already had plans for using this line. By noon June 30 Wilder's bedraggled command was back at Manchester.[10]

Somebody had erred. Generals Polk, Cheatham, and Maney, plus thousands of lesser officers and soldiers within their commands were familiar with this country, even if Bragg was not. They knew that once a Federal force moved from Matt's Hollow onto the Highland Rim the open rolling country beyond was a standing invitation to invasion. Yet this path to the Confederate rear had been left unprotected. Polk first heard of Wilder's destructive raid while in conference with Bragg about 9 A.M. on the twenty-ninth. Bragg explained that the Federal mounted force was too strong to be controlled; therefore, he had decided to fight Rosecrans at Tullahoma. Polk, much disturbed, rode out along the lines until he met Hardee. After telling him of his conference with Bragg, he added that he thought the General's decision "an injudicious one." [11]

At 3 P.M. both Hardee and Polk conferred with Bragg. Bragg asked Polk what he would advise. Polk suggested that the first

[10] Wilder's report, *ibid.*, 457 ff.
[11] Notes of W. B. Richmond, *ibid.*, 621.

step must be to re-establish communications. This had already been accomplished that morning, Bragg replied. How then, Polk inquired, were they to be maintained? " 'By posting cavalry along the line,' " Bragg explained. But there was not sufficient cavalry to do this and cover other necessary points, Polk observed; consequently, the Federals would drive off the cavalry and repossess the railroad within thirty-six hours and this time with forces sufficient to hold it. The Army of Tennessee would then be "as effectually besieged as Pemberton in Vicksburg." There would be no need for the enemy to strike a blow, for the choice would be either to starve or to retreat into North Alabama by way of Fayetteville. Even if retreat should be attempted eventually, men and animals would be so weakened that the whole wagon train, ordnance, and artillery would be in great danger of seizure by the enemy. But supposing that the army could be safely led across the Tennessee River into the hills of North Alabama, it would be without food, for the enemy would have taken Chattanooga, marched into North Georgia without serious opposition, and taken possession of "the heart of the Confederacy."

After listening to this recital of gloomy possibilities, Bragg interrupted: " 'Then you propose that we shall retreat.' " " 'I do, and that is my counsel,' " Polk exclaimed. Bragg then turned to Hardee for his opinion. Hardee expressed great respect for Polk's views but was not ready to advise retreat. He thought that communications might be protected by a combined cavalry and infantry force while awaiting development of the enemy's plans. It was agreed.[12]

Polk returned to his corps and immediately ordered Cheatham and Withers to supply the engineers all necessary assistance in strengthening the breastworks. The army settled down for a night in the mud. The rain continued.[13] At 11 A.M. on the thirtieth Bragg informed Polk that the enemy was approaching by both the Manchester and Hillsboro roads. This dispatch was followed by another at 3 P.M. The enemy plan now seemed clear; so Bragg had decided to retreat to a position south of the Elk River. "Have your wagon train ready to move on Allisona by the road south of the rail so soon as Hardee's train is out of the way," he ordered Polk. The time he thought would be about 10 P.M., but

[12] *Ibid.*, 621–22.   [13] *Ibid.*, 622.

Polk's train actually started moving "by different roads" at 7 P.M. The General left at the head of his troops at about 11 P.M. and arrived at Allisona at 5 A.M., July 1. The train and troops had all arrived by noon.[14] Allisona, the point where the Nashville and Chattanooga Railroad crossed the Elk River, was near the present Estill Springs.

General Bragg had gone by rail to Decherd. "Cross all your command"; he wrote Polk at Allisona, "take position to defend the crossing for cavalry on dirt road bridges; destroy railroad bridges thoroughly, superstructure and piers; send trains here, and ride over yourself." Polk placed Cheatham in command at Allisona and rushed to Decherd for a conference with Bragg, returning at 5 P.M. Two hours later Bragg rushed him a message: "The enemy have reached your front; close up. The question to be decided instantly, Shall we fight on the Elk, or take post at foot of mountain at Cowan? Answer." Polk replied the same evening: "I reply, take post at foot of mountain at Cowan." He added that as much of the wagon train as possible should be moved across the mountain. Feed for animals kept this side the mountain could be moved in by rail.[15] Some time during the day Bragg had already ordered Polk to send his "engineer troops" to repair the mountain road as far as University Place.[16]

About the time Polk was replying to Bragg, Hardee was penning Polk a "confidential" note: "I have been thinking seriously of the condition of affairs with this army. I deeply regret to see General Bragg in his present enfeebled state of health. If we have a fight, he is evidently unable either to examine and determine his line of battle or to take command on the field. What shall we do? What is best to be done to save this army and its honor? I think we ought to counsel together. Where is Buckner? The enemy evidently believes we are retreating, and will press us vigorously tomorrow. When can we meet? I would like Buckner to be present." [17]

Later in the evening Hardee also received an inquiry from Bragg. He too replied "fight at the mountain." He then dashed off another note to Polk: "This decision will render unnecessary the meeting which I sought to-night; we can talk about the matter to-

[14] *Ibid.*, 622–23.   [15] *Ibid.*, 623.   [16] *Ibid.*, 624.
[17] July 1, 1863, 8:30 P.M., *ibid.*, 623.

morrow. I do not desire that any one but Buckner and yourself should know my anxiety." He was somewhat relieved that the apparent decision was to fight at the foot of the mountain, yet in view of the conditions outlined in his previous note, he still thought further retreat the wiser course.[18]

At 1:30 A.M. July 2, Bragg issued orders to fall back from the position along the Elk River. Polk would move through Winchester to Cowan. The reserves under Buckner would precede him. Hardee was to move by Decherd and the road to Brakefield Point. Wheeler's cavalry corps would keep careful watch along the Elk, challenge any enemy attempt to cross over, and cover the rear of the army until it was in position at the foot of the mountain.[19]

Buckner, recently appointed to command in East Tennessee, had notified Bragg at Tullahoma on June 25 that he could come to his assistance with two batteries and probably 3,000 troops. On the following day his chief of staff reported that Buckner would leave that evening to re-enforce Bragg.[20] It was Buckner's troops that Wilder had reported on the cars at Anderson.

By 5 A.M. Polk's troops were in motion. Both the railroad and dirt bridges at Allisona had been destroyed, he notified Bragg. He had furnished a guide for Buckner.[21] By afternoon the Army of Tennessee, re-enforced by Buckner, was falling into battle line on the plain between Cowan and the mountain. The train was ordered across the mountain. But Rosecrans, not wishing to give battle in a position selected by Bragg, had not followed; so during the night Bragg's entire force moved across the mountain.

Polk arrived at University Place at 2 A.M. July 3, and remained there until 4 P.M. before riding off to join Cheatham's division six miles ahead. One can imagine his feelings as he rode about the site of the embryo University, reflecting upon his past efforts, and dreaming of the future.

Wheeler, still protecting the rear of the retreating army, reported to Polk on July 4 that he had been very warmly engaged by enemy cavalry and infantry near the University. Later in the day he suggested that Polk detail some infantry units to block roads down the mountain. His cavalry could retire by a single road and then block it up behind. This would greatly retard pursuit by the

[18] *Ibid.*, 624.   [19] Orders. July 2, 1863, 1:30 A.M., *ibid.*, 624.
[20] *Ibid.*, Pt. 2, 885, 887.   [21] *Ibid.*, Pt. 1, 624.

enemy. But even after stripping his batteries Polk could collect only about a dozen axes. These he sent to Wheeler. He also instructed Wharton to begin felling trees, cutting them "half in two," leaving to the retiring cavalry the task of completing the obstruction. "The descent is exceedingly difficult" Polk reminded Wheeler.[22]

The obstructions did not prove of great importance. Rosecrans was not in hot pursuit, and by the close of the day, July 4, Polk's corps had crossed the Tennessee River near the mouth of Battle Creek. Buckner crossed at Bridgeport. Both were in Chattanooga by July 8. Buckner was back in Knoxville the following day. Before reaching Chattanooga Hardee was relieved of command and ordered to report to General Johnston at Jackson, Mississippi. He would be replaced by Lieutenant General D. H. Hill.

The Army of Tennessee was exhausted, but not from fighting. It was now back at the base from which it had started almost a year earlier, but under much different circumstances. It was now being chased out of Tennessee by the army it had so successfully flanked out of the state the previous year. Retreat had become almost a habit; confidence was at a low ebb. Bragg was being vigorously censured by both officers and troops. Even so, his mistake had not been in retreating but in permitting his army to get into a situation where retreat was necessary. And to add to the gloom came the news that Lee had been stopped at Gettysburg and Pemberton had surrendered Vicksburg.

Army returns dated July 20 showed 51,027 present at Chattanooga. Of this number 38,618 were listed as effectives. Polk reported that his corps was slightly stronger than when the recent retreat began. There had been some straggling and desertion but new recruits and returning convalescents had more than made up this loss. While at Tullahoma, Bragg had created a Volunteer and Conscript Bureau for his department and placed Brigadier General Gideon J. Pillow in charge. With headquarters first at Columbia, Tennessee, and later Huntsville, Alabama, Pillow had rendered very effective service.

On July 21 Polk wrote Adjutant General Cooper again calling attention to a plan he had presented while in Richmond the previ-

[22] *Ibid.,* 625.

ous November. There were enough men in the Confederacy
capable of bearing arms, Polk explained, to give the Confederate
army sufficient strength to defy the enemy and win independence.
The problem was to get them into the service, and the solution to
this problem would require "a more concentrated, direct, and
stringent" effort than had yet been made. He therefore proposed
the creation of a bureau of reserves headed by an officer of "high
grade, of competent capacity and aptitude." The field of activity
embraced the entire Confederacy, subdivided into districts, each
headed by a competent officer. In the hands of this bureau should
be placed the entire machinery of conscription, the recruiting of
volunteers, and the seizure and return of deserters. To perform effectively the last function officers of the bureau would need the
powers of a military police. This bureau might also be responsible
for supplying Negro laborers to those military commanders who
requested their services as teamsters or on public works. "Negroes
so employed would be equal to an addition of so many effectives
to each army corps."

General Bragg, by the creation of his Volunteer and Conscript
Bureau, had made a good beginning, Polk concluded, and General Pillow, the officer in charge, had proved himself eminently
competent and the remarkable results of his efforts had demonstrated the feasibility and value of such a bureau. "No officer
could have proved himself more capable, faithful, and efficient."
Consequently, Polk urgently recommended that Pillow be promoted to major general and placed in charge of such a bureau. He
was convinced that "no measures could be devised which would
compare with this for increasing and strengthening the armies of
the Confederacy." And Pillow's "peculiar fitness . . . and his industry and energy would make his presence promptly felt." [23] The
Bishop-General, by nature kind and forgiving, had conveniently
forgotten his experience with Pillow at Columbus.

Polk's letter to Cooper was forwarded through Bragg, who indorsed thereon his approval, adding, "We cannot retrieve the
losses of the past, but prompt adoption of the remedies suggested
may do much to save the future." [24]

Polk shared the disappointment resulting from retreat but made

[23] *Ibid.*, Pt. 2, 919–22.   [24] *Ibid.*, 922.

no effort to saddle Bragg with sole responsibility. "Of our falling back to this place I have to say I thought it judicious, and advised it," he wrote President Davis. The situation, however, was critical, and he had concluded that little relief could be expected from "prosecuting our campaign in the west on the present plan"; therefore, he wished respectfully to submit some proposed changes. It was reported that a shortage of water had turned Grant back from Jackson to Vicksburg. It was also reported that he was sending a corps to the Virginia front. The remaining troops would likely move against Mobile. Even against this force Polk feared Johnston could not hope to contend successfully. Eventually Mobile would fall and Alabama be overrun in spite of Johnston. If this be valid reasoning, then Johnston's army could be used to greater advantage elsewhere. Why not leave a small detachment to assist in rallying Alabama state troops and transfer Johnston's entire army to Chattanooga?

By adding Buckner's troops from East Tennessee the total force would be more than 70,000 strong. Rosecrans could be crushed, Tennessee repossessed, and Columbus, Kentucky, reoccupied. With the Mississippi River above Vicksburg again in Confederate hands Grant would be "at our mercy." The only great risk would be in leaving Alabama open to occupation, but even that calamity would be greatly outweighed by the successes elsewhere.[25]

While Polk was urging that Johnston's army be moved to Chattanooga, Hardee, who had recently joined Johnston, was discouraged and homesick. He found Johnston's force much reduced by desertion and somewhat demoralized, he wrote Polk. The infantry did not exceed 18,000. Johnston had appeared glad to see him but had no real need for his services. "I fear I will not be able to do as much good as you anticipated. I *know* I wish I were back at Chattanooga with my corps. . . . I think I may venture to say to you in confidence of friendship that Johnston is wanting in all those particulars in which you feared he was deficient, and in addition has a very *inefficient staff*." In closing, Hardee wished "my dear friend" much success and happiness, but could view the present only as "a dark hour for the Confederacy."[26]

Before receiving Hardee's letter Polk wrote him one, reviewing

[25] Polk to Davis, July 26, 1863, *ibid.*, 932–33.
[26] Hardee to Polk, July 27, 1863, Leonidas Polk Papers.

what he had suggested to Davis relative to the concentration of forces at Chattanooga. He had long believed the Army of Tennessee the most important fighting force in the Confederacy, he added, and if "properly strengthened and handled" it would yet accomplish more than any other. But something must be done and that immediately. If Hardee thought well of his suggestion he wished him to pass it on to Johnston.[27]

Weeks passed. The Army of Tennessee rested and fortified Chattanooga. Lieutenant General D. H. Hill arrived and assumed command of Hardee's corps. Withers, of Polk's corps, was transferred to Alabama to organize and train fresh troops. He was replaced by Major General T. C. Hindman. No one in authority seemed to have any plans. It was just another period of waiting, but for what?

Polk became apprehensive, and in private correspondence began to question the ability of Richmond authorities. A letter to his brother-in-law, Kenneth Rayner, began with a survey of the situation, with an injection of views and opinions here and there. Johnston, he thought, was doing the best he could to pull together an army out of the Mississippi *"debris."* But Grant was "making sure of his conquest in Miss.," and would no doubt soon move on Mobile. A court was being called to inquire into Pemberton's surrender of Vicksburg. Little was heard from Kirby Smith's Trans-Mississippi region but that little was favorable. It was reported that Price had resigned. This he thought unfortunate, "not withstanding I had no great confidence in his ability."

These preliminaries out of the way, Polk became confidential. The Confederacy, he explained to Rayner, was fast approaching a crisis. It was generally agreed that "we have lost ground in the last few weeks," making necessary the adoption of emergency measures. "As to the army as it stands—while there may be occasional desertions—we have no fear. We think it may be relied on. But it is not strong enough. It must be increased. (*We have the men & they should be put into the ranks.*) To accomplish this, more vigour is required in the administration. Its action is not decided enough. It does not seem to rise under increasing pressure. Whether it will prove equal to emergencies still more stringent, yet to come, remains to be seen. But the indication which I think most signifi-

[27] Polk to Hardee, July 30, 1863, *Official Records*, XXIII, Pt. 2, 937–38.

cant is *the tendency now manifesting itself in different states among the people to let down."* General Bragg, he said, had heard from his brother, Former Governor Thomas Bragg, that a certain North Carolina newspaper was advocating "yielding and returning to the old Union," and that Former Governor William A. Graham was supporting the movement. "Can this be so?"

There were also reports of similar movements in Alabama and Mississippi "—to say nothing of the state of things in Georgia." The gravity of the situation, he urged, demanded "immediate attention on the part of those *who do not mean to allow our effort to rid ourselves of Yankee rule to fail . . . although I do not think it by any means clear that we cannot succeed single handed,* yet, from the present condition of the army as to numbers; the want of activity and energy on the part of the government in bringing out the military forces of the states; the altered state of public feeling at the north, growing out of Morgan's raid and Lee's invasion— both very ill advised—together with the growing evidences of discontent at the conduct of the war by certain hated agents or officials of the executive; and now, more than all these indications of letting down on the part of the people, I am constrained to say that I feel the time has come when it is safe for us to cast about to see whether we may not (should it become necessary) find *an ally* with power sufficient to help us out. In a word, I think we should take time by the forelock and open communications with *France. . . ."* [28]

On this same day Polk wrote an even more critical letter to his intimate friend Bishop Elliott. "The truth is," he explained, "I am somewhat afraid of Davis. He has so much at stake on this issue that I do not find myself willing to risk his judgment. . . . He is proud, self-reliant, and I fear stubborn." There was no doubt but that the Confederacy possessed the means to defy the Yankees; with proper plans and execution lost ground could still be regained. If Davis would "lean a little less upon his own understanding" and recognize that "there were some minds in the land from whom he might obtain counsel worth having & would push his advantages with greater vigor" the cause would be greatly benefited. [29]

[28] August 15, 1863, Leonidas Polk Papers.   [29] August 15, 1863, *ibid.*

To Rosecrans should go considerable praise for the skillful manner in which he maneuvered Bragg out of Tennessee. Even impatient Washington authorities could smile as they added this accomplishment to the list of recent Federal achievements. But smiles soon changed to frowns; satisfaction again gave way to impatience. Rosecrans just would not follow up. It was expected that with the co-operation of Burnside, who had now moved from Kentucky into East Tennessee, he would be able to deal Bragg a destructive blow before re-enforcements from Johnston could arrive. "You must not wait for Johnston to join Bragg, but must move forward immediately against the latter," Halleck urged on July 24. ". . . There is great disappointment felt here at the slowness of your advance." [30]

Rosecrans refused to be rushed, and even suggested his own removal if the Government had another available general in whom it had more confidence. A month had passed and he had not crossed the mountains out of Middle Tennessee. Finally at noon, August 4, Halleck wired him at Winchester: "Your forces must move forward without further delay. You will daily report the movement of each corps till you cross the Tennessee River." At 5 P.M. Rosecrans inquired "I wish to know if your order intended to take away my discretion as to the time and manner of moving my troops?" Apparently it did, for Halleck shot back: "The orders for the advance of your army, and that its movements be reported daily, are peremtory." [31]

In spite of such definite orders, Rosecrans did not start moving until August 16. Crittenden's corps, which had been based at McMinnville, was directed to cross the mountain into Sequatchie Valley, thence over Walden's Ridge, and threaten Chattanooga from the front. Thomas' and McCook's corps were at Winchester. The former was directed to cross the mountain into Sequatchie Valley by way of Sewanee. The latter would make use of the railroad to Stevenson. Bragg learned that the Federals were on the move, but had no idea of Rosecrans' plans. On August 21 he appealed to Johnston for assistance and soon the divisions of Breckinridge and W. H. T. Walker, 9,000 strong, were on their way across Alabama toward Chattanooga.

[30] *Official Records*, XXIII, Pt. 2, 552.   [31] *Ibid.*, 592.

The enemy had thrown a few shells into town, killing three privates, Polk wrote his wife on August 27. "From our stations on Lookout and Raccoon Mountains, we have the enemy under observation. They consist only of cavalry thus far and artillery, a few pieces. We think Rosecrans is moving up the river to make his attempt to cross *above* Chattanooga; but his plans are as yet not well developed. He has not crossed at Bridgeport and I think will not,

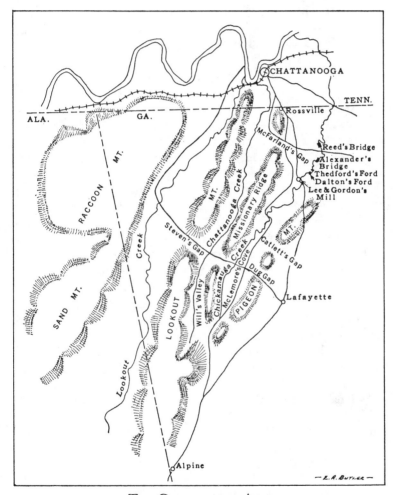

THE CHICKAMAUGA AREA

nor at any other place below Chattanooga. He will wish to cross at a place where, when he gets over, he will find no mountain obstructing him." Re-enforcements were "pouring in" and the Confederate army was "in fine spirits." [32]

Polk proved to be a poor prophet; Thomas and McCook had already reached the Tennessee River and were repairing the railroad bridge at Bridgeport and preparing their pontoons and rafts. They began crossing on August 29. This was truly a mountainous region into which the Federals were moving, and one is inclined to agree with Bragg and his generals in their belief that military operations over such a terrain would be most impracticable. The first barrier was Sand Mountain (the northern portion of which was known as Raccoon Mountain). This was a broad, but not very lofty, range roughly paralleling the river and extending fifty miles into Alabama. Beyond Sand Mountain was Lookout or Wills Valley, down through which ran Chattanooga Creek. Next came Lookout Mountain, a range a hundred miles in length and at points rising to 3,000 feet. From the northern extremity of this range, a point usually referred to as Lookout, one could get a view of the Tennessee River, Chattanooga, and miles of adjacent country. East of Lookout Mountain was a shorter and less lofty range known as Missionary Ridge. Joining the Ridge on the south and forming a hairpin with it was Pigeon Mountain. Inside this hairpin curve was McLemore's Cove. From this Cove flowed Chickamauga Creek to enter the Tennessee River just above Chattanooga. The principal entrance into the Cove from Lookout Mountain was Steven's Gap. Pigeon Mountain, from south to north, was cut by three important gaps—Bluebird, Dug, and Catlett's. About five miles east of Bluebird Gap was LaFayette, Georgia. The road from Chattanooga to LaFayette and points south led through Rossville and crossed Chickamauga Creek at Lee and Gordon's Mill.

As soon as they were across the Tennessee River Thomas and McCook headed straight for the mountains. Rosecrans had no intention of attacking Bragg in his Chattanooga fortification. He had flanked the Confederates out of Shelbyville and Tullahoma. Why not try it again? Thomas was to cross Lookout Mountain at

[32] Polk to Wife, August 27, 1863, Leonidas Polk Papers.

Steven's Gap and move into McLemore's Cove, Negley's division leading the way. McCook would make use of Will's Valley moving first southward annd then eastward. Both would be moving toward the railroad to Atlanta, Bragg's only supply line. Crittenden would then cross the river below Chattanooga and occupy the town, probably without a fight.

Bragg was confused; Rosecrans was doing exactly what he thought the Federal commander would not do. And once Federal troops were within the mountains and protected by them there was no way of telling when or where they would come out. " 'It is said to be easy to defend a mountainous country,' " Bragg observed to General Hill, " 'but mountains hide your foe from you, while they are full of gaps through which he can pounce upon you at any time. A mountain is like the wall of a house full of rat-holes. The rat lies hidden in his hole, ready to pop out when no one is watching. Who can tell what lies behind that wall?' " [33]

As the Federal "rats" were reported at three widely scattered points Bragg immediately sensed the possibility of striking Rosecrans in detail. His first thought was to cross the Tennessee and attack Crittenden while he was still isolated. This plan he outlined to Hill as soon as he learned that Thomas and McCook had crossed east of the river. "What say you?" he inquired. Fords could be located and General Forrest promised to cross infantry on his Cavalry horses. "The crushing of this corps would give us a great victory and redeem Tennessee. . . . Consult Cleburne." [34]

Hill and Cleburne were apparently willing to make the try but Bragg changed his mind. He decided that while his army was chasing Crittenden, who might fall back rather than fight, Thomas and McCook might pop out of the mountains and cut Confederate connections with Atlanta. So instead of going after Crittenden he decided to abandon Chattanooga and fall back toward LaFayette. Polk's corps, composed of Cheatham's and Hindman's divisions, took position at Lee and Gordon's Mill where the road to LaFayette crossed Chickamagua Creek. Hill's corps, consisting of Cleburne's and Breckinridge's divisions, moved to the vicinity of LaFayette, Cleburne taking up watch at the gaps

[33] Daniel H. Hill, "Chickamauga—The Great Battle of the West," *Battles and Leaders*, III, 641 n.
[34] Bragg to Hill, September 4, 1863, *Official Records*, XXX, Pt. 4, 594.

through Pigeon Mountain. Walker was ordered farther south
toward Rome to observe McCook. Buckner, having abandoned
East Tennessee as Burnside advanced, would soon move into the
LaFayette area.

No sooner had Thomas reached the mountains than he began
to pick up information from natives and "deserters," some of them
no doubt supplied by Bragg for this purpose. He first learned of
the arrival of re-enforcements from Mississippi, but this disturbing
news was soon made less important by persistent reports that
Bragg's whole army was in headlong flight southward toward
Rome. Since Bragg was better known for his retreats than his
fights, this sounded reasonable. It was what Rosecrans had expected. He immediately ordered Crittenden to occupy abandoned Chattanooga. McCook was to hasten to Alpine and Sum-
merville and intercept the fleeing Confederates. Thomas would
push through McLemore's Cove to LaFayette and strike them in
the flank.[35]

Negley's division of Thomas' corps had already moved into Mc-
Lemore's Cove. On September 9 Bragg learned of its presence
there. He ordered Hindman's division of Polk's corps to move into
the Cove and attack the following day. Cleburne's division of
Hill's corps, already in the vicinity of the gaps, was to move
through Pigeon Mountain to Hindman's assistance. This was an
excellent plan, but its success depended upon the speed of its execution; Negley must be hit before he could be re-enforced or retire
through Steven's Gap. Hindman was on the move by 2 A.M. the
following morning, supposing Cleburne was also ready, which he
was not. Bragg's order had been five hours late in reaching Hill,
Cleburne was sick, and his brigades were scattered—two were with
Breckinridge and two others on picket duty at other gaps. Furthermore, the Confederates themselves had made the gaps impassable by felling trees to obstruct a possible enemy advance.[36]
Hindman stopped short of attack and remained all day awaiting
assistance. Buckner arrived at 4:45, but it was too late to complete
the assigned task. At 7 P.M. Hindman notified Bragg that he

[35] James A. Garfield to Thomas, September 9, 1863, 10 A.M., *ibid.*, Pt. 3,
483.
[36] Kinlock Falconer to Hindman, September 9, 1863, 11:45 P.M., *ibid.*, Pt.
2, 298–99; Hill to Mackall, September 10, 1863, 4:25 A.M., *ibid.*, 300.

would attack at dawn on the eleventh. An hour earlier Bragg had sent him a dispatch stating that Crittenden had moved out of Chattanooga "in this direction"; therefore, it was necessary to finish the movement in the Cove "as rapidly as possible." In reply Hindman suggested that instead of going to seek Negley he might turn and in co-operation with Cheatham and possibly one of Hill's divisions, "crush" Crittenden.[37]

At midnight Bragg, from headquarters at LaFayette, ordered Hindman to "attack and force your way through the enemy to this point at the earliest hour you can see him in the morning." Polk (Cheatham's division) would protect his rear and Cleburne would attack in front as soon as "your guns are heard."

Hindman's and Buckner's actions on the eleventh are most confusing. Scouts brought reports of heavy enemy concentration in their front. Hindman feared that if he drove deeper into the Cove he would be attacked in the rear from Steven's Gap. There was some skirmishing during the day but no attack. Nightfall found Hindman and Buckner at Davis' Crossroads. Bragg ordered them to LaFayette immediately. Negley retired to safety in Steven's Gap.[38]

About dawn on the morning of the eleventh Polk received orders to march his entire force to LaFayette. He and his staff reached there late in the afternoon, and there he learned that the report of heavy enemy concentration in the Cove was "all bosh." Bragg had gone to Dug Gap, so Polk followed. By this time Bragg had ridden through the Gap and met Hindman and Buckner. He encountered no enemy force. "The bird had flown," noted Polk's aide-de-camp in disgust, "and the farce was complete."[39] Regardless of who was responsible for the confusion and failure to give battle, Negley escaped, and thus slipped away Bragg's first opportunity to defeat Rosecrans in detail. Polk's son-in-law reported that Bragg was "in high resentment" at Hindman.[40] Three weeks later Bragg suspended Hindman from command "for not obeying his orders for the attack on the enemy in McLemore's Cove on the 11th instant."[41]

[37] *Ibid.*, 294–95, 301–302.   [38] Hindman's Report, *ibid.*, 296–97.

[39] Extracts from Notes of Lieut. W. B. Richmond, *ibid.*, 74.

[40] William Dudley Gale to Wife, September 15, 1863, Gale Papers.

[41] Special Orders, No. 249, September 29, 1863, *Official Records*, XXX, Pt. 2, 298.

One opportunity had slipped away, but another was near at hand. As Crittenden moved out of Chattanooga he had divided his corps, taking two divisions with him to Ringgold and sending the other toward Lee and Gordon's Mill. On September 11, while Bragg was marching his troops in the opposite direction, Crittenden's corps was still divided, as if inviting attack. But Bragg, fearing an advance by Thomas through the Cove and by McCook by way of Alpine, had ordered his forces to fall back to LaFayette. However, finding no enemy in the Dug Gap area, he now decided to strike at Crittenden's divided corps.

It was 11 P.M. of the eleventh when the last of Polk's corps arrived at LaFayette. At midnight he was instructed to prepare Cheatham to start northward again. And at 7 A.M. Cheatham's dusty tired division began march for Rock Spring Church eight miles away. Walker's division followed later in the day. Polk arrived at the church late in the afternoon. At 6 P.M. Bragg sent him more information (incorrect) as to the location of Crittenden's division, suggesting that this presented an opportunity, and "I hope you will avail yourself of it at daylight to-morrow. . . . This division crushed, the others are yours. We can then turn again on the force in the cove." Two hours later Bragg gave orders to attack the enemy on the Graysville road near Pea Vine Church "at day dawn to-morrow." A third note arrived later in the evening saying the enemy was approaching from the south; therefore, it was of utmost importance that Polk's morning attack be "quick and decided. . . . Let no time be lost." [42]

Meanwhile, Polk, also relying upon incorrect information, had reconnoitered the ground and dispatched his aide-de-camp with a report informing Bragg of the situation. There were three roads along which Crittenden might advance upon him, and he had learned that there was a division on each. Consequently, he was faced by Crittenden's entire corps. To defend these probable approaches he needed 10,000 men. He urged that Buckner be sent to join him. That would still leave Hill's corps "for any contingency in your quarter." Polk had no doubt but that Crittenden would attack him at dawn. He himself could not be ready to launch an attack at that time, but should Crittenden not attack he would do so without delay. [43]

[42] Bragg to Polk, September 12, 1863 (3 dispatches), *ibid.*, 30.
[43] Polk to Bragg, September 12, 1863, 8 P.M., *ibid.*, 44–45.

Bragg's reply through Aide-de-Camp Richmond was that the attack should not be deferred; Polk was already stronger than the enemy. However, he had reassigned Hindman's division to Polk's corps and would send Buckner to his support the next day. Success, he urged upon Polk, must depend upon promptness and rapidity of movement. Bragg later complained that when he arrived at Rock Spring Church early on the thirteenth that Polk, instead of being prompt and rapid, had made no attack at all, and Crittenden had concentrated his forces west of Chickamauga Creek.[44] The statement was true, but it ignored the facts in the case. Neither Bragg nor Polk knew where Crittenden's divisions were; at the time Polk was to attack, Crittenden had already concentrated west of Chickamauga Creek. There was no enemy force on the Graysville Road. In short, Polk's orders were to attack an enemy force that did not exist.

During the night of the twelfth Polk placed his troops in battle line across the three roads, Cheatham on the left and Walker on the right. When Hindman arrived he moved in between these two. Pegram's cavalry was to cover the right and Armstrong's the left. At 11:30 P.M. Polk issued a special appeal to his troops: "The lieutenant-general commanding cannot permit the troops under his command to engage in the battle now before us without expressing to them his profound sense of importance of the issues which hang upon the result. If we are successful the star of the Confederacy rises in the ascendant. The spirits of our friends everywhere will be cheered and our homes made happy. The thorough defeat of the enemy now would blast the prospects of our cruel invaders. The lieutenant-general knows that the troops he has now the honor to command have long and eagerly desired an opportunity to confront their adversaries. That opportunity is now offered them, and he confidently believes that they have the power as well as the will to make themselves felt as no troops were ever felt before. They will not fail to remember that this is the enemy by whom their property has been destroyed, their hearthstones desolated, their women insulted and outraged, their altars profaned, and they will sternly avenge their wrongs." [45]

Early on the thirteenth Polk threw forward his cavalry brigades to learn the exact location of the enemy to be attacked; no enemy

---

[44] Bragg's Report, *ibid.*, 31.
[45] Circular, September 12, 1863, 11:30 P.M., *ibid.*, 49–50.

was found. The small force reported in that area the previous day
had served its purpose of attracting attention while Crittenden
concentrated on Chickamauga Creek near Lee and Gordon's Mill.
It too had now joined the concentration. It was noon before the
Confederate cavalry located Crittenden.

Bragg later attempted to shift to Polk the responsibility for failure to seize this second opportunity to destroy a Federal force in
detail, but he gave no sound reason why he did not order an immediate attack upon Crittenden on Chickamauga Creek, only a
half dozen miles away. He himself was present at Rock Spring
Church and the full strength of Polk's and Buckner's corps was at
hand. Was this not a sufficient force to handle Crittenden's three
divisions?

The answer to the riddle of Bragg's inaction is that he suddenly
reverted to the real Bragg; his fighting spirit faded into indecision.
Ignorant of McCook's whereabouts and intentions, he feared
every possibility. One cannot escape the recurrence of the question, why did he not at least know McCook's strength and position? There were numerous loyal Southerners who knew the
mountains and were willing to serve as informers. Bragg later explained that, although greatly disappointed over Crittenden's escape, he decided to place his trains and supplies in a safe position
and concentrate his entire army along Chickamauga Creek. In
other words, instead of striking while Crittenden's corps was isolated he would wait until McCook and Thomas came to Crittenden's support. And that is just what they were doing. While Mc-
Cook was marching his troops and dragging his train over fifty
miles of rough mountain road to join Thomas and both were
then moving to join forces with Crittenden, Bragg waited.

After he decided that there would be no battle with Crittenden
on the thirteenth Bragg took Buckner's corps and returned to La-
Fayette. Polk soon followed. For the next four days Bragg did
nothing while Rosecrans concentrated. The only real boost to
Confederate morale during this period of waiting was the news
that Lieutenant General James Longstreet was on his way with re-
enforcements from the Army of Northern Virginia. Confederate
loss of the railroad from Virginia through East Tennessee made it
necessary for Longstreet to come the long route by Augusta and
Atlanta. Although three brigades loaded on the cars on Septem-

ber 9, they did not arrive at their destination until the eighteenth. Others arrived on the following day.

On the seventeenth the Army of Tennessee moved into position along Chickamauga Creek. On the right was Bushrod R. Johnson's brigade, to which would soon be added three brigades from Longstreet's corps. Next came Walker, whose position was opposite Alexander's Bridge. Then came Buckner near Thedford's Ford, Polk opposite Lee and Gordon's Mill, and Hill on the left. The cavalry divisions of Forrest and Pegram covered the right and left flanks.

On the evening of the seventeenth Bragg ordered an advance for 6 A.M. the following morning. (Why he did not wait another day for the arrival of Longstreet is a question that has never been answered.) Johnson was to cross the creek at Reed's Bridge, turn to the left and "sweep up the Chickamauga toward Lee and Gordon's Mills." Walker would move next, crossing at Alexander's Bridge, unite with Johnson, and "push vigorously on the enemy's flank and rear in the same direction." Buckner was to use Thedford's Ford, quickly turn left, and press the enemy "up stream from Polk's front." Polk would cross at Dalton's or Thedford's Ford, as necessity might require. Hill would hold his position, observe, and then attack at the proper time. The cavalry would guard the gaps in Pigeon Mountain, covering the left and rear, and round up stragglers.[46] On paper, this was an excellent plan. Although Bragg did not specifically say so, his idea was to fold Rosecrans back into McLemore's Cove as a clock hand in reverse, cutting him off from escape to Chattanooga or through the gap in Missionary Ridge and Lookout Mountain.

Rosecrans suspected some plan to cut him off from Chattanooga, so during the night of the seventeenth he shifted his line to the left until Crittenden covered the LaFayette-Chattanooga road below Lee and Gordon's Mill. The Confederate advance to cross the Chickamauga did not get underway until midafternoon. Bragg attributed this delay to spirited opposition from enemy cavalry and bad narrow roads, adding that although "several times urged to press forward," the commander on the right did not cross the creek until late afternoon. By that time General John Bell Hood of Longstreet's corps had arrived on the field and succeeded Johnson.

[46] Circular, September 18, 1863, *ibid.*, 31.

In the meantime the enemy had vigorously opposed Walker at Alexander's Bridge and destroyed it. Walker finally crossed farther down stream at Byram's Ford and joined Hood but it was then almost dark.[47]

During the night Rosecrans again extended his line to the left until it overlapped the Confederate right. Bragg, not learning of this shift, expected to resume the fight on the nineteenth where he left off on the eighteenth. During the night and early morning all remaining Confederate infantry crossed the Chickamauga except the divisions of Hindman, Breckinridge, and Cleburne. Cheatham's division of Polk's corps crossed at 7 A.M. and took position in reserve. Polk remained with Hindman's division. Fighting began on the extreme Confederate right about 9 A.M., when Forrest's dismounted cavalry and the forces of Federal General John M. Brannan stumbled upon each other. This Bragg had not expected; no Federal force was supposed to be opposite the extreme Confederate right. Forrest called for assistance and Walker was pulled out and moved to the right. He too was roughly handled and called for more aid. At 11 A.M. Cheatham was ordered to the right. Following some temporary gains these combined forces were compelled to fall back. At noon Bragg ordered Polk to cross over with Hindman's division and to assume "command in person on our right." Polk, quickly concluding that he was confronted by most of Thomas' corps, called for re-enforcements. Stewart's division of Buckner's corps was sent to the relief, arriving as Cheatham, with his flanks exposed, was falling back.

Stewart struck hard in defense of Cheatham's left flank, thus giving Cheatham an opportunity to reform his lines. Thomas was now confronted by Walker on his left, Cheatham in front, and Stewart on his right. Cleburne's division of Hill's corps arrived about 6 P.M. and Polk sent it into line in front of Walker's battered division. At dusk Polk ordered Cheatham and Cleburne to renew the attack. Short gains were made before darkness intervened. But the small gain was too costly; Brigadier General Preston Smith of Cheatham's division, an "active, energetic, and brave" veteran of two and a half years of service, was mortally wounded.[48]

[47] Bragg's report, *ibid.*, 31–32.
[48] Reports of Bragg, Cheatham, Walker, Stewart, Cleburne, *ibid.*, 26 ff., 77 ff., 239 ff., 360 ff., 153 ff.

Hood, in the Confederate center, saw little action until mid-afternoon, and then his small gains came at a heavy cost in casualties. The divisions of Breckinridge, Hindman, and Preston on the left saw little action. They could have done heavy damage to the flanks of enemy columns moving to the relief of the Federal left, but this was not in accordance with Bragg's plan to roll Rosecrans back into McLemore's Cove. There was truth in Hill's later statement that fighting on the nineteenth resembled "the sparring of the amateur boxer" rather than "the crushing blows of the trained pugilist." Attack was piecemeal, never general. Bragg could truthfully say that "night found us masters of the ground," but this was only the ground over which the contenders had fought during the day. There had been little change in the general lines of the two armies.[49]

During the evening of the nineteenth Bragg called the "proper commanders" to headquarters. He had received information that more of Longstreet's brigades had arrived from Virginia and that the General himself would report during the night. In view of Longstreet's arrival Bragg decided to divide the Army of Tennessee into two wings—the right to be commanded by Polk and the left by Longstreet. Polk's wing would consist of the corps of Hill (Cleburne's and Breckinridge's divisions) and Walker (Walker's and Liddell's divisions) and Cheatham's division. Longstreet's wing would include Buckner's corps (Stewart's and Preston's divisions), the divisions of Hindman and Johnson, and five brigades commanded by Hood. Forrest's cavalry was attached to Polk and Wheeler's to Longstreet. The plan of battle was to be similar to that of the nineteenth; Bragg was still determined to roll Rosecrans back into McLemore's Cove. Polk was given verbal orders to attack at dawn, the units on the extreme right leading off and others joining the attack "in succession rapidly to the left." Longstreet did not arrive at Bragg's headquarters until after the other generals had left. He received instructions, rested a few hours, and then moved on to find his troops and reconnoiter the area in which he was to operate.

Polk, accompanied by Breckinridge, arrived at his own headquarters near Alexander's Bridge at 11 P.M. Along the way he met

[49] Hill, "Chickamauga—The Great Battle of the West," *loc. cit.*, 650; Bragg's report, *Official Records*, XXX, Pt. 2, 32.

one of Hill's staff officers, through whom he relayed the plan to attack at dawn and also a request for Hill to call at wing headquarters. At 11:30 P.M. Polk issued orders to Hill, Cheatham, and
Walker. Hill and Cheatham would attack simultaneously "at daylight." Walker would hold his corps in reserve.[50] Copies of this order were sent to Hill and Cheatham by special couriers; Walker
called by headquarters and received his in person. The courier
sent to Cheatham delivered his order immediately; the one to
Hill did not return until dawn and then reported he had been unable to locate him. And Hill had not reported to wing headquarters
during the night. Polk dashed off an order to Hill's division commanders—Cleburne and Breckinridge. Unable to locate General
Hill, he explained, he must give them orders direct to "move upon
and attack the enemy as soon as you are in position." [51]

The order was placed in the hand of Captain J. Frank Wheless
with instructions to "ride as rapidly as possible." Passing by Cheatham's headquarters Wheless left him a copy and kept moving. He
found Generals Hill, Breckinridge, and Cleburne around a camp
fire in the rear of Cleburne's command. Upon reading the order
Hill complained that Polk had failed to leave a guide at the
bridge to direct him to wing headquarters. He then dashed off a
note to Polk.

On his return trip Wheless met Polk and delivered Hill's note.
"My divisions are getting their rations," Hill explained, "and will
not be ready to move for an hour or more. Breckinridge's wagons
seem to have been lost. . . ." [52] It was now 7 A.M. Polk relayed
to Bragg the contents of Hill's note and then rode on to the front.
There he found that another reason for delay was Hill's misappre-
hension as to the position of Cheatham's line, which he erroneously believed to be formed at right angle to his own.[53]

This was Polk's story, and it tended to shift to Hill the blame for

[50] Circular, *ibid.*, 52.   [51] *Ibid.*, 52.
[52] Since Breckinridge was on the left the previous day and was now ordered to fight on the right, he had some difficulty in making the shift during
the night.
[53] Polk to George William Brent, September 28, 1863, *Official Records*,
XXX, Pt. 2, 47; Thomas M. Jack to Cleburne and Breckinridge, September 20, 1863, 5:30 A.M., *ibid.*, 52; Hill to Polk, September 20, 1863, *ibid*,
53; John Frank Wheless to William Dudley Gale, October 8, 1867, Leonidas
Polk Papers.

failure to attack at dawn. Naturally, Hill was not pleased with the implication. There was no explanation as to why Hill was not present at the meeting of "proper commanders" at Bragg's headquarters on the nineteenth. He later reported that he was with Cleburne and his brigade commanders until 11 P.M. Since he had no orders for the following day he then set out to find Bragg's headquarters, but was unsuccessful. In the meantime, he sent a staff officer to direct Breckinridge to move over to Cleburne's right. About midnight a staff officer reported that Hill's corps had been placed under Polk as wing commander and that Polk wished to see him at headquarters near Alexander's Bridge. After resting until 3 A.M., Hill then set out to find Polk's headquarters. There was no courier at the bridge to show him the way; consequently, he could do nothing but ride to the front, which he reached "a little after daylight." He found Breckinridge, who had spent a portion of the night resting at Polk's headquarters, still not in position. The troops were hungry, some not having eaten for twenty-four hours; so he ordered that rations be issued.

"At 7:25 A.M." he was shown an order from Polk directing his division commanders to attack at once. He immediately reported to Polk that there would be some delay. Polk, who soon arrived on the scene, offered no objection to the delay. "At 8 o'clock General Bragg himself came on the field, and I then learned for the first time that an attack had been ordered at daylight." Bragg remarked angrily: " 'I found Polk after sunrise sitting down reading a newspaper at Alexander's Bridge, two miles from the line of battle, where he ought to have been fighting.' " Hill later claimed that Polk did not tell Breckinridge of any order to attack at daylight, although he spent several hours at Polk's headquarters. Breckinridge himself said only that he left Polk's headquarters "two hours before daylight." Polk had informed him that he was "to prolong the line of battle upon the right" of Cleburne.[54] This was Hill's story.

According to Bragg's account, he and his staff were ready for the saddle before dawn. "With increasing anxiety and disappointment" he "waited until after sunrise without hearing a gun." He then sent a staff officer to find Polk and learn the reason for de-

[54] Hill's report, *Official Records*, XXX, Pt. 2, 140–41; Hill, "Chickamauga," *loc. cit.*, 652–53; Breckinridge's report, *Official Records*, XXX, Pt. 2, 198.

lay. The staff officer later reported that after searching in vain for
Polk at the front he finally found him "at a Farm House three
miles from the line of his troops, about one hour after sunrise,
sitting on the gallery reading a newspaper and waiting, as he (the
Genl.) said, for his breakfast." Going in person to the right wing,
Bragg sent for Polk, renewed his order, and urged "prompt and
speedy movement." [55]

Since Bragg was sour on both Polk and Hill, this mix-up gave
him an opportunity to be critical of both. Hill had been much
disappointed by conditions within the Army of Tennessee. Accustomed to the efficient leadership of Lee and "Stonewall" Jackson, the deficiencies were even more startling to him. No doubt
Bragg knew of his attitude. And by nature Hill was not the type of
subordinate who willingly obeyed orders to the best of his ability.
Bragg, a comrade in arms during the Mexican War, had not welcomed Hill upon his arrival at Chattanooga. Hill seemed surprised, and the reason for Bragg's coolness is obscure. Since that
time he had neither requested Hill's advice nor paid him any particular attention. Hill and Polk were the only lieutenant generals
in Bragg's army, yet Hill was not called into conference on the
nineteenth, although some major generals were apparently present.[56] Then when Bragg decided to assign Longstreet to command
of the left wing and subordinate Hill to Polk he did not even
notify Hill of his new status. In fact no general received written
notification that the army had been divided into two wings.[57] In
view of these facts, Hill's lack of enthusiasm, bordering on disobedience, is understandable, although not justified in military
sense.

The only possible key to this puzzling mix-up would be the
time element. But unfortunately the hour and minutes were not
noted on many dispatches, and the testimonies of participants conflict as to time. There are a few things, however, which are certain.
Hill could have found Polk's headquarters during the night if he

[55] Bragg's report, *ibid.*, 33; Bragg to E. T. Sykes, February 8, 1873, copy
in Leonidas Polk Papers.

[56] Polk's son later stated that Bragg was irritated against Hill for failing to
give Hindman proper support in McLemore's Cove.

[57] A few weeks later Bragg's, Longstreet's, and Polk's assistant adjutant generals searched their files in vain for a copy of such an order. Thomas M. Jack
to Polk, October 28, 1863, *Official Records*, XXX, Pt. 2, 69–70.

had made an earnest effort. Polk was with the troops at "one hour after sunrise," not three miles away sitting on the front porch of a farm house reading a newspaper and waiting for breakfast. The troops were not ready to attack at dawn. Bragg's order was not executed. There also remains one baffling question. Did Polk inform Breckinridge during the night that he was to attack at dawn? If so, why did Breckinridge continue to sleep at Polk's headquarters until two hours before dawn when he must have known that his division was not in position? If Polk did not so inform him, why?

There was no attack at dawn but it is by no means certain that an early attack would have substantially affected the outcome. While dissension, distrust, and confusion prevailed within the Confederate camp, Rosecrans, frightened by exaggerated rumors of Confederate re-enforcements, was busy readjusting his lines. And throughout the night the sound of axes and falling trees could be heard by Bragg's troops as the Federals constructed log breastworks. Rosecrans with his back to Missionary Ridge now had his entire army north of Lee and Gordon's Mill and astride the road to Chattanooga (the State Road). Thomas, on the left was east of the road; McCook was west of it. To the rear of Thomas' position was a group of hills known as Horseshoe Ridge. Another road, which crossed Chickamauga Creek at Alexander's Bridge, passed through the middle of the Federal lines, a gap in Horseshoe Ridge, and McFarland's Gap in Missionary Ridge, and then turned down the valley toward Chattanooga. This road would be heavily used by Rosecrans' troops before the close of the day.

When the Confederate line was formed Polk's right wing was opposite Thomas. And behind his log breastworks Thomas had packed four divisions. It was about 9:30 A.M. when Breckinridge, supported by Forrest's dismounted cavalry, opened the attack on the extreme right. Cleburne was next to move. It was an unequal fight—two divisions against four. Although vigorously pushed, the attack was stopped and the Confederates were hurled back with bloody results. Thomas, feeling the power of the thrust, called for help and remained behind his breastworks. Rosecrans responded by pulling units from his right and transferring them to the left, an act that would be repeated again and again and would prove his undoing before the close of the day. Delay in action on the part of Longstreet's left wing, which was in accordance with Bragg's plan, gave the impression that the heavy Confederate concentration was before the Federal left.

Longstreet, noting that the "battle seemed to rage with considerable fury, but did not progress as had been anticipated," grew impatient. He dispatched a courier to Bragg to inquire if he should put the left wing in action. But before the courier returned, Stewart, acting under direct orders from Bragg, made a fierce attack, but was thrown back. Longstreet then rushed Hood into action. This division, moving in column of brigades, by chance struck an opening that had been left by the removal of a Federal division to the support of Thomas, and thus pierced the Federal defense. This breakthrough was not a part of Bragg's plan. It should not have happened until Thomas had been rolled back that far by Polk's right wing.

Longstreet now joined the ranks of those generals who found it necessary to change Bragg's orders; instead of turning to his left he turned to the right. Hood fell severely wounded (losing a leg) but the fierce attack upon the enemy's right flank and rear continued. McCook and Crittenden fell back, eventually in great confusion. Rosecrans' headquarters (the Widow Glenn's House) was captured. When the fleeing Federals reached the Dry Valley road they headed for McFarland's Gap and Chattanooga. Among them were Sheridan, McCook, Crittenden, and even Rosecrans. "Bull Run had nothing more terrible," an excited Federal official wired Washington.

Longstreet's wing, fighting fiercely, swept everything before it until it reached Thomas. This "Rock of Chickamauga," with the field left to him, had taken position along Horseshoe Ridge, where he had been re-enforced on his left by Gordon Granger's corps, which, although without orders, had moved up from Rossville. Recognizing the need for fresh troops to deliver a finishing blow, Longstreet appealed to Bragg for some idle brigades from the right wing. He later quoted Bragg as replying: "There is not a man in the right wing who has any fight left in him." Bragg then returned to his headquarters at Reed's Bridge leaving his commanders to solve their own problems.

It was not true that there was no fight left in the right wing.

Cheatham's division, except for John K. Jackson's brigade, had not yet been in action. In its original position it had been found to overlap Stewart, so was pulled back in reserve. The other right wing divisions had fought furiously, gained little ground, and suffered heavily, but they were still able and willing to fight.

According to Bragg, about 2 P.M. he had sent written instructions to Polk "to again assault the enemy in his front with his whole force and to persist until he should dislodge him from his position." Subsequently, he said, a second staff officer was sent to urge "a prompt and vigorous execution of my written order." At 3:30 Polk ordered Hill to begin the advance. Polk's son, who was present, later recalled that Polk's plan was for Cleburne to open a heavy cannonade on the enemy front while Hill took Cheatham, Walker, and Breckinridge to "assail the enemy's left on the State road." Hill, not pleased with the plan, "showed a singular unwillingness to act," and the order had to be twice repeated. Hill later attributed the delay to shortcomings and misunderstandings on the part of Jackson, Cheatham, and Breckinridge.

The delay was short and probably of little importance. By 4 P.M. the general advance of the right wing was under way, and in the words of Hill, the troops "sprang eagerly forward." Cleburne did more than shell Thomas' front. Led by Lucius Polk's brigade [58] his division broke through the enemy's defense while Breckinridge, Walker, and Cheatham fell heavily upon the enemy's left. With his front crumbling and his wings folded back, Thomas had no choice but to withdraw while there was yet time. This he did in an orderly fashion as darkness made further Confederate attacks more dangerous to friend than foe.[59] The bloody battle of Chickamauga was over. More than 34,000 men lay dead or wounded or dragged their torn bodies away to safety.[60] Neither commanding general

[58] Son of General Polk's half brother, William.

[59] Reports of Bragg, Longstreet, and Hill, *Official Records*, XXX, Pt. 2, 26 ff., 287 ff., 136 ff.; Horn, *Army of Tennessee*, 257 ff.; Polk, *Leonidas Polk*, II, 271 ff.; Hill, "Chickamauga," *loc. cit.*, 638 ff.; Williams, *Lincoln Finds a General*, V, 255 ff.

[60] The Tenth Tennessee Regiment reported 68 per cent casualties; the Second, Fifteenth, and Thirty-seventh, 60 per cent; the Sixth and Ninth, 58 per cent; the Fifth Georgia, 61 per cent; the Sixteenth Alabama, 59 per cent. Horn, *Army of Tennessee*, 273. General Hill later recalled "I have never seen the Federal dead lie so thickly on the ground, save in front of the sunken wall at Fredericksburg." Hill, "Chickamauga," *loc. cit.*, 658.

was present to witness the closing scene. Rosecrans was in Chattanooga; Bragg was far to the rear at his Reed's Bridge headquarters. The former thought his defeat more complete than it was; the latter had no idea that the Army of Tennessee had won a brilliant victory.

The victorious Confederates, Polk among them, bivouacked for the night on the field. Polk sent his son-in-law William Dudley Gale to find the Bishop's nephew, Lucius Polk. Lucius was not found, but Gale gave a vivid description of what he witnessed as he rode over the battlefield:

> The moon was shining as clear as possible and gave a most unearthly appearance to this horrid scene. Wounded, dying, and dead men and horses, were strewn around me & under me everywhere for the field was yet hot & smoking from the last charge, and thousands were lying insensible, or in agony, where a few short moments they stood in battle array. I can never forget the horrid indecency of death that was pictured on their agonized faces upturned in the pale moonlight as I spurred my mare over and around their prostrate forms. Ten thousand fires lit up the scene and revealed still more vividly this hideous carnival of Death.[61]

Polk sent out scouts to locate the position Thomas had taken after withdrawal from Horseshoe Ridge. They found no Federal troops. Thomas had also fallen back on Chattanooga. This information Polk relayed to Bragg. He was then called to Bragg's headquarters for consultation. It was almost midnight when Polk and his aide arrived. Bragg was in bed. Polk insisted that the enemy had been routed and was " 'flying precipatately from the field' " thus presenting an opportunity for Bragg to capture or destroy the entire Federal army before it had time " 'to reorganize & throw up defences at Chattanooga.' " [62] The appeal failed; Bragg was himself again, totally lacking in aggressiveness. Disgusted and despondent, Polk rode away to rejoin his troops.

Again Bragg would fail to complete the task of turning a brilliant advantage into a complete victory. General Hill was probably correct when he later recorded that of all the blunders at Chickamauga the greatest was failure to pursue the enemy on the twenty-

[61] Gale to Wife, September 28, 1863, Gale Papers.
[62] *Id.* to Mecklenburg Polk, March 28, 1882, Leonidas Polk Papers.

first. There were still bloody battles ahead, Hill concluded, "But it seems to me that the *elan* of the Southern soldier was never seen after Chickamauga—that brilliant dash which had distinguished him was gone forever." [63]

After years of thought and increasing bitterness, Polk's aide-de-camp son-in-law William Dudley Gale confided to Polk's son "I can forgive Mr. Davis for all the blunders he made & persisted in during the war—except the infernal sin he committed in placing Bragg at the head of the army of Tenn & keeping him there, as he did. I believe Bragg lost us our independence and the future student of history will so decide, in my judgment. Next after him came Joe Johnston. What had we done that we should have had *two* such Generals sent to us, either one of whom was enough to ruin our cause. B[ragg] was Cruel yet without courage, Obstinate, yet without firmness, Restless, yet without enterprise, Crafty, yet without strategy, suspicious, envious, jealous, vain, a bantam in success & a dunghill in disaster, and yet in command of a better army than Hanibal [*sic.*] & Scipio had to conquer Rome or Carthage." [64]

Writing from his field headquarters early on the twenty-first, Polk reported to his wife that he and his staff had come through two days of battle without injury. Rosecrans was retreating toward Chattanooga. "We shall pursue as soon as we are refreshed. The Lord has been very gracious & merciful to us & has blessed us!" A week later he needed to make some corrections in his earlier report. His "dear & faithful and attached young friend" aide-de-camp Richmond was among the casualties. On the morning of the twenty-first his body was found within sixty yards of headquarters. Polk still thought the battle of Chickamauga a "great success," but felt that "We should have made more out of it." The enemy had not been pursued. Instead, he himself was now atop Missionary Ridge looking down into Rosecrans' camp. "I do not think we will attack him but will turn his flank. That I think the most judicious. But we are tired of the delay." [65]

Polk was probably correct. No doubt a flanking movement at this time would have been more judicious than a direct attack upon

[63] Hill, "Chickamauga," *loc. cit.*, 662.
[64] Gale to Mecklenburg Polk, March 28, 1882, Leonidas Polk Papers.
[65] Polk to Wife, September 21, 27, 1863, *ibid.*

the Chattanooga fortifications, much of which had been constructed under Polk's supervision. Rosecrans had expected an attack on the twenty-first and had spent the day strengthening his
fortifications and moving his trains out of enemy reach. At 11:30
A.M. General Forrest reported to Polk that the "sound of axes in
great numbers" indicated that the enemy had fallen back into
Chattanooga and was cutting timber from the ridge to strengthen
the fortifications. Later in the day Forrest reported from atop
Missionary Ridge. He could "see Chattanooga and everything
around. The enemy trains are leaving, going around the point of
Lookout Mountain." From prisoners he had learned that two pon-
toon bridges had been thrown across the Tennessee River. "I think
they are evacuating as hard as they can go." [66] This information
was referred to Bragg, yet he failed to take advantage of the enemy's difficulties. He merely moved the Army of Tennessee in
closer to Chattanooga and waited while the Army of the Cumberland received sufficient supplies and re-enforcements to extri-
cate itself from a most precarious position.

Again after Chickamauga as after Perryville and Murfreesboro
a war-weary public wanted to know why Bragg had failed to make
more out of his victory. Discontent within the army, especially
among the high ranking officers, reached new heights. Again
Bragg looked for a scapegoat. Polk was still at hand, more distrustful of Bragg's leadership than before. Hill and Hindman, recent additions to the Army of Tennessee, had also fallen under
Bragg's displeasure. And by the close of one day of fighting Longstreet had concluded Bragg was not equal to his assignment.

On September 26 Bragg's three lieutenant generals held a conference "to consider what should be done in view of the palpable
weakness and mismanagement manifested in the conduct of the
military operations of this army." It was agreed that Polk should
write President Davis urging that Bragg be superseded by Robert E. Lee or some other competent general. Longstreet would
write Secretary of War Seddon making the same suggestion. Polk's
letter to Davis has not been located but he referred to it in a subsequent letter as having been written on the twenty-seventh.

Longstreet wrote Seddon on the twenty-sixth explaining the

[66] Forrest to Polk, September 21, 1863 (two dispatches), *Official Records*,
XXX, Pt. 4, 675, 681.

situation within the Army of Tennessee. He pronounced the victory at Chickamauga the greatest of the war, except perhaps First Manassas. Since Chickamauga, however, Bragg had proved a complete failure, doing only what "he ought not to have done." Longstreet had found the General unable to "adopt and adhere to any plan or course, whether of his own or of some one else." He was "convinced that nothing but the hand of God can save us or help us as long as we have our present commander. . . . Can't you send us General Lee?" [67]

Polk also wrote directly to General Lee. The two generals had spent some time at West Point together, but since they were two classes apart they were not close associates. As Lee later related, he saw Polk only once after West Point days and that was when the two visited Richmond in the spring of 1861. "Allow me to unite with him [Longstreet]," Polk began his letter to Lee, "in an earnest appeal to you to give us the benefit of your skill and judgment and experience at this most important crisis. We have gained a signal victory under God's blessing over our enemy, but I greatly fear we are about to lose the fruits of it for want of necessary capacity to reap them. I speak advisedly, and after a very familiar acquaintance with the mind and character of the officer commanding this army, when I say we must have a change before any permanent success can be had in this region. The eyes of all would look to you could you come. Longstreet thinks that you can without serious detriment to the interests of Virginia, leaving it in the hands of one of your well-trained lieutenants. If both armies were driven back to the Mississippi, and Tennessee—not to say Kentucky—freed, and we on Grant's line of communications and in connection with the trans-Mississippi army, we might, by moving south, make short work of the army of the latter. May I not then, general, again beg you to give this matter your respectful and serious attention, and see whether, as a question of duty to our suffering command, it be not proper for you to come over and help us." [68]

A month passed before Lee replied. Polk's letter had arrived just as he was preparing to move against Meade. In the meantime, Bragg had removed Polk from command. "I am indebted, I know,

[67] *Ibid.*, 705–706.   [68] *Ibid.*, 708.

entirely to your kind feelings for the proposition made to me," Lee began. "I wish I could be of any service in the west, but I do not feel that I could do much anywhere. In addition to other infirmities, I have been for more than a month a great sufferer from rheumatism in my back, so that I can hardly get about. I hope the President has been able to rectify all difficulties in your army, and that Rosecrans will at last be obliged to abandon his position. I trust you are again with your command, and that a merciful God will continue His blessings to us and shield us from any danger. That He may have you and your brave army under His care is my earnest prayer." [69]

Polk had not been restored to his command and by this time was many miles from the Army of Tennessee. On September 22 Polk received a note from Bragg requesting a written explanation of his failure to attack at dawn on the twentieth. Polk, busy moving his troops toward Chattanooga, delayed reply. On the twenty-fifth Bragg sent a reminder. Three days later Polk sent a presentation of his version of the mix-up. Bragg pronounced this explanation "entirely unsatisfactory," removed Polk from command, and ordered him to Atlanta.[70]

Bragg also suspended Hindman and sent him to Atlanta, and a few days later he wrote President Davis, urging that a "more efficient organization and command of his army" demanded that General Hill be relieved of duty with it. Hill was also accused of "want of prompt conformity to orders." He was relieved. Years later Bragg explained that after Polk's removal he learned that Polk *had* issued orders to Cleburne and Breckinridge to attack at dawn but that "Hill, being present in person, countermanded the order, without notifying either Polk or myself." [71]

Bragg immediately wired Adjutant General Cooper of his action regarding Polk and Hindman. Davis indorsed on the telegram that Bragg had exceeded his powers, which were limited to arrest and the preferring of charges. Cooper then informed Bragg that suspension from command must be "considered punishment

[69] *Ibid.*, Pt. 2, 69.

[70] Polk to Brent, September 28, 1863, *ibid.*, 47; Special Orders, No. 249, *ibid.*, 56.

[71] Bragg to Davis, October 11, 1863, *ibid.*, 148; Bragg to E. T. Sykes, February 8, 1873, copy in Leonidas Polk Papers.

without trial." Davis sent a note of advice. "I think it was unfortunate that the evil resulting from delay had not been pointed
out to the lieutenant general to prevent its recurrence, and confidence preserved by abstaining from further action. It is now believed that the order in his case should be countermanded." [72]
Bragg wanted no advice, not even from the President; he was determined. He had taken action in Polk's case only after "an unsatisfactory written explanation," he replied. 'The case is flagrant
and but a repetition of the past. If restored by you to his command the amnesty should extend to all. In the crisis now upon
us might he not be exchanged for Hardee? . . . My personal feelings have been yielded to what I know to be the public good, and
I suffer self-reproach for not having acted earlier." [73] Bragg then
preferred charges against General Polk, accusing him of disobedience and neglect of duty. [74]

The distrust of Bragg by his generals, the request of his lieutenant
generals that he be removed from command, and his drastic action against Polk and Hindman placed President Davis in a di-
lemma. How could he continue such an officer in command of
one of the two great armies of the Confederacy? When one's
ability is questioned by a few, discipline might be effectively applied; when distrust becomes unanimous, removal from command
would seem to be the only solution. If Bragg could only be persuaded to change his attitude toward his generals he might even
yet win their support, Davis wishfully reasoned.

He could appreciate the fact that disappointment might result
from delay or disobedience, he wrote Bragg, yet he feared that
such drastic action against Polk would "entail further evil" rather
than "heal the injury." Knowing that Polk "possessed the confidence and affection of his corps, . . . his influence in your favor
should be preserved by a lenient course." From the information
before him, the President could find no intentional disobedience,
and there might never be repetition of the "objectionable conduct." If Bragg persisted in his present course then there must be
an investigation with all sorts of "criminations and recrimina-
tions." And he would remind the General that opposition to him

[72] *Official Records*, XXX, Pt. 2, 55; *ibid.*, LII, Pt. 2, 533.
[73] Bragg to Davis, October 1, 1863, *ibid.*, 534.
[74] *Ibid.*, XXX, Pt. 2, 55–56.

"both in the army and out of it" had become so great a public
calamity as greatly to impair his capacity for usefulness. The President had hoped that the great victory at Chickamauga would
produce harmony within the army and "just appreciation" on the
part of the general public.

It would be rare indeed, Davis continued, if a great battle were
fought without errors, the absence of which would have produced
more important results, yet "the exposure of these diminishes the
credit due, impairs the public confidence, undermines the morale
of the army, and works evil to the cause for which brave men have
died, and for which others have the same sacrifice to make." He
regretted that Bragg did not consider Polk's explanation sufficient
to justify his overlooking the offense, and he wished to point out
that he was "at a loss to see how the delay of one general should
be regarded as a higher offense than the disobedience of orders
by another officer of the same grade." Surely Bragg must know
that those persons already "predisposed to censure" him would
connect the present controversy with a former one said to have
resulted from his questioning his generals. In conclusion, President
Davis stressed that "It not infrequently happens that in a state of
excitement one believes himself impelled to do that which a calm
observer will regard as easily pretermitted." [75] Never did a President give better advice to a general less willing to accept it.

On the day following the penning of this sound advice to General Bragg, the chances for harmony between him and his generals received another setback. The general officers of the Army of
Tennessee signed a round robin presenting to President Davis the
deplorable situation. After a glorious victory troops eager to complete the task of destroying the enemy had been held waiting in
line of battle for almost two weeks while the Federals were being
greatly re-enforced. The time had now arrived when, unless rescued by re-enforcements and a competent commander, this proud
army, "stricken with complete paralysis," must soon be "thrown
strictly on the defensive" and would be fortunate to escape without disaster. Without discussing the merits of General Bragg, his
generals thought it sufficient to say that poor health rendered him
unfit for field command. They realized that the step they were

---

[75] Davis to Bragg, October 3, 1863, *Official Records*, LII, Pt. 2, 535.

taking was unusual among military men, but they considered it a patriotic duty from which they should no longer shrink.[76] What part Polk had in this petition is uncertain. He was now in Atlanta. General Hill later told President Davis that "Gen. Polk got it up and it was written by Gen. Buckner." [77] There is no evidence that this is true.

[76] *Ibid.*, XXX, Pt. 2, 65–66.
[77] Hill to Davis, October 30, 1886, Dunbar Rowland, *Jefferson Davis, Constitutionalist* (Jackson, Miss., 1923), IX, 498–500.

(16)

Maneuvering in Mississippi

IN RETIREMENT AT Atlanta General Polk had ample time to nurse his grievances. To Secretary of War James A. Seddon he wrote requesting "a court of inquiry at the earliest moment practicable." He also protested against the legality of Bragg's action, insisting that the General's power was limited to placing him under arrest, which had not been done.[1] To President Davis he sent a note again denouncing Bragg as incompetent. Of the failure to follow up the Chickamauga victory, he averred that "General Bragg did not know what had happened, and allowed the whole of the fruits of this great victory to pass from him by the most criminal negligence, or, rather, incapacity, for there are positions in which weakness is wickedness. If there be a man in the public service who should be held to a more rigid accountability for failures, and upon the largest scale, than another, that man is General Bragg." He himself would welcome a court of inquiry in order that he might have not only an opportunity to vindicate his own conduct but also "of establishing the truth and justice" of his charges relating to Bragg's "lack of capacity as a commanding general."[2]

In preparation for a probable court of inquiry Polk and his Assistant Adjutant General, Thomas M. Jack, set to work collecting reports and statements from fellow generals and staff members. But Polk's real feelings in the matter can be determined by reading his family correspondence. Bragg's action was a part of a "long-cherished purpose," he assured his wife. "I think my way very clear before me and am unmoved. I defy his motive . . . & the pitiful effort by which he has so long attempted to vent it. I beg

[1] *Official Records*, XXX, Pt. 2, 68, 69.
[2] October 6, 1863, *ibid.*, 67–68.

you to be assured that I am entirely quiet and undisturbed by this demonstration." His fellow officers, he explained, agreed that he had been done an injustice. General Hill, "who was chiefly culpable," had assured him " 'I take the blame of the omission to attack.' " [3] Walker thought it "ridiculous" that Polk should be suspended "for the omission of Hill." And Buckner pronounced the whole thing "absurd." "The truth is," Polk concluded, "General Bragg has made a failure notwithstanding the success of battle & he wants a scape goat." [4]

Another week of waiting and reflecting increased Polk's self-assurance and indignation. On October 10 he wrote one of his daughters that having done his duty, he had no fear of an inquiry or an investigation. Response of friends, especially those in the army, had been most gratifying. "The poor man who is the author of this trouble is I am informed as much to be pitied or more than the object of his ill-feeling. I certainly feel a lofty contempt for his puny effort to inflict injury upon a man who has dry nursed him for the whole period of his connection with him and has kept him from ruining the cause of the country by the sacrifice of its armies."

The President passed through two nights earlier on his way to Bragg's headquarters, and had stopped for a conference with Polk. "I gave it to him plainly & simply." The President expressed regret at the unfortunate and unnecessary action taken by General Bragg. This strengthened Polk's confidence. "I never was in better health," he reassured his daughter, "and am also, as my friends say, in marvelously fine spirits." [5] His spirits were given a further boost when he was joined by Mrs. Polk and their daughter Sally.

In light of evidence of almost unanimous distrust of Bragg on the part of his general officers, President Davis felt compelled to visit the Army of Tennessee for an on-the-scene investigation. He reached Atlanta and conferred with Polk on the night of October 8 and moved on to Bragg's headquarters the following day. In view of the delicacy of his mission, he probably could not have

[3] This is not in accordance with Hill's statement of September 30 in reply to a query from Polk—"No staff officer of mine or yours communicated any order to me to attack at daylight." *Ibid.*, 64.

[4] Polk to Wife, October 3, 1863, Leonidas Polk Papers.

[5] *Id.* to Daughter, October 10, 1863, *ibid.*

committed a greater blunder than he did by bringing along General John C. Pemberton. Since he surrendered Vicksburg this general had been unemployed and his popularity was at a very low ebb. His accompanying Davis to Chattanooga at this time suggested a plan to assign him to command of Polk's corps. But Bragg's chief of staff told Pemberton bluntly that "there was not a division in this army that would be willing to receive him." [6] Certainly the men of Polk's corps, being already distressed over the treatment accorded their popular leader, were in no mood to accept Pemberton.

Davis' investigation was unusual, to say the least. Longstreet, Hill, Buckner, and Cheatham were called into conference and questioned in Bragg's presence. According to Longstreet, Davis asked each general for his opinion of Bragg's fitness to command. All agreed that a change in commander was necessary.[7] But Davis, instead of removing Bragg, approved the removal of Hill and the transfer of Longstreet and Buckner to East Tennessee. The only thing for which the Army of Tennessee had to be thankful was that Davis did not leave Pemberton at Chattanooga.

On his return trip through Atlanta Davis again conferred with Polk, and apparently with Bragg's consent, suggested that he resume command of his corps. This Polk refused to do. No doubt Davis expected a refusal. Polk's aide-de-camp son-in-law sat through the conference and was much gratified by "the assurance of the perfect friendship, confidence, and harmony existing between them." He thought instead of losing "in this collision with Genl Bragg" Polk had "gained immensely." [8]

From Atlanta Davis went to Mississippi to visit Johnston's army. Before leaving Atlanta he "pretty plainly indicated" that the charges preferred by Bragg would be dismissed and that there would be no court of inquiry. This disappointed Polk, for he wished to present a mass of evidence unfavorable to Bragg. If the case should be dismissed without a hearing, Polk wrote his brother-in-law, Kenneth Rayner, "I am at the end of my row." He did

[6] *Official Records,* XXX, Pt. 4, 742.

[7] Longstreet, *Manassas to Appomattox,* 465.

[8] Polk to Daughter, November 15, 1863, Leonidas Polk Papers; William Dudley Gale to William E. Huger, October 31, 1863, *ibid.*; Kenneth Rayner to Thomas Ruffin November 26, 1863, Hamilton (ed.), *Papers of Thomas Ruffin,* III, 346.

not expect Bragg to request an inquiry. But come what may, Polk told Rayner, he would retain his commission and "serve out the war, should my life be spared." [9] Davis apparently told Polk nothing of his plans, except that Bragg would be retained as commander of the Army of Tennessee.

After conferring with Johnston, and probably Hardee, Davis wrote Polk from Meridian, Mississippi, on October 23, officially relieving him of duty with the Army of Tennessee and assigning him to command of Hardee's corps in the Department of Mississippi, which was commanded by General Johnston. Hardee would assume command of Polk's corps in the Army of Tennessee. In closing, Davis stated that he would leave that evening for a two days visit to Mobile and then proceed by rail to Montgomery. He would be pleased to meet Polk at either place.[10]

Polk met the President in Montgomery. "The interview was as friendly and cordial as ever," reported Gale, and Polk was pleased with the transfer. Gale thought there was "no doubt a field here where reputation can be made provided old Joe Johnston is not in the way." But he added that President Davis did not think Johnston would be "in any body's way"; he would be "only too glad to have somebody of life and energy enough to relieve him of all responsibility." Davis "intimated," however, that if things did not work out well he would create a separate department for Polk.[11] Gale's distrust of Johnston was clearly not a reflection of Polk's opinions. It might have been a result of Johnston's earlier failure to protect the Mississippi country against the Yankee invasion which drove the Gale family from their beloved "Holly Bend."

Polk returned to Atlanta in the President's private coach. The two must have conversed freely along the way. Before departing for Richmond, Davis addressed a personal note to Polk: "After an examination into the causes and circumstances attending your being relieved from command with the army commanded by General Bragg, I have arrived at the conclusion that there is nothing attending them to justify a court-martial or a court of inquiry, and I therefore dismiss the application. Your assignment to a field of

[9] Polk to Rayner, October 17, 1863, Gale Papers.
[10] Davis to Polk, October 23, 1863, *Official Records*, XXXI, Pt. 3, 582.
[11] Gale to Wife, October 27, 1863, Gale Papers.

duty, alike important and difficult, is the best evidence of my appreciation of your past service and expectations of your future career." [12]

While at Atlanta Polk received the disturbing news that his family was no longer safe at Asheville. Confederate retirement from East Tennessee loosed upon the mountainous area numerous roving bands of "bushwhackers," who had little regard for either life or property. Raids and rumors of raids cast a dark shadow of fear. The Polk family became worried about their valuables, especially their silver; so Hamilton and a friend sealed them in the rock wall of a basement, where they remained unmolested until long after the war. Negro slaves, although not numerous in the Asheville area, became a problem. Some ran away; others remained to cause trouble. "Josh" was suspected of having set fire to the Polk home because he became angry with one of the girls. Other servants and neighbors extinguished the blaze before much damage was done.

When Gale read aloud to Polk a letter from Katherine telling of their plight tears appeared in the General's eyes and his voice became husky as he cried out " 'put your trust in God, for he is willing and mighty to save. God is stronger than men, yes God is stronger [than] devils.' " Mrs. Polk was visiting her husband in Atlanta at the time; so the General dispatched Gale to Asheville to check up on matters and see what could be done to assure the family safety. A few days later Polk wrote one of his daughters "May God give you all grace to know how to bear up under the trials and griefs and calamities of this life, and enable you to faithfully and truly to discharge the duties of this life as to be prepared for the rewards and the happiness of that which is to come!"

As for Josh, the General was much surprised at his conduct, for at New Orleans he had begged on bended knees that he might be permitted to accompany the Polk family in its flight. "But the race to which he belongs," Polk explained, "is in its peculiarities really unfathomable, and I can believe almost any thing of them." He wished Gale to arrest Josh and send him farther into the interior "beyond reach of the Yankees." Or he might send him to Augusta and sell him as an experienced cook from New Orleans. "If I could have sufficient proof to establish his guilt in the matter of

[12] Davis to Polk, October 29, 1863, *Official Records*, XXX, Pt. 2, 70.

setting the house on fire, I would of course see that he was hung."
But there was no proof; it might have been the act of some other
servant or "some of the tories."[13] Gale did not send Josh into the
interior or sell him but instead took him to General Polk in Mississippi. But Josh soon ran away.[14]

Mrs. Polk, the General, and his staff left Atlanta for Mississippi
on November 7. They stopped for a day with General Withers at
Montgomery, spent a few days in Mobile, and arrived at Enterprise, Mississippi, on the thirteenth, where they took quarters in
the home of General O'Ferral. Sally joined her parents on December 5.[15] Two days after arrival in Mississippi Polk took a parting
shot at General Bragg, confiding to a daughter at Asheville: "He
is a poor, feeble minded, irresolute, man of violent passions . . .
uncertain of the soundness of his conclusions and therefore timid
in their execution. He is withal without elevation of character and
capable of petty evasions to cover his incapacity and blunders.
. . . I had a contempt for his military capacity and his personal
character, & should forfeit my self respect if I should after what
passed return to his command."[16] Bitterness and declining confidence in the ultimate success of the Confederate cause were cast-
ing a gloomy shadow across the cheerful and optimistic disposition
of the Bishop-General.

No doubt Polk was pleased that he was no longer subject to
Bragg's command, yet he could scarcely have been enthusiastic
about prospects in Mississippi. Upon arrival at Enterprise his principal task became the rounding up and reorganization of paroled
and exchanged Confederates who had surrendered at Vicksburg
and Port Hudson. The number was estimated to be about one
brigade. Gale laughingly remarked that this should be the "best
drilled" brigade in the Confederate army since its line of command from the top down was General Johnston, Lieutenant General Polk, Major General Forney, and Brigadier General Mackall.
But Gale confided to his wife: "The truth is my dear that we are
laid on the shelf for the present and no mistake."[17] One suspects
that the aide-de-camp was almost quoting his general.

[13] William Dudley Gale to Wife, October 27, 1863, Gale Papers; Gale,
"Recollections"; Polk to Daughter, November 15, 1863, Leonidas Polk Papers.
[14] Gale, "Recollections."   [15] Polk, "Leonidas Polk, A Memoir."
[16] Polk to Daughter, November 15, 1863, Leonidas Polk Papers.
[17] Gale to Wife, December 8, 1863, Gale Papers.

By the time Gale made this observation, however, events had occurred which would quickly take Polk off the shelf. General Bragg had failed miserably in the battle of Lookout Mountain and Missionary Ridge and at his own request had been relieved from command of the Army of Tennessee. The sound of the "universal voice of army and country" calling for Joe Johnston had reached Mississippi, and Gale (and Polk) was already speculating on the benefits that would result should President Davis "yield" and transfer Johnston to Georgia and elevate Polk to command in Mississippi.[18]

At the same time Gale was writing to his wife, Polk was drafting a letter to President Davis. He had learned that Bragg had been relieved of command of the Army of Tennessee and had also heard much speculation as to who would succeed to that command. Again, "in the frankness of the intercourse which had characterized our long acquaintance," he wished to urge the appointment of General Johnston. Such a recommendation, the President would recall, had previously been made when his relationship with General Johnston had been quite different; therefore, it could not be considered as a part of any scheme for personal advancement. Understanding the feeling of the army and the country as he himself did, he thought it the President's duty "to yield to this general desire. . . . I think your friends and history would justify you in this, and that magnanimity perhaps may require it at your hands." [19]

Perhaps letters from friends like Polk had some influence; Davis did yield, reluctantly. On December 16 he wired General Johnston to turn over to General Polk the command of his department and proceed immediately to Dalton, Georgia, and assume command of the Army of Tennessee.[20] A week later the transfer was made at Brandon, Mississippi. After reassuring his "brave comrades of his full appreciation of the high soldierly qualities they have exhibited," Johnston placed them in the hands of "one who on so many bloody fields has proved himself worthy of such troops as constitute this army." [21]

Shortly before Johnston left for Dalton, Polk had a confidential talk with Edwin J. Harvie, a member of Johnston's staff. They discussed at length the possibility of bringing about a better feeling

[18] *Ibid.*   [19] *Official Records*, XXXI, Pt. 3, 796.   [20] *Ibid.*, 835.
[21] *Ibid.*, LII, Pt. 2, 579–80.

between President Davis and General Johnston. During the conversation Polk no doubt learned the details of Harvie's previous efforts in behalf of reconciliation.[22] A few weeks after Harvie's departure Polk wrote him a lengthy letter on the subject. That there were misunderstandings between the President and General Johnston was now generally known, he commented. He himself was not prepared to say who was at fault, but "at a time like this, when a cordial support should be given the generals by the President, it is desirable that both parties should rise to a point that is high above all that is merely personal, and bury the past in a united and cordial devotion to the future."

In view of Johnston's present popularity with the army Polk felt that the General could well afford to take the initiative. Perhaps he could write to a mutual friend, expressing regret for any contribution he had made to the lack of cordial relations between himself and the President, and proposing that "in view of public interest," he was "prepared to waive all that was past."

Polk had no doubt that such an overture would be received by the President "in the best spirit" and that the results would be both satisfactory to their mutual friends and "eminently conducive" to military success. Such a course would no doubt involve sacrifices of feelings but Polk thought "the sacrifices might well be tendered an as instance of becoming magnanimity." [23] No good came from the efforts of the peacemakers; relations between Davis and Johnston grew worse, not better.

In assuming command in Mississippi Polk reminded his troops that "Our cause is not less the cause of truth, of honor, and of God now than it was the day we first took up arms against the barbarous horde of fanatics and of Puritan and German infidels who have for three years sought to despoil us of our political rights, rob us of our property, destroy our social life, and overturn and crush our altars. The hate of these men has not been abated by the plunder and desolation and bloodshed upon which it has fed, but . . . [it has] rather been deepened and intensified. From them, should they succeed, we are to expect nothing but universal confiscation of our property, abject social and personal degradation or death." There must be trust in God, but, he warned, all must

[22] See Govan and Livingood, *A Different Valor*, 229.
[23] January 21, 1864, *Official Records*, XXXII, Pt. 2, 593–94.

"remember that it was a maxim of the religion of the heathen that the gods helped those who helped themselves; a maxim which the teachings of a purer and truer faith have served to confirm and establish." [24]

The department which Polk had been chosen to command was without name. In his first general order he referred to it as the Department of the Southwest, but in petitioning Richmond for an official name he explained that he used this term because there was no other. It was not until January 28, 1864, that the region became officially known as the Department of Alabama, Mississippi, and East Louisiana.[25] Polk established department headquarters at Meridian, Mississippi. His army was nearby. The two divisions of infantry were commanded by Major Generals William W. Loring and Samuel G. French. The cavalry was commanded by Major Generals Stephen D. Lee and Nathan Bedford Forrest. Polk soon divided the territory in which the two cavalry forces would operate by drawing a line across Mississippi passing through Prentiss. Forrest would operate north of the line and Lee to the south.

There was no serious enemy threat to the department at the time Polk assumed command. The most disturbing problem was that created by roving bands of deserters, draft dodgers, and renegades in general, who were terrorizing whole counties in Mississippi. "The military police of this department I find very defective," Polk informed Secretary of War Seddon. He proposed a "thorough reorganization of the provost-marshal's department." Experience in that department had proved, he explained, that officers charged with rounding up deserters and conscripts should report to the department commander rather than to Richmond. This had been the case previously when General Pillow headed that service and he wished it continued under Pillow's successor.[26] Thus began a fight with Richmond that Polk was not destined to win.

Polk spent Christmas with his wife and daughter Sally at Enterprise.[27] There was little celebration even though that area had

[24] *Ibid.*, XXXI, Pt. 3, 857–58.   [25] *Ibid.*, 857 n.
[26] Polk to Seddon, December 28, 1863, *ibid.*, 875.
[27] Mrs. Polk later recalled that during her stay in Mississippi her husband spent much time "daily fitting for heaven. . . . He had always had a great horror of death,—I mean the separation of soul and body. And when I would

not yet been visited by the invader. Some paroled and exchanged prisoners who had been forcibly collected there were in an especially bad mood. Polk had them formed in a huge square, and then with Generals Forney and Mackall and Aide-de-Camp Gale standing by, he mounted a table in the center and delivered them a two hours "Stump Speech," after which he was applauded with "three cheers." He returned to his Meridian headquarters on January 1.[28]

On January 9 came a wire from President Davis. He had learned "from a person of high standing" that Union Admiral David G. Farragut was planning an attack upon Mobile. Confederate Major General Dabney H. Maury at Mobile wired that he had received similar information through Havana. Polk, in acknowledging both bits of information, urged Davis that since "the pressure is on me rather than him just now" Johnston "should send me assistance." This was a request for the return of two brigades transferred from Mississippi to Georgia before Polk assumed command. Davis agreed and so ordered. Polk sent the two brigades to re-enforce Maury at Mobile.[29]

Maury, with Polk's support, worked feverishly to strengthen the fortifications at Mobile. The services of 5,000 were needed immediately, he urged, for the erection of defenses. Polk appealed to the Governors of Mississippi and Alabama for assistance in securing these laborers and issued orders for impressment. But as preparations for defense increased the threat of immediate attack subsided. On January 31 Maury informed Polk that he was unable to learn of any "visible preparation for any attack on Mobile." Although there were still rumors that Farragut would attempt "to force the passage of the outer line," there was no evidence that the Federal Admiral had so powerful a fleet as would be required "to attack successfully the Bay batteries." [30]

---

remark upon the sadness of life, he would say he did not think so at all; that there was so much to be thankful for in the daily gifts of life, and that the knowledge that we were daily doing the will of God brought with it such entire happiness, he was, if left to himself, unwilling to exchange it for a state of which he knows little." Polk, "Leonidas Polk, A Memoir."

[28] Gale to Wife, January 3, 1864, Gale Papers.
[29] *Official Records*, LII, Pt. 2, 592, 596, 601; *ibid.*, XXXII, Pt. 2, 542.
[30] Polk to Thomas M. Jack, January 28, 1864, *ibid.*, 629; *id.* to Governor Watts, *ibid.*; Maury to Polk, *ibid.*, 638.

This was welcome news to Polk, for he was now receiving reports of a strong enemy concentration along his western front. On January 12 Sherman (at Memphis) wired Halleck and Grant: "I think by the 24th I can make up a force of 20,000 men to strike Meridian, and it may be Selma. Infantry will move via Vicksburg, Jackson, and Brandon; cavalry down the Mobile and Ohio Road from LaGrange, they meeting about Chunky River." Three days later Grant replied, approving the proposed movement and enclosing a copy of a letter to Halleck, which he said "contains all the instructions I deem necessary to you in your present move." In this letter to Halleck Grant had stated: "I shall direct Sherman . . . to move out to Meridian with his spare force (the cavalry going from Corinth) and destroy the [rail]roads east and south of these so effectually that the enemy will not attempt to rebuild them during the rebellion. He will then return unless the opportunity of going into Mobile with the force he has appears perfectly plain. . . . Sherman will be instructed, while left with large discretionary powers, to take no extra hazard of losing his army or of getting it crippled too much for efficient service in the spring." [31]

Sherman's plans were explained more fully in a letter from him to General Nathaniel Banks at New Orleans. He hoped to move into the interior as far as Demopolis and by a thorough destruction of the railroads "close the door of rapid travel and conveyance" from Mississippi to the eastern portion of the Confederacy. This would leave Mobile completely dependent upon the Alabama River. Since all portions of the Memphis and Charleston Railroad were either in Federal hands or destroyed the only link between Mississippi and Alabama and Georgia was the single track railroad from Meridian, Mississippi, to Selma, Alabama. His aim was to destroy this link, and he thought he would "surely succeed" unless General Polk was "too heavily re-enforced from Mobile and Atlanta." [32]

As early as January 11 one of Forrest's scouts reported that an advance into Mississippi was being planned. Forrest rushed the information to Polk. And by February 1 Forrest and Polk possessed reliable information that there were Federal advances from Vicksburg, up the Yazoo River, and from Collierville, Tennessee, on the

[31] *Official Records*, XXXII, Pt. 2, 75, 100, 105.   [32] *Ibid.*, 113–15.

Memphis and Charleston Railroad.[33] Polk ordered Lee to pull back his cavalry units operating along the Mississippi and to destroy the railroad between Vicksburg and Jackson, "beginning as far west as you can. . . . Let it be done thoroughly." [34] French's division was ordered to Jackson. Loring was already at Canton.

On the morning of February 4 Polk left for Mobile on an inspection tour. Upon arrival he received news that Sherman's troops had moved out of Vicksburg on the previous day. There was no opposition except a few minor attacks by Lee's cavalry. "Detain the enemy as long as possible from getting into Jackson," Polk wired Loring early on the fifth; re-enforcements from Mobile were on the way. He himself would return to Meridian that evening and come to the front immediately. To French he wired: "Continue the work vigorously. I am sending help." French replied at 12:30 P.M. "Your dispatch received. It is impossible to comply." The enemy was already at Clinton.[35] On February 7 Polk sent his wife and daughter back to Asheville and joined his troops at the front. Mrs. Polk reported to the family that for the first time General Polk showed great concern about the eventual outcome of the war.[36]

Sherman's advance entered Jackson at sunset on the fifth. Loring and French crossed over Pearl River and fell back toward Morton. Lee's cavalry remained west of the river to operate on the enemy's flank and rear.[37] Polk appealed to both Johnston in Georgia and Beauregard in South Carolina for any aid they could give. Both felt their own positions hard pressed, so could promise no help. But when President Davis learned of the serious threat to his home state he ordered Johnston to "Keep in communication with General Polk, and do what you can to assist him, either by sending him re-enforcements or joining him with what force you can." [38]

Sherman's divisions under McPherson and Hurlbut, more than 20,000 strong, crossed Pearl River on February 7 and continued eastward. Loring and French continued to fall back. Upon reaching Morton the Federals turned southward. Polk now decided that Sherman intended to strike the Mobile and Ohio Railroad

---

[33] *Ibid.*, 557, 648.   [34] *Ibid.*, 648.   [35] *Ibid.*, 676, 679.
[36] Polk, "Leonidas Polk, A Memoir"; Gale, "Recollections."
[37] French to Polk, February 5, 1864, 4 P.M., *Official Records*, XXXII, Pt. 2, 679.   [38] *Ibid.*, 716.

south of Meridian and then move on Mobile. He notified Maury at Mobile that the brigades recently brought up were being returned; others would follow. Lee was instructed to use his entire cavalry force to protect the Mobile and Ohio until these troops had passed down.[39]

On February 11 Polk received a message from Forrest in North Mississippi. The expected enemy advance from Collierville was underway in the direction of Pontotoc, the corn producing prairie country, and the Mobile and Ohio Railroad.[40] This cavalry force, estimated by Forrest at 10,000, was commanded by General William Sooy Smith, whom Grant had recently sent from Middle Tennessee. It was now quite evident that Smith was to destroy the Mobile and Ohio Railroad as he moved southward and join Sherman at Meridian, for Sherman had not continued toward Mobile but had again turned in the direction of Meridian.[41]

Greatly outnumbered, Polk decided not to give battle to Sherman's infantry. He ordered Lee northward to co-operate with Forrest against Sooy Smith's advancing cavalry; he had hopes of destroying that arm of the Federal force. To French and Loring, however, he gave "discretionary orders" to fall back whenever expedient. "My intention is to fall back on the Tombigbee at Demopolis." [42] The best he hoped for was that the enemy might be checked long enough for the removal of stores across the Tombigbee. All the railroad rolling stock was to be sent to Mobile.[43] "I see nothing left me but to fall back on Alabama and take advantage of events," Polk informed Davis and Johnston.[44]

Polk's infantry and trains moved out of Meridian on February 14. Two nights later they crossed the Tombigbee at Lewis's Ferry, twenty-five miles below Demopolis. And two days later they were in Demopolis. This was a well-timed and well-directed withdrawal. All stores at Meridian and all at Enterprise "except corn in the shuck" were saved. All shop tools and rolling stock "except eight or ten cars" were likewise moved to safety. "The whole movement was conducted with the utmost coolness and

[39] Polk to Maury, February 9, 1864, *ibid.*, 701; *id.* to Lee, February 9, 1864, *ibid.*, 700; *id.* to Davis, February 9, 1864, *ibid.*, Pt. 1, 335.

[40] *Ibid.*, Pt. 2, 720.

[41] Polk to Lee, February 11, 1864, *ibid.*, 718; *id.* to Loring, February 11, 1864, *ibid.*, 717.   [42] *Id.* to *id.*, February 12, 1864, *ibid.*, 725.

[43] *Id.* to Maury, February 13, 1864, *ibid.*, 733.   [44] *Ibid.*, 729.

deliberation, and was entirely successful," reported the general superintendent of the Mobile and Ohio Railroad.[45] Sherman moved into Meridian the day Polk moved out.

On the day that Polk's infantry arrived at Demopolis he received telegrams from Seddon and Johnston. "You will be re-enforced. Employ all means within your power to obstruct and delay the enemy and to collect supplies and stores for your coming forces," urged the Secretary of War. Johnston wished to know "where re-enforcements can find you and of the enemy's movements." Polk was unable to decipher Johnston's telegram but was expecting re-enforcements. "Guessing at your cipher," he wired, "I reply they can meet me at Demopolis. Enemy at last account still at Meridian breaking up railroad." Seddon's warning about adequate stores was of little concern to Polk, for his was the best fed army in the Confederacy at that time. His brief reply was that Maury had a "six months' supply" at Mobile and he was that day shipping him another half million pounds of bacon and a large quantity of corn.[46]

On the next day Hardee's corps of Johnston's army, composed of Cheatham's and Cleburne's divisions, began arriving in Montgomery. Where should he go? Hardee wired Polk, who ordered him to Demopolis and called up enough boats from Mobile to transfer the re-enforcements from Montgomery to Selma.[47]

Sherman was still at Meridian, waiting for the arrival of Sooy Smith's cavalry, tearing up railroads, and destroying most of the business property of the town. Forrest and Lee were still blocking Smith's path, skirmishing often but not risking a decisive fight. It was of the "highest consequence," Polk urged Forrest and Lee, that this cavalry force be destroyed. If this could be accomplished Sherman's whole army "must come to a bad end." He urged that the people of the country be aroused. "Let them form companies or join those already with you, if for only temporary service. Let them ambuscade the enemy and assail him in bodies or singly." Sherman was "lying quietly at Meridian awaiting . . . that column. If it be possible, let him not see it." [48] "It was obvious," Polk later recorded, "that if Sherman was deprived of its presence and Services to procure forage & Subsistence for his army

[45] L. J. Fleming to Polk, February 19, 1864, *ibid.*, 768.
[46] *Ibid.*, 755, 763.   [47] *Ibid.*, 769, 782.
[48] Polk to Lee and Forrest (two letters), February 20, 1864, *ibid.*, 779, 781.

it must Starve and destruction by Starvation was as Effectual as destruction by battle." [49]

Smith moved as far as West Point and stopped. Already several days behind schedule and hearing exaggerated reports of the strength of the Confederate concentration between himself and Sherman, he decided not to march his "encumbered command into the trap set for me by the rebels." [50] On February 21 he began a retreat toward Memphis. Forrest stung him all along the way but did not deliver a crushing blow.

On the same day Smith began his retreat Sherman also moved out of Meridian on his return trip to Vicksburg. Without knowing of Smith's retreat Polk dispatched 600 re-enforcements to Forrest, and ordered Loring and French to recross the Tombigbee. Hardee's corps was ordered back to Dalton. Polk made no effort to overtake Sherman, but set about repairing the damage the Federal invaders had done to the railroads.

Gale gleefully reported to his wife that "The country breathes free again. The Yankee army baffled and whipped, almost without a battle, have retired and thus closes one of the most brilliant efforts of the war on the part of a Confederate Genl and his brave little army." He was certain that General Polk would "gain great credit" for his skillful operations. [51]

Polk was also well pleased with his own efforts. " 'Mine enemies compassed me in on every side, they compassed me in I say on every side, but in the name of the Lord have I destroyed them,' " he wrote his wife on March 9. "Thus sang the Psalmist and thus by the grace of our God am I enabled so to sing." There had never been a more gloomy prospect than that which faced him when the enemy began moving in; never was there a brighter day than that which followed the "defeat and rout of that advancing army. . . . It was the Lord's doings and it is marvelous in our eyes."

Polk recalled that as he parted with his wife on leaving for the front to meet Sherman she had noted that the expression of despair on so many faces filled her with apprehension, "for it seemed

[49] Polk to Wife, March 9, 1864, Gale Papers.
[50] Smith's report, *Official Records*, XXXII, Pt. 1, 256–57.
[51] William Dudley Gale to Wife, February 25, 1864, Gale Papers.

as if it were as Goliath against David." As he moved to the front these words had stuck in his mind. "I so trusted myself and felt all the Smooth Stones from the brook were not exhausted and so by the power of God it proved." He thought that "considering the disparity of forces" the result was "wonderful." [52]

Polk and his aide had cause to be proud of their accomplishment, but the terms they used to describe Sherman's plight were exaggerated. He had not been "whipped" or "routed"; neither was there evidence that he was "baffled." He had planned to return to Vicksburg if conditions were not favorable to a move on Selma or Mobile. The failure of Sooy Smith's cavalry to join him at Meridian and the arrival of Hardee's corps to re-enforce Polk left the Federal commander in an untenable position. Polk deserved credit for skillful maneuvering that saved both his army and supplies, but Sherman took a considerable toll in the destruction of public and private property, leaving "a swath of desolation 50 miles broad across the State of Mississippi, which the present generation will not forget." [53]

Polk correctly considered Sherman's Mississippi campaign but a precursor of a Federal advance from Chattanooga upon Johnston at Dalton. He was also correct in his belief that Grant would soon call Sherman's veteran army to Chattanooga. On February 28 he sent President Davis a private letter setting forth his views and plans for assisting Johnston. As matters stood, he considered Johnston's force inadequate to resist the Federal advance, yet the "remoteness of Chattanooga from the enemy's base" offered an opportunity. He himself wished to fall upon this long flank and supply line running westward to Nashville. To enable him to do this he proposed that Cheatham's division be detached from Johnston and assigned to his command. This division of Tennesseans, "raised by me" from the middle and western sections of the state, was about 4,000 strong. Polk would send it as close as possible to these home sections for recruiting service and feel confident of doubling its present strength by the addition of those who had quit its ranks and gone home during the past three years plus many others who had never been in the service. To this number

[52] Gale Papers.   [53] *Official Records*, XXXII, Pt. 2, 498.

he hoped to add enough troops from Alabama and Mississippi to increase the infantry column to 15,000. He was also confident that he could get together another 15,000 of cavalry.

As for his own department, Polk believed it would be safe with a few cavalry operating along the Mississippi provided Kirby Smith would seriously threaten Banks west of the Mississippi. He would then throw his army of 30,000 across the Tennessee River and strike the Federal flank and rear. At the same time Longstreet, aided by Morgan's cavalry should move across the mountains and strike the enemy's left flank. These combined operations, he believed, could "break up Grant's expedition effectually, if not shatter his army." [54]

Although Polk's suggestion had definite merit, Davis apparently was not impressed. Sherman later wrote that "The Atlanta campaign would simply have been impossible without the use of the railroads" from Atlanta to Louisville.[55] The question is whether or not Polk could have destroyed this life line. There is good reason to believe that he could have. No one has yet satisfactorily explained why the tunnel at Cowan, Tennessee, was never blown up. Grant and Sherman carried with them railroad materials and laborers but they had no machinery that could open up a caved-in tunnel through a limestone mountain within a reasonable time. If it were true, as Sherman said, that his Atlanta campaign depended upon the railroad from Chattanooga through Nashville to Louisville, then it was lost by the Confederates at Cowan, not in the vicinity of Atlanta.

On the day following his letter to President Davis, Polk addressed Secretary of War Seddon on another topic. "The existing organizations of the War Department for collecting and accumulating subsistence and quartermaster stores in this military department are working inefficiently for the objects proposed," he began, "and operate so as to hamper exceedingly the freedom of the military dispositions and movements of the commander of the department. The objects proposed are good, but the modes of effecting them are faulty." Officers performing these services had no consultation with the department commander. As he understood it,

[54] *Ibid.*, 813–14.
[55] William T. Sherman, *Memoirs of William T. Sherman* (New York, 1875), II, 398.

it was the object of the War Department to collect all stores required by the armies. The surplus above the needs of a department was stored in depots subject to shipment to "other armies in distant fields." Officers in this subsistence and quartermaster service constituted an independent organization responsible to Richmond. The military commander in the department in which they functioned knew nothing of their plans or operations. And his acquaintance with the personnel was limited to that intercourse necessary in drawing upon them "for such supplies as they may happen to have."

Polk considered it both inconvenient and hazardous for a department commander to be dependent upon officials not under his supervision to supply his subsistence and commissary needs. And the evil was further increased by an order from the War Department directing that all requisitions for stores must first be sent to Richmond for approval before they could be honored. "The truth is the system cannot be worked," Polk exclaimed; "it must be broken down and disregarded by the necessities of the case or it will break down the armies in the field."

A further objection, Polk charged, was that by doubling or tripling the number of agents needed in this service the system "swells the ranks of idlers and drones." All of these evils could be corrected if the collection of stores were placed under control of the department commander, who in turn would be responsible for its efficiency and thoroughness. Let all subsistence and quartermaster agents be members of the department commander's general staff and report directly to his headquarters. Under such a system the commander would always have exact information as to the quantity and location of available stores.

Every department commander was already required to make trimonthly reports of his troops; he could easily be required to do the same for supplies in his depots. Authorities at Richmond had the power to transfer these troops at will; they might have the same power over supplies. Such a new system might also be applied to field transportation.

During the recent enemy invasion, Polk concluded, the weakness in the supply system had been painfully apparent. The problem of saving stores had been greatly increased by the necessity of first locating them. Since the existing system had been inaugurated as an experiment he saw no reason why it could not be discarded in favor of a more efficient one.[56]

Seddon could not approve Polk's proposal. A similar plan, he explained, had prevailed before the adoption of the present system and had been abandoned because of its evils. Department commanders often had been slow about collecting more stores than they needed and at times had refused to give permission for the transfer of supplies to other departments. As long as needed items were plentiful throughout the Confederacy this lack of co-operation was not serious. But when supplies became scarce in some departments while in others there was an abundance, an equitable distribution became absolutely necessary. Such a distribution could be administered only through centralized control; consequently, he was convinced that the existing system was "right in itself" and could be made to work efficiently. He trusted that reflection would induce General Polk "to concur in the superiority of the general plan," and make every effort to assist in its efficient execution.[57]

Without waiting for Seddon's reply, Polk had shifted to still another important subject, addressing letters to Seddon and Adjutant General Cooper, the third member of the Richmond triumvirate. "We must have more fighting men," he told Seddon, and this need could be met from the large amount of conscript material within the department. Judicious and energetic prosecution of the work of conscription could greatly increase the armed strength within sixty days. However, under the system in use, the officers of the Conscript Bureau were not subject to orders from the department commander and the whole organization was a source of "inconvenience and embarrassment." The only apparent remedy was to intrust to the commander full control over conscription.[58]

In his letter to Cooper, Polk went into greater details. The inefficiency of the Conscript Bureau, he charged, had resulted in bands of conscripts and deserters terrorizing sections of the Mississippi country. In Jones County they had "killed the officer in charge . . . of conscription and dispersed and captured his supporting

[56] *Official Records*, XXXII, Pt. 2, 814–16.
[57] Seddon to Polk, March 15, 1864, *ibid.*, LII, Pt. 2, 639–40.
[58] March 1, 1864, *Official Records*, XXXII, Pt. 3, 574.

force." They were daily increasing in numbers and boldness; they had "destroyed the houses of many loyal men by fire, plundered others," and attacked wagon trains, "helping themselves largely to Government and other stores." Authority to suppress their activities and arrest these outlaws was instructed to the Conscript Bureau, but "The administration demanded for such work is far more vigorous than can be exercised by a bureau having its seat at Richmond." The department commander must therefore "turn aside" sufficient field forces "to put down this combination." If the duty of "collecting and conscribing these men and arresting these deserters" was intrusted directly to the department commander one body of troops would be sufficient for all requirements. But under the present arrangement, "I have to detail a force for the conscription officers and another to arrest deserters, absentees and paroled men, and keep down . . . rebellions."

There should be no troops in his department not under his direct control, Polk concluded. He could not be held responsible for the proper administration of his department when "the power to control its affairs is divided between me and another officer." Consequently, he urged that he be given complete control over all military operations within his department.[59]

General Cooper did not reply to Polk's letter but indorsed thereon: "To comply with the suggestion in this letter would but add to the military responsibilities of General Polk, and would not lessen the evil complained of, inasmuch as it would require the same amount of force to enforce conscription and apprehend deserters, to which the general here objects." [60]

Secretary Seddon replied at length. He understood the embarrassment resulting from inefficient administration of the conscript law, yet he was inclined to believe the situation was a result of irregularities during General Johnston's tenure as department commander. Johnston had requested authority similar to that Polk suggested and it had been granted. He in turn placed it in the hands of General Pillow, who although acting "with characteristic energy and zeal," disregarded legal exemptions and restrictions and resorted to something near military coercion. Authori-

[59] March 3, 1864, *ibid.*, 580–81.   [60] *Ibid.*, 581.

ties at Richmond, bombarded with well-founded complaints,
deemed it necessary to revoke Pillow's authority and place conscription again in the hands of the Conscript Bureau.

Seddon was confident that this return to "the more regular and
simpler administration of the law" would soon result in "less dissatisfaction yet more thorough enforcement of conscription." He
would not say that the authority requested by Polk would not be
granted but he preferred, for the present at least, "to request your
serious reconsideration of the matter, with the hope that fuller information may convince your judgment of the inexpediency of
such power." [61]

Although he had received no favorable response from Richmond on his suggestions, Polk presented still another idea. A few
weeks previous President Davis had requested him to consider a
plan submitted by one Colonel Reid of Arkansas for the recapture
of New Orleans. Reoccupation of New Orleans was greatly desired by General Polk, but he knew it would be impossible as
long as the enemy controlled the Mississippi River.

On March 21 he wrote Davis at length, setting forth a plan for
seizing control of the river from Cairo down. He would divide the
distance into sections fifteen miles long and assign to each section
a force of mounted infantry "composed of persons of all ages living within the enemy's lines and near them on the banks of the
Mississippi." Equipped with long range rifles and rifled field pieces,
these squadrons could destroy enemy commerce on the river and
serve as a police in preventing trade with disloyal residents and
enemy cultivation of plantations. Polk was confident that he could
raise the 6,000 men that would be required for such a venture.

Once the patrols were in operation along the river, Polk next
proposed "to attempt the passage of the river." The Federals had
divided the river into sections each patroled by a gunboat. He
would learn the exact location of each boat. Next he would purchase in St. Louis a transport regularly used in trade down to
Memphis. At some designated woodyard landing near Fort
Pillow the transport would be seized by 500 picked men. As was
the custom, this transport would "hail and round-to alongside" the
first gunboat met, which would likely be anchored, as if to ex-

[61] Seddon to Polk, March 16, 1864, *ibid.*, 644–46.

change mail. Gunboats carried only 80 to 100 men; so there would be little difficulty in capture. With most of the "500" secreted aboard the captured boat it would then steam down the river repeating the performance again and again, for there was neither system of signals between gunboats nor telegraphic connections along the river. Captured boats would be kept well to the rear unless needed in putting down resistance. The shore patrols would also be in position ready to assist, but would not be informed of the plan.

If the venture proved successful all river ports could be reoccupied and it would be worth any expenditure required in its execution. If it failed the loss would be small. The President would recall, Polk reminded, that the first commission given him was to " 'take charge of the land and water defenses of the Mississippi River.' " [62]

Polk must have been conscious of all of the difficulties that might be encountered in such a daring venture, yet more bizarre plans have sometimes succeeded. The rapid change in events during the next few weeks, however, would have prevented much progress even if the proposal had been approved. But General Bragg, now military adviser to the President and understandably sour on any suggestion from Polk, pronounced both the "practicability and policy" of the proposal "doubtful." [63]

Appeals for protection from deserters and other lawless elements arrived at Polk's headquarters almost daily. Especially desperate were the Confederate agents who were attempting to collect the "tax in kind" levied by an act of Congress. One agent reported that "the deserters have overrun and taken possession of the country, in many cases exiling the good and loyal citizens or shooting them in cold blood on their own door-sills." The agent in Jones County, Mississippi, had not been heard from since he was ordered to leave the county. In Covington County deserters had notified the agent "to desist from collecting the tithe" and to distribute among their families what he had already collected. A group raided Augusta in Perry County and destroyed the public stores collected there.[64] One suspects that not all of those opposing the tax collector were deserters.

[62] *Ibid.*, XXXIV, Pt. 2, 1064–67.   [63] *Ibid.*, 1067.
[64] James Hamilton to T. M. Jack, March 31, 1864, *ibid.*, XXXII, Pt. 3, 727–28.

Polk interpreted his recent letter from Seddon to mean that while he had no direct control over conscription, his power to ferret out and return deserters was unlimited. He divided his department into military districts, and with the co-operation of General Maury at Mobile, sent detachments of troops to round up these "deserters and traitors." In some of the Pearl River counties they met with defiance and open rebellion, but the application of stringent and "very summary measures" soon brought results. Some deserters fled to the bottoms, threatening to return with Yankee assistance; others professing to have returned to reason and loyalty, surrendered themselves.[65]

Since it was reported that many were afraid of punishment and had not heard of an earlier presidential offer of amnesty, the Mississippi Legislature petitioned Polk to issue a proclamation of pardon to those who voluntarily returned. This he did on April 16. Full pardon would be granted to absentees who would return to their commands within ten days after learning of this proclamation, provided they were not commissioned officers or had at any time joined the service of the enemy. "The lieutenant-general commanding desires to add the expression of the hope that this last opportunity now presented for wiping out the disgrace which attaches to the characters of these men, and must follow and brand their posterity after them, will be availed of by them, and that he will thus be relieved from the painful duty of making examples of those who, in contempt of the claims of their country upon their services, and in defiance of all law, have not only deserted their standards, but by banding themselves together have rendered the property and lives of peaceable citizens insecure and reduced society to the condition of lawlessness and violence." [66]

By April 30 General Polk was able to report to President Davis that more than 1,000 deserters had been returned to their commands. He was determined to continue his efforts until his department was free from absentees.[67]

There was a lull in military activities in Polk's department after Sherman returned to Vicksburg. Lee's cavalry followed the retreating Federals and assumed about the same position it had occupied

---

[65] Polk to Davis, March 21, 1864, *ibid.*, 662–63.   [66] *Ibid.*, 785–86.
[67] *Ibid.*, 855–56.

before the invasion. The infantry soon moved back to the Pearl River region. Forrest was sent into West Tennessee and Kentucky on a short campaign that was to have brilliant results. Polk's headquarters remained at Demopolis. The most important question for speculation was what would be Sherman's next move. Many reports were soon in circulation. A portion of Sherman's army was said to be moving to New Orleans from which it would no doubt assist in an attack upon Mobile. Another report had him taking his whole force up the Red River in a campaign against Kirby Smith.[68] Still another announced that most of Sherman's army had gone up the Mississippi on furlough. What these furloughed troops would do when they returned to active duty was still another question. "Information of Sherman's movements is important to me," Johnston wired Polk. "You will oblige me greatly by giving it as it comes to you." [69] Polk did as requested.

The movement of greatest immediate concern to Polk was the reported concentration of troops along the Tennessee River in North Alabama. The coal and iron region of central Alabama, with its foundries, shops, and depots, was a vital spot in the Confederacy. Polk had earlier feared a Federal advance southward from Huntsville but none was made. By mid March, 1864, however, he was receiving reports of a concentration about Decatur. On April 2 Governor T. H. Watts of Alabama reported the enemy fortifying at Decatur and "inflicting great injury" upon the surrounding country. An advance toward central Alabama appeared certain.[70] On this same day, apparently before receiving Watts' disturbing message, Polk wrote optimistically to his daughter: "Things look encouraging in the Confederacy generally and every body in these parts is in a good humor. We cannot but hope that this year will wind up our troubles." [71]

Upon receiving Watts' report Polk immediately ordered General Loring to begin moving his infantry division to Montevallo, Alabama. General Lee was instructed to take the main body of his cavalry to Tuscaloosa, send out a part of his command to Elyton (present site of Birmingham) in Jones Valley, and to scout the country northward to the Tennessee Valley. He would also or-

---

[68] A portion of his force did join General Banks in this campaign.
[69] March 10, 1864, *Official Records*, XXXII, Pt. 3, 605.   [70] *Ibid.*, 735–36.
[71] Leonidas Polk Papers.

ganize expeditions "against the deserters and tories" in the North
Alabama hill country. On April 18 General French was also ordered to move his division to Tuscaloosa, thus completing the
concentration in central Alabama, except for Forrest's command
which was still in North Mississippi.[72]

Polk, estimating his own strength at 8,000 as opposed to a potential enemy force of 20,000, renewed his plea that Major General Cheatham's division be sent to him. "They are very anxious to
come and I to have them." He still believed that if this division
was moved near the Tennessee line its number would be doubled
by the return of absentees. His combined force could then block
any advance into central Alabama and could strike the enemy's
flank should an advance be made on Johnston at Dalton.[73] Davis
referred this request to Bragg; Bragg objected. "The transfer of
the division to that locality," he endorsed, "would soon see another
large portion of them on stolen horses marauding over the country." [74] The intense loyalty of Cheatham's division to Polk had
never been a source of pleasure to Bragg.

Instead of transferring Cheatham to Polk, Bragg suggested that
Polk send Loring's division to Johnston. Polk objected. As long as
the enemy threatened central Alabama, he thought Loring could
not be spared. But the enemy did not advance on central Alabama;
the obstacles were too great. As one of Loring's scouts reported, it
was difficult to find subsistence stores for even one horse and rider
in that "barren and desolate" hill country between the Tennessee
Valley and Jones Valley.[75] Even the residents of that area, heavily
Unionist in sympathy, were suffering from a lack of essential supplies since so many deserters had sought safety among them. Polk
was still trying to catch or drive out these deserters but was finding
it slow business. The lack of roads and forage made the use of
cavalry less effective than infantry. And since these "traitors" were
seldom found in groups, it was necessary to chase them down individually. When a policy of leniency and amnesty failed to work,
Polk ordered that those offering armed resistance should be "put
to death upon the spot." [76]

[72] *Official Records*, XXXII, Pt. 3, 733, 770, 791.
[73] Polk to Davis, April 18, 1864, *ibid.*, 790–91.   [74] *Ibid.*, 791.
[75] Loring to Thomas M. Jack, April 24, 1864, *ibid.*, 815.
[76] Douglas West to J. D. Bradford, May 2, 1864, *ibid.*, XXXVIII, Pt. 4,
657–58.

Polk and his generals gradually concluded that the Federal concentration at Decatur was for the purpose of protecting the railroads and preventing Polk from sending re-enforcements to Johnston. On April 25 Forrest reported that reliable scouts had observed the Federals moving everything toward Chattanooga via the Nashville and Chattanooga and the Tennessee and Alabama railroads.[77]

The scouts were correct. Sherman had assumed command at Chattanooga and trains from Nashville were bringing in troops and every type of supplies essential to a successful campaign. Johnston's scouts were reporting this disturbing news, and by May 1 they were certain that a Federal movement was imminent. It began on the second with Federal cavalry driving Confederate units from Ringgold back upon Tunnel Hill. Johnston called for help, and Cooper wired Polk: "The President directs . . . that you move with Loring's division, and any other available force at your command, to Rome, Ga., and there unite with General Johnston to meet the enemy." [78] Polk wired Johnston that he was coming with all available forces—10,000 infantry and 4,000 cavalry.[79] Bragg complained that it appeared Polk was taking more troops than was intended. Polk referred him to the President's instructions and kept moving.[80] General Lee was left in command of the department.

For weeks Bragg kept up a running argument, claiming that Polk had weakened the Alabama-Mississippi front too much by taking too many troops to Georgia. Polk replied that the President, through Adjutant General Cooper, had ordered him to take all available forces. Bragg wanted to know why Polk had changed his mind; a short while earlier he had opposed sending one division of 4,000 and now he was taking 14,000. Polk explained that it was not a change of mind but a change of situation. Relief from pressure in Alabama and increase in pressure on Johnston at Dalton made the shift of troops necessary and proper.[81] So ran the argument. Bragg was not pleased with either Polk or Johnston. The latter had declined to accept Bragg's proposal for an offensive

[77] Lee to Jack, April 24, 1864, *ibid.*, XXXII Pt. 3, 814; Forrest to Polk, April 25, 1864, *ibid.*, 822.   [78] *Ibid.*, XXXVIII, Pt. 4, 661.
[79] *Ibid.*, 670.   [80] *Ibid.*, XXXIX, Pt. 2, 585; *ibid.*, XXXVIII, Pt. 4, 684.
[81] *Ibid.*, 733, 735, 737, 740.

movement; Bragg opposed sending him extensive re-enforcements for the mere purpose of defense.[82]

Polk was ordered to move his troops to Resaca, where he arrived in person with Loring's division on May 11. On the following day he officially took command of his combined forces, which he styled the Army of the Mississippi, consisting of infantry divisions under Major Generals Loring and French and Brigadier General James Cantey. The last had been moved up from Mobile. The cavalry under command of Brigadier General W. H. Jackson, was composed of the brigades of Armstrong, Ferguson, and Ross. Soon finding himself unable to use cavalry effectively in the task to which he was assigned, Polk turned the cavalry over to Johnston for reassignment.

At Resaca Polk relieved Hood who was to move up to command the right wing of the Army of Tennessee at Dalton. Thirty-two, dashing, and full of fight, Hood had recently returned to active duty after recuperating from the loss of a leg at Chickamauga. On the evening of Polk's arrival the two rode to Johnston's headquarters. There was a general feeling that a great battle was impending. Hood was more serious than usual, and before arriving at Dalton he informed Polk that he wished to be baptized. Nothing could have been more pleasing to the Bishop-General. "The scene was a touching one," Polk wrote his wife. "He with one leg[,] leaning on his crutches—a veteran in the midst of his & my officers & I the officiating minister. His heart was fully in it." [83]

Polk's old friends and troops of the Army of Tennessee received him "with cordial demonstrations of pleasure. . . . I hope I appreciate it properly," he confided to his wife. As attested by an observing staff officer, Polk the man and the soldier was indeed much respected by officers and troops alike:

> Wrapped in his old gray hunting-shirt, with slouched hat and sabre, he sat his horse and received the leaden compliments of the enemy with complacent yet not indifferent good humor. He had a habit of shrugging his shoulders when a Minie ball came too close to his ear, and sometimes he would drop a chance word as though in reply. But he never got out of the way of them, and, if there was anything interesting at hand, was wholly indifferent

[82] See Horn, *Army of Tennessee*, 317 ff.
[83] Polk to Wife, May 21, 1864, Leonidas Polk Papers.

to their importunities. In battle he was a daring old man, with his heart in the fray, and his best faith on the result; riding through shot and shell from point to point, unconscious of danger, directing the movements of his line with a quiet self-possession which bespoke knowledge. At Shiloh, at Perryville, at Murfreesboro, at Chickamauga, and at Resaca, he was to be seen constantly at the front, at every part of his line, supervising the progress of events with his own presence. . . . He was kind and considerate of his men; he was approachable and self-denying in his own person; and he did not know the name of fear. He possessed that faculty of inspiring all who came about him with courage. . . . He was proverbial for getting into "hot places"; and he seemed to be able to pass along a line of fire like the children through the fiery furnace, untouched. His staff loved him most fondly. He was every inch a gentleman, without mannerism or assumption,—simple and innocent, yet dignified and imposing.[84]

Resaca was located at the point where the railroad to Atlanta crossed the Oostenaula River. It was particularly vulnerable to a flanking attack, and such attacks would be the plan of Sherman's operations all the way to Atlanta. Johnston's Army of Tennessee was along the line of Rocky Face Ridge, Hood on the right and Hardee on the left, with Wheeler's cavalry protecting the right flank. If Sherman had wished immediately to settle the issue with Johnston he could have approached Dalton by way of the Chattanooga road. Instead, although outnumbering Johnston two to one (about 100,000 to 45,000), he chose to maneuver him out of position.

While Thomas and Schofield threatened Johnston along the ridge, Sherman planned to send McPherson's force of 25,000 through Snake Creek Gap on the right to destroy the railroad at Resaca, fall back and wait for Johnston's inevitable retreat, and then strike him in the flank. Although McPherson had a gap through which to move he found the country rugged and without roads. These obstacles delayed him long enough to permit Cantey's division of Polk's army to get into position to receive him. Surprised by this opposition McPherson fell back before reaching the railroad.

[84] Statement by Henry Watterson, an aide on Polk's staff, later a prominent newspaper editor, quoted in Polk, *Leonidas Polk*, II, 352–53.

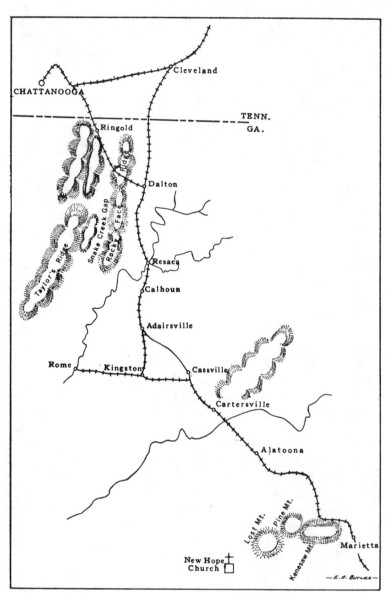

THE ROUTE TO ATLANTA

Disappointed but determined to destroy Johnston's life line, Sherman decided to move his entire army through Snake Creek Gap. Wheeler observed the movement and reported to Johnston. Johnston now had no choice but to fall back to Resaca and hurriedly fortify against Sherman's advance. He took position west of the railroad opposite Resaca, Hood on the right, Hardee in center, and Cantey's and Loring's divisions of Polk's army on the left. French's division had not yet arrived, but Polk was urging him to hurry.[85]

There was heavy skirmishing between the opposing forces throughout May 13 and 14, with little gained or lost. During the fifteenth fighting became heavier, but no great battle developed. During the night it was learned that a Federal force had crossed the Oostenaula below Calhoun. Johnston called a council of war and it was decided that another withdrawal was necessary. Polk covered the retreat and destroyed the Resaca bridge when no longer needed. Unable to find a suitable defensive position, Johnston moved southward to Adairsville. There the road divided, one branch going directly to Cassville and the other to the same place by way of Kingston. Johnston divided his forces, sending Hardee to Cassville by way of Kingston and Polk and Hood along the direct route. He hoped that Sherman, seeing the Confederate army had used both routes, might also divide his forces. If Sherman fell into this trap, then Johnston with his columns reunited at Cassville could fall upon the Federal columns separately. By the afternoon of the eighteenth Johnston's army was well in hand at Cassville.[86]

Again when a great battle appeared imminent a general wished to be baptized. In response to a plea from his wife General Johnston made this request of Bishop-General Polk. "You are never too much occupied I well know to pause to perform a good deed," Mrs. Johnston wrote Polk from Atlanta, "& will I am sure, even whilst leading your soldiers on to victory, lead my soldier nearer to God. General Johnston has never been baptized & it is the dearest wish of my heart that he should be & that you should

[85] Polk to French, May 13, 1864, *Official Records*, XXXVIII, Pt. 4, 706, 708.

[86] For a detailed account of Johnston's defensive maneuvering see Govan and Livingood, *A Different Valor*, Chapter XIX.

perform the ceremony would be a great gratification to me—I have
written to him on the subject & am sure he only waits your leisure.
I rejoice that you are near him in these trying times. May God
crown all your efforts with success and spare your life for your
country & friends." [87]

Late in the afternoon, May 18, in the presence of Generals Hood
and Hardee, General Johnston was baptized by Bishop-General
Polk. "It was a deeply solemn scene & what a passage for history!"
Polk wrote his wife. "God seems to be drawing our hearts to
Him. . . . Our trust is not in charriots [*sic.*] or horsemen but in
the living God. May he take and keep all our hearts unto that
day." [88]

During the night of the eighteenth Johnston's army moved into
position. This time Polk was in the center with Hardee, who had
moved from Kingston, on the left. Early on the following morning
Johnston had a stirring message read to all the troops, assuring
them that "Your communications are secure. You will now turn
and march to meet the advancing columns."

Thomas' and McPherson's corps had followed Hardee to Kingston; Schofield's had taken the more direct route. It was Johnston's
plan to assume the offensive as soon as the Federals moved out
of Kingston toward Cassville. Hood was to take the lead, striking
the Federal left flank. Polk was to strike the front. About mid-
morning a courier took a message to Hood to begin the attack,
but he found him already falling back. He had sighted Federals
in "heavy force" on his right. If the Federals were already on
Hood's flank the Confederate plan could not be executed. Johnston doubted the accuracy of Hood's report, but ordered the whole
army to fall back to defensive position. It was soon revealed that
the "heavy force" was a small band of cavalry that had lost its
way. Johnston later blamed Hood for failure before Cassville.[89]

Late in the afternoon Polk sent his chief engineer, Captain Walter J. Morris, who had that day arrived from Alabama, to inspect
the position his forces now held. When Morris returned Polk sent
Gale to invite General Johnston "to sup" with him. Hood was
already at Polk's headquarters. After the generals had examined

[87] May 16, 1864, Leonidas Polk Papers.   [88] May 21, 1864, *ibid.*
[89] Johnston to William Dudley Gale, May 24, 1869, quoted in Polk,
Leonidas Polk, II, 355–57.

Morris' notes and sketches Polk decided that French's division, which had finally arrived from Rome, could not hold its position one hour under enemy artillery fire. Hood thought his force could not hold out two hours. Both favored either an offensive movement or withdrawal. They preferred the former, but Johnston thought he was in no position to take the offensive; so he ordered withdrawal south of the Etowah River to Allatoona. When Hardee arrived later in the evening he was not pleased with the views of the other generals, insisting instead that the present position could be held, but the decision to withdraw stood.[90]

From Allatoona Polk wrote his wife that he thought it "cannot be many days" before Johnston would offer battle. It had been a hard campaign, with much marching and little sleep. The troops were in "fine spirits and feel quite confident of their ability to succeed to the utmost of their wishes." [91] A week later he was at New Hope Church still expecting a "pitched battle." The troops were still "in exceedingly fine spirits & very confident"; relations between Johnston and his generals were "very pleasant. . . . our whole hope and confidence is in God upon whom we lean and in whom we trust. We consign ourselves, our army and our cause to Him who sitteth on the throne of judging right. . . ." [92]

Sherman had left the railroad which now ran to the southeast and was moving directly southward toward the Chattahoochee River. This forced Johnston to shift to the left to New Hope Church to block his progress. There the Confederates took position in much the same order as at Cassville. Through days of intermittent fighting in rain and mud Sherman gradually extended his line eastward toward the railroad. To prevent being overlapped Johnston extended his line in the same direction until it rested on the small mountains west of Marietta.

There was growing dissatisfaction, especially in Richmond, with Johnston's failure to force a real battle with Sherman. But if this dissatisfaction was shared by the troops, Polk and his staff knew nothing of it. The army was fully prepared to meet the enemy wrote Gale, and all were confident of its "ability to gain a great victory. Genl Johnston still has the entire confidence of the whole

[90] *Ibid.*; Morris to W. M. Polk, June 25, 1878, quoted in *ibid.*, 376–82.
[91] May 21, 1864, Leonidas Polk Papers.
[92] Polk to Wife, May 27, 1864, *ibid.*

army." [93] "I think I have never seen the troops, one and all, in such fine spirits and condition as they now are," commented Polk on June 1, "and am of the very common opinion that under God we shall beat them when the collision shall take place. Indeed, the army is just ready to go along itself when it shall be put at its work. Their numbers are somewhat larger than ours, but the difference is not such as in our opinion to affect the result. I think it likely we shall find it expedient to pass the Chattahoochie, but the battle may happen on this side."

A week later Polk had lost none of his confidence. The enemy still preferred to operate on the Confederate flanks, he commented, but Johnston would likely "terminate this shortly." His own force was stronger than when the campaign began. In spirit, organization, and equipment it was "as fine as I could desire, great harmony prevailing everywhere." [94]

Four more days passed and no great battle. Polk had "never known the army to be so well clad and shod and fed . . . or so well organized or so easily handled. . . . It is very gratifying to find that the troops and the country appear to have undiminished confidences in the ability and skill of General Johnston & he seems to be managing things very prudently." [95]

[93] Gale to Wife, May 27, 1864, Gale Papers.
[94] Polk to Wife, June 1, 7, 1864, quoted in Polk, *Leonidas Polk*, II, 364–66.
[95] Polk to Daughter, June 11, 1864, Leonidas Polk Papers.

(17)

Atop Pine Mountain

On June 12 the rain poured. Military activities were at a stand-still. General Polk "seemed more abstracted to day than usual," his son-in-law confided to his journal. During the early part of the morning he remained in his room reading from the Bible and a small prayer book prepared by Chaplain Quintard for use by soldiers. About 10 a.m. he came out and announced he wished to read the church services to members of his staff. This he did with "dignity and solemnity worthy of a prophet of old" and then led the singing of a hymn and a psalm. "In a voice tremulous with emotion he read the concluding prayer, and, asking a blessing, sat down in profound silence." [1]

The rain continued on the thirteenth. Polk again remained in his quarters, writing letters, one of which was to his daughter Lilly who a few weeks earlier had married William E. Huger:

> You have now, my dear child, entered upon a new field, and under God's blessing (upon which, if you look to Him, you may count) your future happiness and success will depend very much upon yourself. Do always what is right, not calculating what is expedient, but try and find out what is right, and with a pure heart and true devotion go straight forward and do it. Be always kind and considerate of the feelings and rights of others, and you will be very apt to have your feelings and rights respected. Watch against impatience of spirit. If you keep your heart always under the dominion of the grace of God's spirit you will be very apt to have your own power of self-control complete and perfect. That is a thing to be cultivated, and is the fruit of watchfulness and prayerfulness. Let it be the business of your life to strive for large attainments in that way. It will be your greatest safety from

[1] Notes of William Dudley Gale, Leonidas Polk Papers.

yourself, the world, and the devil, and will be a shield and tower of strength for you. . . .

May the good Lord bless and keep you and yours, my dear child, in all your coming experiences and trial of life, and afterward receive you to glory, is the prayer of your affectionate father.[2]

During the afternoon Polk rode to General Johnston's headquarters for a conference. While there he was requested to join Johnston and Hardee on an inspection tour to the top of Pine Mountain the following morning. The rain was gone by the morning of June 14 when the generals set out. Pine Mountain, more hill than mountain, stood as a salient toward the Federal lines. A Confederate battery was stationed on its summit, but it was within range of Federal guns.

As the generals approached the summit they were warned of the danger. The tour, as conducted, was a foolish act. Although from atop the mountain there was full view of the enemy lines, it was no place for three high-ranking generals. As they viewed the enemy location and preparations a shell exploded nearby. They shifted to a safer place and continued serious conversation. Polk then moved a few feet nearer the crest as if to get a final view. As he stood, arms folded, "a cannon-shot crashed through his chest, and opening a wide window, let free that indomitable spirit." As his fellow generals knelt beside the fallen Bishop-General, Hardee remarked "this has been a dear visit . . . little did I think this morning that I should be called upon to witness this." Johnston sighed "I would rather anything than this." [3]

As blood rushed from the open wound and saturated the clothing of the dead Bishop-General it stained the leaves of three little volumes in his pocket. These tracts, prepared by Chaplain Quintard and entitled *Balm for the Weary and Wounded,* had been inscribed to Generals Johnston, Hardee, and Hood "with the compliments of Lieutenant General Leonidas Polk, June 12, 1864." No doubt Polk intended to deliver them that morning. Two days later Assistant Adjutant General Douglas West did deliver them. Gen-

[2] Quoted in Polk, *Leonidas Polk,* II, 367–68.
[3] Johnston to C. T. Quintard, October 9, 1885, University of the South Library; Notes of William Dudley Gale, Leonidas Polk Papers.

eral Johnston replied: "The autograph and noble blood which almost effaced it makes it a souvenir truly precious, one which I shall cherish whilst the Almighty leaves me on earth." [4]

As staff officers bore the body of their fallen chief down the slopes of Pine Mountain one led "Jerry," a "strawberry roan with black legs" that Polk had ridden regularly since Shiloh. The horse would be sent to the plantation of Frank S. Lyon at Demopolis to graze out a peaceful existence. [5]

In the afternoon General Johnston issued a short address to the troops:

> Comrades, you are called to mourn your first captain, your oldest companion in arms. Lieutenant-General Polk fell today at the outpost of this army, the army he raised and commanded, in all of whose trials he shared, to all of whose victories he contributed. In this distinguished leader we have lost the most courteous of gentlemen, the most gallant of soldiers. The Christian patriot soldier has neither lived nor died in vain. His example is before you; his mantle rests with you. [6]

Immediately after General Polk's death Gale left for Asheville to escort Mrs. Polk and the girls to the site of burial. The body was taken to Atlanta and then to Augusta where it lay in state in St. Paul's Church. The venerable Bishop Elliott, Polk's intimate friend for many years, delivered the burial address, using as his subject "The Master is come and calleth for thee," and concluding:

> And now let us commit his sacred dust to the keeping of the Church of the Confederate States until such time as his own diocese shall be prepared to do him honor. . . . And he shall then receive a prophet's reward! His work shall rise up from the ashes of the past and attest his greatness. A diocese rescued from brutal dominion by the efficacy of his blood!—a Church freed from pollution by the vigor of his counsels!—a country made independent through his devotion and self-sacrifice!—a university sending forth streams of pure and sanctified learning from

[4] Arthur Howard Noll (ed.), *Doctor Quintard, Chaplain, C. S. A., and Second Bishop of Tennessee, Being His Story of the War, 1861–1865* (Sewanee, 1905), 97; Johnston to West, June 16, 1864, Gale Papers. In the Gale Papers are also the replies from Hood and Hardee.

[5] See Leonidas Polk Papers for notes on "Jerry."

[6] *Official Records*, XXXVIII, Pt. 4, 776.

its exuberant bosom—generations made better and grander from his example and life, and rising up and calling him blessed! [7]

The body was lowered to rest beneath the chancel window at the rear of the church. As the slab closed over the grave and the battery fired a final salute to the fallen Bishop-General, Bishop Elliott, his head bowed in grief, walked away, taking Mrs. Polk and Sue home with him for a visit.[8]

The death of General Polk was a severe blow to the morale of his army; however, this is not to say that had he been spared, the Atlanta campaign would have had different results. He was much beloved by his officers and men for his personal qualities; he was respected for his bravery and industry and his competence in inspiring troops to their best efforts. He was not a thorough student of military science. During the period from West Point days to the beginning of the Civil War he showed no interest in military affairs. Unlike many West Point men, he was not strongly tempted to become a participant in the Mexican War. In fact, in his extant correspondence he made no reference to that conflict. He much preferred the life of a planter and service within the Church. As a planter he was a near approach to failure; as a churchman he was a powerful influence in the development of Christianity and education. His acceptance of a commission in the Confederate army was in response to a sincere desire to be of service in a cause he believed just. He never doubted the right of Southern states to secede, and to him the defense of that right was a duty.

Polk was a competent corps commander, yet his frequent disagreements with Bragg would seem to indicate that he was at times hesitant in executing the orders of his superior. This charge, however, becomes less serious in view of the fact that all high ranking officers within the Army of Tennessee, distrusting Bragg's competence as a field commander, supported Polk in his apparent disregard of orders. Left unanswered was the question of whether or not the orders of a superior should be executed regardless of

[7] *Funeral Services at the Burial of the Right Rev. Leonidas Polk, D.D.* (Columbia, S. C., 1864).

[8] The other members of the family, including Altimore, Polk's faithful servant throughout the war, went back to Asheville. In 1875 Mrs. Polk was buried by the side of her husband. In 1945 both remains were at last claimed by the Diocese of Louisiana and reinterred in Christ Church Cathedral, New Orleans.

conditions or circumstances. Through it all, Polk's forgiving spirit was put to a severe test as he came to believe Bragg wished to saddle him with the responsibility for failure of the Army of Tennessee to win the victories expected of it.

After the Confederate failures during the summer and fall of 1863 Polk almost despaired of eventual success. His removal from command and subsequent transfer to Mississippi contributed to this despondency. He lost some of his ability to make "every thing bright and joyous around him." Then upon his return to Georgia his hope was somewhat revived. Again and again, in private correspondence, he pictured his army as being in fine spirits and quite confident, yet he always stressed that "our whole hope and confidence is in God."

When death came it was not as Bishop-General Polk would have wished it. He had no desire to die on the field of battle. If death was inevitable he would have preferred it while in service of his Church and that his body be laid to rest in the quiet little cemetery at St. John's Church near Ashwood. But he did not wish to die. Devoted husband, father, and friend, he loved life among his people. He asked nothing more than the privilege of serving the cause of Christianity and religious education. When his wife once commented on the sadness that was the common lot of man, his reply was that he was thankful for the gift of life even with its seeming hardships; he was not eager to exchange it for a state of which he knew nothing. His prayer was for faith sufficient to sustain him on earth. The future was entirely in God's hands.

Yet with all of his faith, as his wife later recalled, he "always had a great horror of death." And for several months prior to his passing he appeared to have a premonition that death was near. While Mrs. Polk was at his Mississippi headquarters they talked at length of what she should do should his life be taken. One morning he rather abruptly remarked " 'To think that this arm, so full of life, must one day be quiet in the grave; that this right hand must lose its cunning, and this brain cease to think!' " When she replied "But the soul does not," he added: "I know in another sphere or form; but what pain and suffering may attend the change.' " In later years Mrs. Polk felt that probably the manner of the Bishop-General's passing was "in mercy."

Polk's ability to accept disaster as the will of God would have been strength and comfort to him had he survived the war. His qualities of leadership would have proved helpful in his diocese and probably throughout the South during reconstruction years. Only in the movement to restore unity within the Episcopal Church would his presence have been of doubtful value. Northern clergymen would scarcely have welcomed leadership by a Southern bishop who had left his diocese to take up arms in support of "rebellion."

Critical Essay on Authorities[*]

In 1893 William Mecklenburg Polk, M.D.,[1] son of Leonidas Polk, published a two volume work entitled *Leonidas Polk, Bishop and General.* In 1915, after the *War of Rebellion Records* had been published, Dr. Polk brought out a revised edition of his work. Although the title page gives the name of William M. Polk as author, at least two other persons should have shared that honor.[2]

In 1881 Bishop William Stevens Perry, then in process of compiling a history of the American Episcopal Church, requested the Reverend John Fulton, Rector of St. George's Church, St. Louis, to write an article on the church in the Confederacy. Fulton had been a close friend and associate of Bishop Leonidas Polk in New Orleans during the 1850's. Much pleased with the opportunity to do justice to his late friend and bishop, he wrote Dr. Polk for material. It was unfortunate, he commented, that no good life of Bishop-General Polk had been published; however, he had heard that Dr. Polk was collecting material for that purpose. If a manuscript had been prepared he would welcome an opportunity to read it.

Dr. Polk had not completed his manuscript, but he sent some material, which Fulton thought quite satisfactory. He regretted that his article in Perry's forthcoming volume must of necessity

---

[*] Only those items found helpful in the preparation of this biography are included in this essay. A few works from which single bits of information were secured are given in full in the footnotes, but are not included in this bibliography.

[1] Later Dean of the Medical School of Cornell University.

[2] Hidden away in the Preface there is an expression of "indebtedness to the Rev. John Fulton, D.D., for the valuable aid rendered."

be quite short, Fulton replied, and he was eager that Dr. Polk's proposed biography be as "perfectly prepared as possible." He was especially eager that the portion dealing with ecclesiastical matters be "intelligently edited."

Later in the spring of 1882 Dr. Polk sent Fulton the manuscript of his proposed biography of Bishop-General Polk. In an accompanying note he remarked that he had been unable to find a publisher. After reading the manuscript Fulton replied that the failure to find a publisher was fortunate, for there should be no publication until the manuscript was "thoroughly revised." In fact, it must be completely rewritten. "It would be better that the historian of the future should be left to form his judgment of your father even from imperfect data," Fulton explained, "than that your father should be misrepresented by an unfortunate presentation of facts and documents." The writing of biography, he added, required "a perfect *rapport* between the biographer and his subject, quick insight, delicate discretion, great self-restraint, fine tact, and a certain dramatic instinct in grouping facts and persons." The manuscript at hand failed to give "an intelligent idea" of Bishop Polk's career during the years 1855–61. It also failed to relate Polk to the times in which he lived; it gave nothing of his political connections; his university scheme was not adequately developed; and his general views on education were neglected. Furthermore, the manuscript was "loosely strung together, with no proper arrangement and with not the least art of any kind." It failed to do justice to Bishop Polk as a "farsighted statesman," although it did contain valuable material.

Fulton proposed that Dr. Polk secure the services of an "expert literary man" to put the biography together. He suggested the Reverend Doctor B. F. De Costa of New York as general editor and agreed that he himself would contribute to the 1855–61 period. He did not want future historians to consider Polk more soldier than bishop, he explained. De Costa was not employed, but Fulton did begin his own chosen duties.

In December, 1883, Fulton chanced to be at dinner with one E. J. Biddle of St. Louis, who introduced himself as a grandson of Charles Biddle of Pennsylvania and nephew of Commodore Nicholas Biddle. During the course of conversation Biddle referred to his recent accomplishment in preparing a manuscript for publication. Fulton then explained Dr. Polk's problem and needs. A few days later he placed in Biddle's hands the first 250 pages of Polk's manuscript and then wrote Polk recommending that Biddle be employed to edit the work.

On January 11, 1884, Biddle wrote Dr. Polk that the material was very good but that the manuscript would "have to be entirely rewritten." As it now stood, the manuscript was usable as notes only. Biddle offered to re-write the complete manuscript and prepare it for the press for the sum of $500. An agreement was made. Biddle was to write the portion prior to 1855, Fulton that from 1855–61, and Dr. Polk the chapters on the war years. Biddle was also to serve as general editor.

Biddle worked rapidly. He had re-written the chapter on Thomas Polk twice, he explained to Dr. Polk on April 3, 1884, and was still not satisfied with it. When would Dr. Polk send some chapters on the war years? A month later he sent to Dr. Polk chapters five through seven to be read and returned. Since Bishop Polk's letters were "excellent and characteristic," Biddle had adopted a plan of "stringing together his letters with as few words as possible, because he himself tells the story better than anyone can do for him."

For the chapter on life at Leighton plantation Biddle had secured long accounts written by a Louisiana neighbor of the Polks and by a former governess, but they were so poorly written as to require extensive revision. He debated how to use this material and then, recognizing the interest that was generally attached to accounts by eye-witnesses, decided to re-write the sketches and quote the revised version.

After calling upon Dr. Polk again and again for more money for special services, Biddle finally finished the first part of the manuscript. But in June, 1884, Fulton became seriously ill and Biddle was forced to complete the chapters covering the period 1855–61. He was disgusted with the two hundred manuscript pages Fulton had prepared. "That mess injected into the middle of the book," he complained to Polk, "will be, financially, decidedly injurious." He finally decided to leave most of Fulton's "original matter" much as it was but to delete the documents. The biography was ready for a publisher late in 1886, but it did not appear in print until 1893. The reasons for this long delay are not known.

During this period of delay and negotiations with prospective publishers another problem arose. Shortly after the war Mrs. Leonidas Polk had agreed to furnish one Winchester Hall material for a biography of her late husband. Hall apparently completed his work about the time Polk, Biddle, and Fulton finished their task. In some way Dr. Polk got access to the Hall manuscript. He was furious. He threatened to take legal action to prevent the publication of such an unfair treatment of the Bishop-General. In the end, Dr. Polk, acting through Fulton, purchased Hall's manuscript and all materials collected by him plus a promise never to publish anything on the subject. The price was $1,500.

As published in 1893, *Leonidas Polk, Bishop and General* was the work of Dr. William M. Polk, E. J. Biddle, and John Fulton, with possibly some assistance from the Hall material. The principal value of the work is in the documents, especially letters, that it reproduced, yet they must be used with caution. Some of the originals of the letters have either been lost or are still in private hands. Most of them, however, are found in the several manuscript collections listed below. But the value of the Polk volumes is greatly reduced by the fact that the letters therein are not correct reproductions of extant originals. The wording, punctuation, spelling, and sentence structure were frequently changed; sentences and even paragraphs were sometimes omitted without proper indication. In some instances Bishop-General Polk was made to say the opposite of what he actually said. It is impossible to fix the responsibility for this violation of sound scholarship.

Several persons have interested themselves in certain phases of Bishop-General Polk's career. In 1949 Vera Lee Dugas published in the *Louisiana Historical Quarterly* (vol. XXXII) an article entitled "The Ante-Bellum Career of Leonidas Polk." This was a revision of a master's thesis at Louisiana State University. *The Historical Magazine of the Protestant Episcopal Church*, vol. VII (1938), carried the following articles: Walter H. Stowe, "Polk's Missionary Episcopate"; William S. Slack, "Bishop Polk and the Diocese of Louisiana"; William W. Manrose, "Early Life and Presbyterate of Leonidas Polk"; and James P. Jervey, "Leonidas Polk, the Confederate General." None of the authors of these articles made use of the Polk family papers.

Manuscript Collections

The Leonidas Polk Papers are in the Archives of the University of the South, Sewanee, Tennessee. This extensive collection of manuscript letters and miscellaneous documents includes the large batch of material brought together by Dr. Polk and his associates while preparing their biography of the Bishop-General. Subsequently other materials were added.

A much larger collection of Polk family papers is in the Southern Collection of the University of North Carolina. The following are rich in manuscript letters: Polk-Yeatman Papers; George W. Polk Papers; Dillon-Polk Papers; Polk-Brown-Ewell Papers; Gale Papers; and Kenneth Rayner Papers. A small number of important letters are in the Kirby Smith Papers. Much valuable manuscript material is also found in the North Carolina State Archives, especially the William Polk Papers, Devereux Papers, and Pollok-Devereux Papers. A few letters to and from Thomas Polk are in Nathanael Greene Papers (Clements Library, University of Michigan) and Horatio Gates Papers (New York Historical Society).

Manuscript records of family business transactions are in the courthouses of Maury and Franklin counties, Tennessee, Wake County, North Carolina, and LaFourche Parish, Louisiana.

Printed Correspondence and Documents, Official and Private

The greatest storehouse of information on military figures of the Civil War period is *The War of Rebellion: A Compilation of the Official Records of the Union and Confederate Armies* (128 vols., Washington, 1880–1901). Numerous items relating to Polk's military career were also printed in Dunbar Rowland (ed.), *Jefferson Davis, Constitutionalist: His Letters, Papers and Speeches* (10 vols., Jackson, Miss., 1923), but most of them are duplicates of the *Official Records*. A few letters of interest pertaining to the University of the South are in Lilly Baker, *et. al.* (eds.), *Sewanee* (Sewanee, 1932) and J. G. de Roulhac Hamilton (ed.), *The Papers of Thomas Ruffin* (4 vols., Raleigh, 1918–20). The principal documents relating to the founding of the University of the South were printed as individual pamphlets and copies are available in the Leonidas Polk Papers. The same documents are also found in Telfair Hodgson (ed.), *Reprints of the Documents and Proceedings of the Board of Trustees of the University of the South Prior to 1860* (Sewanee, 1888).

Bishop Polk's reports on church matters were published in *The Spirit of Mission*, IV (1839), *Journal of the Proceedings of the Bishops, Clergy, and Laity of The Protestant Episcopal Church in the United States of America in Convention* (1840–60), and in the *Journal of Convention* of the Dioceses of Tennessee and Louisiana.

The most valuable sources on the business and military careers of Thomas and William Polk are William L. Saunders (ed.), *The Colonial Records of North Carolina* (10 vols., Raleigh, 1886–90), Walter Clark (ed.), *The State Records of North Carolina* (16 vols., Winston and Goldsboro, 1895–1905), H. M. Wagstaff (ed.), *The Papers of John Steele* (2 vols., Raleigh, 1924), and William Henry Hoyt (ed.), *The Papers of Archibald D. Murphey* (2 vols., Raleigh, 1924).

Diaries, Autobiographies, Memoirs, and Reminiscences, Manuscript and Published

Shortly after the Civil War Mrs. Leonidas Polk recorded some interesting memories of her late husband entitled "Leonidas Polk, A Memoir Written by His Wife for Their Children." The original manuscript is in the Leonidas Polk Papers. Although very sentimental, it gives facts and sidelights that cannot be found in any other source. Polk's daughter, Katherine Gale, also recorded her "Recollections of Life in the Southern Confederacy, 1860–1865." A copy is in the Southern Collection of the University of North Carolina. This item is extremely valuable for information relating to family affairs during the war period.

In the University of the South Archives there is a copy of "Mrs. I. H. Hilliard's Diary." Mrs. Hilliard's identity is uncertain, but she gave some interesting glimpses of life on the Polk plantation in Louisiana. Early in 1861 Bishop Polk himself began a "Diary for 1861." The entries, brief but important, stopped when he entered the military service. The original is in the University of the South Archives.

A few published diaries, reminiscences, and memoirs contain a limited amount of information pertaining to Polk's career. All deal with the war years. The more important are Joseph E. Johnston, *Narrative of Military Operations, Directed, During the Late War Between the States* (New York, 1874); Ulysses S. Grant, *Personal Memoirs of U. S. Grant* (2 vols., New York, 1885); William T. Sherman, *Memoirs of W. T. Sherman* (2 vols., New York, 1892); James Longstreet, *From Manassas to Appomatox* (Philadelphia, 1896); John B. Jones, *A Rebel War Clerk's Diary* (2 vols., New York, 1935 reprint); Basil W. Duke, *Reminiscences of General Basil W. Duke* (Garden City, 1911); Samuel G. French, *Two Wars—An Autobiography* (Nashville, 1901); Jefferson Davis, *Rise and Fall of the Confederate Government*, (2 vols., New York, 1881); Arthur H. Noll (ed.), *Doctor Quintard, Chaplain, C. S. A., and Second Bishop of Tennessee, Being His Story of the War, 1861–1865* (Sewanee, 1905); Walter Lord (ed.), *The Fremantle Diary, Being the Journal of Lieutenant Colonel James Arthur Lyon Fremantle, Coldstream Guards, on His Three Months in the Southern States* (Boston, 1954); G. Moxley Sorrel, *Recollections of a Confederate Staff Officer*, edited by Bell I. Wiley (Jackson, Tenn., 1958); John Bell Hood, *Advance and Retreat* (New Orleans, 1880.).

Biographies and Sketches of Military Campaigns

A few standard biographies and campaign sketches of General Polk's associates and opponents should be listed: William Preston Johnston, *Life of Albert Sidney Johnston* (New York, 1878); Alfred Roman, *Military Operations of General Beauregard* (2 vols., New York, 1884); Arndt M. Stickles, *Simon Bolivar Buckner* (Chapel Hill, 1940); John P. Dyer, *The Gallant Hood* (Indianapolis, 1950); Don C. Seitz, *Braxton Bragg, General of the Confederacy* (Columbia, 1924); T. Harry Williams, *P. G. T. Beauregard, Napoleon in Gray* (Baton Rouge, 1954); Robert S. Henry, *"First With the Most" Forrest* (Indianapolis, 1944); Gilbert E. Govan and James W. Livingood, *A Different Valor, The Story of Joseph E. Johnston, C. S. A.* (Indianapolis, 1956); Thomas Jordan and J. P. Pryor, *The Campaigns of Lieutenant General N. B. Forrest and of Forrest's Cavalry* (New Orleans, 1868); Freeman Cleaves, *Rock of Chickamauga, Life of General George H. Thomas* (Norman, Okla., 1948); Irving A. Buck, *Cleburne and*

His Command (New York, 1908); Cecil F. Holland, *Morgan and His Raiders* (New York, 1942); Joseph H. Parks, *General Edmund Kirby Smith, C. S. A.* (Baton Rouge, 1954); John P. Dyer, *"Fightin' Joe" Wheeler* (Baton Rouge, 1941); Hudson Strode, *Jefferson Davis, Confederate President* (New York, 1959).

Articles

Much genealogical material of importance is found in Mrs. Frank M. Angelotti, "The Polks of North Carolina and Tennessee," *New England Historical and Genealogical Register*, LXXVII, LXXVIII, and Mary Winder Garrett, "Pedigree of the Pollock or Polk Family," *American Historical Magazine*, III (1898).

Of value in the study of Polk as a churchman are John Fulton, "The Church in the Confederate States," in William Stevens Perry, *The History of the American Episcopal Church, 1587–1883* (2 vols., Boston, 1885), II, George W. Polk, "St. John's Church, Maury County, Tenn.," *Tennessee Historical Magazine*, VII (1921), and Tresvant P. Yeatman, Jr., "St. John's—A Plantation Church of the Old South," *Tennessee Historical Quarterly*, X (1951).

Isabel Howell, "John Armfield of Beersheba Springs," *Tennessee Historical Quarterly*, III (1944) is useful in the study of the founding of the University of the South.

The most extensive and important articles of the campaigns of the Civil War are in Robert U. Johnson and Clarence C. Buel (eds.), *Battles and Leaders of the Civil War, Being for the Most Part Contributed by Union and Confederate Officers* (4 vols., New York, 1884–88). Many other articles of value are found in the *Southern Historical Society Papers*. Of less importance but of some interest are the files of the *Confederate Veteran*.

Histories and Monographs

Considerable information on family background and business activities is found in William Harrison Polk, *Polk Family and Kinsmen* (Louisville, 1912), Daniel A. Tompkins, *History of Mecklenburg County and the City of Charlotte from 1740–1903* (2 vols., Charlotte, 1903), John H. Wheeler, *Historical Sketches of North Carolina to 1851* (Philadelphia, 1851), William Henry Foote,

Sketches of North Carolina, Historical and Biographical (New York, 1846), William Henry Hoyt, *The Mecklenburg Declaration of Independence* (New York, 1907), Albert Ray Newsome, *The Presidential Election of 1824 in North Carolina* (Chapel Hill, 1939); Thomas P. Abernethy, *From Frontier to Plantation in Tennessee* (Chapel Hill, 1932); Kemp P. Battle, *History of the University of North Carolina* (2 vols., Raleigh, 1907).

Church affairs with which Bishop Polk was closely connected are covered in Arthur H. Noll, *History of the Church in the Diocese of Tennessee* (New York, 1900), Herman Cope Duncan, *The Diocese of Louisiana: Some of Its History, 1838–1888* (New Orleans, 1888), Joseph Blount Cheshire, *The Church in the Confederate States* (New York, 1912), Hodding and Betty Carter, *So Great a Good, A History of the Episcopal Church in Louisiana and of Christ Church Cathedral* (Sewanee, 1955).

There are two good works on the founding of the University of the South: George R. Fairbanks, *History of the University of the South* (Jacksonville, Fla., 1905) and Arthur B. Chitty, Jr., *Reconstruction at Sewanee* (Sewanee, 1954).

Useful information on many Confederate military leaders is given in George W. Cullum, *Biographical Register of the Officers and Graduates of the United States Military Academy* (2 vols., New York, 1868) and Ellsworth Eliot, *West Point in the Confederacy* (New York, 1941). The most extensive account of Confederate military operations is Clement A. Evans (ed.), *Confederate Military History* (12 vols., Atlanta, 1899). Those volumes covering the campaigns in Kentucky, Tennessee, and Georgia were especially useful. The best account of the campaigns of the Army of Tennessee is Stanley Horn, *The Army of Tennessee* (Indianapolis, 1941). A readable general treatment of the 1861–62 campaigns is Shelby Foote, *The Civil War: A Narrative. Fort Sumter to Perryville* (New York, 1958). Extensive accounts of the campaigns of the opposing Federal armies are Kenneth P. Williams, *Lincoln Finds a General* (5 vols., New York, 1949–59) and Bruce Catton, *Grant Moves South* (Boston, 1960).

Index

Adams, D. W., 289
Adams, John, 42
Adams, John Quincy, 46
Adams, Thomas, 42
Alexander, Abraham, 19 n.
Alexander, Adam, 19 n.
Alexander, John McKnitt, 19–20,
    19 n.
Alexander, Joseph McKnitt, 17
Alexander, Moses, 4
Alexander, Nathaniel, 2 n.
Altimore (Polk's servant), 163,
    278, 384 n.
Ammen, Jacob, 232
Anderson, Patton, 223 n., 254, 255,
    256, 266, 268, 271, 272, 287,
    290, 301, 302
Anderson, Robert, 144, 184
Armfield, John, 127, 134, 137, 141,
    142 n., 149
Armstrong, John, 13, 18
"Ashwood," 66 n., 75, 79, 85, 90,
    94, 98, 99, 100, 107, 385

Badger, Catherine, 73
Badger, George, 23 n., 46, 49, 56 n.,
    62, 65, 73
Badger, Mary Brown Polk (Mrs.
    George), 14 n., 23 and n., 32,
    46, 47, 65, 66, 73
Badger, Sally, 73
Bainbridge, William P., 24
Banks, Nathaniel, 358
Barbour, James, 31, 33–34
Barnard, Frederick, A. P., 151
Barney, Charles R., 130, 132, 134,
    136–38, 141, 145, 150
Bass, John M., 127, 146
Beatty, Samuel, 290
Beauregard, P. G. T., 208–209, 210,
    214, 359; assigned to West,
    206–207; ordered to Colum-
    bus, 211; illness of, 211, 213,

245; plans offensive, 216–17;
confers with Polk and Bragg,
218; at Corinth, 219, 220,
243–44; at Shiloh, 223 ff.; and
Island No. 10, p. 241; relieved
of command, 245
Beersheba Springs, 127, 130, 132,
    141, 141 n.–142 n., 149
Bell, John, 307
Belmont (Mo.), battle of, 189–95
Beltzhoover, Daniel, 190, 191
Benjamin, Judah P., 179, 201, 203,
    204, 206, 210, 211, 215
Berrien, John M., 50 n.
Biddle, E. J., 104 n.
Blake, Frank, 91 n.
Bledsoe, Albert Taylor, 147, 148,
    208
Blythe, A. K., 234
Bowen, J. S., 223, 227
Bowman, Alexander H., 144
Bragg, Braxton, 218, 243, 322, 384,
    385; at Shiloh, 223 ff.; ap-
    pointed to command, 245; and
    aid to East Tennessee, 248,
    249; trains army at Tupelo,
    249–50; moves to Chattanooga,
    250; and Kentucky campaign,
    251 ff.; at Murfreesboro,
    279 ff.; called to Richmond,
    279; and Battle of Stone's
    River, 284 ff.; retreats, 292;
    asks for vote of confidence,
    293; controversy with gen-
    erals, 293 ff.; reports on Stone's
    River, 300; charges Polk with
    disobedience, 300–301, 302;
    described by Fremantle, 304;
    reviews troops, 304; confirmed
    by Elliott, 307; and defense
    of Tullahoma area, 309, 310,
    311 ff.; retreats to Elk River,
    314; ability of, questioned by

Bragg (*Continued*)
Hardee, 315; falls back to mountains, 315–16; retreats to Chattanooga, 316–17; and conscription, 317–18; appeals for aid, 322; confused by Rosecrans, 325; falls back into Georgia, 325–26; at Chickamauga, 327 ff.; removal of, urged, 342–43; removes Polk and Hindman, 343–44; advised by Davis, 344–46; and round robin, 346; denounced by Polk, 348–49, 353; visited by Davis, 349–51; removal of, 354; disapproves Polk's plans, 369, 372, 373

Bragg, Mrs. Braxton, 298
Bragg, Thomas, 321
Branch, John, 49, 50 n., 62, 63
Brannan, John M., 332
Breckinridge, John C., 243, 249, 282, 284, 295, 322, 325, 326; at Shiloh, 223, 233 ff.; at Stone's River, 286 ff.; advises change of commanders, 294; resents Bragg's innuendo, 300; supported by Kentucky, 300; reviews troops, 304; at Chickamauga, 333 ff.

Brevard, Ephraim, 2 n., 19 and n.
Bright, John M., 151
Brown, Daniel, 2 n.
Brownell, Thomas C., 94
Buchanan, James, 154–56
Buckner, Simon Bolivar, 185, 186, 187, 207, 211, 249, 251, 254, 255, 256, 257, 258, 259, 262, 268, 269, 272, 315, 316, 319, 326, 327, 350; replies to Bragg, 301; re-enforces Bragg, 316; returns to Knoxville, 317; at Chickamauga, 328 ff.; and round robin, 347
Buell, Don Carlos, 208, 209, 230, 234, 238, 239, 242, 246–47, 248, 249, 280; moves to join Grant, 222; and Kentucky campaign, 251 ff.; removed from command, 282

Buford, Napoleon B., 193, 194, 195, 214 n.
Burke, Thomas, 10
Burnside, Ambrose E., 322, 326
Butler, Benjamin F., 277 n.
Butler, Edward G. W., 50
Butler, John, 10

Cabell, R. L., 147, 148
Calhoun, John C., 27, 65
Cambreling, Churchill C., 41
Canning, George, 25
Cantey, James, 374, 375, 377
Carroll, Charles M., 191
Caruthers & Harris, 88–89, 105
Caswell, Richard, 12
Catron, John, 42 n., 71, 90
Catron, Mrs. John, 90
Chalmers, J. R., 223 n., 256–57, 286, 288, 289
Cheatham, Benjamin F., 173, 187, 211, 213, 219, 254, 256, 257, 258–59, 267, 268, 269, 270, 272, 275, 276, 282, 284, 293–94, 295, 304, 311, 312, 313, 314, 315, 325, 350, 361, 363, 372; at Belmont, 191; at Shiloh, 222 ff.; and Kentucky campaign, 251 ff.; at Stone's River, 284 ff.; advises retreat, 291; replies to Bragg, 301; at Chickamauga, 328 ff.
Chickamauga, Battle of, 327 ff.
Chickasaw Treaty, 16
Christmas celebrations at Murfreesboro, 283
Churchill, Thomas J., 251
Clark, Charles, 222, 224, 227, 234, 239
Clay, Henry, 26–27, 46, 48
Cleburne, Patrick, 99, 250, 251, 261, 263–64, 266, 284, 295, 307, 325, 326, 361; at Shiloh, 223 ff.; at Stone's River, 286; advises change of commanders, 294; at Chickamauga, 332 ff.
Cobbs, Nicholas Hamner, 133, 306 n.
Colonization Society, 48
Coltart, J. G., 287
Columbia Institute, 90 and n., 99, 101